Inside Novell NetWare, Special Edition

Debra Niedermiller-Chaffins

NEW RIDERS
PUBLISHING

New Riders Publishing, Carmel, Indiana

Inside Novell NetWare, Special Edition

By Debra Niedermiller-Chaffins

Published by:
New Riders Publishing
11711 N. College Ave., Suite 140
Carmel, IN 46032 USA

Printed in the United States of America   2 3 4 5 6 7 8 9 0
Library of Congress Cataloging-in-Publication Data is available

About the Authors

Debra R. Niedermiller-Chaffins is Education Director for Computer Data, Inc. in Madison Heights, Michigan. Ms. Niedermiller-Chaffins started the education department at Computer Data in 1988 to help organizations develop autonomy and self-sufficiency in training future Certified NetWare Engineer (CNE) operations. She is a Certified NetWare Instructor (CNI) and a CNE, specializing in training future CNEs. Aside from teaching, Ms. Niedermiller-Chaffins also supports a small client base, which provides her with a background of real-world networking scenarios. She is the author of *Inside NetWare Lite* also published by New Riders Publishing.

Brian Chaffins is Technical Director for Computer Data, Inc. in Madison Heights, Michigan. He believes that network users are best served by committing himself to providing quality services and technical excellence. Mr. Chaffins was one of the first three CNEs in Michigan and has earned a reputation of being an ace troubleshooter. He also is the co-author of *Inside NetWare Lite* published by New Riders Publishing.

New Riders Publishing extends special thanks to the following contributors to this book:

Timothy A. Gendreau, who contributed the first half of the Command Reference. Mr. Gendreau is president of Training Solutions, a Novell Authorized Education Center located in Tempe, Arizona. He is a Certified NetWare Engineer and a Certified NetWare Instructor and is active in teaching many aspiring CNEs and CNIs.

Danny R. Kusnierz, who contributed the second half of the Command Reference. Mr. Kusnierz is a Novell Certified NetWare Engineer with more than 13 years' experience in the personal computer industry. He is a computer consultant with an emphasis on local area networks. His experience in the computer industry includes computer sales, end-user training, programming, and systems engineering.

Richard Leach, who contributed to the development of Appendixes A and B and served as a technical editor. Mr. Leach is a technical support specialist for Prentice Hall Computer Publishing, located in Carmel, Indiana. He is a Certified NetWare Engineer.

Acknowledgments

I want to dedicate this book to the many people who helped and supported me through this project. Special thanks to my parents for always believing that I had it in me. I also want to thank everyone at Computer Data, Inc. for putting up with and supporting me. Finally, thanks to my husband, Brian, without whom I could not have done it.

New Riders Publishing would like to express its sincere thanks to the following people, for their contributions to this book:

David Solomon, for initial development of the text.

Drew Heywood for inspiration and development of this expanded Special Edition.

John W. Pont for managing the authoring team.

Cheri Robinson for editorial support and guidance.

NRP Production Editor Geneil Breeze for managing the editing and preproduction preparation of the text.

Editors Sandra Blackthorn, Tim Huddleston, Peter Kuhns, Rob Lawson, Mark Montieth, Nancy Sixsmith, and Rob Tidrow, for their careful and rapid work.

Karen Opal, for editorial assistance wherever needed.

The production staff of Prentice Hall Computer Publishing for the expeditious handling of materials.

Trademark Acknowledgments

New Riders Publishing has made every attempt to supply trademark information about company names, products, and services mentioned in this book. Trademarks indicated below were derived from various sources. New Riders Publishing cannot attest to the accuracy of this information.

ARCnet is a registered trademark of Datapoint Corporation.

AT&T is a registered trademark of AT&T.

CHECKIT is a registered trademark of TouchStone Software Corporation.

CP/M, DR DOS, and FlexOS are registered trademarks of Digital Research, Inc.

CRAY is a registered trademark of Cray Research, Inc.

IBM and Micro Channel are registered trademarks, and NETBIOS is a trademark of International Business Machines Corporation.

NetWare, NetWare Name Services, and Novell are registered trademarks, and LAN Workplace is a trademark of Novell, Inc.

LaserJet is a registered trademark of Hewlett-Packard Co.

Microsoft Windows is a registered trademark of Motorola Inc.

Post-it is a trademark of 3M Company.

UNIX is a registered trademark of AT&T.

WaveLAN is a trademark of NCR Corporation.

Trademarks of other products mentioned in this book are held by the companies producing them.

Warning and Disclaimer

This book is designed to provide information about the Novell NetWare program. Every effort has been made to make this book as complete and as accurate as possible, but no warranty or fitness is implied.

The information is provided on an "as is" basis. The author and New Riders Publishing shall have neither liability nor responsibility to any person or entity with respect to any loss or damages arising from the information contained in this book or from the use of the disks or programs that may accompany it.

Table of Contents

3 Examining NetWare's Benefits 53

7 Adding Users and User Security to the System 185

9 Setting Up the NetWare Environment for Users .. 295

10 System Administration and Troubleshooting 351

Introduction

The computer industry has evolved considerably from the days of the multimillion dollar machines of the 1950s. Today, the norm is *distributed processing* moving from the heavily controlled and guarded atmosphere of the large IBM mainframes operated by the priests in white lab coats, to separate, independently maintained personal computers, or "PCs." The personal computer became popular unexpectedly to many of the early computer engineers. At one point, it was believed that the world would some day be run by a single large computer, or at least one large computer per country. Now, as computer prices continue to drop almost daily, the personal computer is becoming the computer of choice.

As the PC began to overtake the mainframes as the primary means of business computing, the need arose to connect isolated PCs together so that they could work together in a manner similar to the terminals on a mainframe. From this need came the idea of merging PC and networking technology. Since the introduction of the local area network (LAN), LAN technology has matured and local area networks continue to flourish.

Networking was first conceived in the late 1960s, when the U.S. Department of Defense began developing the Advanced Research

Projects Agency (ARPA). From this agency was created ARPANET, which was the first packet-switched network. The first version of ARPANET began operations in 1969. This project was a success and developed into what is today called the capital "I," or Internet.

In 1983, Novell, Inc. released a network operating system that revolutionized the computer network. The system was created by a group of Brigham Young University graduates who called themselves "Superset Software." This operating system was known by many names, but was the forerunner of the network OS known as NetWare.

Current networking technology offers a cost-effective method for distributing services and sharing equipment. From the early ARPANET project, networking has found its way into small family businesses and large corporate environments.

Many companies start with a small workgroup system that is designed to solve the needs of a small department. As productivity and effectiveness increase, so does the need for more networks and workstations. *Inside Novell NetWare, Special Edition* is not only a tutorial on the administration of Novell NetWare but also a collection of techniques, methods, and procedures that have enabled many businesses to effectively operate a NetWare network.

Who Should Read this Book?

Inside Novell NetWare, Special Edition is written for individuals that need to learn more about Novell NetWare because of a job responsibility, and for those who are curious about NetWare. The following chapters contain information and procedures for the average networked computing environment. This information is the product of many installations and many hours spent assisting people in controlling and administering their networks.

What Versions are Covered?

This book includes the most current information available on NetWare v2.2 and v3.11. The DOS-related information in these chapters includes MS-DOS and PC DOS versions 3.1 through 5.0, and DR DOS

6.0. All these versions of NetWare and DOS have been tested and operate as described in this book, when installed properly.

What Topics are Not Included?

Inside Novell NetWare, Special Edition is intended to introduce and familiarize you with Novell NetWare v2.2 and v3.11. Unfortunately, however, this book cannot cover all troubleshooting and debugging practices. The procedures for properly repairing advanced problems would require a book twice the size of this one. Although you will learn the majority of the system administrative utilities, you will not be bored with details about every little feature. Learning is always a pleasure, and with the many details in the NetWare operating system, you can be sure to enjoy it for many years.

The Details of this Book

You can flip quickly through this book to get a feel for its organization. The book begins by laying a conceptual foundation, on which you can build an understanding of NetWare and networking. The text then builds on that conceptual information through topical chapters that present a practical view of setting up NetWare and customizing it for your needs. The book then presents appendixes that help you install NetWare v2.2 and v3.11 and a syntax-based command reference. You can read the chapters in order, or choose the order that you want to use. Wherever possible, examples and figures are included to help you become more familiar with the NetWare interface. The following is an overview of each chapter in this book.

Chapter 1, "Understanding Networks," discusses the advantages of networking and illustrates the fact that a well-planned network can maximize the use of all your equipment, including older, less-effective computers that you otherwise would retire. Chapter 1 also discusses the benefits of sharing expensive peripherals and centrally protecting your information.

Chapter 2, "Building a Network," discusses the necessary equipment for building a network and helps you determine which equipment is best for your work environment. Chapter 2 assists you in choosing a file server and workstations, and provides information on cabling systems and peripherals, such as printers, modems, and network FAX servers. Finally, the chapter helps you decide between NetWare v2.2 or v3.11 for your network operating system.

Chapter 3, "Examining NetWare's Benefits," focuses on NetWare's reliability. The areas discussed in this chapter include security, performance, and expandability areas in which NetWare has proved itself to be the most reliable network operating system on the market today.

Chapter 4, "Gathering Workstation Software," discusses the software components required to connect the workstation to the network. You learn about different operating systems, the IPX protocol and NETX, XMSNETX, and EMSNETX shells, whether you need NETBIOS or Novell's ODI solution, and whether you can use diskless workstations.

Chapter 5, "Accessing the File Server," discusses the utilities and methods used to log in (attach) to a file server located on your network. Also, this chapter shows you how to create the shells necessary for a network. You also learn how to log in to the network through DOS and Windows 3.x, and by using commands such as ATTACH and LOGOUT. This chapter defines and discusses each of the options that can be used in the NET.CFG file. Finally, you find some interesting tips in this section if you use UNIX, OS/2, or Macintoshes on your network.

Chapter 6, "Managing Directories," discusses the way the NetWare operating system works with the directory system. You learn about the required NetWare directories and how to effectively manage them. The chapter also examines attributes and related commands.

Chapter 7, "Adding Users and User Security to the System," shows you how to set up users on the system and create user names and groups. This chapter also gives you an understanding of rights-related commands.

Chapter 8, "Printing on a Novell Network," shows you the many ways to implement network printing. You are shown how to effectively use the printing systems included with NetWare v2.2 and v3.11. You learn about the advantages of core printing versus print servers, the way to install Novell print servers, and the way to direct printer output. In addition, Chapter 8 shows you how to customize your print output by using the PRINTDEF command, and the way you can create print jobs by using PRINTCON-related commands.

Chapter 9, "Setting Up the NetWare Environment for Users," shows you ways in which you can optimize the performance of your network. A poorly designed user environment can significantly decrease productivity. Chapter 9 describes how to increase performance for system administrators and users. This chapter also shows you how to master drive mappings, develop usable login scripts, create custom menus, and work with utilities and related commands.

Chapter 10, "System Administration and Troubleshooting," shows you the way to administer the network. You also are shown basic troubleshooting methods supplied with NetWare. You will find that monitoring network performance helps to maintain a trouble-free system. This chapter discusses monitoring and maintaining the network by using the SET commands which are defined and discussed in depth, as well as using such commands as BINDFIX, FCONSOLE, and COMCHECK.

Chapter 11, "Management Concerns," discusses data recovery and data protection. This chapter provides information on backing up the file server and recovering from data disasters.

Chapter 12, "Network E-mail," presents the Message Handling System (MHS) engine for running e-mail applications on the network. In this chapter, you learn what MHS does and are introduced to some actual packages. Finally, a short section on e-mail etiquette is presented to help you get your point across with style.

Appendix A, "Installing NetWare v2.2," steps you though an installation of a NetWare v2.2 file server. You learn how to generate the operating system files and to modify the system when required. The topics covered include preparing the hardware, installation methods, using the command line options, and configuring the system. After the system is set up, you learn how to modify the v2.2 installation.

Appendix B, "Installing NetWare v3.11," discusses NetWare v3.11 installation by describing a common installation. This chapter examines such installation-related issues as hardware preparation, loading SERVER.EXE disk drives, and following the install module. You also learn about LAN drivers, modifying the v3.11 installation, and upgrading to a v3.11 file server.

Appendix C, "History of the NetWare DOS Shell," shows the path that the IPX.COM file has taken. Make sure to check this section against the IPX versions you are currently running to see if there are potential problems with your applications. Each version of IPX is listed along with the problems that it fixed.

Appendix D, "Using the Programs on the Bonus Disk," contains brief descriptions of and installation instructions for the programs contained on the *Inside Novell NetWare, Special Edition* disk. These programs are designed to help you manage and use your NetWare network.

The Command Reference is an alphabetized directory of NetWare commands and their syntax. You will find the Command Reference a valuable asset while using this book and while using NetWare commands on your network. The Command Reference describes each NetWare command, explaining the command's purpose and syntax, and offering examples of the command at work. You learn when to use a command and find notes that clarify issues of the command's use or actions. You will want to keep this book close to your workstation and file server for easy access to the Command Reference.

Conventions Used in this Book

Certain conventions are used in this book to help you more easily understand the discussions. You will find special notes, technical asides, and author notes throughout the text, as well as special typesetting conventions that will help you distinguish NetWare prompts and messages, as well as information that you need to enter.

Notes appear with a special margin icon. These special bits of text contain "extra" information that can help you boost your system's productivity or provide additional details about NetWare commands and features.

Technical asides and author notes appear in special shaded boxes. Technical asides are notes that contain technical information and definitions to help you understand NetWare, DOS, and computing in general. Author notes are notes that contain information culled from years of consulting and installation experience that will help you understand NetWare and the best way to set up your network.

Special Typefaces

This section describes the special typefaces used in *Inside Novell NetWare, Special Edition*:

Typeface	Meaning
`Special font`	This font is used for NetWare and DOS commands, the names of files and directories, and system output, such as prompt signs and screen messages.
`Bold, special font`	This font is used for user input, such as commands, options to commands, and names of directories and files used as arguments.
`Italic, special font`	This font is used for names of variable elements to which values are given by the user.
`ALL CAPS, SPECIAL FONT`	This font is used for screen output.
`ALL CAPS, BOLD, SPECIAL FONT`	This font is used for user input.

Command Reference Conventions

This book's Command Reference uses the preceding conventions and others to show you the way to use NetWare's commands. The first line of each command entry contains the command name and the following special indicators:

A>	Indicates a DOS executable command
F>	Indicates a workstation command
:	Indicates a console command
:DOWN	Indicates a command that must be issued from a downed file server
:LOAD	Indicates a NetWare loadable module
MENU	Indicates a menu-based utility

The first line of each command also contains the NetWare version on which the command works. If the command works on both v2.2 and v3.11, a version is not specified on this line.

The Command Reference also contains notes, tips, and warnings. Notes contain "extra" information that provides additional details about NetWare commands and features. Tips and warnings appear with special margin icons. Tips contain information that can help you boost your system's productivity. Warnings contain information that warns you of potential danger to your system.

Learning More about Networks and Operating Systems

Unfortunately, a single book cannot concentrate at the same time on NetWare, DOS, Windows, and other operating systems. If you have a greater need for information in one or more of these areas, you will find that NRP offers a variety of books that suit your needs.

To supplement the discussions in *Inside Novell NetWare, Special Edition* pick up NRP's *Novell NetWare On Command*. *Novell NetWare On Command* is a task-oriented guide to Novell NetWare performance. Organized according to tasks, *Novell NetWare On Command* gives you tips on sharing data and ensuring system integrity. *Novell NetWare On Command* also provides a complete coverage of essential NetWare commands and utilities.

If you are an AutoCAD user who is managing a networked AutoCAD environment, NRP's *Managing and Networking AutoCAD* is an ideal book to use to help you set up and manage AutoCAD workstations. *Managing and Networking AutoCAD* teaches you how to improve CAD performance through effective, centralized CAD system administration. *Managing and Networking AutoCAD* also shows you how to integrate Novell NetWare into your AutoCAD system.

If you have been using MS-DOS 5, or if you are just beginning but are a fast study, then NRP's *Maximizing MS-DOS 5* has content tailored for your needs. *Maximizing MS-DOS 5* brings you an inside approach to developing the most powerful DOS system possible. *Maximizing*

MS-DOS 5 also shows you how to customize DOS 5 and how to network your DOS system to maintain peak power.

If you are a Windows 3.1 user, or you are just beginning, then NRP's *Windows 3.1 On Command* deserves a spot on your bookshelf. *Windows 3.1 On Command* is a task-oriented guide to Windows performance that helps you set up and customize your Windows environment. *Windows 3.1 On Command* also covers networking concepts and real-world networking tasks.

If you have been using Windows 3.1, or you are just beginning but are a fast study, NRP's *Maximizing Windows 3.1* will help you improve your performance on your PC. *Maximizing Windows 3.1* shows you how to change the appearance of your Windows environment, dynamically link spreadsheet data with word processing reports, and network your windows system and maintain peak power. *Maximizing Windows 3.1* also provides tips for system and network administrators.

If you work with Berkeley or SCO UNIX, then you will benefit from NRP's *UNIX On Command*. *UNIX On Command* is a task-oriented guide to UNIX utilities, shell programming, and sessions. *UNIX On Command* gives you tips for UNIX productivity with more than 100 reference entries.

Understanding Networks

network is a number of computers connected by cable that can share information and peripheral devices, such as printers. *Networking* is a communications system that enables users to transfer or share similar types of data and programs. Networking also applies to any multiuser system. *Local area networking* (LAN) connects PCs together for sharing real-time information, storage, applications, and peripherals. Novell NetWare puts these networking functions together and offers a wide range of products for networks of any size. In this chapter, you learn that networking is the latest phase of computer technology and that networks offer many interesting opportunities. You also will be introduced to the following features and benefits of networks:

- Seeing the growth of networks from mainframe and mini-computers

- Getting updated information immediately

- Using new technology while keeping your existing equipment

- Using networks to share programs, data, and backups among different users

- Protecting vital information by using networks
- Sharing expensive peripherals on networks

To become acquainted with networking, first examine the origins of the networking trend.

Networking: The Latest Phase of Computer Technology

Businesses first adopted *mainframe computers* for their computing needs. Mainframe computers, known simply as *mainframes*, are extremely powerful and can sift through numbers and generate reports that might frighten the average accountant. Even today, mainframes provide the computing power for large corporations' processing needs. Mainframes have multiple-processing units and can support a large number of users.

The biggest drawback to using a mainframe is the cost. Companies owning mainframes also need full-time personnel to run them—not to mention large sums of money for software systems. You may notice that your local computer store normally stocks only programs for personal computers. The reason for this is that mainframes only fit the budgets of large corporations and scientific communities.

The *minicomputer* was the next step for finding solutions to business problems. Minicomputer systems are smaller in size and support fewer users. Minicomputers still need full-time support people (just not as many), and they still do not yet have their own section in computer stores. Although minicomputers fit the needs of medium-sized corporations, such as engineering firms, small companies still relied on pencils and calculators.

After the minicomputer came the *personal computer*, or *PC*. The public liked the PC's ease of use and relative affordability, but found that if several PCs were placed in one room, it was difficult to get them to communicate with each other.

The need arose to return to the technology of bigger computer systems, such as mainframes, because they have the capability to communicate with each other. The search for a system that enables PCs to speak with each other led to *networking*.

About Mainframe Computers...

Local area networks (LANs), which primarily consist of personal computers, will not take over the computer industry—at least not in the near future. Many intense calculations needed in scientific and engineering work still will be performed by mainframes and minicomputers.

Many computer analysts use the term *downsizing* to indicate that the mainframe's time has come and gone. This probably is not true. Downsizing means that a company restructures the use of its current computer system. Most corporations that maintain mainframes need the mainframe's raw horsepower to manipulate large applications that service offices across the country, and they also need mainframes to maintain millions of company records. The restructuring process usually involves enabling the mainframes and minicomputers to perform what they do best— number crunching—and assigning such tasks as spreadsheet calculations and word processing to the LAN.

Companies also are downsizing their use of minicomputers. Some PCs are available that are considered high-end, which means that they are exceptionally fast in processing information. High-end PCs can outperform many low-end minicomputers.

Networks also make wonderful specialized nodes on mainframes and minicomputers. (A *node* is any device connected to a network, such as a workstation or file server.) Instead of wasting valuable nodes on the larger systems to word processing people, you easily and cost-effectively can add a network to support those users with a gateway into the mainframe or minicomputers if necessary. A *gateway* refers to software and hardware that a network uses to communicate with a mainframe or minicomputer. For more information on file servers and workstations, see Chapter 2.

Examining Networking Opportunities

Networking offers a variety of elements that enable you to communicate within a wide range of computing environments. Some of these features include simple printer and file sharing, minicomputer and mainframe access, and remote links to other PCs and networks. Figure 1.1 illustrates a network's capability to communicate with other computing systems, including mainframes and minicomputers.

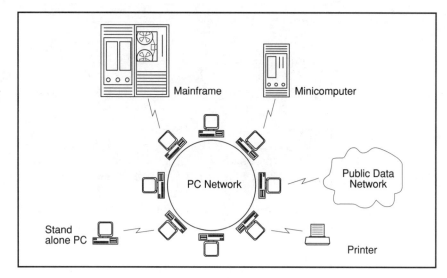

Figure 1.1:
A PC network, connecting to other multiuser systems.

Networking can be as simple or as complex as you need for your company. Small offices can use the network for sharing data and printers among users. With medium-sized networks, you can have gateway links to minicomputers from multiple vendors and links to offices across town or across the country. Because each type of multiuser environment has its own rules and utilities, gateways enable dissimilar systems to communicate with each other through hardware and software connections (see Chapter 3 for more information about gateways and their places in networking).

Even large networks, commonly referred to as *enterprise networks*, enable users to access data located throughout the world from any number of minicomputers, mainframes, or remote LANs.

If you use a network in your company, data can be made available where it is needed, when it is needed, and at a relatively low cost. Instead of asking the accounts payable department to print a 400-page vendor list for the purchasing department to reference, for example, the purchasing department can access the vendor list whenever the data is needed. The accounts payable department can examine purchase orders as soon as they are created instead of when vendor invoices arrive. Depending on the size and structure of the organization, the accounts payable and purchasing departments can use separate PCs in separate offices, or even on separate types of computer systems.

A Note from the Author...

One network my firm is implementing will connect more than 4,000 PCs to 80 departmental networks interconnected with a high-speed fiber optic link. This particular organization has in place a wide variety of UNIX systems and IBM mainframes, and even a Cray Supercomputer. When this project is completed, any of the 4,000 users can access data anywhere within the enterprise. A user, for example, will start a batch job on an IBM mainframe, enter transactions on a UNIX system, and transfer a file from a remote file server to his or her local hard disk without rebooting the PC and with only a single physical connection to the network.

Getting Updated Information Immediately

One benefit of networking is that you can enter information and see results immediately. This type of feedback is called *interactive processing*. Interactive processing enables users to enter data into an application and immediately see how it affects other data. This feature is not available with all computer systems.

Companies with large computer environments still commonly make users perform *batch processing*, which involves updating and processing the day's data so that changes are available for the next day. This procedure usually is performed in the evening or during periods of low activity to provide adequate processing power. Batch processing may be satisfactory for many companies, but with today's industry competition, the company with updated information first has an advantage over other companies.

 An interactive system provides data in a manner that is natural to the way people communicate. Receiving an answer to a question within a reasonable time period is natural. In most businesses, time is money, and waiting even one day for results can cost plenty.

If your goal is to have all your data and statistics *now*, networks meet this goal admirably. In many cases, an effectively designed system can provide information within minutes, which is a big change from the days when you submitted your request to the computer people in white lab coats and then waited days for your answer.

Networking provides your company with the capacity to process information in the most timely and effective manner.

Using New Technology with Existing Equipment

Networking is intended to be expanded. Companies rarely find that they do *not* need computing expansion. Each time a new person is added to a firm, another computer generally is needed. Forecasting when and how you may outgrow your current configuration is not easy. Because planning for the future usually is done without knowing what the future holds, the best you can hope for is an easy path for growth. Expandability and the capability to use many different types of computers from different manufacturers are prime objectives for networking.

Although the initial investment in a network may appear expensive, existing equipment can be used in most cases. A network thrives on the distribution of computers. Workstations, print servers, and gateways require a computer as the basic building block. In a network, older systems rarely are ever scrapped. Instead, older PCs are demoted to less important or less demanding tasks. Existing equipment can be functional for a group of users.

When a user's workstation requires replacement, the PC is simply upgraded to provide greater processing power. The older computer then can complete its service life by processing less demanding information.

The capability to transfer seemingly outdated computers to positions in which they still are usable is a new concept in most mainframe system installations. Corporations using mainframes are familiar with retiring older equipment after upgrading to new technology. When networking, you even can use old mainframe equipment as specialized nodes on a network by using the equipment as a mass storage medium.

> ### A Note from the Author...
>
> The same principles used in restructuring a mainframe network
> hold true for network boards and cabling. In most cases, as you
> add newer workstations to your network, you do not have to re-
> place the entire cabling scheme to accommodate newer or faster
> technologies. My office provides a prime example.
>
> When we moved into a new building, we wired the entire office
> for twisted-pair Arcnet. We chose this method because the cable
> is easy to install and is cost-effective. As our office grew, we
> needed faster technology for testing and education. When we
> added a new classroom, we cabled for 10BaseT (or Ethernet us-
> ing standard telephone wire). We did not need to scrap our pre-
> vious cabling because we still could use it for our medium
> processing needs. Now we can choose whichever topology fits
> the needs of new users.

As PC hardware technology advances, you can expand your current
system without using your existing computers as paperweights. With
minimal down time, you can upgrade your existing file server to one
with a faster processor. The existing system can become a powerful
workstation for one of the end users. The oldest system in this chain
can be made into a low-end router or print server.

Sharing Programs, Data, and Backups

In the past, legal restrictions required you to have a separate copy of
an application for each workstation. An *application* is a software program or package that enables users to perform a specific task, such as
an accounting or word processing job. Many software vendors now
offer site licenses that enable you to purchase a copy of the software
for your file server and manual sets for workstations. Many variations
of site-licensing options are available at a substantially lower cost than
that of purchasing individual copies. Each application has its own
method of implementing site-licensing. More information can be obtained from software vendors.

Along with licensing costs are the costs for individual local hard
drives. Most hard disk drives used in stand-alone PCs are not

designed to operate for extended periods, and, in most situations, the stand-alone PC user does not perform backups as often as needed. Although most users try to form good computing habits, lessons often are learned the hard way. Ask any veteran computer user why backing up his computer is necessary, and you likely will hear a story about what happened when a backup was not performed. Such stories usually do not have happy endings.

By placing all data and applications on a common, controlled, secured medium, networks offer much better protection than what most stand-alone computers can provide by themselves. This action also provides a convenient means for updating programs for all users. To update new versions of software in stand-alone computer environments, you need to repeat the same procedure for each PC using the old software. This is one of the major reasons that many companies with non-network PCs are not using current software. Upgrading is simply too much work.

Networking enables you to place one copy of an application on the network file server. If an update is needed, you can update one program, and then everyone can use that version. If you have several copies of a single-user application for copyright reasons, and these copies are on the network, you can update these versions from any PC that you are using, eliminating the need to hunt down individual computers for revisions.

With networking, you easily can monitor and update information on the file server. Simplicity in use and a centralized point of supervision can make administration a breeze. This benefit holds true with hardware as well as software. One way that networks offer ease of use and versatility is through adherence to local and international rules.

Protecting Information

Networking enables you to secure your data on the file server. You can do this procedure from any node on your network, and it takes effect immediately. You probably have discovered that safeguarding data is harder when it is scattered among many PC local hard drives.

Many ways are available to protect system data and limit users' access to PCs. Most methods add and use functions that DOS, a single-user operating system, was not designed to provide. These types of system-protection applications include password protection, inquiry only, and similar features.

The previously mentioned, safeguarding methods generally work nicely as long as the user is in the application, but these methods provide no protection to data accessed at the DOS prompt. Any curious or malicious user easily can do damage.

Applications and data located on a Novell NetWare file server can be controlled on a per-user basis. Along with all the options NetWare provides, a properly designed and implemented security system can supply a secure environment. The key is design and implementation. This issue is covered in detail in Chapters 6 and 7.

Sharing Expensive Peripherals

On the surface, networks may seem expensive to implement. The expense of *not* implementing a network is not as evident. You should take the time to calculate the cost of preparing floppy disks, transporting data, and interrupting work flow. Remember to include the cost of reconciling printer codes with different software packages and different versions. Many organizations can rationalize the expense of a network based on peripheral sharing alone.

Printer codes are control characters that the printer interprets for output. *Control characters* can signify bold, italic, landscape orientation, or any other functions and features that the printer is capable of printing.

Peripherals are devices that enable users to put in and take out computer data in a usable format. Peripherals include printers, modems, and other devices that are connected to a computer.

You can use networks to share many types of peripherals, such as modems for communicating in remote locations and fax servers that enable you to send documents to fax machines at another location from within an application.

Three options currently exist for printing in an office with stand-alone computers. The first option is to put a printer on the desk of each person who needs to print (see fig. 1.2). This procedure usually requires purchasing low-cost printers so that everyone is accommodated.

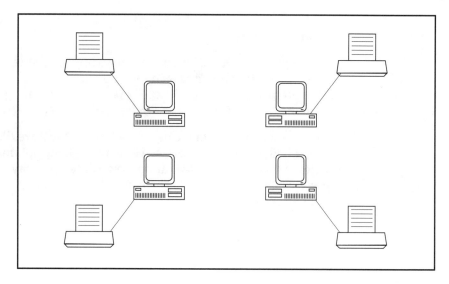

Figure 1.2:
A stand-alone
computer
environment, in
which each PC has
an attached printer.

The second option is to buy a few high-quality printers and institute a *sneaker-net*, which is created when users without printers must put information on a floppy disk and move to a different workstation that has a printer. A surprisingly large number of offices currently use this method.

The third option is to install manual or electronic data switches. A *manual data switch* is similar to an A/B switch, which is a switch that must physically be changed from A to B. Manual switches work fine with light use but quickly become cumbersome with heavy use. PC users get impatient when they must wait for a printer to become available and constantly move a switch to a new location. An *electronic data switch* detects the need to change and automatically switches to A or B. Electronic switches are better but usually require a user to wait for an available printer—especially when a buffer is full.

In the Novell NetWare environment, many options are available for adding printers to a network. With NetWare's printer-sharing facilities and the abundance of third-party options, you can install a printer anywhere on a system conveniently and reliably. When they are set up properly, network printers can supply high speed and quality for all those who need to use them.

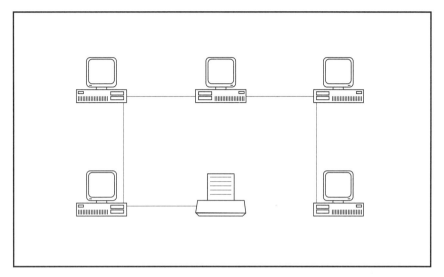

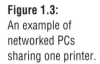

Figure 1.3:
An example of
networked PCs
sharing one printer.

You will see in Chapter 8 how to set up the printing environment for users. Chapter 8 also discusses the setup procedure for print servers and provides information on every print utility in NetWare.

Networking also enables you to share other peripherals, such as modems and fax servers. Currently available are some high-performing add-on network products, ranging from PC add-on cards and software to dedicated units that use Motorola 68000 series processors. These units can supply high print quality and handle a large volume of pages without a wait at the fax machine.

Fax servers come in several varieties. Some are simply add-in boards that send faxes. Others actually use Motorola Mc68000 chips to increase the speed and intelligence of the fax server.

Some high-quality fax servers not only supply a printout with 300-by-300 dots-per-inch resolution quality, but they also emulate any Hewlett-Packard laser printer and most PostScript printers. These fax servers enable you to print directly from within an application and to use soft fonts. These fax servers also can double as high-performance print servers, enabling multiple printers to be connected directly to the fax server. Although these units are impressive, many companies still do not take advantage of their capabilities.

You also can share fax services across a network. Suppose, for example, that a railroad company needs to fax the entire manifest for a train to each stop before a train can leave the station. Before implementing a shared fax server, the company had to print the manifest and then repeatedly fax it to all stops for which the train was scheduled. By integrating the shared fax services into its network, the company eliminated the need to fax documents manually. In this case, the railroad company reduced its personnel requirements for this operation by 50 percent.

Although modems and fax servers that you can share are fairly new to networking, their quality and performance are constantly improving. With additional software, you can set up a pool of modems that any user can access. Instead of setting up a modem for each user, you can set up a few modems and telephone lines for all users to share. Modem servers have been available for a while now, but sometimes their performance and functionality have been marginal.

Currently, the highest performing modem servers communicate directly through Novell's IPX, which is a translation method that PCs use to communicate with a NetWare file server. IPX is a de facto standard supported by many manufacturers of modem servers. Novell is moving closer to implementing the OSI model for networking, which is the international standard that uses Open Data-Link Interface (ODI) drivers. As Novell changes to OSI to take advantage of its capabilities, so too will the previous standards change.

Looking for Software Availability

To get an idea of how popular PCs are compared to mainframes and minicomputers, walk into any mall and you will find stores that are stocked wall-to-wall with software programs—programs that you can use right off the shelf. If none of the programs appeal to you, pick up any computer magazine and browse through the hundreds of ads for software. If neither option provides what you are looking for, open a phone book and look under "PC Software Consultants." Thousands of programmers around the world make their living by writing and customizing PC software. All of these applications are available for thousands of dollars less than the cost of performing the same functions on mainframes and minicomputers.

In addition, you can find software for networks much more easily than software for larger computer systems. Many software vendors who used to write for mainframes and minicomputers are now writing programs that can be used on networks.

Many books provide information on the design and operation of application software. Many professionals also make their living on that subject alone.

Recommending software packages is difficult. Generally, different packages are best for different users. If a package works for you, use it. Low-quality software packages do not last long on the market. In today's PC marketplace, you often hear the same software titles over and over again. In most cases, these products are good choices for your needs.

When you are looking for a database, accounting, or manufacturing system, start by contacting a value-added reseller (VAR) or consultant to check into the product in detail. A *value-added reseller* is a company that sells products, such as NetWare, and provides support for the product by answering technical questions and providing trouble-shooting services and spare parts. Check into local users' groups for input, also. Any major software purchase can be costly if you make a poor decision in the beginning.

Before you choose any software for your network, you must become familiar with the various types of software available. The following are the four types of software currently available for the PC:

- **Stand-alone software.** This type of software cannot seem to get around the files that a NetWare server requires the system to load. These files usually are IPX.COM or NETX.COM. Several software houses make separate versions of an application, usually one for non-networked PCs and one for networked PCs. A non-networked PC application often looks to see if IPX.COM was loaded at the workstation. If it is found, the load is aborted. Other programs are hard-coded to bypass DOS. NetWare does not always catch these programs.

- **Single-user software.** This type of software is made for single PCs but can run on networks. The limitation of single-user software is that setup configurations often are set globally for all users and cannot be customized. It is possible for data to become corrupt if more than one user tries to modify a common file.

- **Network-compatible software.** If a program does not mention NetWare in the documentation, a red flag should go up in your mind. If NetWare is not mentioned in the documentation, the software may not run on a NetWare network. If the software does run, chances are that you will have to manipulate the NetWare environment before it works smoothly on your system. Programs that are written to run on any generic network often require the system administrator to make non-supported network changes, such as requiring users to have more rights than is safe.

- **NetWare-aware software.** This type of program has special features that enable you to manipulate the NetWare network environment from within the program. This type is the best selection because the software company has tested the software for you on a Novell NetWare network.

When examining any software package, always ask whether the product is *network compatible* or *NetWare aware*. Doing so can save you time if the application has been written and tested to operate on a network. Often, people install a program on a network, flag the files as shareable, and then wonder why the program does not work correctly when several people try to access and change the data. Aside from violating the copyright laws that state that applications written for non-networked PCs can be run on a network providing only one person at a time uses the application, not all applications are multiuser applications.

Summary

In this chapter, you learned that many reasons exist for networking your stand-alone PCs. Whatever your computing requirements are, networking should fit your needs. One of the most important reasons for networking is that it enables you to share your data and applications, eliminating the need for redundant software.

When you install your network, you can keep your equipment up-to-date without eliminating existing equipment. Hardware chosen today for your network may be replaced with different technology tomorrow. Networks enable you to make use of what you chose today, while still retaining the capability to add newer, faster, and more reliable equipment tomorrow.

Networking also enables versatility in communicating with other systems, meaning that you are not locked into a single vendor's solution. Networks provide the capability to expand from most manufacturers' mainframes and minicomputers to other vendors' computers and networks. Peripherals also do not need to come from the same vendors, but can be mixed and matched to customize your network to your needs.

Networks also alleviate security dilemmas. With a network, you can control the security from a central point of administration. Networks can eliminate the repetitive aspects of system maintenance, so that more time can be devoted to other tasks. These topics are covered in detail in Chapters 6 and 7. Networks can be easy to administer when they are set up correctly.

Now that you have decided to try networking, you need to know the requirements. The next chapter examines the equipment and software you need to build your network.

Building a Network

hether you are planning to purchase a network or currently have one in place, this chapter can help you make sure that your network does what it is intended to do. The preceding chapter provided an overview of networking. This chapter examines the specific parts and pieces that make up a network.

In this chapter, you examine the following features of networks:

- What makes up a good file server
- What to look for in a workstation
- Which operating systems can be used
- Which cabling topologies can work for you
- Which peripherals are available

This chapter helps you examine Novell NetWare's networking features and what you need to build a system that fits your needs.

Understanding File Servers

File servers are the center and heart of today's networks. A *file server* is a PC that controls network activity, such as printing, file sharing, and security. The file server becomes the most important PC in the office. It controls printing, data and program sharing, and security access.

Examining File Servers

Because the file server's operation is critical, you should make your file server selection carefully. Reliability and serviceability should be your highest concerns. After looking at various file servers, clients often say, "I want to use this one because it's the fastest." After the clients carefully inspect the fast file server, however, they do not always receive the news they expect. Clients often are informed that the file server they want is unapproved. These servers are not of a quality that would normally be acceptable for reliability and performance. File servers of this type often do not work with commonly used high-performance network boards or drivers. They also have problems with many disk drives.

Not all computers are built alike. This factor usually becomes evident after you install NetWare. Many computers that are used as file servers randomly lock up or do not operate in a nondedicated mode when you try to run NetWare on them. A nondedicated v2.2 file server must be 100 percent IBM-compatible to operate properly in this switched mode.

 Some versions of NetWare do not work with some IBM PS/2 models. NetWare 386 lists its requirements as Compaq 386 or 100 percent compatible.

So that you do not make a poor purchasing decision, you need to know the proper procedure for choosing a file server.

Reviewing Standard File Server Options

Novell publishes an extensive list of computers and networking components approved with the NetWare seal of approval. Examining this list is always a good place to start. Check whether your PC or peripheral has been accepted. You should be concerned about a PC's capacity to function as a Novell file server.

Keep in mind that you must consider the Novell approval in terms of the conditions in which the tests were performed. Equipment tested and approved with NetWare v2.15 may not necessarily operate properly with v2.2 or v3.11. Most reputable resellers will supply a copy of the Novell report, as well as written proof that the equipment functions properly.

During the process of selecting a file server, consider the types of applications, number of users, and total amount of possible disk space to be used, as well as whether you may need communication with a different computer environments, such as mainframes or minicomputers.

The 286 file server still works well in small offices with a couple of users who need to share word processing documents and spreadsheets. In this type of environment, a PC with an 80286 processor, 3M (megabytes) of memory, and an 80M hard disk drive probably is fine.

Offices with large numbers of users or database-intensive applications, such as accounting programs, certainly require more horsepower. In this type of environment, the individual components can make a big difference in performance.

When selecting the PC itself, consider processor speed, memory-access time, and bus type and speed. With 486 systems becoming the current standard and 386DX and 386SX systems becoming the workstations of choice, you must weigh all these performance items against your budget. Currently, you can choose from the Intel 386- and 486-based systems. These systems operate at speeds of 20Mhz (megahertz), 25Mhz, 33Mhz, and now even 50 or 66Mhz.

Although speed is generally always good, some of the newer 50 and 66Mhz computers have not quite got it right yet. Make sure that these computers have been fully tested and certified to operate as a NetWare file server.

Then you must examine the ISA (Industry Standard Architecture), MCA (Micro Channel Architecture), and EISA (Ehanced Industry Standard Architecture) busses. Each one offers its own set of advantages when used in the right places.

The 386SX is a cost-effective limited version of the standard 386DX microprocessor. The SX processor only provides a 16-bit bus, which is half that of the DX. This computer makes a good data processing workstation.

Generally, faster processors provide faster memory-access times. Because NetWare relies heavily on disk caching for performance, fast processors become an important factor as well.

When examining bus options, consider performance, budget, and availability of service parts. The ISA bus has been available since the introduction of the first IBM PC. The ISA bus still offers the largest selection and greatest availability of service parts, but varies greatly in performance. A 486 file server operating at 33MHz with a standard 8MHz ISA bus may not support a large number of database users.

IBM's MCA was introduced with the IBM PS/2 computer and has a large number of installed units. Generally, MCA bus computers are IBMs, but MCA clones are becoming available.

A Note From the Author...

I have found that the MCA bus performs better than the standard ISA bus, but the cost for the computer and the required MCA network interface cards is higher. MCA cards are available from most manufacturers but may not be immediately available from local dealers.

The newest available bus option, the EISA bus, offers high performance if it is set up correctly. EISA is compatible with older ISA-type cards. The EISA standard is becoming the preferred choice among professionals in the industry because of its compatibility and its capability to be slowly integrated by using existing controllers. For these reasons, many PC manufacturers support this standard. The EISA bus can provide 33MHz bursts at the bus level—with a hefty price tag attached. The cost of EISA bus disk controllers and LAN cards starts at nearly $1,000.

You need to keep in mind that the EISA bus provides this performance only when it is used with EISA cards. The EISA bus standard also enables you to use 16-bit cards with some performance compromise. 16-bit cards, which are ISA, operate at 8MHz. If they are used, any performance advantages you hoped to gain by using EISA architecture are lost.

Some manufacturers make PCs with an ISA bus that can provide bus speeds up to 16.5MHz. These computers can move data across an ISA bus at rapid rates. You can measure up to a 30 percent increase in disk input/output (I/O) merely by changing the bus speed on these ISA systems.

Later in this chapter, you examine how to make a file server selection.

Examining Workstations

When you are using a network, the workstation is where most of the processing takes place. Novell NetWare provides a *distributed-processing environment*, which means that each computer provides the processing power required to operate the desired program at the personal level.

Workstations come in many shapes and sizes, and they operate with many diverse local operating systems. With Novell NetWare, many popular workstation systems can share network resources. Whether it is a DOS, Windows, OS/2, Macintosh, or UNIX computer, Novell NetWare offers connectivity.

Workstations come in desktops, towers, and portables, and many manufacturers offer the interfaces to connect to networks. With such a large selection of computer workstations available, making a good choice becomes difficult. Your most important concern should be support. Who will provide service if the workstation breaks?

The market is flooded with PC manufacturers who offer deals. You need to ask yourself this question: "What is better for my company—getting a rock-bottom low price today and then getting the workstation serviced tomorrow, or paying the price for a quality system today to ensure years of trouble-free service in the future?"

When you choose a workstation, keep in mind your need and application performance. Many people make purchases based on cost only. What often is not clear is that a lower-cost, lower-performance PC may cost more in the long run. With the 8088, 80286, 80386, and 80486 processors currently available, applications developers take advantage of the power required to complete their tasks in a timely fashion.

Some of the newer technology databases and graphics interface programs need a great deal of power. In this case, a 386SX or 386DX is appropriate. The amount of memory and type of video system you use depend on the requirements of the applications chosen. You should ask the software developers what to use to get the best results.

Novell offers users various facilities and functions—including file and print services—on Macintosh, OS/2, and UNIX systems. With Novell's optional NetWare for Macintosh, OS/2 Requestor, and new NetWare v3.11 NFS systems, users can operate with the appropriate workstations and can share network peripherals from any of the previously mentioned platforms.

The safest and most common choice is a 386SX workstation with a Video Graphics Array (VGA) color monitor and 4M of memory. The SX computers are a limited version of a regular 80386 computer and are a cost-effective solution to computing needs. SX computers run all the currently popular software packages, including Windows and OS/2.

Choosing a Cabling System

The next important feature of a network is the way that the computers are connected. This is known as the *cabling system*. When installing a cabling system, many cabling topologies are available, such as Arcnet, Ethernet, and Token Ring. Personal computers must be connected for them to communicate. The method that is used to interconnect computers is referred to as the *topology*. To make the best choice, you should find a compromise between what works, convenience, cost, and standards for connectivity.

 Connectivity is the capability to hook computers together and have them share data and peripherals.

After you select a topology, you need to examine the various cabling types available. Current options include coaxial cable, unshielded twisted-pair, shielded twisted-pair, fiber optics, and even wireless connections for cableless-connection systems. Different cable types are discussed in the next section.

Shielded Twisted Pair

Shielded twisted-pair wiring has been available the longest. Its roots start with mainframe terminals. Currently, shielded twisted-pair wiring is most popular with IBM Token Ring and is known by such names as Type 1 and Type 6 cabling. Generally, this type of cabling is used for up to 16 megabits of data transmission, but new engineering enables transmission speeds up to 100 megabits.

 A speed of 16 megabits is 16 million bits of data sent through a cable in one second.

Because IBM's standard is shielded twisted-pair, this type of cabling is prevalent in companies that have IBM computers. This usually is because the company is a dedicated IBM customer with IBM PCs, mainframes, or both.

Coaxial Cable

Various types of coaxial cables, known simply as *coax* cables, are available. Coax cable types, such as RG58 and RG62, each have particular electrical characteristics and must be selected to work with the chosen cabling topology.

Whether it is Arcnet, Ethernet, or a proprietary system such as G/net, the proper coax type must be installed. Coax cable has been available for years and is used throughout the electrical industry. Coax cable is used in radios, televisions, and communications whenever a high-frequency signal is used and high-interference rejection is needed. One of the most common uses of coax today is with cable television. If you subscribe to cable television, you have coax cable connected to your cable box or directly to your television set.

Coax still is used as a network cabling system in which a high level of electrical interference is present or as a "backbone" to provide a common segment for connecting multiple file servers.

Although new coax installations are increasingly rare, coax is by no means becoming obsolete. In many installations, coax cable provides high performance and reliability. Coax cable has been perfected through the years and now has provided a solid step to the next level of network cabling.

Unshielded Twisted Pair

Everywhere that you see network ads, you see the letters UTP. *Unshielded twisted-pair* (UTP) wiring currently is the cabling system of choice. UTP systems predominantly follow the AT&T Primisus wiring standards, but variations exist. Most people assume that UTP network cabling is merely telephone wiring, which is mostly correct. The problem is that telephone wiring, which was installed before the AT&T standard, does not necessarily meet the specifications required to pass high-speed data. If you plan to use an existing telephone wiring system as a high-speed network medium, have the system tested and certified before proceeding. Most reputable network resellers can supply this service.

UTP is convenient and easy to manage if designed and installed properly. With UTP, office and workstation moves are painless (these moves always are a problem with coax systems). UTP can provide a high-performance and reliable data connection. With the high-quality hubs and concentrators also comes the capability for a high level of cabling diagnostics.

 A *connector* is a piece of hardware that connects a cable end to a hardware device or another cable. A *hub* is a central connecting point for cables. A *concentrator* is a type of hub.

UTP cabling currently works with all of the common topologies: Arcnet, Ethernet, and Token Ring. Arcnet provided a UTP system first; Ethernet and Token Ring followed later. Arcnet UTP is currently a de facto standard. Not all manufacturers' products supplying the UTP option can communicate with each other, because no real standard exists for this method. At this time, two ways are available for operating Arcnet over unshielded twisted-pair: SMC and Thomas Conrad. Both manufacturers hold a substantial share of the market, and each has valid reasons why its product is better.

For Ethernet to communicate over UTP, two methods also are available: LatticeNet and 10BaseT. Synoptics is a manufacturer that supported Ethernet on UTP well before the current 10BaseT standard.

Synoptics also became popular in large corporations because of the system interfaces available. Synoptics has supplied enough connectivity options to create an installed base large enough to become another de facto standard. Since the release of the 10BaseT standard, Synoptics has expanded support to include both topologies.

 10BaseT is an IEEE standard that enables Ethernet technology to be used over twisted-pair cabling.

With 10BaseT now an IEEE standard, most companies using Ethernet are migrating toward 10BaseT. With the current wave of manufacturers now supplying 10BaseT equipment, deciding to move to 10BaseT cabling makes sense.

Token Ring is installed predominantly with shielded twisted-pair or IBM Type 1 and Type 6 cabling. Most manufacturers support the operation on UTP, but no confirmed standard exists. Most manufacturers use a simple impedance matching device, such as a balun, to enable UTP operation. This method greatly reduces the maximum cable lengths that can be used, but it is still quite popular despite this drawback.

 A *balun*, or balanced/unbalanced device, converts impedance of one interface to the impedance of a second interface. An example would be coax cable to twisted-pair. The impedance of a cable is the resistance the wire offers to a change in current.

Underwriters Laboratories Listed Cable

UL (Underwriters Laboratories) has developed a program that covers all UL-listed communications cable. This program currently identifies five levels of performance for the UTP 100-Ohm cable type. You must be aware of these cable ratings when you design or install a LAN. The cables are divided into five levels, and each has distinct performance differences, as shown in the following list:

- **Level I** cable is intended for very basic communications and low-level power functions. This level has no performance rating.

- **Level II** cable covers cable with 2 to 25 twisted pairs and is similar to IBM Type 3. This cable level can be either 24 or 22 AWG (American Wire Gage) and covers both shielded and unshielded cables. This level of cable is designed for slower speed communications and is only rated at speeds to 1Mhz.

- **Level III** is the first true data grade cable. This cable complies with the data-transmission standards set by the Electronic Industries Association (EIA) for commercial building telecommunications standards. This is the minimum level cable that should be considered in any LAN environment. Level III cable can be 24 or 22 AWG and carries a rating of up to 16Mhz, but provides only adequate performance to 10Mhz. This level provides good performance for UTP Arcnet LANs.

- **Level IV** cable complies with the current requirements of the National Electrical Manufacturers Association (NEMA) and is considered a Low-Loss Telecommunications Cable. This level is very common in today's LAN environment and provides adequate performance for 10BASE-T and 4Mbs Token Ring networks. Level IV also is available in both 24 and 22 AWG. Although this level is rated to 20Mhz, reliable operation over 10Mhz in a LAN is questionable.

- **Level V** cable is currently the cable of choice when implementing a 16Mbs Token Ring system over UTP. Level V cable is available in both 24 and 22 AWG, and supports transmission speeds to 100Mhz. Level V cable is referred to as Low-Loss Extended-Frequency Premises Telecommunications Cable. Although Level V loses much of its performance after 20Mhz, it does offer a very clean media up to that point. It is currently the highest certified cable available. Any Level V cable should be clearly marked stating its Verified Level.

Examining Topologies

Now that you have examined the cabling options and the various topologies that can be used on each type of cable, you need to determine which protocol best fits particular situations. Each topology discussed in this section has benefits and drawbacks that vary with each installation.

Arcnet

Arcnet, developed by Datapoint Corporation, operates in a star or bus configuration, as shown in figure 2.1. Arcnet uses a token passing or token bus protocol and is extremely popular with one of the largest installed bases. Arcnet enables operation on both coax and UTP, which adds to its appeal. Arcnet is popular in small-to-midsized companies because of its low cost and reliability.

 Token Passing or Token bus is a network-access method that puts a token on the cable that workstations look for to give requests, commands, or data. Workstations must give information to empty tokens. Tokens are passed from a network node to the next highest node address. Node addresses are set manually with switches on the board in Arcnet systems. The numbers range from 1 to 255.

Figure 2.1:
An example of
Arcnet cabling.

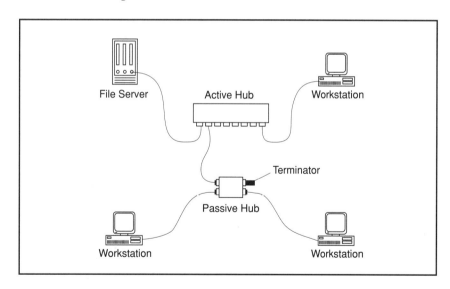

Arcnet does have drawbacks. When Arcnet is installed with a large number of users or used on a very busy system, its performance tends to drop fairly fast, with a total bandwidth of 2.5M. A user on an Arcnet system can expect approximately 50K- to 80K-per-second throughput, which drops off sharply as demand goes up. Arcnet also offers little in the way of large system connectivity and therefore is suited for small-to-midsized companies that do not require a standard into the mainframe or minicomputer environment.

A group of manufacturers is working on an implementation of Arcnet to supply a 20 megabits-per-second standard. When this standard is completed, Arcnet may become one of the fastest networking topologies commonly used. Thomas Conrad currently offers TCNS, a 100 megabit-per-second implementation of Arcnet over fiber optics. Although this is a proprietary solution, it does offer a high-speed option for graphic workstation applications such as computer-aided design (CAD).

Ethernet

Ethernet can provide connectivity with most computer systems manufactured today, regardless of their size. Ethernet operates in a bus configuration and uses the Carrier Sense Multiple Access/Collision Detection (CSMA/CD). Ethernet is a widely used standard that enjoys success with mainframes, minicomputers, and many UNIX systems. Figure 2.2 shows a thick Ethernet cabling system.

Figure 2.2:
An example of a thick Ethernet cabling system.

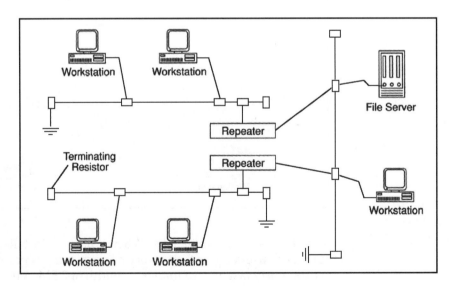

CSMA/CD stands for Carrier Sense Multiple Access/Collision Detection. CSMA is the way each workstation listens for communications on the cable. If there is nothing on the cable, the workstation sends its information to the cable. Data on a network can collide because multiple workstations can transmit their data at the same time. The Collision Detection scheme is the means by which a network detects collisions on the network and tells the sending workstation to retransmit the information.

The Ethernet topology was developed in 1980 by Digital Equipment Corporation, Intel, and Xerox Corporation. Currently, the Ethernet specification is V2.0 or Ethernet II. Although Novell and other companies use the IEEE 802.3 standard as a default, a difference exists in the way the data frames are formed. Both standards are widely used, which is why Novell provides support for each.

Until recently, normal Ethernet installations used RG8 (thicknet) or RG58 (thinnet) coax. With the recent standardization of 10BaseT, many people are installing the new UTP system rather than coax. Ethernet is a robust system, providing high throughput in short bursts. Ethernet's 10M bandwidth enables it to supply workstations with speeds between 90K- and 200K- per-second of data throughput. Ethernet's performance varies greatly with the amount of traffic on the cable. If a collision is detected, the sending node waits a predetermined amount of time and resends the data.

 Data Frame is a group of bits that make up a basic block of data for transmission on a network.

This retransmitting of data causes the network performance to vary. Some 10BaseT systems provide a method of *collision elimination* (CE) or *collision avoidance* (CA). This service is provided by the 10BaseT concentrator. The device acts as a traffic cop for the system, preventing packets from colliding on a heavily used system and therefore preventing the need to resend data.

Ethernet has a great deal to offer when you need a connection to a larger system. Most manufacturers support Ethernet, and it works well in small-office systems and large-enterprise systems. Ethernet returns a high level of reliability, provided that you protect the coax cable from damage. In a bus system, a damaged cable can cause the entire segment to fail. The 10BaseT UTP system not only adds a convenient way to connect workstations, but also adds protection from cable damage due to its star configuration. If one cable breaks, only one workstation loses the connection, not the entire network. Figure 2.3 shows a star configuration.

Figure 2.3:
An example of a
star configuration.

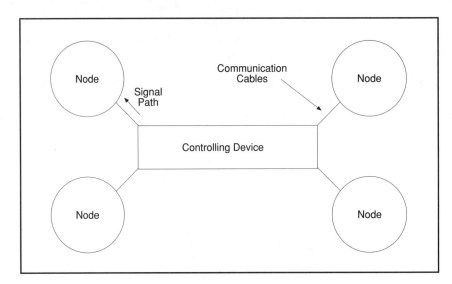

The equipment required for installing an Ethernet network varies greatly, depending on the performance and diagnostic features included in the 10BaseT concentrator. Many 10BaseT suppliers are emerging. Remember to keep the cost in perspective. The cost shown on paper is not always the cost that you pay. Hidden costs always emerge if you choose hardware and cabling that are not the best quality. Frequently, these costs accumulate when everyday use shows the weaknesses of the system. Keep in mind that the cabling system acts as the artery system to the heart, which is the file server, that provides the life force to your company. Chapter 11 discusses ways to can choose a consultant who can help you avoid the pitfalls of an improperly chosen cabling system.

Token Ring

Another protocol option is Token Ring. IBM Token Ring operates in a star-wired ring and uses IBM Type 1, IBM Type 6, and UTP cabling.

The Token Ring protocol provides a consistent data flow and can deliver a performance that is much higher than Arcnet or Ethernet. IBM made the Token Ring topology popular by providing support to all of the company's product lines. Figure 2.4 shows a star-wire ring.

Figure 2.4:
An example of a star-wire ring.

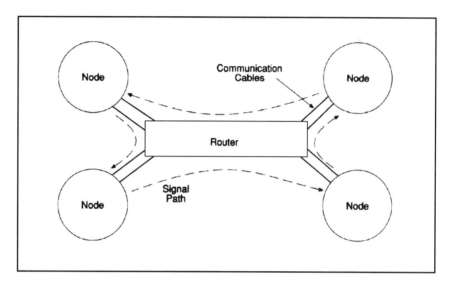

Token Ring operates at either a 4M or 16M bandwidth, depending on the hardware you use. With the performance that Token Ring offers, you may wonder why it is not the most commonly used protocol. Token Ring's drawbacks are cost and cabling. In most cases, the cost of Token-Ring equipment nearly doubles that of Ethernet and triples that of Arcnet. IBM's Type 1 and Type 6 cables are difficult to work with, and Token Ring UTP greatly reduces the cable distances allowed when designing a system. Cost and difficulty generally outweigh performance. Figure 2.5 shows a Token-Ring configuration.

 Bandwidth is a range of frequencies that can pass over a given circuit. The greater the bandwidth, the greater the amount of information that can be sent.

This chapter's discussion has been concentrating on options that are popular in most installations. Networking is not limited to the options examined so far. Other options are available, including fiber optics and wireless connections.

Figure 2.5:
A Token-Ring
configuration.

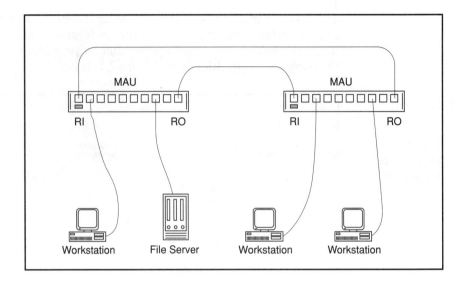

Fiber Optics

Fiber optics is fairly new to the network industry. In the past, the cost of fiber optics—both material and installation—has kept it out of all but the largest companies and academic environments. Fiber optics can deliver data at a 100-megabit bandwidth, is not susceptible to electrical noise, and enables transmission distances not available with any other cabling system. The cost of all these features exceeds what the average network installation budget can handle.

It is becoming apparent that the need and performance outweigh cost because fiber optics is becoming more and more popular. Fiber optics has offered large corporations and campus environments performance and reliability that was previously unavailable. With the Fiber Distributed Data Interface (FDDI) standard on the horizon, the possibilities are almost endless.

 FDDI, or Fiber Distributed Data Interface, is a new standard that permits 100 megabits-per-second (Mbps) of data transfer.

As with fiber optics and other cabling methods, the person that installs your cable should be a qualified cable engineer who is experienced with the installation of the topology that you choose.

CDDI (Copper Distributed Data Interface) is a recent technological advancement. CDDI provides the capability to transmit 100Mbps over copper cable. Currently, this is implemented using *STP (Shielded Twisted Pair)* or IBM Type 1 cable, but work is being done to determine the possibility of operating FDDI over UTP.

Wireless Connections

The newest popular "cable" system is the *wireless connection* system. Currently, two companies provide products for wireless environments. Both NCR and Motorola have systems that enable workstations to communicate with the file server without a physical connection.

NCR's WaveLAN, which requires that transmitting and receiving devices be mounted on each workstation, offers a proprietary or non-standard solution to networking. Motorola's Altair Plus system offers a wireless connection with a full 10M Ethernet connection to workgroups using cellular telephone technology. The Altair system uses a frequency band allocated for its use in the 18Ghz (Gigahertz) range. This product is currently available in two different product lines. The standard model provides limited distance for use in the office environment. The external version, with a remotely located antenna, provides an extended distance of up to 500ft to offer a building-to-building connection.

Wireless connecting products will not eliminate the cabling system. You should use them as an expansion or portable addition to your corporation's permanent system.

Sifting through the Options

You must consider standards, performance, cabling types, and topologies when selecting a system. Fitting a performance level to your company's needs can be a difficult task. Usually, you also must keep in mind the company's budget. You should not, however, make the final choice based only on budgetary concerns.

Many good cabling solutions are available. If your company does not have a standard for cabling, your best bet for finding the most effective system is to use an outside consulting engineer. The cabling system you choose today may need to be expanded tomorrow. By carefully selecting an option that can grow with your company, you can avoid spending excess dollars in both service and engineering costs later.

The installation of the actual cable must be performed within the guidelines set by the particular topology. Improperly installed cable is the source of many network problems. The cost of a qualified cable engineer can prevent additional costs later.

Networking for the Small Office

Suppose that you are researching a network for an office with four computer users. Their main needs are word processing, occasional spreadsheet work, and moderately simple accounting. The workload is fairly steady; these users process approximately 25 orders a day for one of the 150 items maintained in stock, and they send out approximately 75 to 100 letters per day to new prospects.

With this caseload, a 286 file server probably would provide adequate performance. With the reasonable price of 386 computers, however, the company would profit more by fitting a 386 system into the budget. Doing so ensures high performance and enables system growth without the need to upgrade the file server later. A computer with a standard ISA or MCA bus provides good performance to an *modified frequency modulation* (MFM), *run length limited* (RLL), or *enhanced small device interface* (ESDI) disk controller and drive. These are all data-encoding methods. The ESDI controller offers the highest data-access time.

Small offices often consider running the file server in a nondedicated mode. If this solution is the only one available to you, then you need to be aware of the dangers.

A *nondedicated* file server divides its central processing unit time (CPU time) between file server functions and DOS workstation functions, doubling as a workstation and file server. The DOS workstation portion can require as much as 70 percent of the CPU's power. Another potential problem is that any software that locks up the workstation causes the file server to lock up or crash. A nondedicated file server crash is the equivalent of unplugging all running workstations simultaneously, which can lead to data corruption in the files that were open.

One possible solution is to place the user with the lightest work load on the file server/workstation computer. Using this method, you can alleviate much of the bottlenecking that occurs when the computer acts as a workstation. Nondedicated file servers work if you take necessary precautions.

Networking the Large Corporation

Now examine a company that has slightly larger needs. Suppose that Evolution, Inc. currently has 25 employees using stand-alone PCs, and the company needs a network to continue its fast-paced growth. At present, the company's employees do word processing on 15 PCs and work with fairly large databases on 10 of the workstations. These databases are loaded on each local drive and vary in size from 1M to 6M. The capability to generate reports from all the databases to assist in sales projections would be beneficial. Evolution, Inc. also wants two people in the accounting department to work from a shared system.

The word processing users in Evolution, Inc. have the least amount of network packet traffic, but the database users' workload is substantial. Because the company's growth averages 50 percent each year, a growth path is essential. In this case, nothing short of a 386 or 486 33MHz computer will work. This type of system provides plenty of horsepower for NetWare v2.2 or v3.11. The 486 system performs the best, but the 386 fits more easily into most budgets.

Another consideration is a disk subsystem—preferably one that uses a *Small Computer Systems Interface* (SCSI). A *disk subsystem* is an external box that houses up to four disk drives and provides an interface from the drives to the file server. The SCSI bus controller can be used to operate multiple disk channels and supports up to seven devices per channel. MFM, RLL, and ESDI generally only offer two drives per controller. SCSI disk controllers also are available with disk coprocessors that can offload some of the file server's work performed by the main processor. SCSI offers a high performance I/O (Input/Output) channel for your file server's disk drives at speeds of up to

5MB-per-second. Because new high-speed disk drives and computers are appearing constantly, an even higher-performance disk channel was needed—thus appeared SCSI-2 and now FAST SCSI-2.

SCSI-2 provides additional commands. Although these commands may not be noticed by the operators, they help the future of interoperability. FAST SCSI-2 offers features that are seen by most users. FAST SCSI-2 uses different timing to push the disk throughput to speeds of up to 10MB-per-second. Because the new FAST SCSI-2 must be understood by both the controller and the disk drives, all equipment must support the new standard to get the full benefit.

Choosing the System

As you can see, multiple solutions sometimes are available for a particular case. Some solutions work better than others, and the solutions vary from dealer to dealer. Most manufacturers have *benchmark programs* that make them look good. A benchmark program determines the speed of a piece of equipment by placing various loads on it. The majority of computers made today use a static cache built into the hardware. When tested, these computers perform well. The dilemma is that many times the cache must be disabled for this type of system to operate as a NetWare file server. Disabling the cache sometimes cuts performance by as much as 50 percent.

New types of computers are made practically every day. Currently available are *superservers*, computers operating with up to 100 megabit busses, 386 disk coprocessors, and cabinets that compare with minicomputers. These computers are designed as file servers. They are intended to be used as dedicated file servers and not as workstations. Superservers are expensive but effective.

When you are planning to buy a file server, your best approach is to ask questions. References are usually better than paper statistics. Good resellers operate from experience—tap into their knowledge. If all else fails, at least a file server that you may have now will make a great workstation in the future.

Using Printers

In this fast-paced corporate world, reports, correspondence, and presentations play a major role. Every office has a need to print. Regardless of whether the item is simple correspondence or a financial statement, printed copies are a necessity.

In non-networked computerized offices, printers are one of the main reasons for *sneaker-net*, an environment in which users must run to other computers to use specific printers. You probably want to be able to print your final copy on a laser printer or print your 100-page report on the fastest dot-matrix printer.

On a NetWare network, printing problems are a thing of the past. With NetWare services and many third-party products, you have several printing options. Anyone connected to the LAN can share the device, regardless of whether it is a laser printer, dot-matrix printer, or high-performance plotter.

With Novell NetWare, you can connect high-usage printers directly to the file server or operate them from a dedicated print server. The number of printers supported by these servers depends entirely on the PC hardware.

Printers that are seldom used may be located in or near a department where other users can make use of them. If these printers are attached to a network, anyone can use them from any workstation. The workstation to which the printer is connected can service that printer as a background task. This setup is convenient and eliminates the need to install special cables to remotely locate the printer.

NetWare's print-queue services provide the flexibility to manage security and administrative functions with each printer.

Printing to a network can improve productivity greatly because the workstation can send print jobs to the network faster than a local printer can accept the same data. With the print services provided by NetWare, you no longer need to install many printers to support each user.

Using network technology, you now can purchase high-quality, specialized printers that can support many users in a more productive manner. For more detail on setting up your printers in NetWare, see Chapter 8.

Using Modems, Scanners, and Fax Machines

A great deal of time and space would be needed to discuss thoroughly the vast amount of network peripherals available. You can select products to share modems, printers, CD ROMs, fax machines, and much more. In this section, you receive an overview of products that suit most users' needs.

Modems

In most cases in which modems are not used constantly, users can share them on a network. By doing so, users eliminate the need to have more telephone lines installed in each office or workstation. Also, productivity can be increased because more people can share the new high-speed V.32 and V.42 modems, for example.

Several methods are available for sharing modems. The first and most economical method is with simple peer-to-peer software. Many of these packages are available. When examining one of these programs, be sure to check all its features and limitations.

 Peer-to-peer networks enable workstations to use printers and hard drives attached to other workstations. Information is sent over cabling without the need of any type of server.

Peer-to-peer programs enable workstations to use another workstation's hardware, such as a modem.

The most common method for sharing modems on a network is through a dedicated *asynchronous communication server* (ACS). The ACS has as many as 16 serial ports that enable connections to modems or host computers. A logical connection is established between the PC workstation and the ACS port by use of DOS's Interrupt 14, which is the DOS programming standard for modem sharing, or Novell's *NetWare Asynchronous System Interface* (NASI) standard. After a virtual connection is made, the modem appears to be connected to the workstation's COM port. In other words, it seems to be attached to the local port when it actually resides in another station. Many ACSs are available, including the *Novell Asynchronous Communication Server* (NACS).

Most asynchronous servers provide both dial-in and dial-out services, along with PBX-like functions, which is the capability to automatically hunt for and find the next available port.

When considering a particular brand, be sure to check all the options because they vary from model to model. The right set of options, such as line pooling, line groups, and line request queues when busy, can make all the difference in managing and monitoring these services.

Fax Servers

Network fax servers have evolved from simple single-user PC cards to high-performance dedicated fax servers. Any office that relies on faxing documents daily and always has a line at the fax machine can benefit from a shared network fax server.

Network fax servers are simple to use when set up properly, and they can increase productivity almost instantly. Most high-quality systems require a dedicated PC to perform as a server or are sold as a proprietary fax computer. These systems simply attach to the network in the same manner as a workstation and accept a modular phone connector as any fax machine does. Most similarities stop there. Differences in functions, performance, and user interfaces become more evident as fax servers are examined.

Some network fax servers provide services for outgoing documents, some provide document-routing services for incoming documents, and some just dump documents into a common directory. Most network fax servers enable direct printing from the application by way of a memory-resident interface, and others require printing files from a special program. The capability to fax a document directly from the application can greatly reduce the extra work required when paper facsimiles are sent. Another important feature is the capacity to operate in both the DOS and Microsoft Windows environments. Because of Windows' popularity, this function is becoming a requirement.

Note The term *memory resident* refers to a program that is always available. These programs are generally activated by pressing a special combination of keys and are available to the user without the need to exit the application.

Most high-quality fax servers provide a queueing service, which enables multiple users to send documents at the same time. Another nice feature is the capability to send documents to a group with a single procedure.

One of the highest performing fax servers currently available is the FaxPress made by Castelle. This machine provides incoming/outgoing faxing, queueing, confirmation, viewing faxed documents, and a hot-key telephone book with corporate and private phone numbers. This product also can fax to groups of phone numbers. This unit fully emulates an HP LaserJet printer and works perfectly with downloadable soft fonts. In addition to all these features, this unit also operates as a dedicated printer and comes complete with a built-in network interface.

As you can see, fax servers vary from a simple fax board that can be shared to a complete system that can handle all your faxing needs. Also keep in mind that most network fax servers require optional scanners if original hard-copy documents are to be transmitted. Most fax servers are used for computer-generated documents and usually do not replace the standard office fax machine.

When you are selecting a fax server, the best approach is to locate a reputable reseller and rely on his or her experience. Most full-service resellers also can set up a demonstration that enables you to test a particular unit in your environment.

CD ROMs

Because many companies now provide data on CD ROMs, which are high-capacity optical drives, the need to share these devices is becoming a requirement. Novell provides the *Network Support Encyclopedia*, which includes all Novell documentation, technical bulletins, patches, and fixes, along with many third-party manuals. Other companies provide CD ROMs with dozens of trade publications listed by topic, data, magazine title, and much more.

In the past, CD ROMs have been difficult to implement on a network. Currently, some clean and efficient methods are available. Some systems require dedicated CD ROM servers, and Novell recently certified drivers that enable CD ROMs to operate directly off the server. This setup enables the CD ROM to use the Novell disk cache for performance.

This section briefly examined a few popular shared peripherals. The main objective was to give you an overview and perhaps to spark a few ideas of your own.

Now you know the requirements for putting together a Novell NetWare network. Appendixes A and B provide guidelines for installing NetWare. Refer to the appropriate appendix to install your own network.

Summary

This chapter examined the individual pieces that make up a network. You must examine many different elements to create a reliable, productive file server. The choices are not easy, but networks are flexible. If an option does not work as well as planned, additional options are available to meet your requirements.

You always can upgrade a well-planned network as new technology produces better equipment. Old equipment can be reused throughout the network. New and different cabling types can be mixed with existing systems. Workstations can become routers, servers can become workstations, and the network improves.

In the next chapter, you examine the reasons to choose Novell NetWare. You learn what makes NetWare reliable, fast, and secure. You also learn why you should be impressed with your decision to purchase NetWare.

Examining NetWare's Benefits

N ovell NetWare provides all the networking features examined in Chapters 1 and 2. Novell NetWare also offers
much more. Novell's diverse operating systems can meet
the needs of all users, both within small companies and
large companies. If your company has simple needs, such
as sharing processed information and printers, the 286-based operating system works well. If, however, your company needs to communicate with other computer systems and to have a more flexible
security system, a 386-based operating system is a better choice.

In this chapter, you examine whether NetWare v2.2 or v3.11 is best for
you. You also examine the following NetWare features and benefits:

- Reliability and system fault tolerance
- Network security
- Performance
- Network expandability.

You then look at specific features to examine why NetWare is reliable, dependable, and fast.

Deciding between NetWare Versions 2.2 and 3.11

Planning for the future for your network is often a concern of NetWare administrators. If you currently have only 286 computers and cannot purchase a 386 or 486 computer, then v2.2 is your only option. If you are not limited to a specific processor type, your choice can be based on preference. This section examines the similarities and differences between the two operating systems.

Version 2.2 Features

NetWare v2.2 offers four different versions of the operating system. The newest 286-based operating system offers several combinations of user versions and connection amounts.

Connections, as defined by Novell, are taken up by print servers, communications, and specialized processes. *Value added processes* (VAPs) take up most of the connections. VAPS are programs that increase the functionality of the server. Common VAPs include printing servers and file server keyboard software locks. Depending on the functionality of the VAP, it can take up several connections, as follows:

- The five-user version provides up to 32 connections.
- The 10-user version provides up to 32 connections.
- The 50-user version provides up to 64 connections.
- The 100-user version provides up to 116 connections.

> ### *About Macintosh Connections...*
> NetWare v2.2 includes Macintosh 2.0 VAPs. V2.2 supports Appletalk Phase II and Tokentalk. Novell enables several Macintosh file attributes to be carried over into the NetWare environment for compatibility.

About Limitations of NetWare Versions...

Early NetWare versions, called *entry-level solutions* (ELSs), limited the functionality of the products. The newer versions limit only the number of users and none of the other features.

The only real limitation of features occurs when a file server runs in a nondedicated mode rather than a dedicated mode. Dedicated file servers are SFT Level II and provide transaction tracking system services. Nondedicated file servers are SFT Level I only. SFT levels are discussed later in this chapter. Memory managers, such as those included with DOS 5.0 and DRDOS 6.0, are not supported on an NON-Dedicated 2.2 file server. The Non-dedicated workstation is limited to the standard 640K of memory.

The file-server requirements for v2.2 are the following:

- 80286-, 80386-, and 80486-compatible computer
- 2.5M of RAM (more for hard drives larger than 80M)
- 10M hard disk (minimum)
- 1.2M floppy disk drive

For information on selecting the proper file server, refer to Chapter 2.

Workstations need to be 8086-compatible computers or better. The faster the workstation, the faster the network works because of distributed processing. The workstation processes a large amount of information for programs, so an 80386 system always outperforms an 8086 computer.

V2.2 is intended to be a workgroup solution, specializing in fitting the simple needs of small departments. This version works well as a specialized node in 386-based networks when a workgroup does not need connectivity to other systems.

About Industry Direction...

The computer industry currently is working toward enhancing the 386-based operating systems. These efforts do not mean that v2.2 is a dead product. If your future network plans are limited to DOS or Macintosh workstations, and if you never expect to have more than 20 PCs, v2.2 is a good choice.

Version 3.11 Features

The file-server requirements for v3.11 are the following:

- 80386- or 80486-compatible computer
- 4M of RAM (more for drives larger than 80M)
- 20M hard disk (minimum)
- 1.2M floppy drive

NetWare v3.11 offers four different user quantities:

- 10-user version
- 20-user version
- 100-user version
- 250-user version

The only difference in functionality between the different user versions of v3.11 is the number of users that can access the file server at one time.

V3.11 enables you to use any 8086-compatible PC or better as a workstation. You should keep in mind that 486 and 386 systems currently are the best systems for local processing, which NetWare relies on heavily.

One major advantage to networking with v3.11 is your ability to communicate with multivendor computers. TCP/IP and NFS connections are not possible with v2.2. This means that the v2.2 system is severely limited in the methods available to communicate with other computer systems. V3.11 provides the means to communicate with diverse single- and multiple-user systems. V3.11 is a corporate solution, meaning that it provides networking features that work for the entire company, as opposed to a single workgroup within the company. Table 3.1 compares features between v2.2 and v3.11.

Examining Reliability and System Fault Tolerance

Equipment failure is like paying taxes; it is something everyone experiences sooner or later. With proper planning and protection, equipment failure does not have to be a painful experience.

Table 3.1
A v2.2 and v3.11 Comparison Chart

NetWare feature	v3.11	v2.1x
Logical connections supported on each file server	250	100
Concurrent open files on each file server	100,000	1,000
Maximum files using TTS concurrently	10,000	200
Volumes on each file server	64	32
Hard disks on each volume	32	1
Hard disks on each server	2,048	32
Directory entries on each volume	2,097,152	10,240
Maximum file size	4G	256M
Maximum volume size	32TB	256M
Maximum addressable RAM memory	4G	12M
Maximum addressable disk storage	32TB	2G

In a productive network, any equipment failure produces costly interruptions. Novell NetWare currently uses state-of-the-art technology in preventing and reducing failures of many kinds. NetWare implements several *system fault tolerance* (SFT) features, such as duplicate disk directories, duplicate file allocation tables (FATs), and read-after-write verification. These features ensure that each block written to disk can be recovered at the time it was written.

NetWare also implements many other features that provide added reliability and added performance. These features include a transaction tracking system (TTS), dynamic bad block remapping (a hot fix), disk mirroring, channel mirroring (duplexing), and file server mirroring.

The Transaction Tracking System

The transaction tracking system (TTS) protects against loss or corruption due to incomplete transactions. The TTS tracks data-update operations and enables data files to return to the point in time just before the incomplete transaction was performed.

A *transaction* is a set of write requests that must be complete for file and data integrity to be maintained. *Write operations* usually consist of index and key files that must be in sync with the main data files. The TTS guarantees that all write operations making a transaction are written in their entirety or not at all.

During system installation, the system administrator selects a volume to use as the TTS work space. The space is used for the record-keeping tasks needed to implement the TTS. The TTS is disabled automatically if disk space drops below what is required. Files to be included in the TTS must be flagged as transactional by using the NetWare FLAG command.

The start and end of a transaction are either implicitly or explicitly defined. *Implicit* transactions are started automatically by NetWare when the workstation does its first write operation to a locked record. When all records related to the operation are unlocked, the TTS assumes that the transaction has ended. *Explicit* transactions are activated by a TTS function call made by the software developer. The explicit transaction ends with either an end transaction function call or an abort transaction function call.

When an implicit or explicit transaction begins, the TTS performs the following steps:

1. **Begin transaction**. When the "begin transaction" call is received, a marker is written to the TTS work file. All open transactional files are added during this process. If a system fault occurs, the TTS can black out any file change up to this point.

2. **Read original**, **write original**. During the TTS process, write requests are sent to the file server. Before this action is performed, the original data is reread from either cache or disk and then appended to the TTS work file, which enables the TTS to black out all changes if a transaction fails.

3. **Write update**. After the original data has been written to the work file, the next write request is completed.

4. **End transaction**. After the TTS is sure that all write requests have been performed, an "end transaction" marker is written to the work file. At this time, an acknowledgment is sent back to the application to confirm that the transaction has been written successfully to disk.

The overhead of NetWare's TTS is shielded because all its operations are written to cache, which prevents any unnecessary delays or performance loss.

SFT Level I

Hard disk media failures are common and can cause many problems if the defect occurs in a data file. Although defects usually are found during disk formatting and surface analysis, new bad blocks appear with age. NetWare's SFT I is a group of techniques designed to detect and solve this problem. TTS is not supported in SFT level I.

The first level of protection is *read-after-write verification*. This procedure guarantees that the written data can be read successfully at least once. This single function can prevent data-file corruption simply by verifying everything that is written.

The next layer of protection is called a *hot fix*. A hot fix occurs when NetWare detects and handles bad disk blocks on the fly. NetWare accomplishes this task by creating a "bad blocks to good blocks" table in system memory. The hot fix requires two percent of each disk to be set up as a redirection area for bad blocks. When read-after-write verification fails, the disk block is marked as bad and the data is written to the known good redirection area. Read operations of the redirection area are handled automatically. If a disk block becomes corrupted, the server attempts to read the data, copy it to a known good block, and mark the faulty block as bad. This procedure ensures that in the future, no attempt is made to use the bad block.

In addition to the hot fix and read-after-write procedures, several redundant components are available. Volume directories and FATs are duplicated and mirrored during normal operation. During the file server boot process, these tables are compared and validated. If an error is found, the system switches to the good copy and a message is sent to the console. You can use the Novell VRepair utility to repair the problems or you can replace the bad component.

SFT Level II

SFT Level II is the next level of protection. With this level, you can mirror disk drives or a complete disk channel.

You perform *disk mirroring* by installing two drives or sets of drives and logically operating them as one. All data written to the primary disk also is written to the mirrored disk. Disk mirroring—along with the hot fix—guarantees data integrity. If a read error occurs, the server simply retrieves the data from the mirrored disk and adds the bad block to the table. All these events occur transparently in the background.

Channel mirroring, or *duplexing*, operates similarly to disk mirroring. The exception is that when you duplex, the complete disk channel is duplicated. When duplexing is used with intelligent disk controllers or disk coprocessors, four separate disk I/O channels can be operated in parallel.

Disk duplexing not only offers redundant hardware protection but also offers optimized performance. NetWare can delegate concurrent read operations to either controller, which in some cases can supply as much as a 50 percent increase in read performance during peak loads.

The biggest difference between mirroring and duplexing is that mirroring enables two pairs of drives to be managed by one controller; duplexing, on the other hand, manages pairs of drives on multiple controllers.

SFT Level III

For years, the public has heard about SFT Level III, which is a system for mirroring complete file servers to provide nonstop processing. In this configuration, you have two complete file servers operating in a mirrored mode. If any component in the file server fails, the backup server steps in and enables all processing to continue.

At this time, SFT III is still under development, and only a few engineers actually have seen this system operate. Currently, you must use automatic copy programs and high-end disk archiving systems for nonstop processing.

Using Network Security

In this section, you examine the various layers of NetWare security. In the process, you learn the reasons that NetWare can reliably provide the right protection for any company.

Login/Password-Level Security

NetWare enables you to use passwords as a measure of security. At least a dozen parameters are available for this feature, and each parameter can be set for individual users or as a default for all users.

NetWare offers a defense measure before the password ever comes into play. Suppose, for example, that you want to log on to a network. Because most small to midsized companies use first names for login names, you might assume that a login name is "Ann" and try to log in with that name. The system responds to this request by asking for a password. You try using common passwords, but each time, the network denies access.

You can try different passwords continually, and NetWare never lets you know whether a user named Ann is on that system. This feature is NetWare's first line of defense against hackers (unauthorized users). Instead of responding with a message that Ann is not a valid user name, NetWare simply asks you for a password.

Parameters for the following items are available and are examined in Chapter 7 of this book:

- How many days a password is valid
- How short a password can be
- Whether users change their own passwords
- When changing a password, whether you can repeat previous passwords or whether they must be unique
- How often passwords need to be changed
- How many times users can put off changing their passwords before the system locks them out
- How many times users can type their passwords incorrectly before the system is alerted of a possible intruder
- How many workstation users can log in to with the same user name
- Which workstations users can log in from
- During what time periods users can log in to the network
- Whether users' accounts are currently active for use

System supervisors can control these parameters conveniently from one menu utility. Both users and supervisors can change passwords from either a menu utility or a command-line utility. Ease of configuration and ease of use are important factors.

About Selecting Passwords...

The following are some ideas you can use when deciding on a password standard:

One option for selecting passwords is to choose two words that are completely unrelated to each other—VELVETKITE, DIAMONDBIRD, and MARBLEDATE, for example. Another safety feature is to put a number between the words—DUMB5COMPUTER, LATE7BLUE, and OCEAN4CAR, for example. Adding numbers and letters to passwords makes them harder to break. Passwords having anything to do with your name or your spouse's, children's, or pets' names are the easiest to figure out. Birth dates and anniversaries also are fairly easy to guess.

Another method for selecting passwords is to choose a short sentence of 7 to 10 words—something meaningful, preferably with numbers in it. Then use the first letter of each word to construct your password. If you choose the sentence *I have worked with computers for over 9 years*, for example, your password becomes IHWWCFO9Y.

The beauty of this system is that it is relatively easy to remember and virtually impossible to guess. This system takes more thought to set up, but it really works.

NetWare's default size for passwords is five characters, which can be upper- or lowercase. Without much effort, people can remember words and numbers of seven characters. Think, for example, of how many 7-digit phone numbers you can remember. Passwords shorter than five characters can be guessed too easily. NetWare's default for changing passwords is every 30 days. Any time period shorter than 30 days frustrates users and causes them to forget more frequently.

About Making Passwords Too Difficult...

When setting up standards for your company, do not make the passwords too difficult to remember and do not change them too often. I have found that people often deal with rules that are too stringent. I have seen countless offices in which all the computers are covered with Post-it Notes containing users' passwords, because the users never can remember what their passwords are.

NetWare does not enable you to see passwords for any network user. Supervisors can change users' passwords without knowing the previous password. Users must type an old password correctly before a new one can be assigned. These rules are for the security of the network and cannot be changed.

Passwords are a big part of network security. Whatever your needs are for securing user names, NetWare enables you the flexibility to design the system. But password protection is not all that is available. Directory-level security is discussed next.

Directory-Level Security

You can set up security for each directory, as well as for each user in a directory. Several different elements can be used.

User Rights

Trustee rights are the rights users or groups have in a directory. These rights also are referred to as *privileges*. Seven trustee rights exist in v2.2, and eight trustee rights exist in v3.11. Trustee rights are the keys each user has for a directory. The seven rights common in both v2.2 and v3.11 are the following:

Right	Function
Read	Enables the user to see the contents of a file and to use the file.
Write	Enables the user to alter the contents of a file.
Create	Enables the user to make new files and directories.

Right	Function
Erase	Enables the user to delete existing files and directories.
File Scan	Enables the user to view files and subdirectories in a directory. Without this right, you cannot see files in v2.2 or v3.11.
	In v2.2, you still can see subdirectories, even if you are denied rights. V3.11 hides subdirectories from the user.
Modify	Enables the user to change the attributes of a file in v2.2. With this right, the user can change a file from read/write to read only or from nonshareable to shareable. In v3.11, this right also enables the user to change the attributes for directories.
Access Control	Enables the user to give any of the preceding rights to other users on the network.

About the Extra Right in v3.11...

V3.11 has an eighth right, Supervisory, which gives all the other rights to the user or group. This right makes the user a directory supervisor, or someone who has control over what happens to a branch of the directory structure.

Directory Rights

Directory rights, also known as the *maximum rights mask*, are the same as trustee rights, but directory rights belong to the system—not the users. Directory rights override trustee rights.

Suppose, for example, that a user has the Erase trustee right to a directory and the directory enables the Erase right; the user then can erase files. If the directory does not enable the Erase right, however, no user can erase files in that directory even if he or she has the Erase trustee right.

Effective Rights

You can think of directory rights as locks that you can put on your system. NetWare gives each directory a full set of locks by default.

You can think of trustee rights as keys that fit the directory locks. Each user can have his or her own set of unique keys. As an example, think of your own key ring. You have your own house key, car key, and so on. Chances are that no one has the same keys as you. Everyone has different locks that need to be opened. The same concept applies to networks. You have specific needs in directories. Some users have the same needs, and others have different needs. Each user can have his or her own set of keys, or rights.

Effective rights are the trustee rights (keys) that actually match available directory rights (locks). If a lock exists and you do not have a key, you cannot perform the function. Likewise, if you have a key and no lock exists, you cannot perform the function. The only way you can use a right is to have matching locks and keys.

File-Level Security

The status of individual files ultimately determines which functions you can perform. Earlier, you learned that if a directory enables the Erase right and a user has that right, files are subject to deletion. If a file is a read-only file, however, trustee rights and directory rights have no effect. Read-only files cannot be deleted, so the file's status takes precedence.

File-level security is attained through the attributes. Although some attributes can be placed on directories, most attributes are designed to be placed on files. The attributes also apply globally to all types of users, including system supervisors. No one is exempt from file attributes.

Security Level Assignments

V2.2 and v3.11 offer a wide range of administrative and user security-level assignments. Some systems require a significant amount of security, and others have more lenient requirements. With NetWare, you can customize the environment to fit your needs.

The End User

The end user holds only the rights needed to perform his or her every-day jobs. End users cannot change their working environments them-selves. These users also generate the most questions for supervisors.

End users are the backbones of the system. By giving end users a mini-mum number of rights to programs they use, you protect the systems while still enabling them to function. If you can make something work for the typical end user, you generally can make it work for any net-work user.

The Print Queue Operator

Any system user can become a print queue operator. Print queue op-erators can manipulate and delete print queues. These users also can enable or disable the operation of queues. This designation does not enable the user to create print queues. By default, system supervisors are automatically print queue operators.

These users can ensure that printing on the network flows smoothly. If a user needs to print a job immediately, a print queue operator can manipulate the order in which jobs are printed. These users also can assign the queue to be serviced by a print server.

The Print Server Operator

Any user can become a print server operator. This type of user can manage print servers attached to the network. Print server operators can manipulate printer accounts that are controlled by the print server and disable the print server. A print server operator also must be a supervisor equivalent to create new print servers.

Only this type of user can disable a print server. Print server operators can reconfigure print servers and monitor the progress of print jobs. They make sure that the print servers are operational.

The User Account Manager

A user account manager is an end user who has been assigned specific users and groups to oversee. Account managers can be individual us-ers or groups of users.

These managers cannot create new users and groups. They also cannot grant more rights than they have been granted. User account managers can create login scripts and account restrictions for users that they have been assigned to manage. They can grant rights to managed users and assign them to managed groups. User account managers also can assign managed users or groups as user account managers.

Most companies have found that delegating power is an effective management tool. Most account managers are departmental employees who have an understanding of which rights users need to operate programs. By using account managers, companies can reroute end users to an interdepartmental employee for help. Minor user problems can be handled quickly and without the need for a supervisor.

The Workgroup Manager

A workgroup manager can be any user or group of users on the system that needs to create users and groups but does not need to change the operating-system environment. Workgroup managers can create, delete, and manipulate users and groups. They can assign disk space and volume restrictions for the managed users and groups.

Workgroup managers cannot delete users and groups that they did not create unless a supervisor assigns them as managed users or groups. Workgroup managers cannot create other workgroup managers or grant more rights than they have been given on the system.

Workgroup managers are assistant network administrators. These users can do almost everything on the network except administrative tasks, such as creating print queues and print servers. They also cannot use the supervisor options of Syscon or FConsole. These managers can oversee the network environment for users but cannot manage all users on the system.

The Supervisor Equivalent

The supervisor equivalent user has full privileges to the entire network. Supervisor equivalents can log in with a unique name.

Several security risks can occur when multiple users log in as the supervisor. If you are using the accounting features of NetWare, for example, you track usage by individual users; having multiple users logged in as the supervisor defeats this purpose. By creating supervisor-equivalent users, you can track more easily where users are logged in and what files and directories they create.

Creating many supervisor-equivalent users is never a good idea. The best method for managing supervisor equivalents is to use them as "back door" users, which means that the only time they log in as the supervisor equivalent is when they need to perform supervisor functions. This setup reduces the chances that the supervisor's password will be discovered. Another potential risk occurs if a workstation where a supervisor equivalent is logged in is left unattended. By only using supervisor equivalents occasionally, you protect the security structure.

The Supervisor

The supervisor is the omnipotent system user. By default, the supervisor inherits all rights to the system.

Some programs require a user to log in as the supervisor for the installation. Supervisor-equivalent users occasionally do not have sufficient rights to the network. In these cases, the supervisor has the necessary rights to the system.

Even the system supervisor must abide by directory rights and file attributes. The difference between the supervisor and the other system managers is that the supervisor automatically has the right to change directory rights and file attributes.

This user is created automatically when the operating system is generated. The supervisor cannot be deleted from the system.

The Directory Supervisor

The directory supervisor can be any type of user. Directory supervisors have a full set of rights to a branch of the directory tree, which enables them to change file attributes and directory rights for other users. This position is most often given to supervisor-equivalent users, workgroup managers, and user account managers.

In v2.2, directory supervisors have the Modify and Access Control rights. In v3.11, directory supervisors have Supervisory, Modify, and Access Control rights.

Checking Performance Issues

In 1982, Novell introduced the NetWare file server operating system. At that time, no other operating system offered all the attributes required to make a complete, distributed-processing environment. These attributes consisted of reliable file service, high performance, and the capacity for adding specialized network services such as SFT, TTS, and connectivity tools.

Novell realized that an optimized operating system is available only through specialization. Through this specialized network operating system, the multiuser, distributed processing environment became available to personal computers.

NetWare obtains its performance by using a "polite" approach. This approach enables a process to maintain control of the central processing unit (CPU) until finished. This process reduces control overhead and assumes that all processes have equal priority.

The NetWare core program, together with the structure of communications and disk channels, provides the performance needed in today's work places. In the heart of any network operating system is the file system. NetWare uses *disk channels* to access data.

In a distributed-processing system, the disk channel is heavily used. Disk-channel optimizing becomes critical because of the CPU time required to support the process. A file server operating at 8MHz with 0 wait states can use as much as one million clock cycles during the time it takes to access the disk twice. In other words, you have to wait longer to access the file server. To overcome this limitation, NetWare uses a multithreaded disk process with caching algorithms to speed throughput and, in many cases, eliminates the need to access the disk hardware. For the user, this method translates into faster responses.

Directory Caching and Hashing

Directory caching and hashing is a service that enables access to files without the physical read of the directory from the disk. *Directory caching* is performed during server initialization and drive mounting. Directory caching is the process of reading the entire directory table into memory. This table is updated continually as changes are made. The table that is created is called a *directory entry table* (DET).

Directory hashing happens in two ways. First, one hashing algorithm is used for indexing each directory structure. The second hashing algorithm is used for indexing the files by volume and subdirectory. Together, directory caching and hashing provide an efficient file-access method.

File Caching

File caching is a system that enables data to be held temporarily in file server memory. The disk system retrieves one block of data at a time. This block may be 4K in a 286 or 386 system and modifiable to 8K, 16K, 32K, or 64K in the 386 system. The average user may require only 512 or 1,024 bytes of data. When the disk system retrieves the data, the system reads a whole block into RAM with the anticipation of any further reads being in the same area. NetWare uses a least-recently-used algorithm system to flush old cache buffers when no cache memory is left for current reads.

User disk read operations greatly benefit from file caching because memory reads are much faster than read-to-the-disk hardware. Disk write requests also benefit from disk caching. When a user disk write request is received, the data is stored in cache, and an acknowledgment is sent to the user. This process enables the file server to accumulate many small write requests before accessing the physical disk. Also, the user only must wait for the data to be written to the cache before being able to return to other tasks.

Cache-buffer size also can be configured during system installation. Generally, cache sizes and disk- block sizes are left at the default of 4K. Individual testing may determine that disk and buffer size need to be varied.

Elevator Seeking

Elevator seeking is a technique used to arrange the order in which data is read from the hard disk. Because disk access is the most common file server request, the disk channel can quickly become clogged with requests.

The elevator-seeking algorithm optimizes disk operation. Each disk driver has a queue that is maintained as disk reads and writes arrive at the queue. The requests are placed in the vicinity of the last request or in the opposite direction, which enables the disk drive heads to operate in a sweeping motion from one disk edge to the other. Elevator seeking improves disk-channel performance by reducing the physical head movement, which is called *thrashing*.

Multiple Disk Channels

NetWare provides another level of performance through multiple disk channels. Standard microcomputers provide a single disk channel through which all disk reads and writes must pass. NetWare provides the support for up to four disk channels that can be used concurrently.

If you have two heavily used databases, for example, you can obtain significant performance improvement by splitting the databases into two disk drives—each on a different channel. In effect, the total disk channel throughput is doubled.

Looking at Network Expandability

The expansion capabilities of networks are virtually endless. The network has grown from enabling small businesses to share PC printers and disk drives to enabling major corporations to connect international computer systems together. The capacity to expand easily is the reason that many businesses have joined the networking movement. Whether your need is for three users to share data or for 200 users to access the company's mainframe and departmental sales records, a properly-implemented network can supply the connectivity requirements.

When purchasing network equipment, always consider its capacity to expand. Many people make purchases based on price alone, without contemplating the possibilities for the future. Many networks have ended up two to three times the size that management originally had planned.

Disk Subsystems

The first issue to consider is storage space. Many types of disk drives currently are available. You probably hear terms like MFM, RLL, ESDI, and SCSI. These terms refer to popular drive interface standards. Each type has advantages and disadvantages.

You should make a drive type selection based on your storage and performance requirements. MFM and RLL drives are considered to be the old technologies and are currently used less frequently. The ESDI format is basically an enhancement of the original MFM drives and offers high performance; the ESDI's disadvantage is that it supports only two drives per controller. See Chapter 2 for more information on disk controllers.

For the best performance, these drives should be of the same model when used on the same controller. This setup can be a problem if a particular model is no longer manufactured at a later date; in this case, you must replace both drives if a hardware failure occurs. If you do not expect your disk requirements to exceed 300M to 600M, ESDI drives can offer high performance at a reasonable cost.

Embedded SCSI drives are the most popular drives used in file servers today. These disk drives have a disk controller included in the electronics of the drive itself. SCSI enables you to attach up to seven devices to each SCSI adapter. The SCSI system also provides performance equal to and, in most cases, higher than a standard ESDI drive.

Currently, SCSI offers both performance and expendability. With the newer SCSI-2 and FAST SCSI-2 systems starting to be readily available, SCSI is the solution used for those seeking performance and future expansion. Unless limited by financial constraints, SCSI should always be used as the file server disk system.

Because of the SCSI drive's popularity and its capacity to use up to seven drives on one interface card, many manufacturers offer disk subsystems. A *disk subsystem* is a self-contained cabinet that includes a power supply and bays to house additional disk drives. Because most standard-configuration file servers provide space for only two drives in the main cabinet, the disk subsystem is the most common method for increasing disk storage.

NetWare can operate with up to four drive channels and a SCSI interface that handles up to eight drives. A fully-configured file server may have up to 32 physical drives attached. The capability to handle multiple drives, when combined with NetWare 386 and the larger 2G drives currently available, can add up to storage capabilities that rival most large computer systems.

Network Boards

One of the most common network growth needs involves cable lengths or user connections. All network topologies have physical restrictions and practical limitations. An RG-58 thinnet Ethernet segment, for example, has a physical cable length of up to 1,000 feet and 30 workstation connections. In most realistic office environments with all 30 workstations used daily, performance would be a problem due to traffic and Ethernet collisions.

 Note   Most cards can handle 1,000 feet of cable. IEEE, however, recommends only 600 feet.

Novell NetWare handles this problem efficiently by providing support for multiple network interface cards in the file server. NetWare enables up to four interface cards in a 286 file server and up to eight interface cards in a 386 file server. These limits are susceptible to the slots available in the file server and to the available I/O address and interrupt settings required by the cards. In most cases, you can overcome the limitations of board settings by intermixing manufacturers' products that enable you to set different settings.

Novell traditionally used the term *bridging* to refer to adding multiple boards to a file server. With the release of NetWare V2.2 and v3.11, Novell has changed the terminology to *routing*. Novell's bridge is more accurately defined as a *router*. A router supports the interconnection of both similar and dissimilar topologies, whereas a true bridge connects similar topologies and protocols together.

Adding an additional network card of a different topology also is common. Whether the card is for a special workstation that needs higher performance or for taking advantage of new technology when expansion is needed, NetWare handles all communications with the internetwork router. Figure 3.1 shows a simple internal bridge.

Bridges and Routers

Both bridges and routers are common in large networks consisting of multiple workgroups, departments, and file servers. Routers and bridges divide groups of workstations to reduce LAN cable traffic, to isolate for cable failure protection, and to connect dissimilar topologies together.

Novell includes its router software with v2.2 and v3.11. The NetWare router provides a good solution for most situations. When designing a system with Novell routers, keep in mind that the advantages of the router come with a cost. Each time a user must pass through a NetWare router, the user can experience a substantial decrease in throughput. If the system is designed with too many router hops required to get from point A to point B, the performance loss can be detrimental (see table 3.2).

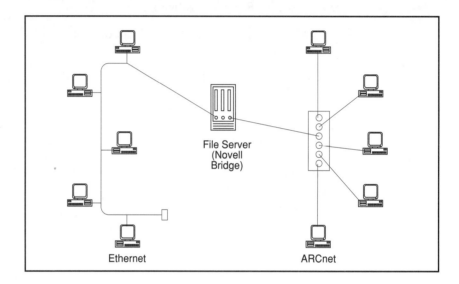

Figure 3.1:
A simple Novell internal bridge.

Table 3.2
Bridge Performance

Number of Bridges	1	2	3	4	5	6
Performance Drop	43%	52%	60%	72%	76%	81%

Performance loss usually can be avoided with proper design of the network layout. If your network needs a bridge or router that is required to pass heavy traffic, you may want to consider one of the many proprietary hardware bridges or routers available. In many cases, under heavy traffic these hardware devices perform much better than Novell's software solution (see table 3.3).

A Novell router transfers a maximum packet size of 512 bytes. This is the primary reason for the performance loss experienced with each router hop. Most network protocols today make use of packet sizes larger than 512 bytes. Because a Novell router has no way of knowing what size packet the other nodes on the network can use, the smallest size of 512 is sent. This is to prevent network errors that result when packets larger than the receiving host or file server can handle are sent.

Although this may appear to be a good reason not to use Novell routers, there are benefits. In Chapter 10, you learn tips on getting the most from your Novell router. When you configure a network, try to keep bridges and routers to a minimum. These devices are intended to isolate and filter network packet traffic. Use only what is required to provide the desired network management.

Gateways

A *gateway* is required for a connection to any minicomputer or mainframe system. A gateway is one of the most commonly used network expansion devices. Dozens of third-party packages are available to help with this type of connectivity. Figure 3.2 illustrates a section of a large corporate network. In this example, users are connected in smaller workgroups with a router or bridge, which provides isolation from the main corporate network. In the figure, all users may also have access to the company's IBM AS400 through a gateway.

Table 3.3
NetWare Bridge Performance/Reliability

Option	Reliability	Performance	Restrictions
No bridge	High	100%	Traffic cannot be split.
Internal	Medium	40% - 60%	Bridging server can get tied up while routing.
Dedicated External	Medium	60%	None.
Nondedicated	Low	30% - 40%	Applications can hang up External bridge. Performance on nondedicated bridges can be as low as 10 percent.

Figure 3.2:
An example of a
large corporate
network.

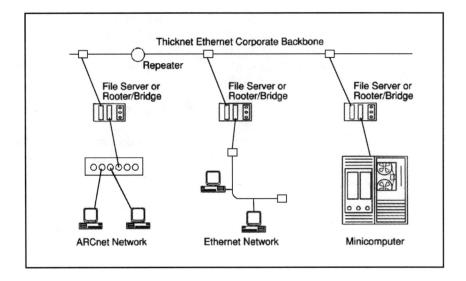

You can use gateways to enable dissimilar LANs or to enable LAN-connected hardware to communicate. Gateways must convert protocols from one system to another, and they have many uses. They can provide connections into IBM SNA environments via SDLC, coax, or Token Ring. They can enable a NetWare IPX LAN to communicate with a TCP/IP UNIX system. They can provide an X.25 connection into a public data network that can provide worldwide connectivity.

 All local area networks use a specific communication method called a *protocol*. The protocols referred to in this chapter are all common and are used by major manufacturers. IBM's Systems Network Architecture, for example, is used with IBM's large host-based systems.

TCP/IP or Transmission Control Protocol/Internet protocol was designed by the Department of Defense (DOD) and is widely accepted with computers running UNIX and with companies like Digital Equipment Corporation and their VAX machines.

Novell systems rely on Internetwork Packet Exchange (IPX) for communication. The X.25 protocol is widely accepted as a method for high-performance communication through telephone lines.

> ### About Repeaters...
>
> A *repeater* is available for most topologies in one form or another. A repeater simply receives and retransmits packets of information. You can use repeaters to extend the maximum distance a particular cabling system may have. You must follow specific rules to use repeaters. In some cases, the only way to extend a cable for a destination node is by using a repeater.

Summary

In this chapter, you were presented with a quick rundown of the features and benefits that have made Novell NetWare the most popular network operating system in use today.

NetWare satisfies most networking needs due to its user accessibility, equipment supported, reliability, security features, and expansion options.

The following chapters expand on the information presented in this chapter. In the computer world, a particular concern may have no end or exact answer. The information provided in the following chapters will help you decide how to effectively use available technology for your network.

4

Gathering Workstation Software

As you learned in Chapter 1, a *workstation* is a personal computer that is attached to a network. When you communicate on a network, your PC is no longer just a personal computer; it is an extension of the network that enables you to access the services and equipment provided on the network.

At the same time, your PC is adding to the network and, in some cases, providing services for others. For this added service to occur, communication must be established between the personal computer and the network file servers and other related equipment.

Because not all networks are created equally, several configuration options are available. Each option enables a network to function differently. Some personal computers have more memory than others, so most of the options come with memory-saving parameters. Other options increase your network's communication options.

You should look at each workstation as a unique piece of the network. Evaluate each workstation's connectivity options, as well as the programs to be run, in terms of the amounts of memory they require.

When attaching a PC to a network, you need to examine various software issues. In this chapter, you examine the following:

- How to choose an operating system
- NetWare's IPX, NETx, XMSNETX, and EMSNETX
- NetBIOS, Novell's ODI solution, and diskless workstations

Choosing an Operating System

To understand the workstation concept, you need to start with the PC operating system, which is the managing force at the local level. Various operating systems currently are available for the personal computer. The most common operating system is the Microsoft disk operating system (MS-DOS).

DOS

DOS manages and works with programs and data files at the hardware and user levels. DOS has evolved a great deal since its first introduction to the public. Novell provided only limited support of DOS's first editions, V1.x and V2.x.

Currently, DOS 5.0 and DRDOS 6.0 are firmly placing themselves in the PC workstation; DOS 3.x and DOS 4.x are slowly becoming outdated. Both DOS 3.1 and 3.3 are still solid operating systems and provide good support to the older network workstations. DOS versions 3.2, 4.0, and 4.01 each experienced various problems when used on a Novell network and should be replaced if still operating on your network.

DOS 5.0 provides many new features and a much-needed memory-management system that previously was available only from third-party developers. DOS 5.0 combines many popular and necessary utilities and tools into one common package. Because DOS 5.0's main focus is on the Intel 286, 386, and 486 workstation, upgrading the older

8088 or XT computers used on networks is questionable. The kernel or memory resident portion of DOS 5.0 is substantially larger than that of DOS 3.x and will cause the loss of precious memory.

Windows

Microsoft Windows 3.0, which actually runs on top of DOS, is another popular operating system. Windows contains a *graphical user interface*, or GUI (pronounced "gooey"). A GUI provides icons, dialog boxes, check boxes, and buttons. The Windows environment is designed to be used with a pointing device, such as a mouse. The Windows operating system resides on top of DOS, and not only provides a friendly user interface, but also stable multitasking when set up properly. With Windows, you can cut and paste portions of screens from one application to another.

Windows enables you to see and run multiple applications on-screen simultaneously. In most cases, the Windows environment provides an enjoyable interface that can increase productivity and decrease fatigue.

About Windows Performance...

Setting up the Windows environment is not as simple as copying files onto your workstation. Although Windows operates on 8088 through 80486 computers, it functions best when used on an 80386 or 80486 computer with at least 4M of extended memory and a VGA video system.

In many large companies, this workstation configuration is becoming a standard. However, companies that invested in 8088 and 80286 workstations with monochrome video systems to support text-oriented applications may need to make a large investment to provide enough hardware for Windows. These companies must weigh the possible productivity increases against the cost.

In addition to DOS and Windows for the personal computer, two other systems—OS/2 and UNIX—are used in many multiuser environments. Novell provides connectivity solutions for both systems.

OS/2

OS/2 is similar to Windows, but OS/2 does not reside on top of DOS. OS/2 is a completely rewritten operating system that requires special OS/2 versions of applications to take advantage of its true multitasking capability. OS/2 has experienced its share of benefits and drawbacks, but it still continues to play a large part in supplying a high-performance, multitasking environment. Generally, OS/2 is used when a specialized application requires it. Although many popular programs are available in OS/2 versions, OS/2 still holds a small percentage of the market.

About OS/2 and Requestor Versions...

To provide NetWare services to OS/2 v1.1 and 1.2, Novell developed the OS/2 Requestor v1.1 and v1.2. The most recent version of Requestor, v1.3, can be used with all prior versions of OS/2.

Novell's OS/2 Requestor provides full support for any OS/2 workstation. Included are OS/2 versions of Syscon, PConsole, and Filer so that network administrators can manage the LAN from an OS/2 workstation. The OS/2 Requestor also supports the OS/2 and DOS Named Pipes, which provide support for Microsoft SQL servers to both OS/2 and DOS workstations.

UNIX

UNIX was developed initially for large systems. In 1983, however, System V was released and included support for microcomputers. UNIX is a powerful multitasking system that is prominent in scientific and engineering communities. UNIX is in no way similar to DOS or Windows and requires all applications to be written for UNIX. The traditional UNIX was a text-oriented system that provided two- and three-letter commands, which was the reason that many people referred to it as a "user-hostile" environment. Because the X Windows environment provides services similar to Windows, UNIX has moved into the GUI environment.

About UNIX Development...

The UNIX system has evolved from its origins as a program for text editing. Bell Laboratories first developed UNIX in the early 1970s. The UNIX operating system and the C language were developed to exploit each other's power.

Both OS/2 and UNIX require Novell's ODI solution to obtain a connection into the network. (Novell's ODI solution is examined later in this chapter.) Novell provides the OS/2 Requestor with current versions of NetWare. Novell has additional products for use with UNIX systems. LAN Workplace for DOS enables DOS workstations to access the UNIX environment, and NetWare NFS enables UNIX users to access a NetWare v3.11 file server. Figure 4.1 depicts a fully integrated corporate network using multiple operating systems. For more information on these products, contact Novell or your NetWare dealer.

Because of recent activities of Novell and Digital Research, you should examine another DOS alternative: DR DOS v6.0.

Figure 4.1:
An example of an integrated network.

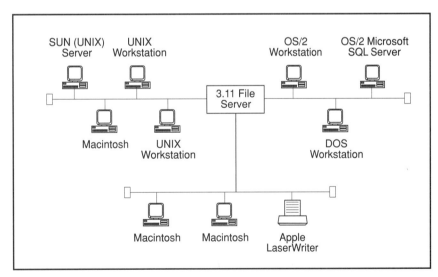

UNIVEL is a joint venture between Novell and USL (UNIX System Laboratories). The first product scheduled for release is UnixWare. UnixWare is a graphical UNIX operation system that offers complete integration with Novell's NetWare.

UNIVEL's first release of this product is based on UNIX System V Release 4.2. UnixWare offers a full *GUI (Graphical User Interface)* and desktop manager that provides compatibility with OSF/MOTIF, OPEN LOOK, XENIX, SunOS, SCO UNIX, and all previous releases of UNIX System V. UnixWare also supports MS-DOS and DOS Windows applications to further provide compatibility with a wide range of user applications. UnixWare is the first version of UNIX to natively support the NetWare IPX protocol and provide reliable communications as both a specialized server or UNIX workstation.

DR DOS V6.0

In July 1991, Novell and Digital Research announced that they were merging. This merger may provide one of the largest changes to the Novell NetWare product. The merger allows Novell to include an operating system for workstations. Digital Research provides the operating systems DR DOS v6.0, FLEXOS, and DR Multiuser DOS. The company also developed the popular CP/M operating system used with PCs several years ago.

Currently, DR DOS v6.0 offers strong competition to MS-DOS v5.0. DR DOS v6.0 provides all the features of MS-DOS v5.0, plus many additional utilities, and it maintains 100-percent compatibility with MS-DOS v5.0. Rumors have circulated that Novell and Digital Research are incorporating the IPX and shell programs required for NetWare into DR DOS. This setup can provide a new level of performance and functionality so this may be a good time for you to take a serious look at DR DOS.

Introducing IPX

When operating in a DOS or Windows environment, NetWare requires two programs to be loaded: IPX and NET*x*. These programs provide the link between the local operating system and the NetWare operating system. IPX is examined in this section, and NETX is examined in the following section.

IPX, which stands for *internetwork packet exchange*, is a protocol that is configured for specific network-board configurations. A *protocol* is a set of standards, rules, and regulations on data exchange. To illustrate a protocol, consider a cable TV station. The equipment at a cable company sends data via satellite to a local distribution center. The cable company then sends that data through a cable to your house. The method that is used to send the data through the cable is that of *protocols*. When you turn on your TV, the show that is on and the language of the show is irrelevant concerning the way the data was sent (the protocol).

In NetWare, to configure IPX you need to know the settings for base memory, interrupts, and base I/O; and whether the card uses direct memory access (DMA).

IPX.COM includes Novell's IPX protocol stack. It also has the lower-level hardware drivers linked to this file. IPX.COM breaks the message into packets, following the rules of the IPX protocol. The other part of IPX.COM takes the created packets and formats them for proper delivery to the network interface card.

NET*x* sits between the user or the application and IPX. NET*x* intercepts all requests and decides if the request should be routed to the local operating system (such as DOS), or if it should be redirected to the network.

Exploring NET*x*, XMSNETX, and EMSNETX

NET*x*, XMSNETX, and EMSNETX are referred to as the *shell*. The shell is a program that provides the capability to send information to the file server and receive information from the file server. After IPX, the shell is the next program you load. There are three versions of the NetWare shell. The three shell files, NET*x*.COM, XMSNETX.COM, and EMSNETX.COM, are discussed in the following sections.

NET*x*

NET*x* functions much like an usher at a theatre. When you arrive at the theatre, for example, you give the usher your ticket. The usher reads the ticket and tells you in which aisle and row your seat is located.

NET*x* functions in a similar capacity. If a command is packeted by IPX for DOS, then the command is passed through to DOS. Likewise, if the information is packeted for the network, DOS does not need to know about it, and the information is routed over the network cable to the file server for processing.

> **More about NETx...**
>
> NETx is at vector 21h in your workstation's memory. All DOS commands pass through this portion of memory on the way to their destinations. At this position, NETx can catch *all* commands and determine whether they are DOS or network commands.

Because several versions of Netx are available, you need to know which one to use. Prior to the summer of 1991, you needed to use the version of Netx that was specific to the version of DOS loaded on your workstation. Therefore, DOS V2.x required NET2, DOS V3.x required NET3, and so on. In August 1991, a new version of Netx, simply NETX, was released. You no longer need to replace the *x* with the DOS version number. This newest release of NETX is self-configuring, which makes it the most versatile NETX to date.

NETx.COM is the "standard" version of the shell. NETx loads into DOS or "real" memory, which is below the 640K limit. Together, IPX and NETx can use as much as 70K of DOS memory, which, in some cases, can be a problem.

XMSNETX and EMSNETX

Many new databases and large-scale applications require as much memory as you can provide. The XMSNETX and EMSNETX shells were provided to ease memory problems; these shells can be loaded into special memory that may exist.

The XMSNETX shell takes advantage of the *extended memory specification* (XMS) by loading itself into the extended memory located above 640K. This version can provide a memory savings of about 30K. To use XMSNETX, you must install an extended memory manager, such as Microsoft's HIMEM.SYS, in DOS.

As an alternative, you can use the EMSNETX shell if extended memory is not available. This version takes advantage of the *expanded memory specification* (EMS) by loading itself into expanded memory.

About LIM EMS...

LIM EMS is a specially accessed memory standard, designed by Lotus, Intel, and Microsoft, and should conform to the LIM EMS 4.0 standard for proper operation.

In most cases, you experience a slight performance loss when using the EMSNETX shell. This performance decrease may or may not cause a problem in your application. It is a good idea to test each shell on a workstation to evaluate which shell performs best.

Both XMSNETX and EMSNETX are optional replacements for the standard NET*x* requirement. Because DOS V5.0 and DR DOS V6.0 are now available, both IPX and NET*x* can be loaded successfully into extended memory, which enables DOS to reclaim 70K for use by system applications.

Deciding Whether To Use NetBIOS

NetBIOS, developed by IBM, is a networking communications standard. Many networking companies comply with this standard simply to maintain multivendor functionality. NetBIOS is to IBM what IPX is to NetWare.

 BIOS is a standard computer term for *basic input output system*. This system facilitates the transfer of data and control instructions between the computer and peripherals, such as disk drives.

If a network communications application is written to speak NetBIOS, the application can operate on any NetBIOS network. The NetBIOS.EXE program, provided by Novell, is basically a front and back end to IPX. This program fully emulates NetBIOS, receives the information, and passes it to IPX. In turn, IPX receives the data and passes it to NetBIOS.EXE, which presents the data to the application as NetBIOS packets.

You must have additional memory available to load NetBIOS.EXE, but you can unload the program when it is no longer needed. The NetBIOS emulator is required only if a specialized application needs to use it.

Table 4.1 lists various shell memory configurations.

Table 4.1
Shell Memory Configurations

Memory Configuration	Required Workstation Programs
Standard memory (640K)	IPX.COM and NETx.COM
Extended memory (XMS 2.0)	IPX.COM and XMSNETX.EXE
Expanded memory (LIM EMS 4.0)	IPX.COM and EMSNETX.EXE
Application uses NetBIOS	One of the preceding requirements plus NetBIOS.EXE

Examining Novell's ODI Solution

A new acronym is circulating among NetWare "techrooms" these days: ODI, which stands for *open data-link interface*. ODI is Novell's interface technology that enables more than one protocol, such as IPX or TCP/IP, to run at the same time on the same network interface card.

Internally, ODI is broken down into layers that conform to the open systems interconnect (OSI) network architecture model. Figure 4.2 shows the placement of ODI in the OSI model.

At the lowest level is the *multiple-link interface driver*, or MLID (pronounced "emlid"). The MLID manages the hardware for a specific network card. Next is the *link support layer* (LSL). The LSL manages communications between one or more protocol stacks and the MLID. The LSL operates at the OSI data-link layer of the OSI model and acts as a switchboard, routing information packets between MLIDs and stacks, and supporting access to multiple frame types.

About the MLID...

The MLID is made up of both the *media support module* (MSM) and the *hardware support module* (HSM). These modules are the lowest level of the architecture and are developed by the network interface manufacturer.

Figure 4.2:
Novell's ODI to OSI placement.

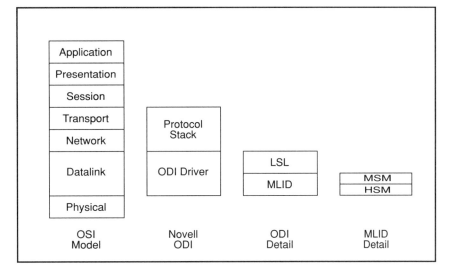

You may wonder what ODI means to you as a network administrator. The new Open Data-link Interface (ODI) may not affect you immediately. If your network does not have a TCP/IP gateway or if you do not need access to a UNIX NFS host, then ODI drivers are currently not necessary. If you want to stay current with changing technology, however, the memory-saving benefits of ODI may be the answer.

About the Future of Network Technology...

NetWare's future is with the ODI technology. Novell has announced that, in the near future, development of IPX drivers will be discouraged and development efforts within Novell will be focused exclusively on ODI drivers. Currently, all high-level communications products sold by Novell, such as TCP/IP, require ODI drivers to operate.

For the standard DOS or Windows workstation, you need to have five files available: LSL, an MLID for your network board, IPXODI, NET*x*, and a NET.CFG file. ODI network card drivers are not generated like the IPX.COM file. The MLID file will be provided by the manufacturer of the network card, not Novell. Check to see if the card you selected has support for ODI. All hardware parameters are listed in the NET.CFG file and read at the time they are loaded.

ODI drivers are examined in more detail in Chapter 5.

Examining Diskless Workstations

NetWare enables a workstation to boot or load both DOS and network-related files directly from the file server via the network interface. This capacity is provided by a special boot program that resides in *read-only memory* (ROM). ROM is a programmable integrated circuit that can store a program for later retrieval.

The diskless workstation has been received with mixed feelings. The first diskless workstations were an attempt to provide a less expensive PC, but this issue became insignificant as hardware costs dropped.

Currently, diskless PCs are most commonly found in environments in which security is an issue. Diskless workstations are available in almost any configuration. These workstations can provide performance for any applications, while preventing unauthorized access. The diskless workstation also enables the system administrator to have tight control of the DOS configuration. Often, an untrained user makes changes to his or her boot disk and causes problems.

Summary

This chapter presented the available PC operating systems and the programs needed to attach the workstations to the network.

As you have seen, NetWare can communicate with many different operating systems and with different PC configurations. This capability to integrate different operating systems and configurations increases the number of options available to you as you put your network together. Many of the computers you already have can use the network because of NetWare's capability to handle different operating systems.

NetWare also helps you make the most efficient use of memory in the workstation. By providing several shell files that work with different memory types, you can customize the workstation network files to make the best use of RAM and maintain performance.

Finally, you saw some alternatives to the basic NetWare workstation configuration. These alternatives enable you to use the newest technology of Open Data-link drivers to have your network "talk" to other computer systems easily.

Chapter 5 takes you to the next step in configuring your network. In the next chapter you will see the steps involved in actually configuring the workstation software and logging on to the network.

5

Accessing the File Server

t this point, your network hardware is in place and your operating system is installed. The next step in putting your network together is to log in to the system. The method you use to log in depends on your workstation operating system and whether you need connectivity to OSI-compliant systems.

This chapter shows you how to log in to the network from either a DOS or Windows workstation, and discusses the login requirements of the Macintosh, OS/2, and UNIX environments.

In this chapter, you get hands-on practice with the following tasks:

- Running WSGEN to generate IPX
- Using JUMPERS
- Logging in through DOS
- Logging in through Windows
- Logging in through ODI drivers
- Logging in with a Macintosh, OS/2, or UNIX workstation
- Using other connection services

93

To start, the following section shows you how to use the *workstation generation program* (WSGEN) to generate the required IPX driver.

Running WSGEN To Generate IPX

The WSGEN utility configures a file that DOS workstations must use to gain access to the network. When you use WSGEN, you generate a file called IPX.COM. IPX stands for *Internetwork Packet Exchange*.

> ### About Linking...
>
> The WSGEN program and the NetWare 2.2 install program are actually menu-driven *linkers*. These programs enable you to select the program modules created by Novell and other developers and link them into the customized executable files that are needed. In the case of WSGEN, you are linking the network board drivers to form IPX.COM.

You can run the WSGEN program from a floppy drive or hard disk. If you run the program from a floppy drive, you first must create a copy of the original disk. The original Novell disk is write-protected, and WSGEN needs to create a new IPX.COM file for you. Novell supplies a number of network card drivers with the WSGEN program. If the driver you need is not included with the Novell disks, you also need a driver disk from the hardware manufacturer. Network card drivers generally are located on a disk shipped with the interface card and need to be placed on a floppy disk with the electronic label LAN_DRV_*xxx*, in which *xxx* is a three-digit number designated by the manufacturer.

> ### About the DOS LABEL Command...
>
> The syntax for the DOS LABEL command is LABEL A:LAN_DRV_*xxx*. Refer to your DOS reference manual for more information.

When WSGEN runs, it searches all floppy drives for disks with these labels and includes the appropriate drivers in the lists presented to you for selection.

System administrators can set up a directory on their local hard drive or on the network to provide a fast method for creating network shells when needed. To set up the required directories, you need a main directory. You can name this directory SHELLS, for example.

After you use the DOS MD command to create a SHELLS directory, create a subdirectory named WSGEN. Then copy the contents of the Novell WSGEN disk into the \SHELLS\WSGEN directory. If any optional LAN drivers are required, you must copy them into directories that have the same name as the floppy disk that contains the drivers. To allow for a floppy name with more than eight characters, place a period (.) before the last three characters or numbers, as in the following example:

```
SHELLSWSGEN
    |
    |-LAN_DRV_.001
    |
    |-LAN_DRV_.002
```

Novell's WSGEN program looks for this label to locate the driver files.

Next, copy the WSGEN.EXE file into the SHELLS directory. You then can execute the WSGEN program from this directory by typing **WSGEN** and pressing Enter. NetWare displays a screen like the one shown in figure 5.1.

When this screen appears, press Enter to continue.

About Workstations that Lock Up...

If WSGEN appears to lock up while searching the floppy drives, reboot the computer and check your directory structures. This problem is common when you are running the WSGEN program from the wrong directory.

The next screen that appears is the driver-selection screen (see fig. 5.2). At this screen, you select the appropriate network board driver required by your network interface card. Simply use the arrow keys to scroll up or down until you find the correct driver.

Figure 5.1:
The WSGEN
opening screen.

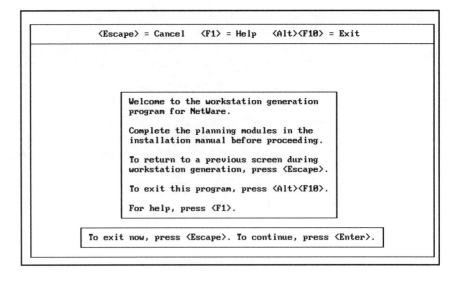

Figure 5.2:
The driver-selection
screen.

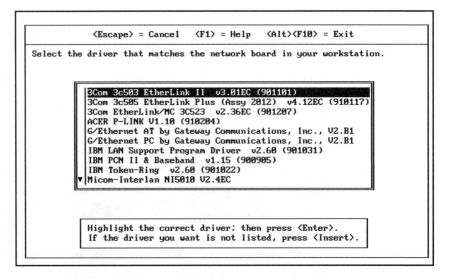

When you locate the desired driver, press Enter. The screen shown in
figure 5.3 appears.

About Additional Drivers...

If the driver you need does not appear in the selection window, the driver may not be included with NetWare or the driver disk may not be installed correctly. If you install a LAN_DRV_.xxx directory, make sure that the underscores (_) and the period (.) are correct. If you create a LAN_DRV_.xxx directory, be sure not to confuse the underscore character (_) with the dash character (-).

Another way to handle the addition of new drivers is to press Ins while the driver-selection screen is visible. NetWare then prompts you to insert the disk that contains the additional drivers. The new drivers are then added to the list of available drivers.

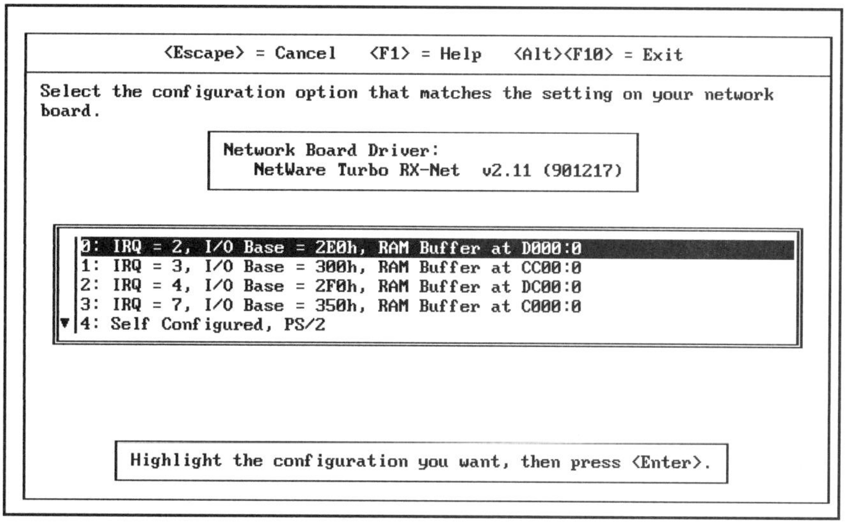

Figure 5.3:
The hardware-configuration screen.

```
        <Escape> = Cancel    <F1> = Help    <Alt><F10> = Exit

Select the configuration option that matches the setting on your network
board.

              Network Board Driver:
                 NetWare Turbo RX-Net  v2.11 (901217)


  0: IRQ = 2, I/O Base = 2E0h, RAM Buffer at D000:0
  1: IRQ = 3, I/O Base = 300h, RAM Buffer at CC00:0
  2: IRQ = 4, I/O Base = 2F0h, RAM Buffer at DC00:0
  3: IRQ = 7, I/O Base = 350h, RAM Buffer at C000:0
▼ 4: Self Configured, PS/2


        Highlight the configuration you want, then press <Enter>.
```

You need to know a few things about the particular workstation you are working with. This screen provides you with the hardware options supplied by the interface manufacturer. These options include interrupts, base memory address, I/O address, and DMA channels. The default option, 0, is usually a good choice for a standard workstation configuration. If your workstation has a modem, terminal emulator, or other special hardware, you need to have all the equipment settings available. When selecting a configuration option, you need to be aware of all the additional interface card settings in the computer.

> **About Avoiding Conflicts...**
>
> You should make a list of all card settings. This list can help you locate unused hardware settings, which your network interface can use.
>
> If none of the available choices appears to provide all the settings, select option 0. From here, you should be able to install a customized configuration with the JUMPERS utility, which is discussed later in this chapter.

Use table 5.1 to determine the standard PC hardware settings. The table includes I/O addresses, memory addresses, interrupts, and DMA channels used by common equipment.

After selecting a configuration option, press Enter to begin the linking process. After you select the hardware option, NetWare displays your choice and prompts you for confirmation. Select Yes to confirm your selection or No to abort (see fig. 5.4).

Figure 5.4:
Confirming your selection.

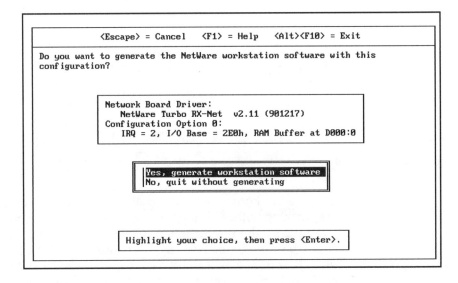

Table 5.1
Common Hardware Configurations

Device	INT	I/O Decode (h)	MEM Decode	DMA
Com1	4	3F8-3FF	-	-
Com2	3	2F8-2FF	-	-
LPT1	7	378-37F	-	-
LPT2 (cannot be used with XT controller)	5	278-27F	-	
If LPT3 exists,				
LPT1	7	3BC-3BE	-	
LPT2	5	378-37A	-	
LPT3	-	278-27A	-	-
XT controller	5	320-32F	C800:0000-3FFF	3
AT controller	14	1F0-1F8 170-177	-	-
Floppy controller	6	1F0-1F8 3F0-3F7	-	2
Tape controller	5	280-28F	-	3
Novell disk coprocessor	11.10, 12, or 13	#1 340-347 #2 348-34F	-	-
Novell SCSI adapter	2, 3, or 5	340-343 (enhanced only)	D000:0000-7FFF	1, 3, or none
EGA	2	3C0-3CF	A000:0000-1FFFE or B000:0000-7FFF or B800:0000-7FFF	0
Monochrome adapter	-	3B0-3BF	B000:0000-7FFF	0
Color graphics adapter	-	3D0-3DF	B800:0000-7FFF	0
Hercules monochrome (286A server)	-	3B4-3BF	B000:0000-7FFF B800:0000-7FFF	- -

If the link process runs without error, NetWare displays a screen informing you that workstation software generation is complete. At this time, you can copy the IPX.COM file from the \SHELLS\WSGEN directory to your workstation boot disk along with the appropriate shell NETX.COM, XMSNETX.EXE, or EMSNETX.EXE.

Using JUMPERS

Before logging in to the file server, you need to know about the Novell JUMPERS utility.

The JUMPERS utility is designed to patch an IPX program to the selected hardware settings without requiring you to rerun WSGEN. JUMPERS also enables you to mix and match options, so that you can create custom options for tightly configured workstations.

 Note   Not all network card drivers are compatible with the JUMPERS utility. Currently, the best method to determine compatibility is the trial-and-error method. JUMPERS informs you if you choose a driver that cannot be configured.

The JUMPERS utility is in the WSGEN directory, and you can use it to change the option setting of IPX files that were linked with JUMPERS-compatible drivers.

To start JUMPERS, type **JUMPERS** at the DOS prompt and press Enter. The JUMPERS opening screen appears, as shown in figure 5.5.

When you press F1, NetWare displays the license agreement. To see the next screen, which lets you specify the file to be modified, press Esc. When JUMPERS prompts for the file to modify (see fig. 5.6), enter **IPX.COM**. Remember to include the COM file extension.

The JUMPERS utility then reads in the current hardware settings and displays a list of these settings in a menu format. Figure 5.7 shows an example of an Arcnet IPX using I/O port 300, interrupt 5, and memory address DC00:0. This driver also is configured for large packets with the setting 4096.

Figure 5.5:
The JUMPERS
opening screen.

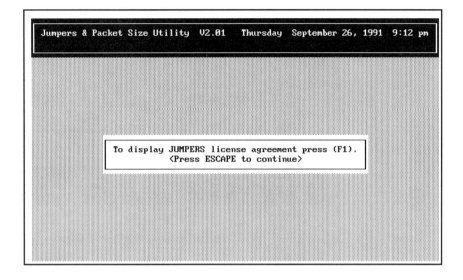

Figure 5.6:
Specifying the file
to modify.

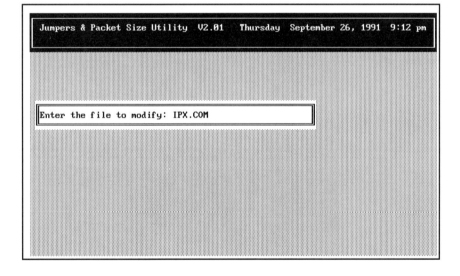

About Arcnet Packet Sizes...

Currently, a de facto standard referred to as Arcnet TURBO-II exists. This standard enables Arcnet cards to use packet sizes other than the standard 512 bytes. You can set these sizes to larger sizes provided that the file server accepts them to increase performance.

Figure 5.7:
The current
configuration.

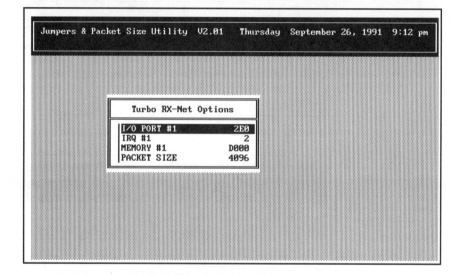

```
Jumpers & Packet Size Utility  V2.01   Thursday  September 26, 1991  9:12 pm



                    Turbo RX-Net Options

                 I/O PORT #1          2E0
                 IRQ #1                 2
                 MEMORY #1           D000
                 PACKET SIZE         4096
```

About Changing the Packet Frame Type...

When configuring a jumpers-compatible Ethernet driver, you also have the option of changing the packet frame type. This option enables you to change between the standard 802.3 frame and the Ethernet-II frame, which is common in UNIX and DEC environments. This feature is important in systems with both Novell and UNIX users.

To make changes to any of the individual settings, select the desired option and press Enter. NetWare then provides you with a list of supported values that you can choose. Continue this procedure for each option that requires changes. Figure 5.8 shows an example of an Arcnet driver that is being changed to memory address DC00:0.

Figure 5.8:
Changing memory
addresses.

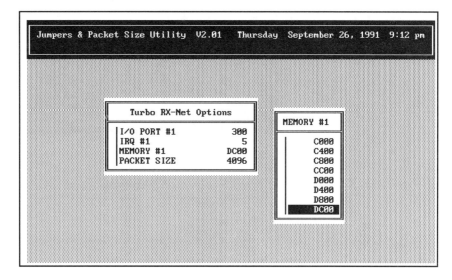

After you make all the changes, press Esc. NetWare prompts you to save your choices. Depending on your selection, JUMPERS exits, saves your choices, and modifies the hardware setting. You then can check the configuration of IPX.COM by using the /I command-line switch after the IPX command. For example, you can type the following at the F:\> prompt:

IPX /I

Logging in through DOS

After you successfully generate your workstation files and copy them to your boot disk, you are ready to attach to the NetWare file server.

You can issue the following commands manually or place them in a batch file in the order listed as follows (you can replace NETX with the optional XMSNETX or EMSNETX):

IPX

NETX

F:

LOGIN *fileserver name/username*

About the First Available Network Drive...

The drive letter F may not be available on some workstations; the number of drive letters available depends on the number of locally attached hard drives or on the CONFIG.SYS file's LASTDRIVE setting. The login drive is the first available unused drive letter.

When you issue the IPX and NETX commands, NetWare displays the information shown in figure 5.9.

Figure 5.9:
A sample screen that appears after you successfully attach to the file server.

```
[DR DOS] C:\SH386>ipx
Novell IPX/SPX v3.04 (910703)
(C) Copyright 1985, 1991 Novell Inc.  All Rights Reserved.

LAN Option: NetWare Turbo RX-Net  v2.11 (901217)
Hardware Configuration: IO: 350; MEM: D800; IRQ: 5 (Jumpers Config)

[DR DOS] C:\SH386>netx

NetWare V3.22 - Workstation Shell (910731)
(C) Copyright 1991 Novell, Inc.  All Rights Reserved.

Running on DOS V3.31

Using configuration file SHELL.CFG
SHOW DOTS ON

Attached to server CDI
09-30-91    5:06:13 pm

[DR DOS] C:\SH386>
```

First, examine the NetWare LOGIN command. The LOGIN command is located in the SYS:\LOGIN directory, and you can issue the command from that directory to access the file server's resources.

After your workstation loads the NetWare shell, it transparently attaches to the nearest file server. After moving to the LOGIN drive (which usually is drive F), issue the LOGIN command. At the F:\LOGIN\> prompt, for example, type the following:

LOGIN

NetWare prompts for your login name and password. After you successfully enter the requested information, you have access to the other services for which you have privileges. If your system utilizes more than one file server, you can prefix your login name with the file server's name. For example, you can type the following at the F:\LOGIN\> prompt:

LOGIN SALES\TOM

After the preceding information is entered, the program prompts Tom to enter his password. After Tom enters his password, NetWare processes the request for access to the SALES file server.

> ### *About Synchronizing Passwords...*
>
> If your login script attaches you to more than one file server, LOGIN determines whether all passwords are valid. If a password has expired, you are prompted to change it. If you change your password, LOGIN asks if you want to synchronize all passwords on all servers. If you answer Yes, the password becomes the same on all attached servers.

The IPX, NETX, XMSNETX, and EMSNETX programs each have optional command-line switches that can simplify the network administrator's job.

IPX.COM provides four options (see fig. 5.10):

- **-I or /I.** Use this option to display an informational screen. This option is handy for determining the version and hardware settings of the IPX you are using (see fig. 5.11).

- **-D or /D.** Use this option to display available hardware settings.

- **-O or /O***x*. Use this option to set IPX to use a hardware setting displayed with the D option.

- **-C or /C.** This option enables advanced users to use a special configuration file rather than the Novell default SHELL.CFG or NET.CFG.

- **-? or /?.** Use this option to display all available options, as shown in figure 5.11.

Figure 5.10:
The IPX options.

```
C:\SH386>ipx ?
Novell IPX/SPX v3.04 (910703)
(C) Copyright 1985, 1991 Novell Inc.  All Rights Reserved.

LAN Option: NetWare Turbo RX-Net  v2.11 (901217)
Hardware Configuration: IO: 350; MEM: D800; IRQ: 5 (Jumpers Config)


Usage: IPX [options]
valid options:
        -I or /I                Display version information
        -D or /D                Display hardware options
        -O or /O<num>           Load using hardware option <num>
        -C or /C=[path]<filename> Use an alternate configuration file

        -? or /?                Display this help screen

C:\SH386>
```

Figure 5.11:
Displaying version information.

```
C:\SH386>ipx i
Novell IPX/SPX v3.04 (910703)
(C) Copyright 1985, 1991 Novell Inc.  All Rights Reserved.

LAN Option: NetWare Turbo RX-Net  v2.11 (901217)
Hardware Configuration: IO: 350; MEM: D800; IRQ: 5 (Jumpers Config)

C:\SH386>
```

> ### *About the Reconfiguration Options...*
>
> The /D and /O*x* command line switches are handy when you need to test a shell or when a shell is included in the batch file. These switches enable you to use any standard configuration without the need to relink the IPX program.
>
> Permanently configuring the IPX program for normal use is still a good idea. Doing so saves confusion if the user attempts to load IPX without the batch file.

NETX, XMSNETX, and EMSNETX provide the following three options:

- **-I or /I.** Use this option to display an informational screen (see fig. 5.12).
- **-U or /U.** Use this option, Uninstall, to remove the shell from memory.
- **-PS or /PS.** Use this option, Preferred Server, to specify the server from which you get the LOGIN command.

Figure 5.12:
Displaying version information.

```
C:\SH386>netx i

NetWare V3.22 - Workstation Shell (910731)
(C) Copyright 1991 Novell, Inc.  All Rights Reserved.

C:\SH386>
```

NetBIOS provides the following two options:

- **-I or /I.** Use this option to display an informational screen.
- **-U or /U.** Use this option, Uninstall, to remove NetBIOS from memory.

About the Uninstall Option...

When using the /U command line switch, make sure that the programs are removed in the opposite order from which they were installed. Also, be aware that you may receive unpredictable results when unloading any memory-resident program that may have another program loaded in after it.

Logging in through Windows

When operating Microsoft Windows 3.0 on a network, follow the same login procedure as for DOS workstations before you load Windows. Currently, logging in or out through a DOS window does not work properly when called from Windows. The procedure may appear to work at times but provides uncertain results.

About Windows Drivers...

The Windows documentation suggests that if your network driver supports logging in and logging out, doing those procedures is OK. The Windows NetWare driver does not support this feature. You should not log in or log out of a file server from the DOS session.

Some shareware versions of the LOGIN command are available, but they currently are not distributed by Novell. These shareware programs should not cause problems if set up properly.

If you follow the Windows network installation recommended in the Windows documentation, all sharable files are placed on the file server. This setup greatly reduces disk-space requirements, but some applications may not operate as quickly as those that are locally installed. Although a slight performance loss results, installing Windows on the network is currently the best way to maintain software integrity and consistency in individual workstation setups. For more information about networking Windows, see *Maximizing Windows 3.1 and Windows 3.1 Networking* by New Riders Publishing.

Using Novell's ODI Interface

Novell's *ODI (Open Data-Link Interface)* driver technology allows multiple protocol stacks to operate concurrently. A *protocol* is a set of rules or a formal process that allows computers to communicate. Novell is now migrating to their ODI solution for the complete Novell product line. ODI is the workstation interface of Novell's future.

Internally, Novell's ODI is broken down into layers that conform as closely as possible, to the *OSI (Open Systems Interconnection)* reference model. Figure 5.13 compares the Novell ODI and the OSI model. As the OSI model becomes accepted by the computer industry, multi-vendor communications will become a reality.

Figure 5.13:
The Novell ODI and the OSI reference model.

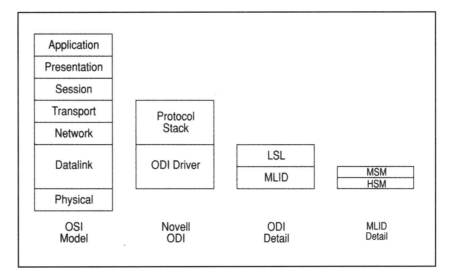

In 1977, the International Organization for Standardization created a committee dedicated to the development of a set of rules or standards to promote interoperability between computer vendors. The OSI reference is the result of these efforts.

The ODI driver is made up of the *Multiple-Link Interface Driver (MLID)*, the *Link Support Layer (LSL)*, and the protocol stack itself. The MLID contains a *MSM (Media Support Module)* and a *HSM (Hardware-Specific Module)*. This software or code makes up the LAN driver and can communicate with more than one protocol stack. The LSL manages the different protocol stacks you are operating.

To further explain the chart in figure 5.13 you need a short explanation on the OSI model itself. The seven layers of the OSI are as follows:

- **Application Layer** communicates directly with the user and relays the data to the layers that follow.
- **Presentation Layer** performs data conversion from a data code to a stream of bits or proper syntax.
- **Session Layer** sets up and tears down communication links as needed.
- **Transport Layer** ensures the quality and reliability of data transmissions.
- **Data Link Layer** packages and unpackages data to be sent through the network; organizes the bits.
- **Physical Layer** controls how the computer interface talks over the network. This layer specifies the electrical specifications.

 Novell has announced that, in the near future, development of the dedicated IPX drivers will be discouraged, and Novell will focus on ODI technology only. Currently all higher level communications products such as SAA and TCP/IP require ODI drivers.

Logging in through ODI Drivers

Implementing ODI drivers requires no generation or linking process. You can control the ODI files' custom configuration by creating a

NET.CFG file. Loading the ODI files is a simple process when you understand what each file supplies.

The Link Support Layer (LSL) is the first program loaded (see fig. 5. 14). This program acts as a switchboard between the network interface driver and the protocol stack. LSL also handles traffic between multiple stacks when they are present.

Figure 5.14:
The Link Support Layer.

```
[DR DOS] C:\NET>lsl
NetWare Link Support Layer  v1.10 (910625)
(C) Copyright 1991 Novell, Inc.  All Rights Reserved.

[DR DOS] C:\NET>
```

About Protocol Stacks...

A *protocol stack* is the process that controls the type of communication taking place. If your PC workstation requires access to both the NetWare file server and your SUN UNIX server, for example, you need to install a Novell IPX and TCP/IP protocol stack.

The TCP/IP protocol was designed by the US Department of Defense and has not been adopted by many large corporate or educational environments.

After the LSL.COM program is loaded, the network interface driver, or MLID (Multiple Link Interface Driver), is loaded (see fig. 5.15). This program, provided by the manufacturer, supplies the hardware support for the individual interface cards. Not all interface cards currently support ODI, but more and more companies are making them available.

Figure 5.15:
The Multiple Link Interface Driver (MLID).

```
[DR DOS] C:\NET>ne2000
Novell NE2000 Ethernet MLID  v1.34 (910603)
(C) Copyright 1991 Novell, Inc.  All Rights Reserved.

Int 5, Port 320, Node Address 1B34C5BE
Max Frame 1514 bytes, Line Speed 10 Mbps
Board 1, Frame ETHERNET_802.3

[DR DOS] C:\NET>
```

About ODI Drivers Suppliers...

Novell currently is supplying ODI drivers for the Novell NE*xxxx* series, EXOS and 3COM Ethernet cards, and SMC-compatible Arcnet and IBM Token Ring interface cards. In the past few months, both Racal-Interlan and Western Digital have provided ODI drivers.

After the MLID is loaded, the protocol stack and shell are loaded to complete the attachment to a NetWare file server. A typical ODI driver loading sequence uses the following files in this order:

LSL

NE2000

IPXODI

NETX

Here, ODI drivers have the advantage over the standard IPX drivers. At this point, you may have loaded a TCP protocol stack if your company uses UNIX hosts. With ODI drivers, however, you can load both the IPX and the TCP stacks to provide both protocols at the same time.

> ### About IBM's LAN Support Program...
>
> If you are using IBM's LAN Support Program on a workstation, you also should use the LANSUP.COM driver.
>
> If you are using IBM's Source Routing, you must load the ROUTE.COM program after LANSUP.COM or TOKEN.COM, but before you load the protocol stack.

The preceding list of commands loads the LSL file and then the MLID required for a Novell NE2000 Ethernet card. At this time, the standard IPX protocol stack is loaded (see fig. 5.16), followed by a normal shell, NETX (see fig. 5.17).

Figure 5.16:
The IPX protocol stack.

```
[DR DOS] C:\NET>ipxodi
NetWare IPX/SPX Protocol   v1.10 (910625)
(C) Copyright 1991 Novell, Inc.  All Rights Reserved.

IPX protocol bound to NE2000 MLID Board #1.

[DR DOS] C:\NET>
```

The NET.CFG file controls Novell's ODI drivers. This ASCII file can be used to modify settings in many of the modules loaded to complete the ODI connection. An example of a simple NET.CFG file is as follows:

```
show dots = on
Link Driver NE2000
    Port 300
    Int 5
```

Figure 5.17:
The NETX shell.

```
[DR DOS] C:\NET>netx

NetWare V3.22 - Workstation Shell (910731)
(C) Copyright 1991 Novell, Inc.  All Rights Reserved.

Running on DOS V3.31

Attached to server CDI
11-21-91    12:39:24 pm

[DR DOS] C:\NET>
```

This file simply provides the necessary hardware settings to the MLID, which in this case is a Novell NE2000 Ethernet adapter. This example also turns on the option "show dots" which is used by Microsoft Windows. This option is explained in the following section.

 Note Any statements previously used in the old SHELL.CFG file can be added to the top of the new NET.CFG in a left-justified format.

The next example of a NET.CFG file is a little more complicated. This one makes use of multiple Ethernet frame types and provides options for TCP/IP support as supplied by Novell's LAN workplace for DOS product:

```
show dots = on
pb buffers = 5
get local target stacks = 3
```

```
Link Support
  Buffers 8 1586
  MemPool 4096

Protocol TCPIP
  ip_address 192.68.205.10
  ip_router        192.68.201.1
  ip_netmask 0.0.0.0
  tcp_sockets      8
  udp_sockets      8
  raw_sockets      1

Link Driver NE2000
  Port 320
  Int 5
  Frame Ethernet_II
  Frame Ethernet_802.3
  Protocol IPX 0 Ethernet_802.3
```

 Notice the third line in the preceding example. The `get lo-cal target stacks` line is very important when you use Microsoft Windows on the network. The default of the setting is 1. Increase this setting for any multitasking program operation.

The order of the programs used in the preceding example are as follows:

LSL
NE2000
IPXODI
TCPIP
BNETX

LSL is the standard Link Support Layer, NE2000 is the MLID or driver for the Ethernet interface, and IPXODI and TCP/IP are both protocol stacks. This is followed with the Burst Mode version of NETX or BNETX.

In the preceding example, a few items must be explained. The first three lines have already been mentioned; these are setup options for Microsoft Windows and Burst mode. Next is the Link Support section. In this section, both the Buffers and Memory Pool have been increased beyond defaults. These settings were obtained from the TCP/IP software and are required for that function. These normally are not used in a simple IPX only connection.

Under the Protocol definition of TCP/IP, you can see both manufacturer set options and system administrator set options. First, you have the ip_address assigned by your UNIX system administrator. Next, is the ip_router required only if you must pass through an IP router to reach your destination. The ip_netmask is not used in this example, but is part of your ip address and is also set up by the UNIX system administrator.

 IP Addressing is much more complicated than the standard Arcnet or Ethernet node number familiar to Novell administrators. If you require further understanding of IP addressing, it would be beneficial to you to purchase a UNIX networking book.

The settings for tcp_sockets, udp_sockets, and raw_sockets are each specified by the protocol stack supplier and should be set accordingly.

In the Link Driver section, you see again the Port and Int settings. These are standard options and are used often. The next lines specify the frame type needed to communicate to the different services. The first frame of Ethernet_II is very common in the UNIX world and is required here for that reason. The next frame type of Ethernet_802.3 is currently the standard frame used by Novell's IPX protocol. The last line specifies which frame to bind the IPX protocol to. With these settings both IPX and TCP/IP communications are provided to the workstation.

Each of the ODI modules provides command-line switches for unloading and for memory-saving loads.

Use /U to unload each module. Figure 5.18 shows the screen display as the NETX shell program is being unloaded.

The IPXODI module provides two extra switches that enable memory savings if full functionality is not needed. Use /D to load IPX/SPX protocols only, without any diagnostic capability; this switch provides a memory savings of 4K. Use /A to load the IPX protocol only; this switch provides a memory savings of 8K. Use /? to display information about any ODI module.

Novell has approved all ODI modules to operate in high memory.

```
[DR DOS] C:\NET>netx /u

NetWare V3.22 - Workstation Shell (910731)
(C) Copyright 1991 Novell, Inc.  All Rights Reserved.

You are being logged out of all servers...
Memory for resident shell has been released.
The NetWare shell has been unloaded.

[DR DOS] C:\NET>
```

Figure 5.18:
Unloading the shell
program.

Figure 5.19 shows the screen display during a successful stack unload. Figure 5.20 shows the display during an unload in which the program module is being unloaded in the wrong order; this type of error results in a "fatal unload."

```
[DR DOS] C:\NET>ipxodi /u

IPX protocol successfully removed.

[DR DOS] C:\NET>
```

Figure 5.19:
A successful
unload.

```
[DR DOS] C:\NET>ipxodi /u
NetWare IPX/SPX Protocol  v1.10 (910625)
(C) Copyright 1991 Novell, Inc.  All Rights Reserved.

FATAL: There is a TSR above the loaded IPX.

[DR DOS] C:\NET>
```

Inside NET.CFG

This section details the LAN DRIVER parameters and their options in the NET.CFG file. Table 5.2 shows the Link Driver hardware parameters. Each option is explained in detail after the table.

Table 5.2
Link Driver Hardware Options

Option
Link Driver **drivername**
CONNECTOR DIX
DMA **channel number**
INT **interrupt request number**
MEM **hex starting address [hex length]**
PORT **hex starting address [hex number of ports]**
NODE ADDRESS **hex address**
SLOT **number**

The Link Driver *drivername* heading must start at the left margin in the NET.CFG file. The drivername is the name of the driver you are using. If you are using the NE2000.COM driver, for instance, then your drivername is NE2000 and the Link Driver statement appears as shown below:

```
Link Driver NE2000
```

The following section defines the Hardware Options that can be used to configure the shell to the hardware settings on the network board. These options must be indented underneath the Link Driver statement.

CONNECTOR DIX. This option is used only with 3COM's 3C503 network board for 3COM EtherLink Series II to change the connector type from thinnet BNC to thicknet DIX. The following example shows how to set a 3C503 board to use the DIX connector:

```
Link Driver 3C503
   CONNECTOR DIX
```

DMA *channel number*. If the network board you are using needs to be configured for Direct Memory Access (DMA), use this option. In the following example, a 3COM 3C505 card is configured to use channel 3:

```
Link Driver 3C505
   DMA 3
```

INT *interrupt request number*. This option is used to state the interrupt—often seen stated as IRQ or INT—that the network board uses. The following example shows how to set an ARCnet board to interrupt 5 using the TRXNET driver:

```
Link Driver TRXNET
   INT 5
```

MEM *hex starting address*. This option specifies the memory range that the network board is configured to use. This number should be entered as a hex value. The following example shows how to set an ARCnet board to use the hex memory address of D000:

```
Link Driver TRXNET
   MEM D000
```

PORT *hex starting address*. This option specifies the I/O port address that the network board is configured to use. This number should be

entered as a hex value. The following example shows how to set an
Ethernet board to use the hex port address of 300:

```
Link Driver NE1000
  PORT 300
```

NODE ADDRESS *hex address*. Some network boards allow the hardware address to be set in the NET.CFG file. The NODE ADDRESS option enables you to define the hex address. This example shows how
to set a Novell Ethernet NE2100 board to use the address of 22A31:

```
Link Driver NE2100
  NODE ADDRESS 22A31
```

SLOT *number*. When using a network board in a slot-based machine,
the driver attempts to locate boards by scanning the slots from the lowest to highest. This option speeds up the process by telling the driver
which slot to look in for the board. In the following example, you see
how to set a Novell Ethernet NE/2 board to use slot 3.

```
Link Driver NE2
  SLOT 3
```

Table 5.3 shows the Link Driver software parameters and the default
options. These options are used to configure the shell to the hardware
settings on the network board. Each option is explained in detail after
the table. These options must be indented underneath the Link Driver
statement.

Table 5.3
Link Driver Software Options

Option	Default
ALTERNATE	
FRAME `frame type`	
LINK STATIONS `number`	1
MAX FRAME SIZE `number`	
NODE ADDRESS `hex address`	
PROTOCOL `name hex protocol ID frame type`	
SAPS `number`	1

ALTERNATE. This option is only used with the LANSUP driver for IBM LAN Support, the TOKEN driver for IBM Token-Ring, or the PCN2L driver for the IBM PC Network II and II/A. It is used when you want the driver to use a network board other than the primary network board. In the following example, the PCN2L driver is configured to use the secondary board.

```
Link Driver PCN2l
   ALTERNATE
```

FRAME frame type. This option is used to enable multiple frame types for network boards. This option only works if the network board supports multiple frame types. Ethernet drivers default to ETHERNET_802.3 frames. Other options include: ETHERNET_802.2, ETHERNET_II and ETHERNET_SNAP. Token Ring drivers default to TOKEN-RING frames, but can support TOKEN-RING_SNAP as well. ARCnet supports only one frame type, NOVELL_RX-NET. The following example shows how to use both the ETHERNET_II and the ETHERNET_802.3 frames with an NE2000 driver:

```
Link Driver NE2000
   FRAME ETHERNET_II
   FRAME ETHERNET_802.3
```

LINK STATIONS *number*. This option is used only with the LANSUP driver for IBM LAN Support. Set LINK STATIONS to allow for all applications using the IBM LAN Support Program.

MAX FRAME SIZE *number*. This option enables you to set the maximum number of bytes that the LAN driver can put onto the network cable at one time. This option is used only with the LANSUP driver for IBM LAN Support or the TOKEN driver for IBM Token-Ring. The default size for TOKEN is 4216 bytes, however, if the board has 8 KB of shared RAM available, the default size is 2168. LANSUP has a default size of 1144, but if the LAN Support program is used with an Ethernet device driver, the default becomes 1496.

Use the following formula to figure the number:

# of bytes for the data packet (1,2,4 or 8K)
        plus
6 bytes for adapter overhead
        plus
The largest possible header (currently 114 bytes)

This number needs to be a multiple of 8. If 4K packets are used, this number will be 4096+6+114, or 4216. To set the maximum size to 4216 using the TOKEN Link Driver, place the following lines in your NET.CFG:

```
Link Driver TOKEN
  MAX FRAME SIZE 4216
```

If you are using TBMI2 or TASKID this option is not available.

PROTOCOL *name hexprotocol frametype*. This option enables existing LAN drivers to handle network protocols. The name of the new protocol is `name`; `hexprotocol` is the protocol ID stated in hex; and `frametype` is the name of the frame the protocol uses.

In the following example, the protocol IPX is assigned the hex protocol ID number 0. To add this protocol to the Ethernet_802.3 frame type, add the following line in the NET.CFG:

```
PROTOCOL IPX 0 Ethernet_802.3
```

SAPS *number*. This option is used only with the LANSUP driver for IBM LAN Support. It enables you to define the number of Service Access Points (SAPs) needed. Set this number to allow for all applications using the IBM LAN Support Program.

Table 5.4 presents the LINK SUPPORT parameters, options, and defaults in the NET.CFG file that are used to configure the shell. Each option is explained in detail after the table.

Table 5.4
Link Support Options

Option	Default
Link Support	
BUFFERS **number [size]**	0 [1130]
MAX BOARDS **number**	4
MAX STACKS **number**	4
MEMPOOL **number**	

ogging

Link Support. This heading must start at the left margin in the NET.CFG file. The the definitions for the Link Support options that can be used to configure the shell are listed below. These options must be indented underneath the Link Support statement.

BUFFERS *number [size]*. This option enables you to configure the number and size of the receive buffers. This number must take into account enough room to hold all headers as well as the maximum data size. Use of the `size` parameter is optional. The minimum is 618 bytes, and the total buffer space must fit into 59KB.

MAX BOARDS *number*. This option enables you to specify the maximum number of logical boards the LSL can handle. The range is from 1 to 16, and the default is 4. If you load all of the possible frame types for Ethernet, you load four frames. Your MAX BOARDS number needs to be set for at least four protocols.

MAX STACKS *number*. Because each protocol stack uses one or more resources, you must define a sufficient amount of stacks or you will receive `out-of-resource` errors. The range is from 1 to 16, and the default is 4.

MEMPOOL *number*. The IPXODI protocol stack does not use this option, however, other protocol stacks may require the size of the memory pool buffers to be adjusted. See the documentation supplied with the protocol for recommended settings.

Table 5.5 defines the Protocol Selection parameters and options in the NET.CFG file. Each option is explained in detail after the table.

Table 5.5
Protocol Selection Options

Option
Protocol *protocol name*
BIND *board name*

Protocol *protocol name*. This heading must start at the left margin in the NET.CFG file. The protocol name is the actual protocol you choose for the LAN board. The definition for the Protocol Selection option that can be used to configure the shell is given below. This option must be indented underneath the Protocol Selection statement.

BIND *board name*. This option binds the protocol to the appropriate LAN board. In the following example, the IPXODI protocol is bound to a Novell Ethernet NE2000 board:

```
Protocol IPXODI
    BIND NE2000
```

Table 5.6 shows the NETBIOS options and defaults in the NET.CFG that are used to configure the shell. Each option is explained in detail after the table. These options should start at the left margin in the NET.CFG file.

Table 5.6
NETBIOS Options

Option	Default
NETBIOS.EXE	
NETBIOS ABORT TIMEOUT=n	540 ticks (30 seconds)
NETBIOS BROADCAST COUNT=n	2
NETBIOS BROADCAST DELAY=n	18 ticks (1 second)
NETBIOS COMMANDS=n	12
NETBIOS INTERNET=on/off	on
NETBIOS LISTEN TIMEOUT=n	108 ticks (6 seconds)
NETBIOS RECEIVE BUFFERS=n	6 buffers
NETBIOS RETRY COUNT=n	10 ticks (~1 seconds)
NETBIOS RETRY DELAY=n	10 ticks (~1 seconds)
NETBIOS SEND BUFFERS=n	6 buffers
NETBIOS SESSION=n	32 sessions
NETBIOS VERIFY TIMEOUT=n	54 ticks (3 seconds)
NPATCH=`byte offset,value`	

NETBIOS ABORT TIMEOUT. This is the amount of time, in ticks (1/18th of a second), that NETBIOS waits for a response before it closes the session. This number needs to be higher than the default of 540 ticks if NETBIOS runs on machines that communicate through asynch or Wide Area Networks.

NETBIOS BROADCAST COUNT. This number reflects the size of your network. This number multiplied by the NETBIOS BROADCAST DELAY determines the total time the network needs to broadcast a name resolution packet. Increase this option if you cannot attach to a gateway. NETBIOS INTERNET directly affects this number. When NETBIOS INTERNET is turned off, the default is 2. When NETBIOS INTERNET is turned on, the default is 4. The entire range is from 2 to 65,535.

NETBIOS BROADCAST DELAY. This number reflects the size of your network. This number multiplied by the NETBIOS BROADCAST COUNT determines the total time the network needs to broadcast a name resolution packet. Increase this option if traffic or packet loss rate is high. Again, NETBIOS INTERNET directly affects this number. When NETBIOS INTERNET is turned off, the default is 18. When NETBIOS INTERNET is turned on, the default is 36. The entire range is from 18 to 65,535.

NETBIOS COMMANDS. This option increases the number of NETBIOS commands available to applications. Increase this number when an error 22 occurs. The default is 12, and the range is from 4 to 250.

NETBIOS INTERNET. If you are running NETBIOS on a single LAN segment, set this option to OFF. If you are communicating with NETBIOS through a bridge, set this option to ON. The default is ON.

NETBIOS LISTEN TIMEOUT. This option sets the amount of time NETBIOS waits before sending out a session-validation packet to request that the other side reply immediately. NETBIOS will continue to send these packets at the interval specified in the VERIFY TIMEOUT option. It will continue until it reaches the specified time limit in the ABORT TIMEOUT option. The default is 108 ticks, and the range is from 1 to 65,535.

NETBIOS RECEIVE BUFFERS. This is the number of IPX receive buffers that NETBIOS uses. Increase this parameter when you use a 3270 gateway or client-server applications. The default is 6 buffers, and the range is from 4 to 20.

NETBIOS RETRY COUNT. This option sets the number of resends NETBIOS performs to establish a remote session. Increase this number when you cannot attach to a gateway or when you have many LAN segments using NETBIOS. NETBIOS INTERNET directly affects this number. When NETBIOS INTERNET is turned off, the default is 10. When NETBIOS INTERNET is turned on, the default is 20. The entire range is from 4 to 20.

NETBIOS RETRY DELAY. This option sets the length of time NETBIOS waits between retries when trying to establish a remote session. Increase this number when you cannot attach to a gateway or when you have many LAN segments using NETBIOS. The default is 10 ticks and the range is 10 to 65,535.

NETBIOS SEND BUFFERS. This is the number of IPX send buffers that NETBIOS uses. This parameter can be increased when you are using a 3270 gateway or client-server applications. The default is 6 buffers and the range is from 4 to 20.

NETBIOS SESSION. This is the maximum concurrent number of supported NETBIOS virtual circuits. The default is 32 sessions, and the range is from 4 to 250.

NETBIOS VERIFY TIMEOUT. This option adjusts the frequency that session-validation packets are sent. The default is 54 ticks, and the range is from 4 to 65,535.

NPATCH=*byte offset,value*. This option patches any location in the NETBIOS.EXE file with any value.

Table 5.7 shows the option used by EMSNETX.EXE and is defined in the NET.CFG. This option must be placed at the left margin in the NET.CFG file.

Table 5.7
EMSNETX.EXE Parameter

Option	Default
ENTRY STACK SIZE=n	10

ENTRY STACK SIZE. This option ensures that the memory page frame sees the code residing in expanded memory. This option is helpful when expanded memory uses TSRs. The default is 10, and the range is from 5 to 40.

Table 5.8 details the IPXODI parameters, options, and defaults in the NET.CFG file. Each option is explained in detail after the table. These options must be place at the left margin of NET.CFG.

Table 5.8
IPXODI Options

Option	Default
CONFIG OPTION=n	
INT64=on/off	on
INT7A=on/off	on
IPATCH=byte offset,value	
IPX PACKET SIZE LIMIT=n	4160 or set by LAN driver
IPX RETRY COUNT=n	20 retries
IPX SOCKETS=n	20 sockets
SPX ABORT TIMEOUT=n	540 ticks (30 seconds)
SPX CONNECTIONS=n	15 connections
SPX LISTEN TIMEOUT=n	108 ticks (6 seconds)
SPX VERIFY TIMEOUT=n	54 ticks (3 seconds)

CONFIG OPTION. This option enables you to change the configuration option used by IPX.COM. Type **IPX /O** at the DOS prompt to find the available option numbers for your IPX. IPX /O lists the interrupt and memory options that you can configure your network board to use. Use of this option is temporary. Use the WSGEN program to permanently change the configuration of the IPX.COM. The default is whatever option the original file was configured to use.

INT64. Certain applications, including earlier versions of NetWare, used this interrupt to access IPX services. Set this option to OFF if an application requests interrupt 64h, or if you have an application that worked with NetWare v2.0a but causes the workstation to lock up with v3.x. The default for this option is on.

INT7A. Certain applications, including earlier versions of NetWare, used this interrupt to access IPX services. Set this option to OFF if an application requests interrupt 7Ah, or if you have an application that worked with NetWare v2.0a but causes the workstation to lock up with v3.x. The default is on.

IPATCH. This parameter enables any address used by IPX.COM to be patched to the specified value.

IPX PACKET SIZE LIMIT. This parameter reduces the maximum packet size set by the LAN driver. Each LAN driver has an optimum packet size. Ethernet's optimum is 1500 bytes, and Token Ring's optimum is the default of 4160 bytes. If this parameter is not configured correctly, the system may be wasting memory for most operations. If this is the case, the workstation experiences `out of memory errors`. The default is 4160, and the range is from 576 to 6500 bytes.

IPX RETRY COUNT. This option enables you to specify how many times a packet can be resent. Use this option if you lose many packets. The default is 20 retries.

IPX SOCKETS. This is the maximum number of open sockets IPX can use. Some programs require several sockets to be opened at the workstation. The default is 20 sockets.

SPX ABORT TIMEOUT. This is the amount of time in ticks that SPX waits for a response before ending the session. The default is 540 ticks.

SPX CONNECTIONS. This option sets the maximum number of SPX connections a workstation can use at one time. If the workstation uses RPRINTER, set this number to 60. The default is 15 connections.

SPX LISTEN TIMEOUT. This is the amount of time in ticks that SPX waits for a response before sending a session-validation packet to determine if the session is still valid. The default is 108 ticks.

SPX VERIFY TIMEOUT. This option establishes the frequency of sending session-validation packets to announce that the session is still active. The default is 54 ticks.

Table 5.9 details the NETX parameters, options, and defaults in the NET.CFG file. Each option is explained in detail after the table. Place these options at the left margin of NET.CFG.

Table 5.9
NETX Options

Option	Default
ALL SERVERS=on/off	
CACHE BUFFERS=n	5 cache blocks
DOS NAME=name	DRDOS or MSDOS
ENVIRONMENT PAD=n	17
EOJ=on/off	on
FILE HANDLES=n	40 open files
GET LOCAL TARGET STACKS=n	1 stack
HOLD=on/off	off
LOCAL PRINTERS=n	# of ports
LOCK DELAY=n	1
LOCK RETRIES=n	3
LONG MACHINE TYPE=name	IBM_PC
MAX CUR DIR LENGTH=n	64
MAX PATH LENGTH=n	255
MAX TASKS=n	31
PATCH=byte offset,value	
PREFERRED SERVER=name	
PRINT HEADER=n	64 bytes
PRINT TAIL=n	16 bytes
READ ONLY COMPATIBILITY=on/off	off
SEARCH MODE=n	1
SET STATION TIME=on/off	on
SHARE=on/off	on
SHORT MACHINE TYPE=name	IBM
SHOW DOTS=on/off	off
SPECIAL UPPERCASE=on/off	off
TASK MODE=n	2

ALL SERVERS. This determines whether all servers are informed of an End of Task or only those servers interacting with the task. When turned ON, End of Task is sent to all servers. The default is OFF.

CACHE BUFFERS. This option can be used to speed up the processing of sequential reads/writes. The option enables you to set the number of 512 byte buffers that can be used for local caching of non-TTS, non-shared files. The default is 5 cache blocks.

DOS NAME. This sets the name of the operating system for up to 5 characters. This option relates to the %OS variable that can be accessed through login scripts. The default is DRDOS or MS-DOS

ENVIRONMENT PAD. This option enables you to increase the number of bytes added to a program's environment space before executing. The default is 17 bytes and the range is from 17 to 512.

EOJ. This option indicates whether locks, semaphores, and files are closed automatically at the end of a job. The default is ON.

FILE HANDLES. This option indicates the number of files the workstation can have open on the network at one time. Set the number of open local files in CONFIG.SYS. Default is 40 open files on the network.

GET LOCAL TARGET STACKS. This option can be configured when using multitasking DOS products, like DRDOS 6.0. Certain applications may require that you increase the number of stacks to communicate with other nodes. The default is 1 stack, and the range is from 1 to 10.

HOLD. When this option is set to ON, it enables workstation files to be held open until you exit from an application. The default is OFF.

LOCAL PRINTERS. This option overrides the number of local printer ports on the workstation. If the workstation has no local printer and no Capture statement was issued, the workstation will lock up. Set this option to 0 to prevent the lockup.

LOCK DELAY. This option sets the amount of time the shell waits before attempting to get a lock. The default is 1 tick.

LOCK RETRIES. This option sets the number of times the shell attempts to get a lock. If the workstation gets receive error messages, try increasing this parameter. The default is 3 tries.

LONG MACHINE TYPE. This option tells the network what type of machine is being used. It works in conjunction with the %MACHINE Login Script Variable. Because the default for all machines is IBM_PC, this option correctly identifies the machine type.

MAX CUR DIR LENGTH. This option enables you to set the maximum length of a directory path in bytes. The default shows 64 bytes of the path with a range of 64 to 255.

MAX PATH LENGTH. This option enables you to set the number of characters in a path name. The default is 255 characters; the range is from 64 to 255.

MAX TASKS. This option sets the maximum number of active tasks. Programs such as Windows or DESQview provide multiple active tasks. Increase this number if you are unable to open additional tasks.

PATCH. This option enables any address in the shell to be patched with any value. This is done when simple changes to the shell have been announced and the code specified.

PREFERRED SERVER. This option is used to force a connection to a specific server. The shell will poll up to five servers for available connections.

PRINT HEADER. This option enables you to set the buffer size for the print header. The information held in this buffer is used to initialize a printer. Increase this buffer if the printer is not receiving all the requested attributes. The default is 64 bytes; the range is from 0 to 255.

PRINT TAIL. This option enables you to set the buffer size for the print tail. The information held in this buffer is used to reset the printer after issuing a print job. If the printer fails to reset, increase this buffer. The default is 16 bytes, and the range is from 0 to 255.

READ ONLY COMPATIBILITY. This option determines whether Read Only files can be opened with an appropriate access call. Older versions of NetWare allowed a Read Only file to be opened and read with the write access, and no error was generated. If an attempt was made to write to the file, an error occurred. The default is OFF. Turn this option to ON, if you want compatibility with older NetWare versions.

SEARCH MODE. This option alters the method used for finding a file not in the current directory. The SMODE command alters the search method for a specific file. You must set this option correctly to find the majority of your EXE and COM programs. Search Mode Options are listed below:

- 0—No search instructions. Default settings used for all executable files.
- 1—If a directory path is specified in the executable file, it is the only one searched. If no directory path is specified, only the default path is searched.
- 2—The executable file searches only the default or specified path.
- 3—If a directory path is specified in the executable file, the executable file searches only that path. If a path is not specified, and the executable file opens data files flagged Read Only, the executable file searches the default directory and search drives.
- 4—Reserved.
- 5—The executable file searches the default directory and NetWare search drives whether or not the path is specified in the executable file. If search mode is set, the shell enables you to search for any extension. Otherwise, DOS searches only for EXE, COM, and BAT files.
- 6—Reserved.
- 7—If the executable file opens data files flagged Read Only, the executable file searches the default directory and search drives whether or not the path is specified in the executable file.

The default drive must be a network drive for SEARCH MODE to function properly.

SET STATION TIME. This option allows the workstation to synchronize with the file server's time. The default is ON.

SHARE. This option allows a secondary process to inherit all the resources of its primary process. The default is ON.

SHORT MACHINE TYPE. This option works in conjunction with the Login Script variable %SMACHINE. The maximum length of this alias is 4 characters. The default machine type is IBM.

SHOW DOTS. The NetWare file server does not have directory entries for . and .. as DOS does. If you are using an application that requires the use of . and .., such as Windows, you must set this option to ON. The default is OFF.

SPECIAL UPPERCASE. The shell does not translate uppercase ASCII characters above 128. If you set this option to ON, the shell asks DOS to translate.

TASK MODE. This option sets the way the shell handles virtual machine task management. Windows 3.x uses 0. Earlier versions of Windows and other third-party multitasking programs need this option set to 1. If you set this option to 0, workstation speed increases if you are not using multitasking programs. The default is 2.

Table 5.10 details the TBMI2 parameters, options, and defaults in the NET.CFG file. Each option is explained in detail after the table. These options must be place at the left margin of NET.CFG.

Table 5.10
TBMI2 Options

Option	Defaults
INT64=on/off	on
INT7A=on/off	on
ECB COUNT=n	20
DATA ECB COUNT=n	60

INT64. Certain applications, including earlier version of NetWare, used this interrupt to access IPX services. Set this option to OFF if an application requests interrupt 64h, or if you have an application that worked with NetWare 2.0a, but causes the workstation to lock up with v3.x. The default is on.

INT7A. Certain applications, including earlier versions of NetWare, used this interrupt to access IPX services. Set this option to OFF if an application requests interrupt 7Ah, or if you have an application that worked with NetWare 2.0a, but causes the workstation to lock up with v3.x. The default is on.

ECB COUNT. This option sets how many nondata event control blocks (ECBs) can be allocated for use by DOS programs. The default is 20, and the range is from 10 to 255.

DATA ECB COUNT. This option sets how many data ECBs can be allocated for use by DOS programs. The default is 60, and the range is from 10 to 89.

TBMI2

Novell's TBMI2 module provides and manages the data buffers required to operate virtual IPX and SPX sessions. TBMI2 is designed for multitasking environments such as the DOS 5.0 DOSSHELL, DRDOS 6.0, and Microsoft Windows.

 Novell's COMCHECK and NetWare 3.11's RCONSOLE cannot be used while TBMI2 is loaded. These applications require too many buffers for this module.

To use TBMI2, simply load it before using a multitasking application and unload it with the /U switch when done. TBMI2's /D switch displays diagnostic information. By using this option, you can determine the proper settings to be used in the NET.CFG file.

DOS Named Pipes

Novell's DOS Named Pipes extender provides the capability to connect to an OS/2 server via a Named Pipe connection. This connection method is used in the OS/2 environment and is common with OS/2 based SQL database servers.

DOSNP.EXE is a *TSR* or *terminate and stay resident program* that must be loaded when a named pipe connection is needed. The DOSNP.EXE program makes use of several commands that can be added to the NET.CFG file. They are as follows:

- **Maximum Machine Names.** This option controls the number of Named Pipe servers that can be communicated with. The allowed range is 4 to 50 with a default of 10. An example of this command is as follows:

```
NP MAX MACHINE NAMES=number
```

- **Maximum Open Named Pipes.** This option controls the maximum number of named pipes that the workstation can have open simultaneously. The allowed range for this option is 4 to 128; 4 is the default. The syntax of this command is as follows:

  NP MAX OPEN NAMED PIPES=*number*

- **Maximum Communications Buffers.** This option controls the maximum number of buffers that can be used when transmitting and receiving data from a named pipe server. The allowed range is 4 to 40 with a default of 6. An example of this command follows:

  NP MAX COMM BUFFERS=*number*

Each of these options is generally suggested by the application developer.

ODINSUP

Novell's newest ODI add-on is ODINSUP. ODINSUP is an interface that enables NDIS (Network Driver Interface Specification) and ODI file server drivers to operate at the same time. The NDIS technology is currently used by OS/2, LAN Manager, and LAN Server. The ODINSUP module does not contain the NDIS driver, but provides compatibility between both methods of communications.

To install Novell's ODINSUP support program, simply copy the ODINSUP.COM program into the same directory as your NET.CFG file. You must then modify the CONFIG.SYS, AUTOEXEC.BAT, NET.CFG, and PROTOCOL.INI files. All but NET.CFG are controlled by your system requiring the NDIS drivers.

 Novell ODI drivers must be dated after May 21,1991 to provide ODINSUP operation. And the LSL.COM program must be version 1.21 or greater. This can be checked by using the ? switch. For example: **LSL ?** <enter>

To load the NDIS drivers, perform the following steps:

1. Set the DOS LASTDRIVE statement in your CONFIG.SYS file by adding LASTDRIVE=<*drive letter*>. This allows

drive pointers for the NDIS network and starts your NetWare drives on the next letter after your LASTDRIVE setting.

2. Load your NDIS protocol manager as follows by including the device statement to your CONFIG.SYS file.

3. Remove all references to the NDIS driver in your CONFIG.SYS file. These are no longer required and will be controlled later.

4. Modify your AUTOEXEC.BAT or the normal file used to load drivers to include Novell's ODI files. These must be loaded in the following order: LSL, <your ODI LAN Driver>, ODINSUP, NETBIND, NETBIOS, IPXODI, and NETX.

 When you load ODINSUP, you must be in the directory that contains your NET.CFG file.

5. Enable the proper Ethernet or Token-Ring frame types as used by your networks. This is performed as shown earlier in the ODI section. A simple example is shown below:

```
Link Driver NE2000
frame ethernet_802.3
frame ethernet_II
```

6. Bind ODINSUP to the proper ODI driver as shown in the following example:

```
Protocol ODINSUP
bind NE2000
```

Both steps 5 and 6 are example sections of the NET.CFG file.

7. Remove all NDIS-related information from your PROTOCOL.INI file as these are not required by ODINSUP. You must then specify the driver you want to bind the NDIS protocol to as in the sample shown below.

```
[XNS]
 .
 .
Bindings=ne2000
```

In the PROTOCOL.INI file, driver names cannot start with a number. If you are using drivers such as those by 3COM, place a letter X in front of the name. For example a 3c505 driver is written X3c505.

After rebooting your computer, you should have the capability to log in to both a LAN Manager server and a NetWare server and to copy or transfer files between the two.

Burst Mode

Burst Mode is a new NetWare NCP (NetWare Core Protocol) designed to speed the transfer of large file reads and writes over wide area network links. This new protocol has been tested with performance results of 10% to 300% increases. The amount of increase you experience depends on your particular setup, but in most cases is significant.

The Burst Mode Protocol operates by overcoming the one-to-one request/response method of communicating over remote routers. When you use Burst Mode, a single read or write up to 64KB in size is sent back-to-back without a response until the last packet is received.

This protocol requires the addition of the PBURST.NLM on the file server or router and BNETX.COM on the workstation. The BNETX.COM also makes use of the NET.CFG command *PB BUFF-ERS=* to configure the proper number of packet burst buffers.

The Burst mode programs are included with Novell's Multi protocol Router or DOS/Windows Workstation Kit.

ODI drivers may appear overly complicated when compared with IPX and NETX. When you understand the flow of the modules, however, you should find that changing a driver's configuration by editing a text file is much simpler and remarkably convenient.

Logging in with a Macintosh, OS/2, or UNIX Workstation

Novell's solution for Macintosh, OS/2, and UNIX workstations enables users to use the services offered by NetWare without compromising their familiar native environments.

Mac users can select the NetWare Server icon from the CHOOSER display as shown in figure 5.21. Here, the Macintosh user can select print devices and available file servers. These servers can be both NetWare and non-NetWare servers.

Figure 5.21:
Typical Macintosh
CHOOSER Screen.

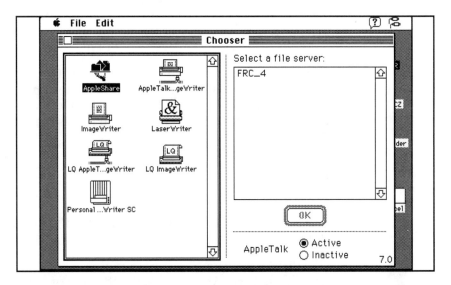

After you select a file server, you are prompted for a login method. The Macintosh provides two methods—Apple Standard UAMs or Encrypted NetWare Authentication. An example of this screen is shown in figure 5.22.

The login screen appears after you select a method. This screen provides the Macintosh user with the required fields to properly attach to the server as either a "guest," or a registered file server user. An example user login screen appears in figure 5.23. When you are connected successfully to the file server, a list of available drives or devices appears as shown in figure 5.24. Select the drives you want to access, and they are placed on your Macintosh desktop along with the other available devices.

Figure 5.22:
Typical Login
Method Screen.

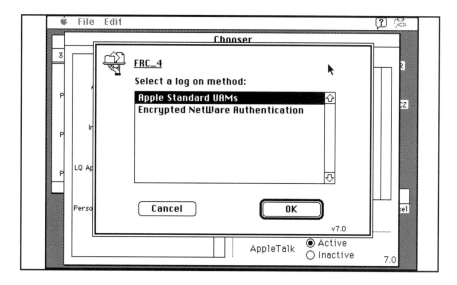

Figure 5.23:
Macintosh System
7 Login Screen.

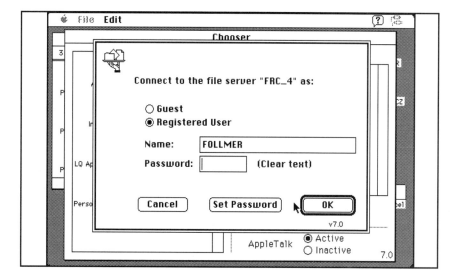

Figure 5.24:
Available drive or
device Screen.

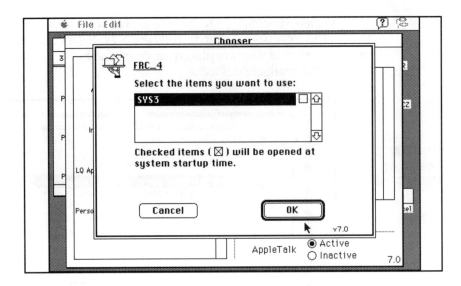

On a UNIX-based workstation, you can connect to a NetWare file server in several ways. Whether you are using the standard UNIX telnet terminal services or the UNIX NFS network services, NetWare can provide the connections.

Figure 5.25 is an example of the screen displayed by the Novell DOS telnet terminal emulator, TNVT220. This example is the product of loading the optional TCP/IP protocol stack and the TELAPI telnet application interface services included with the Novell LAN Workplace product.

As shown in figure 5.25 and 5.26, the DOS version of the telnet terminal emulator provides very functional text-based connections. Figure 5.26 shows a successful connection; the "$" prompt shows it is ready for user commands.

The Novell LAN Workplace product also provides a very good Windows interface. Figure 5.27 shows an example of the opening screen presented by the Windows terminal emulator—the Host Presenter.

The Open Session screen enables you to connect to the UNIX host and implement custom profiles if needed. Figure 5.28 is an example of a successful UNIX host connection. The Windows product provides full traditional Windows functionality.

Figure 5.25:
TNVT220 Initial
Connection Screen.

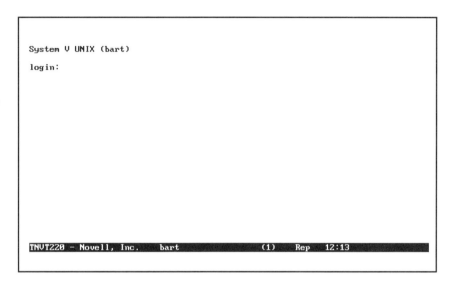

```
System V UNIX (bart)

login:




















TNVT220 - Novell, Inc.     bart                (1)    Rep   12:13
```

Figure 5.26:
Successful Telnet
Login.

```
System V UNIX (bart)

login: bchaffin
Password:
UNIX System V/386 Release 3.2
bart
Copyright (C) 1984, 1986, 1987, 1988 AT&T
Copyright (C) 1987, 1988 Microsoft Corp.
All Rights Reserved
Login last used: Mon Aug 17 17:17:25 1992

/                 :         Disk space:    34.01 MB of    87.00 MB available(39.10%)

Total Disk Space:                          34.01 MB of    87.00 MB available(39.10%)

        Welcome to the CDI UNIX Host.
This System is intended as a training ground
            for Employees
TERM=vt100
$

TNVT220 - Novell, Inc.     bart                (1)    Rep   12:13
```

The UNIX connections services also provide full native UNIX file transfer services by using the FTP or File Transfer Protocol services. This service is available in both DOS and Windows. The DOS product provides services that conform very closely to the standard UNIX interface. The Windows version shown in figure 5.28 has a functional interface that graphically displays both the UNIX and DOS file tree.

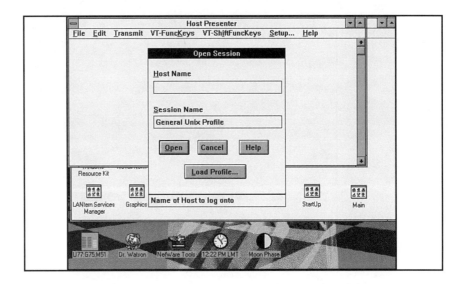

Figure 5.27:
Initial Windows
Host Presenter
Screen.

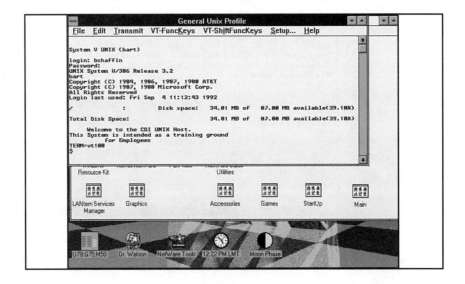

Figure 5.28:
Successful
Windows
Connection.

Figure 5.29:
Windows FTP
Connection Screen.

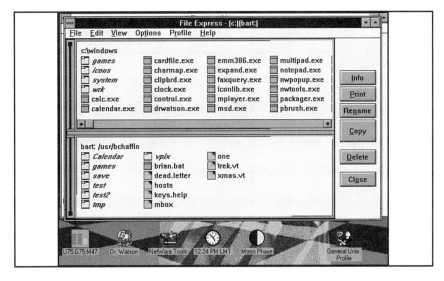

When you use an NFS connection, the functionality is similar to that of other NetWare Name Services. The directory or directories that have been set up for NFS services are mounted and displayed to UNIX users as native UNIX directories.

The NetWare OS/2 Requester provides OS/2 connections to NetWare file servers. This requester is a complete package of both network card drivers and OS/2 utilities that provide various capabilities to the OS/2 client. Table 5.11 is a list of the NetWare utilities provided to OS/2 users. These utilities have been rewritten to provide native OS/2 applications.

The utilities listed in Table 5.11 are copied into special OS/2 directories when the requester is installed. To follow the standard NetWare directory structure, OS/2 places the following directories underneath the related NetWare directories, as shown in the following directory structure:

```
SYS:LOGIN\OS2
SYS:PUBLIC\OS2
SYS:SYSTEM\OS2
```

Table 5.11
OS/2 2.0 Utilities

Allow	Attach	Atotal	Bindfix	Bindrest	Capture
Castoff	Caston	Chddir	Chkvol	Dspace	Endcap
Filer	Flag	Flagdir	Grant	Listdir	Login
Logout	Makeuser	Map	Ncopy	Ndir	Nprint
Nver	Paudit	Pconsole	Printcon	Printdef	PSC
Purge	Remove	Revoke	Rights	Rprinter	Salvage
Security	Send	Setpass	SetTTS	Slist	Syscon
Systime	Tlist	Userdef	userlist	Version	Volinfo
Whoami					

Examining other Connection Services

Both the ATTACH and LOGOUT commands provide services that complement the initial login.

ATTACH

The ATTACH command enables users to attach to additional file servers while remaining logged in to the default server. ATTACH accepts two command-line parameters: *file server* and *login name*. At the F:\> prompt, for example, type the following:

ATTACH ACCOUNTING\TOM

If no parameters are specified, the user is prompted for each one. ATTACH does not provide drive mapping because the system login script is not executed. To map network drives, simply use the MAP command after a successful server attachment.

> ### *About Windows Tools...*
>
> For Windows users, Novell now is providing the NetWare Tools, a group of commonly used NetWare commands in native Windows programs. The Windows Attachment program is simple to use and provides full functionality in the native point-and-shoot Windows style.

LOGOUT

Use the LOGOUT command to log out of all file servers. LOGOUT terminates your access privileges and removes all drive mapping that was set up while you were logged in.

You can log out of a specific file server by typing the name of the file server after the LOGOUT command. At the F:\> prompt, for example, you can type the following:

LOGOUT SALES

This command terminates the access privileges and removes drive mapping to the SALES file server while maintaining all other file-server connections.

> ### *About Logging Out...*
>
> Logging out of all file servers before shutting down for the day is extremely important. If you do not log out of a workstation, some files may not be backed up properly because most tape drives cannot back up open data files.

Summary

A working knowledge of workstation software and its underlying drivers is essential for users who must understand and maintain proper connections with their network. This chapter has introduced you to several types of software that affect the manner in which you log in to and work with your network. Currently, the Novell single-track IPX program is predominantly used with the ODI drivers slowly being released into the larger corporate networks. Novell is now discouraging IPX driver development and is supplying ODI drivers with all new products.

The next chapter focuses on the set up of file server directories, their management, and some of the command-line and menu utilities available to assist you with these tasks.

6

Managing Directories

This chapter discusses designing your directory structure and file security. The process of setting up directories on a NetWare network is similar to setting up directories in DOS. NetWare supports many DOS-based utilities to help manage the structure. The concepts of directories and manipulating them are essential to setting up security properly on your system.

In this chapter, you learn about the following NetWare directory and security items:

- Creating file server names
- Accessing netware volumes
- Understanding required directories
- Managing required directories
- Using recommended directories
- Understanding attributes
- Using directory-related commands

147

If you currently are planning a network, this chapter will help you develop a workable and reliable directory structure. This chapter discusses each of the parts needed to produce the best directory structure for your needs. Although most new applications tell you the way to set up your directories and security for files, many programs still do not provide a complete description of the ways in which network security affects the files that applications use. This chapter shows you the way to set up structures that provide the tools an application needs to work. The directory structures you learn about in this chapter also adhere to the principles of effective networking.

If you already have a network installed, read the following sections for more information on improving the integrity of your system and increasing its performance. Your current directory setup may be convenient, but has it also been reliable? With the help of the information in this chapter, you will be able to evaluate your structural needs and determine which refinements, if any, need to be made to your current system.

The way in which you set up directories on your system determines the stability of your system's security. The next section describes the requirements for addressing your network drives.

Creating File Server Names

File servers must have unique names to "talk" to other file servers. Computers are smart, but they do not understand non-verbal communication. If you are in a room full of people named Chris, for example, you expect some confusion. If you use gestures and eye contact, you can single out one of the individuals with little difficulty. Computers do not have the capability to see and interpret visual clues. If you try to access two computers with the same name, the system locks up because NetWare cannot figure out which system you want.

Before you name a file server, consider how it is to be used and how easily you want users to access it. In most NetWare training classes, the first generic file server is referred to as FS1 and the second as FS2. Some NetWare students are so comfortable with these file server names that they use them in their offices. Server names can be as long as 45 characters. For this reason, most companies use some form of its name or department name for their file servers.

A NetWare network's structure begins with the file server name, which starts the full directory path. The file server name can be from two to 45 characters. The shorter the name, the easier it is for users to move among file servers. File server names resemble DOS labels for hard drives or floppy disks. Like drives or floppy disks, file server names usually indicate the type of information the drive contains.

A full directory path in NetWare uses the following syntax:

FILESERVER\VOLUME:DIRECTORY\SUBDIRECTORY

The directory path **CDI\SYS:PROGRAMS\DATABASE**, for example, starts with a file server name (**CDI**) and then a volume name (**SYS:**). The file server name and the volume are separated with a backslash (\). After the volume name appears the first level, or *parent*, directory (named **PROGRAMS**), then a secondary directory, or *subdirectory*, called **DATABASE**. The full directory path indicates your location on a network or the desired location.

 If your network plans do not include connecting to another file server, you can name your server anything you like. A few clever choices have been Zeus, Thor, Bambi, HAL, and Peabody. In a single server environment, you can leave the file server name out of the directory path. The system assumes that you want to address this file server because you did not specify another server.

Accessing NetWare Volumes

Volumes are the next level in a full directory path. Unlike file server names, volumes are essential to the full directory path.

Volumes, NetWare, and DOS

Volumes are to NetWare what *root drives* are to DOS. In a DOS directory tree, the highest level you can access is the root directory. Root directories are identified by a backslash (\) after the drive indicator. The root drive of C is shown as C:\. To get to this level of the directory structure, tell the system to change the directory to the root by typing **CD**.

Note One of the most common mistakes users make when they change directories is to improperly use the backslash (\). Whenever you type the backslash (\) directly after the CD command, as in **CD**, the system is instructed to find the next directory right off the root directory. If the directory you want to change to is really a subdirectory of the current directory, insert a space after the CD command. In the following example, the directory DATA would be off the root of the C directory.

```
C:\APPL>CD \DATA
            C:
        ____|____
        |        |
        \APPL    \DATA
```

In the following example, DATA is a subdirectory of APPL.

```
C:\APPL>CD DATA
        C:
        |
        \APPL
        |
        \DATA
```

This information on DOS applies to both a stand-alone DOS workstation and DOS used on a network. Keep the directory structure in mind when changing directories. NetWare v2.2 can have up to 32 volumes, and NetWare v3.11 can have up to 64 volumes.

Naming and Setting Up Volumes

When you create and name volumes in NetWare, remember that the volume name must follow certain conventions. The following rules apply to all NetWare volume names:

- Volume names can be from one to 15 characters long.

- With the exception of the * / \ ? @ characters, almost any keyboard character can be used for volume names. The @ sign is new to the unavailable characters list and is reserved for designations made with the NetWare Naming Service product. Novell offers this product for simplifying the login process in multiple-server environments.

- You can use a period (.) in a file server name as long as it is not the first character.
- The first volume on the first drive always is called SYS:.
- Volume names always are followed by a colon (:).

In NetWare v2.2, the largest volume that you can access is 256M. If you have a drive that is larger than 256M, use the remaining space for additional volumes. If you have a 650M drive, for example, one option is to break the drive into two volumes—one volume with 255M, and another volume of 140M.

NetWare v3.11 breaks the 256M limitation, enabling you to create a single volume of up to 32 terabytes. A terabyte is a number with 12 zeros after it (1 terabyte equals 1,099,511,627,776).

Another benefit of v3.11 is the capability to span drives. That is, a volume in v3.11 can encompass multiple drives and can address these drives as a single volume. This capability has several advantages. For one, it is easier for users to stay on one volume than to try and remember which volumes contain which files. Another advantage is that files can now be over 256M. The v2.2 limitation was created under the assumption that you would never need to store files larger than this size.

The main advantage to NetWare v3.11's capability to span drives is the increase in network performance. The number of drives used when spanning a volume can be used as a factor when explaining the increased performance in terms of disk access time. If you have four 20 millisecond drives and span them into one volume, for example, you can divide the access time by the number of drives to calculate the increase in performance. The drive access time, 20, divided by the number of drives, 4, equals 5; therefore, your drive access time has been cut from 20 milliseconds to 5 milliseconds.

The disadvantage of spanned drives is an increased risk of drive failure. The number of drives that span a volume directly affects the increase in performance of disk access times. This is a serious disadvantage because if one drive in the spanned volume fails, the entire volume also fails.

To reduce the risk of drive failure, you can *duplex* your drives. Duplexing uses mirrored disk drives, cables, and disk controllers. Duplexing protects you if a drive failure occurs. Duplexing also increases network performance by 15% due to split seeks. Unless you also are duplexing, do not span volume SYS:. If you lose a drive in a spanned volume other than SYS:, all you lose is the capability to access that particular volume. If you lose a drive in a spanned SYS:, your network will no longer be accessible. The server needs volume SYS: to function; with no available SYS:, the network is inaccessible.

Understanding Required Directories

When NetWare is first installed, four directories are included that are essential to an efficient and reliable system. The SYSTEM, MAIL, PUBLIC, and LOGIN directories are established in the SYS: volume. The next few sections describe these directories and show you how they work within the NetWare environment.

Exploring SYS:LOGIN

LOGIN is the first directory that you can access on a network. It contains the SLIST and LOGIN files. SLIST displays all of the file server names that the routing table is aware of (see fig. 6.1).

Figure 6.1:
Server list using SLIST.

```
M:\MENUS>SLIST
Known NetWare File Servers                    Network   Node Address Status
--------------------------                    -------   ------------ ------
CDI                                           [    FE][         1]Default
CDI286                                        [     3][        A3]
CDI386                                        [   CD1][         1]
FAXPRESS                                      [44000470][    44800470]
LAB1                                          [     1][   1B266F9A]
LAB2                                          [     1][   1B0ABACE]
NORTH286                                      [     5][   1B32CFB2]
NORTH386                                      [    AB][         1]

Total of 8 file servers found

M:\MENUS>
```

LOGIN tells the file server the name you would like to use. When you type **IPX**, you announce your presence on the cable system for peer-to-peer communications. The file server is not aware of your presence, however, until you type in **NETX**, which communicates to NetWare that you want to connect to the server. The file server returns a response similar to, "I recognize you as a node. Here is a directory that you can use to attempt logging into a server in the server list." At this point, you change to the F: drive or the first available network drive, which would be pointing to SYS:LOGIN. You then can view and read any file in this directory.

If any workstations exist on your network without floppy disk drives, the boot image file also resides in this directory. If you have multiple file servers, place this image file in each login directory so that you can find the proper boot file in any server you attach to.

 Use caution when you place files in the SYS:LOGIN directory. Anyone that attaches to the SYS:LOGIN directory will be able to use files placed here.

SYS:MAIL

This directory took its name from a program that Novell used to provide with previous versions of NetWare. Novell used to include a simple mail program written for NetWare that introduced users to electronic mail. This mail program saved messages in each user's ID directory. NetWare no longer includes this program, but the SYS:MAIL directory still is used.

These MAIL ID directories, as NetWare refers to the user's MAIL directory, still exist in current versions of NetWare. The MAIL ID directories reside under the SYS:MAIL directory and part of every user's system. These MAIL ID directories are up to 8 hexadecimal digits long. The system supervisor has the distinct name of SYS:MAIL\1.

These directories hold the user's personal login script. They also contain the PRINTCON.DAT file if the user has print jobs created through PRINTCON.

Two screens in NetWare enable you to view MAIL directories and their corresponding users. Both are options in the SYSCON menu utility.

If you choose the SYSCON option in the User Information menu after you specify a user, two menu options enable you to view ID information (see fig. 6.2). The first option, which shows a User ID number, is located in the Other Information Option. The User ID number is the same as the mail directory. If you compare these numbers to the directories, the preceding zeros are deleted in the directory names.

Figure 6.2:
SYSCON, User Information, and other information windows.

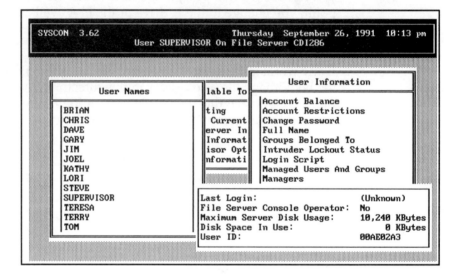

Another option that lists ID information is in the Trustee Directory Assignments list illustrated in figure 6.3. When you become a new user on the network, you automatically are given all rights by NetWare under your USER_ID directory except for Access Control in v2.2 and Access Control and Supervisory in v3.11. Use this option to see the directory under SYS:MAIL in which you have rights. Notice how the system automatically truncates the preceding zeros as SYSCON displays this information.

Users have rights to their own MAIL_ID directories and system managers also have rights to user MAIL_ID directories. By default, system supervisors have rights to all directories. This privilege enables supervisors to create personal login scripts and PRINTCON printing jobs for users.

Figure 6.3:
SYSCON, User Names, and Trustee Directory Assignments windows.

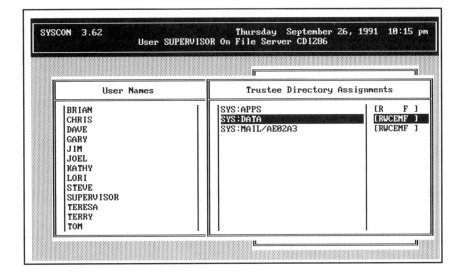

SYS:PUBLIC

The SYS:PUBLIC directory contains all of the network management commands that network users need to access. Each menu utility and the command line utilities available to network users appear in this directory. *Printer definition files* (PDF) and *overlay files* reside in the SYS:PUBLIC directory. The HELP II command by Folio also appears in this directory. HELP II is an on-line reference guide to NetWare.

Although NetWare creates the SYS:PUBLIC directory for NetWare utilities, the system administrator should create a directory structure underneath this directory for COMMAND.COM files used on DOS machines. Follow the procedure in Chapter 9 under LOGIN SCRIPTS to ensure that each workstation is capable of finding the appropriate COMMAND.COM files.

SYS:SYSTEM

This directory contains the command line utilities that only network supervisors can access. The system defaults so that only supervisors and users with supervisor privileges have rights to this directory. A few of the most frequently used utilities put into the SYS:SYSTEM directory are accessed with the following commands:

- **ATOTAL.** Sees the aggregate totals for the system if you are using NetWare's accounting feature. These totals are shown as per day and per week values.

- **PAUDIT.** Lists individual entries for each user who logs into or out of the system.

- **SECURITY.** Compares your system to the NetWare recommendations for securing a system (see fig 6.4). SECURITY displays system supervisor, manager accounts, and user accounts that have not been recently used.

Figure 6.4:
A sample report
from SECURITY.

```
Group SPREADSHEET
  No Full Name specified

User TERRY (Full Name: Terry Roos)
  Does not require a password

User JIM (Full Name: James T. Weyand)
  Is security equivalent to user SUPERVISOR
  Has no password assigned

User JOEL
  Users managed: 2
  Has no password assigned
  No Full Name specified

User KATHY
  Users managed: 1
  Groups managed: 1
  Is security equivalent to user SUPERVISOR
Press any key to continue ... ('C' for continuous)
```

- **BINDFIX.** Attempts to repair bindery problems, then creates new bindery files and renames the previous files with OLD extensions. Use BINDFIX if you suspect corruption of the bindery files.

NetWare v2.2 contains two *bindery files*, NET$BIND.SYS and NET$BVAL.SYS. In v3.11 there are three bindery files, NET$OBJ.SYS, NET$PROP.SYS, and NET$VAL.SYS. These files are hidden system files that reside in the SYS:SYSTEM directory. Bindery files contain security information on users and groups on the system. This security information includes password requirements, station and time restrictions, trustee rights, and security equivalences. If these files are corrupted, random portions of the user and group accounts cannot be modified.

- **BINDREST.** Deletes the newly created binderies created by BINDFIX, renames the OLD files to SYS files, hides the new files, and then makes them system files. Use BINDREST if the BINDFIX command does not fix corrupted files; you then need to put the binderies back to their original state.

Managing Required Directories

When you work with NetWare directories, remember that these directories are created by NetWare. In other words, DOS plays no part in their creation. When NetWare networks are installed, the operating system sets up these directories for its own use. If a user tries to delete or rename these directories within DOS, the results can produce difficulties for the network. For this reason, follow these guidelines when you work with NetWare directories:

- Keep NetWare directories clean.

  Leave these directories for the network. Do not add programs and data files to the default NetWare directories. Place program and data directories elsewhere on the system. Even though it is convenient to place program directories in the SYS:PUBLIC directory, there is no performance advantage.

- Do not modify the installed NetWare directories.

  If you change a NetWare MAIL ID directory name, the directory will be unusable because NetWare uses hexadecimal names, not logical names. Although it is inconvenient to try and match hexadecimal-named subdirectories with logical names in the MAIL program, the system uses these different naming methods to match user names and directories. For this reason, do not change the subdirectory names in NetWare or they may not work.

- Do not move default NetWare directories.

  NetWare knows of only one place to look for the four installed directories. The place for these directories is SYS:.

If you do not modify or move the LOGIN, MAIL, PUBLIC, and SYSTEM directories, you can effectively improve network performance. If these directories are left alone, NetWare does not need to sort through data to find the information it is seeking.

If an application insists on installing itself in one of the essential directories, however, leave the program in the directory. VAPs, or *value added processes*, for example, are programs that need to be in the system directory. VAPs run on the v2.2 server, usually providing extra resources, such as print servers and keyboard locks. Part of the process of booting the server is to look to the SYS:SYSTEM directory to find programs with a VAP extension. A diagnostic program is another type of application that places itself in the NetWare installed directories. These programs are exceptions—most applications should be in other directories.

Do not be afraid to create directories. A good directory structure tells a story about your network. A well-constructed directory tree enables anyone to view your directory tree and instantly know the location of utilities, programs, and data directories for each program.

 When you create directories in NetWare, remember a rule applied to creating DOS directories—not too deep and not too wide. In other words, do not create directories that have too many subdirectories or files. Network users notice that the system slows down when more than 500 files exist in a directory. Back-up programs have been known to choke and fail if a directory has more than 1,000 files.

For easier security administration and to save time and trouble, create categories of directories. The following section examines some categories for directories.

Using Recommended Directories

NetWare supplies the directories that it needs to run properly. The system administrator must decide how he or she wants to manage programs and data directories. This section examines several options to help you determine where to place new directories.

The following four categories of directories can help you organize your system: directories that the system needs, directories required for an application, directories that store data, and directories that users can manage. The previous section discussed the directories that NetWare needs to operate. The next section examines another directory type that is not mandatory to NetWare operation.

Home Directories

Network structures that include home directories for end users can help you monitor users. Although home directories are optional, they are useful on your network for several reasons. Home directories are set up for the user to store personal files. Many companies set up a directory off of SYS: called \USERS. Each user has a directory with a login name. Users usually have all privileges at their home directory level.

First, in v3.11, branches of the directory structure can be limited to a specific amount of file server disk space allowed for the users. In other words, system administrators can decide how much space a user can have for his own work. In both v2.2 and v3.11, space also can be limited per user for the entire volume. Both of these features enable system administrators to monitor file server disk consumption.

Second, providing users with their own directories on the file server enables them to control their files and subdirectories. Users given a branch of the structure that they can modify are less likely to damage the system. If you provide directories that users can manipulate, they tend to stay in those directories instead of wandering around the system.

Finally, from an administrator's viewpoint, knowing where to look for expendable files saves time. If the system supervisor instructs users to place only nonessential data in home directories, it is much easier and safer to delete files in case the system runs out of storage space.

Application Directories

The placement of application directories depends on where the program wants to be located. The installation procedure for an application largely dictates the placement of its directories in the NetWare directory tree. Other applications place themselves anywhere. The designer of your system's security structure ultimately determines where application directories install on the network.

Application directories can be in any volume on the network, which provides the system administrator with several options. If a volume is going to be used primarily by the accounting department, and the accounting programs are only used by the accounting staff, for example, then place the application among directories that pertain to those users. You should place applications within the directory for the department that needs to use the program.

Another option is to place application directories under the SYS: volume because everyone has rights to these directories. If an application on your network is used by everyone, place it in the SYS:PUBLIC or SYS:MAIL directories.

There is no right or wrong place to put application directories. The placement of application directories, however, factors into any security plans for a network. Whatever method you choose, remember that the best planned systems always clearly label the directory's contents.

Data Directories

Never mix applications and data in the same directory. The main responsibility of system administrators is to ensure that end users can work without a system failure. The extra burden of determining which files are data and which files contain applications is a task that can and should be solved early in the life of the network.

If a program needs to be deleted or upgraded, a well-planned directory structure avoids wasted time sorting through directories for data files. By placing data in a separate directory, administrators can easily update the application without losing data.

Numerous options are available for data directories. One option, called a *shared data directory*, places the data directory with the program. With this method, anyone using the program can place the data files in a common directory.

Another possibility for organizing data is to create *departmental directories*. Each member of a department then has a place to put his data files. Departmental directories often are used when departments work mostly on their own.

One other popular method for organizing network data is to have users place their data files in their own home directories. This method usually includes a single shared directory, in which users place files that other users need. Many corporations that employ tight security use this method for their data directories.

Finally, creating a separate volume for data is a practical solution if you have disk drives with large amounts of memory storage. This method maintains a high level of security, but also requires that users have more system knowledge.

The directories discussed in this section are only suggestions to help you organize your network. Not every option can be used on every system. Before you configure a network structure, try it on paper so that you can better understand what your structure should look like. Your network users will quickly let you know what needs to be changed. Fortunately, you can move most applications and modify the system without many problems.

Understanding Attributes

After all program and data directories are created and files are added, the next step is to secure the files and directories. Files are secured by the use of *attributes*, which are conditions put on the files. These conditions help to control what can be done to the files and how the files can be used on the network. Many combinations of attributes are attached to files and directories. This section discusses NetWare attributes and how you can use attributes on your network.

Attributes are handled different ways in NetWare v2.2 and v3.11. NetWare v2.2 supports file attributes only; v3.11 supports directory attributes and file attributes. The next section discusses each attribute and how it works on each version.

File Attributes for v2.2 & v3.11

The following attributes work with both v2.2 and v3.11, except for the Indexed and Private Attributes. The function of the Indexed attribute happens automatically in v3.11. NetWare V2.2 requires that the Indexed attribute be put on specific files.

Archive Needed

NetWare uses the letter A to signify files that have been altered since the last backup. The Archive Needed attribute also is assigned to files that have been copied into another directory. Archive Needed looks for the DOS Archive Bit flag on a file.

Execute Only

Execute Only is designated with the letter X. After this attribute is placed onto a file, it cannot be taken off. This attribute only affects files ending in COM or EXE and is the only attribute that you cannot reverse. Only users with supervisor privileges can assign this attribute.

Execute Only prevents files from being copied or downloaded to prevent application piracy.

 Make sure that you have a copy of a file before you attach the Execute Only flag because this attribute also prevents files from being backed up. In addition, many programs cannot run when flagged with Execute Only.

Hidden File

The Hidden File attribute uses the letter H. Files hidden with this attribute do not show up when you use the DOS DIR command. If a user has the File Scan right, files hidden with this attribute appear.

Read Audit and Write Audit

NetWare still is in the process of perfecting a built-in audit trail on files. Currently, you can flag files with Ra for Read Audit and Wa for Write Audit, but they have no effect.

Read Only and Read/Write

You cannot write to, delete, or rename a Read Only file. The Read Only attribute enables users to read and use files. Program Files are most often flagged with Ro for Read Only.

A Read/Write file enables users to read from the file and write back to the file. This attribute is designated with Rw and is the default on newly-created files. Flagging a file with Read Only deletes the Read/Write attribute. Data files are usually flagged with Read/Write.

When Read Only is used in v3.11, the attributes of Delete Inhibit and Rename Inhibit also are included.

Shareable and Non-Shareable

NetWare uses the letter S to show shareable files. This attribute enables several users to access a single file at the same time. This flag is used most often with Read Only files and database files.

Non-shareable, or Normal, is the system default. If you flag a file with N, you set the attributes as Non-shareable Read/Write. Non-shareable files are assigned normally to program files that are single-user applications. This attribute ensures that only one person can use the file at any one time.

System File

System files, flagged with Sy, are not listed when you use the DOS DIR command. These files cannot be deleted or copied. If you have the File Scan right, you can see these files by using the NDIR command.

Transactional

Files marked with T can be tracked with the Transaction Tracking System (TTS). All database files that need to be tracked while being modified need to have this attribute.

Indexed (v2.2 only)

This attribute uses the letter I on files larger than 256K that need a turbo FAT index to speed file access. Use this attribute on files larger than 1M.

 In v3.11, data files that use more than 64 regular *file allocation table blocks* (FAT blocks) are automatically assigned the Indexed attribute, which increases the access time for the file. The attribute can be assigned to smaller files, but it has no real effect.

File Attribute for v3.11

The following attributes are for use only in NetWare v3.11. Copy Inhibit only works on the Macintosh. Delete Inhibit and Rename Inhibit combine to make Read Only. The Purge attribute keeps a file out of the Salvage utility—a utility used to retrieve deleted files (see Chapter 9).

Copy Inhibit

Marked as a C, Copy Inhibit prevents files from being copied to another directory. This attribute is used only with Macintosh files.

Delete Inhibit

This attribute is one half of the Read Only file designation. Rename Inhibit represents the other half of Read Only. The Delete Inhibit flag, marked as a D, prevents files from being deleted.

Rename Inhibit

Aside from Delete Inhibit, Rename Inhibit is the second Read Only attribute. Marked as an R, Rename Inhibit prevents users from renaming files.

Purge

Purge uses the letter P to show files that are to be considered purged when deleted. If you mark a file with the P flag, you ensure that it cannot be restored after it is deleted.

Directory Attributes for v2.2 & v3.11

You also can use attributes on directories. The following list of attributes can be used on directories in NetWare.

Hidden Directory

The Hidden Directory Attribute uses the letter H. Directories hidden with this attribute do not show up when you use the DOS DIR command. If a user has the File Scan right, files hidden with this attribute appear.

System Directory

System directories, shown with Sy, are hidden from the DOS DIR command. These directories cannot be deleted or copied. If a user has the File Scan right, these directories will appear using the NDIR utility.

Purge Directory (v3.11 only)

This attribute uses the letter P to show directories in which all the files will be considered purged when deleted. This flag ensures that once the directory is deleted, any files in the directory cannot be restored.

Using Directory-Related Commands

The following sections describe several commands that you can use to manipulate directories and files. The utilities discussed in this section are used differently, depending on your security status. The system supervisors are able to use all of the functions, whereas the typical end user may be limited to the functions he can use. This section describes all the options for the directory and file management utilities.

Using the FILER Command

Filer can be used as an alternative to DOS commands when you manage directories. The main screen in Filer enables you to view a specific directory or a directory's contents, specify search options, or look at volume information (see fig 6.5).

The Current Directory Information Menu

The first menu item in FILER, Current Directory Information, enables you to see and assign the following information (see fig. 6.6):

- Who created, or owns, a specific directory.
- When a directory was created.
- The directory attributes that apply.
- The setting of the Maximum Rights Mask in v2.2.
- The setting of the Inherited Rights Mask in v3.11.
- Who has specifically been granted rights to this directory.

Figure 6.5:
The first menu in
FILER.

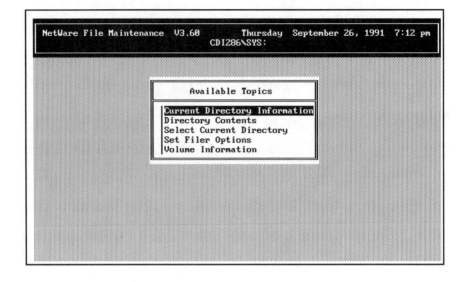

Figure 6.6:
Current directory
information.

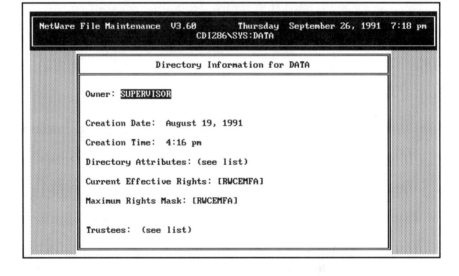

The Current Effective Rights line shown in Figure 6.6 lists current rights for the user; the Maximum Rights Mask line lists the allowable rights. The Maximum Rights field cannot be changed directly. It reflects what you are able to do currently in a directory.

At the DOS prompt, you can change directory attributes by using the FLAGDIR command. Inside FILER, you add attributes by pressing Ins and then choosing from the available list shown in figure 6.7. You can delete attributes just as easily by highlighting the attribute and then pressing Del. Figure 6.7 shows directory information for the \DATA directory. The current attributes show that this directory was flagged by using the FLAG command to immediately purge from the salvage utility any files that are deleted from the directory. By pressing Ins, another menu appears that displays all other available flags that can be assigned to this directory.

Figure 6.7:
Choosing directory attributes.

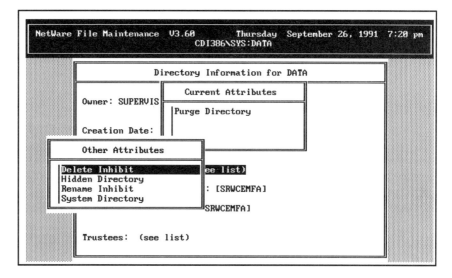

You can assign and manage trustees by using FILER. At the DOS prompt, trustees are managed by using the GRANT, REMOVE, and REVOKE commands. Figure 6.8 shows that two groups are given rights to the directory SYS:DATA. Rights are covered in depth in Chapter 7. By giving groups rights, you make them trustees of this directory.

The Directory Contents Menu

The next option of the FILER main menu, Directory Contents, enables you to perform the following tasks (see fig. 6.9):

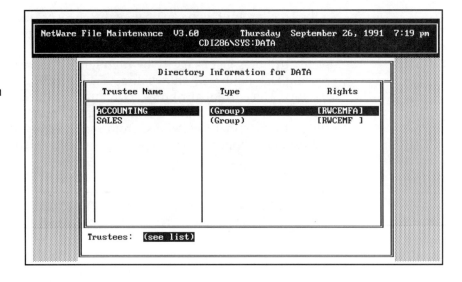

Figure 6.8:
Viewing Trustee
Assignments from
FILER.

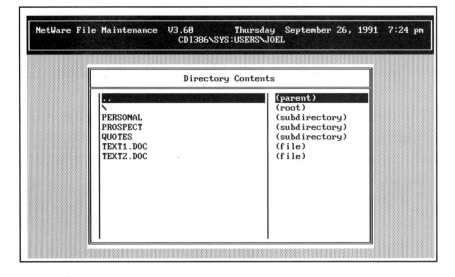

Figure 6.9:
Directory Contents
with subdirectories
and files.

- Create and delete subdirectories
- Copy subdirectory structures
- Move file and subdirectory structures (v3.11 only)
- Copy files

- View and set directory information (see fig 6.10)
- View and set file information (see fig 6.11)
- Change directories

Figure 6.10:
NetWare v3.11
Subdirectory
Options in
Directory Contents.

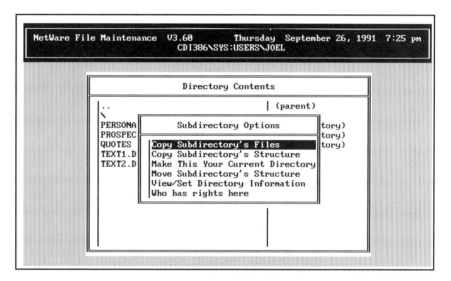

Figure 6.11:
NetWare v3.11 File
Options in
Directory Contents.

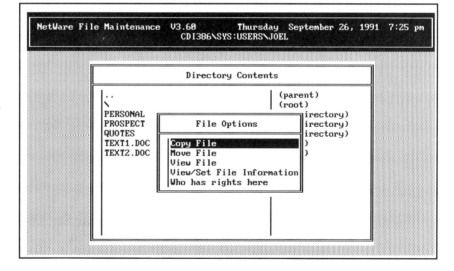

Figure 6.9 shows three subdirectories and two files in the directory SYS:USERS\JOEL. After you highlight a directory and press Enter, you see the menu options shown in figure 6.10. Highlighting a file and pressing Enter shows you the menu options displayed in figure 6.11.

To create directories from the Directory contents screen, press Ins. A box appears where you put the new directory name. Then press Enter. This procedure is the same as using the MD (make directory) command at the DOS prompt.

To delete a directory, highlight the directory to be deleted and press Del. Another menu appears that enables you to choose between deleting files only from this directory and any subdirectories under it, or to delete the complete directory structure underneath the highlighted directory.

Files also can be deleted by highlighting the file and pressing Del. Other function keys work to mark multiple files. Read Chapter 7 to find out more about function keys.

 When you work in DOS, you often may need to delete several directories at once. If you delete directories in DOS, you must specify the directory and the files you want to delete, which can be a tedious process, especially if the directories contain read-only or hidden files. If you use FILER instead, you can delete an entire directory structure, all files in a directory structure, or specific files.

The Select Current Directory Menu

The third option in the main FILER menu, Select Current Directory, enables you to change the directory being viewed (see fig. 6.12). If you are not sure of the exact directory path, press Ins to call up a list of available file servers, volumes, and directories.

The Set Filer Options Menu

The fourth option of the Filer main menu, Set Filer Options, enables you to set the parameters for viewing and manipulating the directory structure (see fig 6.13). In FILER, under Set Filer Options, you can specify letter patterns to view either directories or files. You also can search for hidden and system files and directories under the Search Attributes.

Figure 6.12:
Setting a directory path for viewing.

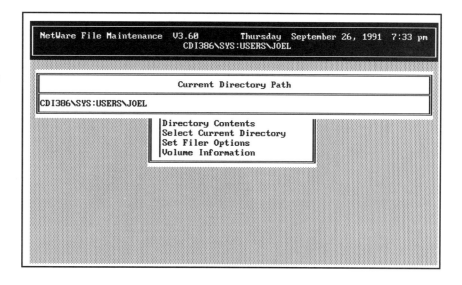

```
NetWare File Maintenance   V3.60        Thursday  September 26, 1991  7:33 pm
                        CDI386\SYS:USERS\JOEL

                       ┌─────────── Current Directory Path ──────────────┐
                       CDI386\SYS:USERS\JOEL

                          │Directory Contents
                          │Select Current Directory
                          │Set Filer Options
                          │Volume Information
```

Figure 6.13:
Filer Settings options.

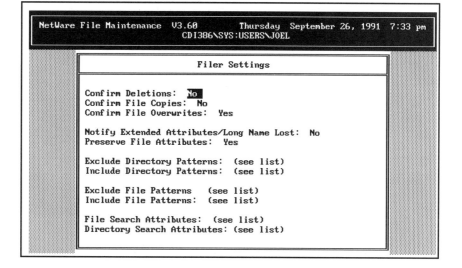

```
NetWare File Maintenance   V3.60        Thursday  September 26, 1991  7:33 pm
                        CDI386\SYS:USERS\JOEL

                    ┌───────────────── Filer Settings ─────────────────┐

                     Confirm Deletions:   No
                     Confirm File Copies:   No
                     Confirm File Overwrites:   Yes

                     Notify Extended Attributes/Long Name Lost:   No
                     Preserve File Attributes:   Yes

                     Exclude Directory Patterns:   (see list)
                     Include Directory Patterns:   (see list)

                     Exclude File Patterns   (see list)
                     Include File Patterns:   (see list)

                     File Search Attributes:   (see list)
                     Directory Search Attributes: (see list)
```

Note

The Extended Attributes/Long Name Lost line in the Filer
Settings box applies to OS/2 attributes (see figs. 6.14 and
6.15). These two figures are examples of help screens that
Novell provides in all the menu utilities and can be accessed
by pressing F1 whenever you need additional information
about a current screen.

Figure 6.14:
A FILER settings
sample Help
screen.

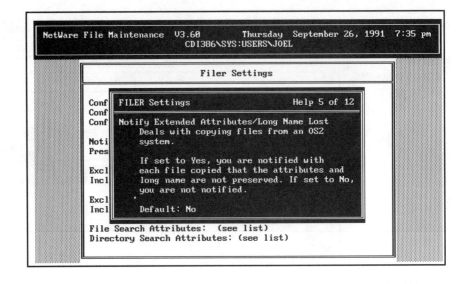

Figure 6.15:
Another FILER
settings sample
Help screen.

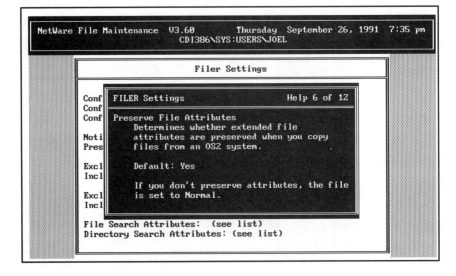

 Any options set in FILER under Filer Settings apply only to
that FILER session. The settings have no effect at the DOS
prompt.

The Volume Information Menu

The last option in FILER's Available Topics menu, Volume Information, displays information about network volumes (see fig 6.16). One reason for using FILER is to clean up cluttered directories for increased disk space. The volume information option enables you to view your progress in cleaning the system. To change the volume being viewed, change Select Current Directory to the desired volume. Figure 6.16 shows information about the current volume SYS: on a file server called CD1386.

Figure 6.16:
Viewing Volume
Information.

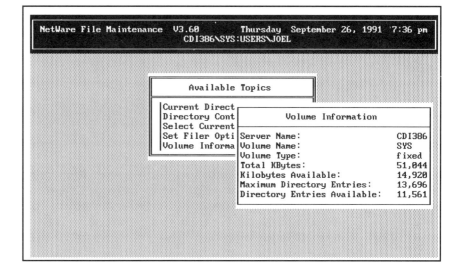

Command Line Utilities

Command line utilities can replace the FILER menu utility. These commands are similar to some DOS commands, but provide network functions and advanced features. The commands that will be shown are NCOPY, FLAG, FLAGDIR, NDIR, and LISTDIR.

NCOPY

This command works similar to the DOS COPY and XCOPY commands. NCOPY has two advantages over the DOS commands. The first advantage is that it is faster.

If User A wants to copy all of the files from the path of P:\DATA\NEW to M:\DATA\OLD using the DOS command, he types the following:

```
COPY P:*.* M:
```

The command first passes to the file server and grabs the necessary tables from memory. These tables then are downloaded to the workstation (pass 2) and the changes in file placement are written to the tables. These tables then go back to the file server (pass 3). Finally, the token returns to the workstation for further instructions (pass 4). The DOS copy command takes four passes on the cable to complete.

 Token is a term used to describe a file server process that tells a workstation that it can transmit any information it may have to the network. The process of sending a token from one node, either a workstation or file server, to another node, is called a *pass*.

If User B wants to transfer files, he uses the same syntax, but adds the letter N in front of the copy command, as follows:

```
NCOPY P:*.* M:
```

NCOPY goes straight to the file server to manipulate the memory tables in the file server's memory instead of the workstation's memory. This process takes only two passes, once to the file server and once back onto the network. This procedure so far is two passes fewer than the DOS copy procedure. The differences between COPY and NCOPY are minimal for small amounts of files, but the time savings are substantial for copying large directory structures.

The other advantage to using NCOPY instead of COPY or XCOPY is that NCOPY displays the source and destination directories. This list is helpful if you often use short cuts when you copy files and you mistakenly copy dozens of files to the wrong place. Figure 6.17 shows the NCOPY command that will copy all files ending in .OVL in the U:\PROGRAMS\UTILS directory to the directory that G: points to, which happens to be SYS1:\STORE. You saw the destination directory because of the way NCOPY works. DOS would not have given you this piece of information.

```
U:\PROGRAMS\UTILS>NCOPY *.OVL G:
From CDI/SYS:\PROGRAMS/UTILS
To   CDI/SYS1:\STORE
     IBM$RUN.OVL    to IBM$RUN.OVL
     $RUN.OVL       to $RUN.OVL

     2 files copied.

U:\PROGRAMS\UTILS>
```

Figure 6.17:
An example of using the NCOPY command.

FLAG and FLAGDIR

FLAG and FLAGDIR are similar to the DOS ATTRIB command. The commands FLAG (see fig. 6.18) and FLAGDIR (see fig. 6.19) by themselves display the current attribute settings for a file or directory. In figure 6.18, typing FLAG with no parameters shows what the files in J:\USERS\JOEL are currently using for attributes. The first command in figure 6.18 shows that the files are flagged as Read/Write and Archive Needed. The second command forces any files ending in .DOC to be flagged as Read Only, which also includes Rename Inhibit and Delete Inhibit. Figure 6.19 shows that the directory J:\USERS\JOEL is flagged as Normal, which means non-shareable Read/Write. The second command in figure 6.19 adds the Purge attribute to J:\USERS\JOEL. To set the attributes of a file, type the following:

FLAG *fileparameters flaglist*

FLAGDIR *directoryparameters flaglist*

Wild cards are acceptable for file and directory parameters.

The default attributes for a file are Non-shareable Read/Write, which is designated with an N. Table 6.1 shows a complete list of flags usable with FLAG and FLAGDIR and the letters used to indicate each flag.

```
J:\USERS\JOEL>flag
        TEXT2.DOC                [ Rw - A - - -- - - -- -- -- -- -- ]
        TEXT1.DOC                [ Rw - A - - -- - - -- -- -- -- -- ]

J:\USERS\JOEL>flag *.doc sro
        TEXT2.DOC                [ Ro S A - - -- - - -- -- -- DI RI ]
        TEXT1.DOC                [ Ro S A - - -- - - -- -- -- DI RI ]

J:\USERS\JOEL>
```

Figure 6.18:
FLAG command
used on a file.

```
J:\USERS\JOEL>flagdir
CD I386/SYS:USERS/JOEL
        JOEL            Normal

J:\USERS\JOEL>flagdir \users\joel p
CD I386/SYS:USERS/JOEL
        JOEL            Purge

J:\USERS\JOEL>
```

Figure 6.19:
FLAGDIR command
used on a directory.

Table 6.1
FLAG and FLAGDIR Attributes

Attribute	Description
A	Archive Needed (automatically assigned)
ALL	All attributes
C	Copy Inhibit (Macintosh only)
*D	Delete Inhibit
*H	Hidden
HELP	Displays all attributes
I	Indexed (v2.2 only)
*N	Normal
*P	Purge
*R	Rename Inhibit
Ra	Read Audit
Ro	Read Only
Rw	Read/Write
S	Shareable
SUB	Views SUBdirectory attributes
*Sy	System
T	Transactional
Wa	Write Audit
X	Execute Only

denotes attributes that also work on directories.

NDIR

NDIR stands for Network Directory Search. You can use the NDIR command to search the network for file or directory parameters (see fig. 6.20).

Figure 6.20 shows the information that can be found about files and subdirectories in the G:\STORE directory. The information that you see includes file names, file size, Last Updated (the last time the file was modified), Flags (attributes), and Owner (who created the file). You also are shown the subdirectory name, Inherited and Effective Rights (discussed in Chapter 7), Owner, and when it was created or copied. Finally, you are shown how many files NDIR found and how much space was taken by the files.

Figure 6.20:
An example of using the NDIR command.

```
G:\STORE>NDIR
CDI/SYS1:STORE

Files:                  Size      Last Updated       Flags              Owner
------------------   ----------   -------------   ------------------   -------
$RUN         OVL        2,288     3-27-86  9:38a  [RoS------------DR]  DEB
IBM$RUN      OVL        2,288     3-27-86  9:38a  [RoS------------DR]  DEB

                     Inherited    Effective
Directories:          Rights       Rights       Owner     Created/Copied
------------------   ----------   ----------   --------   ----------------
NEW                  [SRWCEMFA]   [SRWCEMFA]    DEB        10-24-91   4:32p

         4,576 bytes in     2 files
         8,192 bytes in     2 blocks

G:\STORE>
```

NDIR also can be used to search for specific information. The syntax for the NDIR command is as follows:

NDIR *path* / *options*

Path

You can replace this option with a directory path, wild cards, or up to 16 file names.

Remember to use a back slash (\) for specifying path names and a forward slash (/) for the options.

Sort Parameters

Sort parameters alter the order in which files and subdirectories are displayed to the user.

- **/SORT** (*parameter*). Enables you to sort the directory on selected parameters by using the parameters described in the following section. The parameter that you specify is substituted into the **parameter** variable after you type the SORT option.
- **/REV /SORT** (*parameter*). Reverses the SORT according to the parameters you specify after the SORT option.
- **/UN.** Leaves list unsorted.

Parameters

A complete list of parameters for the NDIR command is shown next. These parameters can be used to gather specific information about files and subdirectories.

Parameter	Description
O	Owner
SI	Size
UP	Update (Last Modified Date)
CR	Created Date
AC	Last Accessed Date
AR	Last Archived Date

Display Formats:

NDIR displays whatever you request. The switches shown below describe specific conditions that can be met using NDIR.

- **/FO.** Displays file names only
- **/DO.** Displays directories only
- **/SUB.** Searches all subdirectories
- **/DATES.** Lists last modified, last archived, last accessed, and created dates
- **/RIGHTS.** Lists inherited and effective rights
- **/MAC.** Lists Macintosh files and subdirectories
- **/LONG.** Lists the long file names for Macintosh, OS/2, and NFS
- **/HELP.** Lists NDIR options

Attribute Searches

If you need to look for files flagged with specific attributes, the following list shows each switch and the attribute it represents.

Attribute	Search Limitation
/A	Archive Needed
/CI	Copy Inhibit
/DI	Delete Inhibit
/H	Hidden
/I	Indexed
/N	Normal
/P	Purge
/RI	Rename Inhibit
/RA	Read Audit
/RO	Read Only
/S	Shareable
/Sy	System
/T	Transactional
/WA	Write Audit
/X	Execute Only

To search for select attributes, place the /NOT option before the attribute.

Restricted Displays

NDIR enables you to restrict displays according to specified conditions.

- **/OW EQ** *name*. Enables you to search for files or directories created by the user's name.

- **/OW NOT EQ** *name*. Enables you to search for file and directory owners that are not the user name specified.

- **/SI** *operator nnn.* Finds all files of a certain size. The *nnn* parameter specifies the number of bytes in a file.

- **/SI NOT** *operator nnn.* Finds all files that do not fall into the category of requested information. To look for files no bigger than 10K, for example, type **NDIR /SI NOT GR10.**

- **/UP** *operator mm-dd-yy.* Finds all files updated before, after, or on a certain date.

- **/UP NOT** *operator mm-dd-yy.* Finds all files that were not updated before, after, or on a certain date.

- **/CR** *operator mm-dd-yy.* Finds all files created before, after, or on a certain date.

- **/CR NOT** *operator mm-dd-yy.* Finds all files created before, after, or on a certain date.

- **/AC** *operator mm-dd-yy.* Finds all files accessed before, after, or on a certain date.

- **/AC NOT operator** *mm-dd-yy.* Finds all files that have not been accessed before, after, or on a certain date.

- **/AR operator** *mm-dd-yy.* Finds all files archived before, after, or on a certain date.

- **/AC NOT operator** *mm-dd-yy.* Finds all files that have not been archived before, after, or on a certain date.

Operators

Operators, that is, basic math concepts, are available when using the NDIR command. NDIR does not accept >, <, or = characters. These operators are used to connect parameters to form specific conditions for NDIR to search.

Operator	Description
GR	Greater Than
LE	Less Than
EQ	Equal To
BEF	Before
AFT	After

LISTDIR

LISTDIR is very similar to the DOS tree command. As shown in figure
6.21, each subsequent subdirectory is indented to see the hierarchy.
You can use this command to view your directory structure.

Figure 6.21:
A sample directory
tree of the SYS1:
volume.

```
The sub-directory structure of CDI/SYS1:
Directory
-----------------------------------------------------------------------------
->DELETED.SAV
->EMAIL
->  ADMIN
->  MAILBOX
->    GDUNCAN
->      GDUNCAN0
->    DNIEDERM
->      DNIEDER0
->    BCHAFFIN
->      BCHAFFI0
->    SBEVERID
->      SBEVERI0
->    JYUNGTON
->      JYUNGTO0
->    BWAITE
->      BWAITE0
->    LMASON
->      LMASON0
->  MAILUSER
->  MHSTEMP
Press any key to continue ... ('C' for continuous)
```

```
LISTDIR /S
```

LISTDIR *path option*

Remember to use a back slash (\) for path names and a forward slash
(/) for options.

Options

LISTDIR also can use several command line switches. The switches
available are listed below. Be sure to place a space after LISTDIR and
the switch.

- **/R.** Lists directory rights and inherited rights masks.
- **/E.** Lists effective rights.
- **/D** or **/T.** Lists both creation date and time.

- **/S.** Lists all subdirectories. Subdirectories show up as indented line items.
- **/A.** Lists all available information.

Summary

In this chapter. you gained information to design a directory structure that you can use in your day-to-day networking environment. You also were shown what directories NetWare creates, what those directories are used for, and how to keep them running well.

Also discussed in this chapter was the menu utility FILER that can be used to manage files and directories. You examined several command line utilities in depth. You discovered that these utilities can be used in place of similar DOS commands and that these network utilities enhance network functionality.

This chapter described setting up your network's directory structure and file security. After you build the foundation, you can easily add your users. In the next chapter, you learn how to add users to the system and create individual security profiles for each user.

Adding Users and User Security to the System

o far, you have seen how to choose network hardware, how to configure the software to log in to the network, how to create workable directory structures, and how to assign attributes to files. The next step is enabling users to get onto the system to use what you have just created.

This chapter takes a look at the different kinds of users on the network and what they can do. The chapter also shows you how to set up users and groups and how to define their restrictions on the network. Finally, you learn about the different levels of management on the network.

In this chapter, you learn about the following:

- Defining security levels
- Setting up user names
- Creating groups
- Using command line utilities

Defining Security Levels

NetWare accommodates seven different types of users that can be on the network. Many of these types combine with other types to fine-tune what a user can do on the system. The following lists the different types of users that can be on NetWare, ranging from the highest-level user to the lowest-level user:

- Supervisor
- Supervisor equivalents
- FCONSOLE operators
- Workgroup managers
- PCONSOLE operators
- Account managers
- End users

Most of these users can be managed by a different type of user. By combining these user types, you can create the administrators and users that can fully utilize your network. Figure 7.1 illustrates the hierarchy of the network administration.

Figure 7.1:
NetWare's subsets of the security divisions and their domains.

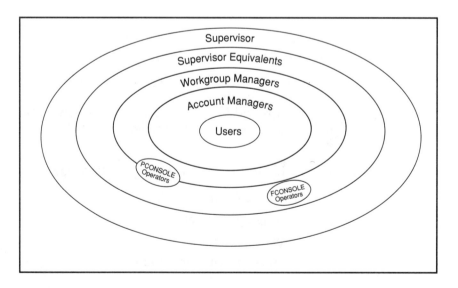

The Supervisor

The supervisor, who has rights to every utility and file on the network, is the highest level network user. Only one user named supervisor is allowed on the network. This user is given all rights and privileges. The supervisor can be viewed as having a *back door* into the network, meaning that he can get into the network in case of an emergency. An example of the supervisor's high status is that a user can delete other users on the network but cannot delete the supervisor. This does not, however, give the supervisor full rights to all files on the network. If, for example, a file is marked as Read Only, the supervisor cannot delete the file until the attribute is changed to Read/Write by the user who created the file.

The supervisor password can be changed by the supervisor or by the supervisor equivalents (discussed in the following section). Many third-party programs that are used to manage the network that have system security still require the login ID of Supervisor and will not run for the supervisor equivalent users.

The Supervisor Equivalent

The supervisor equivalent user is a regular end user who is given the same authority on the system as the supervisor. Supervisor equivalent users can create other supervisor equivalent users.

The FCONSOLE Operator

NetWare's FCONSOLE utility enables you to view certain information about the network. FCONSOLE operators have certain privileges depending on whether they also are supervisor equivalents. FCONSOLE operators that have supervisor equivalence may use all options available in FCONSOLE. FCONSOLE operators that do not have supervisor equivalence, however, cannot clear connections or down the file server from FCONSOLE. Users who are not FCONSOLE operators or supervisor equivalents can use FCONSOLE but are severely limited in what information they can see.

Chapter 10 walks you through all FCONSOLE options and points out which features of FCONSOLE are limited to users who are not FCONSOLE operators.

The Workgroup Manager

Workgroup managers can be either users or a group of users. Workgroup managers can create, delete, and manage user accounts. They can change passwords, account restrictions, and login scripts for users. Workgroup managers, however, can manage only those users and groups that are assigned to them or that they create. Workgroup managers cannot modify users or groups that are not in their list of managed users and groups.

The User Account Manager

User account managers can be either users or groups. User account managers can manage and delete accounts that are assigned to them. Unlike workgroup managers, user account managers cannot create users and groups.

The PCONSOLE Operator

NetWare has two types of PCONSOLE operators. One of them, the print queue operator, can manage and delete print queues. The other, the print server operator, can manage and delete print servers. The only types of users, however, that can create print servers and queues are the supervisors.

Table 7.1 lists the functions that administrators and end users can use on the network and helps you visualize which types of users on the network can accomplish different management tasks.

The End User

End users make up the majority of NetWare users. End users are capable of performing only the functions given to them by the other six categories of users.

Table 7.1
Security Domains

	Create/Delete Supervisor Equivalent	Create/Delete Workgroup Managers	Create Account Manager	Create/Delete Users	Inherits All Rights To Network	Create/Delete Print Queues and Servers	Manage Print Queues (by default)	Manage Print Servers (by default)	Use FCONSOLE (LIMITED) Access	Use FCONSOLE (UNLIMMITED) Access
Supervisor	●	●	●	●	●	●	●	●		●
Supervisor Equivalent	●	●	●	●	●	●	●			●
Workgroup Manager			●	●					●	
User Account Manager			●						●	
Print Queue Operator							●			
Print Server Operator								●		
FCONSOLE Operator									●	

Using the SYSCON Menu Utility

The remainder of this chapter discusses the menu utilities and command line utilities available in NetWare. These utilities help you create users and groups on the network. These commands also enable you to give rights and privileges to the network users to control the users' access to programs, utilities, and data files. The following section discusses the role of SYSCON. At the end of the chapter, you are introduced to NetWare's different commmand line utilities.

The SYSCON menu, which stands for *SYStem CONfiguration*, enables you to set up NetWare's accounting feature, check file server information, create users and groups, and perform administrative network functions. These functions are set up by using the options listed in the Available Topics menu as shown in figure 7.2. Each of these options is described in more detail in the following sections.

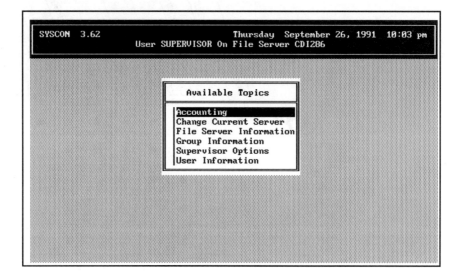

Navigating the Menus

Before you learn the different menus and submenus in SYSCON, however, you should become familiar with the following keys that enable you to navigate the various menus in the utilities:

- **Enter.** Moves you to the next level in the menu or accepts an item from the list.

- **Esc.** Takes you back to a previous level or stops the selecting process.

- **F1.** Shows you the definition of a highlighted item.

- **F1 F1.** Shows you a list of function key definitions.

- **F3.** When highlighting an object or path, F3 enables you to change the name of the object or path.

- **F5.** This is a toggle switch. You can use F5 to choose multiple items from a list, and then press Enter to bring the selected item into the current list. When you select an item using F5, the item blinks on-screen. To deselect an item that you have selected, press F5 a second time.

- **F6.** Enables you to mark a pattern of items.
- **F7.** Enables you to unmark all marked items.
- **F8.** Enables you to unmark a pattern of items.

When you select or mark an item, NetWare places a marker on the object, causing it to blink. You then can delete or copy marked items. Some of these keys do not work in all menu items. F6, F7, and F8, for example, work best in FILER (discussed in Chapter 6), but do not work in SYSCON (discussed in the next section).

Another way to choose an item in a list is to place the highlighter bar on the desired item. You can move the bar by pressing the up or down arrow keys or by typing the name of the item. Just repeat this process until the highlight bar is on the desired name.

When you are in a menu that contains a list of many items, you can go directly to the item you want by typing one letter at a time. If you want to go to a group called SUPERS, for example, simply type the letter **S**. If no other group exists with the letter S, you go directly to SUPERS. If, on the other hand, a group called SALES exists, you would go directly to SALES. In this case, you need to also type in the second letter (**SU**) to go to SUPERS.

The Accounting Option

The first option on the SYSCON menu is the accounting feature. The Accounting option enables you to charge users for use of the network based on the following five areas:

- Blocks read
- Blocks written
- Connect time
- Disk storage
- Service requests

Large installations may cover several departments. In many businesses in which a network is installed, each department is required to pay for part of the network. NetWare's accounting feature enables the system administrator to charge each department for its portion of the total network usage. Users in each department then are charged only for what they do on the network.

To set up accounting on your network, you first need to decide which charge rates from the preceding list you want to use and in what combinations. These areas, which appear on-screen on the Accounting menu (see fig. 7.3), can be combined in any combination to charge different users. NetWare automatically tracks user logins and logouts. The accounting information then is stored in SYS:SYSTEM in a file named NET$ACCT.DAT.

Figure 7.3:
Accounting options
in the SYSCON
menu.

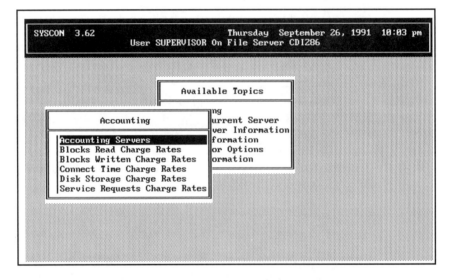

The Blocks Read Charge Rates option in the Accounting menu is used to determine the amount of information users request from the file server. Users are charged for each block of information that is read from the file server. A *block* is the minimum size of a piece of information that NetWare can read and write. The default block size in NetWare is 4K. When you choose this option, the Blocks Read Charge Rates screen appears on-screen (see fig. 7.4). This screen enables administrators to configure the accounting charge rates.

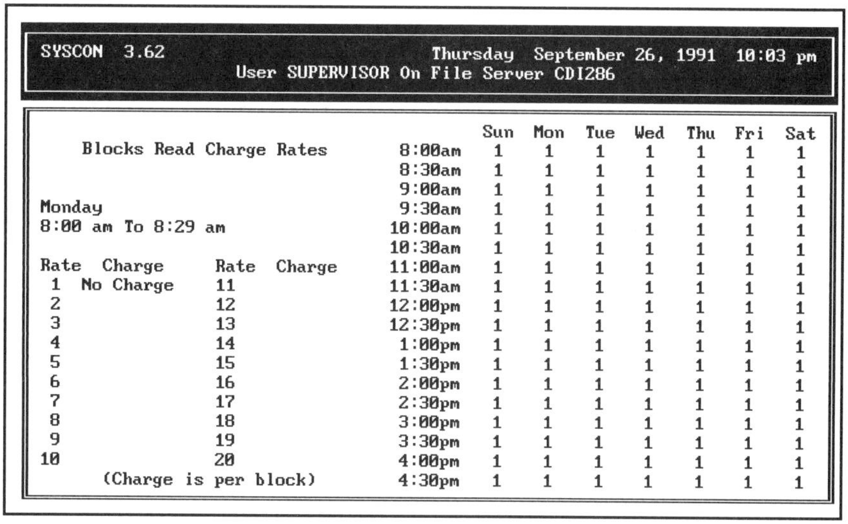

Figure 7.4:
An example of the
Blocks Read
Charge Rates
screen.

```
SYSCON  3.62                        Thursday  September 26, 1991  10:03 pm
                        User SUPERVISOR On File Server CDI286

                                               Sun  Mon  Tue  Wed  Thu  Fri  Sat
        Blocks Read Charge Rates       8:00am    1    1    1    1    1    1    1
                                       8:30am    1    1    1    1    1    1    1
                                       9:00am    1    1    1    1    1    1    1
Monday                                 9:30am    1    1    1    1    1    1    1
8:00 am To 8:29 am                    10:00am    1    1    1    1    1    1    1
                                      10:30am    1    1    1    1    1    1    1
Rate  Charge     Rate  Charge        11:00am    1    1    1    1    1    1    1
 1  No Charge     11                  11:30am    1    1    1    1    1    1    1
 2                12                  12:00pm    1    1    1    1    1    1    1
 3                13                  12:30pm    1    1    1    1    1    1    1
 4                14                   1:00pm    1    1    1    1    1    1    1
 5                15                   1:30pm    1    1    1    1    1    1    1
 6                16                   2:00pm    1    1    1    1    1    1    1
 7                17                   2:30pm    1    1    1    1    1    1    1
 8                18                   3:00pm    1    1    1    1    1    1    1
 9                19                   3:30pm    1    1    1    1    1    1    1
10                20                   4:00pm    1    1    1    1    1    1    1
        (Charge is per block)          4:30pm    1    1    1    1    1    1    1
```

The Blocks Written Charge Rates option in the Accounting menu is used to determine the amount of information that is being written back to the file server. Users are charged for each full block of information that is written to the server.

The Connect Time Charge Rates option in the Accounting menu is used to determine the amount of time a user is logged in to the network. Users are charged for each minute that they are attached to the network.

To determine the amount of disk space each user takes up on the file server, use the Disk Storage Charge Rates option in the Accounting menu. Users are charged for space occupied by files they own.

About the Disk Storage Charge Rate in v2.2...

If you plan on charging for disk storage in v2.2, you should make sure that the Limit Disk Space Option is chosen. This frees up the server if you charge during peak network usage times. This option needs to be run only once or twice a day because users get charged for any files that they own each time this charge is assessed.

The Service Requests Charge Rates option in the Accounting menu is used to determine the amount of network traffic a user generates. Users are charged for each request they make to the file server.

Setting Up a Network Account

When you set up accounting on your network, the charge rates specify the amount each user is to be debited when using the network. A *charge rate* is displayed as a fractional number, such as 1/4. The *multiplier*, or top portion of the fraction, specifies the amount of monetary units that is debited against an account. The *divisor*, or lower portion of the fraction, determines how many units of measure must accumulate before the charge is made. The most common unit of measure is one cent. A charge of 1/4, for example, means that one cent is charged for every four units of measure. A unit of measure can be one minute, one read, one write, one server request, or one block of disk storage.

Before you set the charge rates, you need to know the times during the week that you want to use those rates. You might, for example, want to charge different rates for different days of the week. NetWare enables you to set different rates for different times and different days. When you choose an option from the Accounting menu, a grid appears on-screen that divides each day, including Saturday and Sunday, into half-hour increments (see fig. 7.4). Each increment has a number that corresponds to the Rate column in the lower left corner of the screen. The numbers in the Rate column, in turn, correspond to the rate shown in the Charge column. Each half hour on the grid is set to charge rate number 1 (no-charge rate) by default. To see the times before 8:00 a.m. and after 4:30 p.m., use the up and down arrows and the PgUp and PgDn keys to scroll the screen.

You can change the charge rate of a particular time by highlighting the desired time or block of time and pressing Enter. To highlight a block of time, use the cursor arrows and move the cursor to the desired time and press F5. This marks the upper left corner of the time you want to change. Next, use the right- and down-arrow keys to position the lower right corner of the highlight box. This highlights the block of time that you want to set. Press Enter and a menu appears that enables you to define the charge rate. Up to 20 charge rates can be established using this method of blocking time periods (see fig. 7.5 and fig. 7.6).

```
 SYSCON  3.62                      Thursday  September 26, 1991  10:04 pm
                      User SUPERVISOR On File Server CDI286

                                          Sun  Mon  Tue  Wed  Thu  Fri  Sat
    Blocks Read Charge Rates      8:00am   1    1    1    1    1    1    1
                                  8:30am   1    1    1    1    1    1    1
                                  9:00am   1    1    1    1    1    1    1
 Monday To Friday                 9:30am   1    1    1    1    1    1    1
 8:00 am To 11:59 am             10:00am   1    1    1    1    1    1    1
                                                    1    1    1    1    1
 Rate  Select Charge Rate  ge     New Charge Rate   1    1    1    1    1
  1  N                                              1    1    1    1    1
  2      1  No Charge             Multiplier     1  1    1    1    1    1
  3     Other Charge Rate         Divisor        4  1    1    1    1    1
  4                                                 1    1    1    1    1
  5                15             1:30pm   1    1    1    1    1    1    1
  6                16             2:00pm   1    1    1    1    1    1    1
  7                17             2:30pm   1    1    1    1    1    1    1
  8                18             3:00pm   1    1    1    1    1    1    1
  9                19             3:30pm   1    1    1    1    1    1    1
 10                20             4:00pm   1    1    1    1    1    1    1
       (Charge is per block)      4:30pm   1    1    1    1    1    1    1
```

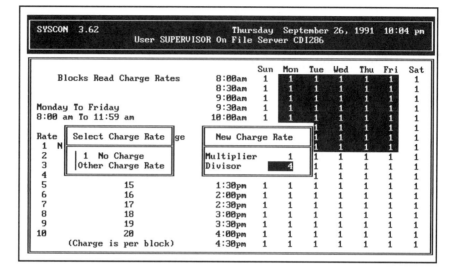

Figure 7.5:
Creating a new charge rate.

```
 SYSCON  3.62                      Thursday  September 26, 1991  10:04 pm
                      User SUPERVISOR On File Server CDI286

                                          Sun  Mon  Tue  Wed  Thu  Fri  Sat
    Blocks Read Charge Rates      8:00am   1    2    2    2    2    2    1
                                  8:30am   1    2    2    2    2    2    1
                                  9:00am   1    2    2    2    2    2    1
 Friday                           9:30am   1    2    2    2    2    2    1
 11:30 am To 11:59 am            10:00am   1    2    2    2    2    2    1
                                 10:30am   1    2    2    2    2    2    1
 Rate  Charge        Rate  Charge 11:00am  1    2    2    2    2    2    1
  1  No Charge        11         11:30am   1    2    2    2    2    2    1
  2  1/4              12         12:00pm   1    1    1    1    1    1    1
  3                   13         12:30pm   1    1    1    1    1    1    1
  4                   14          1:00pm   1    1    1    1    1    1    1
  5                   15          1:30pm   1    1    1    1    1    1    1
  6                   16          2:00pm   1    1    1    1    1    1    1
  7                   17          2:30pm   1    1    1    1    1    1    1
  8                   18          3:00pm   1    1    1    1    1    1    1
  9                   19          3:30pm   1    1    1    1    1    1    1
 10                   20          4:00pm   1    1    1    1    1    1    1
       (Charge is per block)      4:30pm   1    1    1    1    1    1    1
```

Figure 7.6:
Viewing multiple charge rates.

Figure 7.5 shows a block of time marked using F5 (from Monday 8 a.m. to Friday 11:30 a.m.). The Select Charge Rates screen displays. To choose another charge rate, select the Other Charge Rates option and press Enter. The New Charge Rate screen appears. NetWare prompts you for the multiplier and divisor. This becomes the charge rate. After you enter the charge rate, press Esc to save your entries. In the example shown in figure 7.5, the charge rate is set to 1 monetary unit for 4 network usage units used. Figure 7.6 shows that the time period marked in figure 7.5 is now set to a charge rate of 2, which is set to 1/4.

Determining Charge Rates

The supervisor determines the costs of maintaining the system and decides how much to charge for system usage. To determine what your charge rate should be, you first must establish three factors: the amount of dollars to be returned, the services to charge for, and the average units used.

To decide which services you want to charge depends on the way you want to monitor users. If you are concerned with the amount of traffic a user is generating, then you should charge for the service by using the Service Requests Charge Rates option. To track the amount of time a user is logged in, use the Connect Time Charge Rates option. If you want to determine the amount of hard drive space a user occupies, use the Disk Storage Charge Rates option.

NetWare also enables you to charge for combinations of the five charge rates. The supervisor determines how much each charge rate affects the total. If 40% of your charges stem from service requests, 35% from disk storage, and 25% from connect time, for example, then you should recoup that percentage of the total from these different areas.

You can determine the average units used by using the ATOTAL command line utility. ATOTAL shows the total system usage per day and for the week (see fig. 7.7). You should run ATOTAL for three to four weeks after you set the ratios as 1/1 in the services you are planning to charge for. The 1 to 1 ratio gives an accurate usage accounting.

ATOTAL needs to be run from the SYS:SYSTEM directory and does not require any command line switches. This report can be lengthy if accounting has been installed for a long time. The output can be redirected to a printer or to a file to be printed at another time. Use the DOS > command to redirect the printout. To redirect the output to a file called ACCT.RPT, for example, type the following statement at the SYS:SYSTEM directory:

```
ATOTAL > ACCT.RPT.
```

```
     Connect time:        10     Server requests:      6603
     Blocks read:        395     Blocks written:          0
     Blocks/day:           0

01/09/1992:
     Connect time:       250     Server requests:     42621
     Blocks read:       2468     Blocks written:         29
     Blocks/day:           0

01/10/1992:
     Connect time:     49813     Server requests:     25061
     Blocks read:       1614     Blocks written:        172
     Blocks/day:           0

Totals for week:
     Connect time:     54298     Server requests:     88162
     Blocks read:       4919     Blocks written:        209
     Blocks/day:           0


F:\SYSTEM>
```

Figure 7.7:
An example of
ATOTAL results.

Accounting information is kept in a file called NET$ACCT.DAT. This file grows automatically as data is accumulated. NetWare enables you to delete the data in this file. As the accounting program gathers new information, however, this file is re-created.

The second file associated with accounting in NetWare is NET$REC.DAT. This file translates the compressed binary information that is kept in the NET$ACCT.DAT file. You should not, however, delete this file.

After determining the factors for accounting and running the ATOTAL command for several weeks, you should replace the 1/1 ratio with a ratio that enables you to calculate accounting changes for each user. To determine what your new ratio should be, use the following formula:

$$\frac{\text{Amount to charge for total system use per week}}{\text{Estimated average amount of charge used per week}}$$

You might, for example, want to receive $200 per week for the time ten users spend logged in to the network. All ten users work 40 hours a week. In NetWare, the connect time is calculated in minutes that a user is logged in to the network. In this case, 40 hours is 2,400 minutes. Multiply the minutes by the number of users ($2,400 \times 10$ users) to get the number of minutes on the network per week (24,000 minutes) for the ten users.

You now need to calculate the amount of money you want to charge each user. In this case, the unit of measure is one cent. To recoup or get back the $200 per week for the usage of the network, you need to calculate the number of pennies in $200, which is 20,000 pennies. This makes the numerator 20,000, or the amount to be charged for total system use per week. The ratio before reducing is 20000/24000 (20000 for the charge rate and 24000 for the minutes used on the network). Reduced, this ratio is 5/6, or five cents charged for every six minutes a user is logged in to the network.

 The numbers that you use to determine your ratios will change. For accurate accounting measures, you should reevaluate your system every six to 12 months. The accounting feature gives you accurate totals about individual user's usage of the system. As the user's responsibilities change, however, so does your account ratios.

A typical case can be a growing company in which one department grows large over a short period of time. This department's use of the system causes the total network use to increase. A reevaluation at this time is necessary to determine if you need to recoup more monies from this department because of a larger load put on the system by the new users.

Establishing Account Balances

One more step is required before you can begin to charge users for use of the network. (Time is only one of five things to be tracked.) You must establish an account balance for each user. When you open a checking account at your local bank, for example, you must first give the bank a sum of money before you can debit the account. This banking procedure is the same for NetWare accounting. The beginning balance is arbitrary. The system uses the balance to establish an account that is depleted as the user works on the system. If the balance is not limited, the account acts as an odometer by tracking the amount of units that are used. The maximum number of units for an account balance is 99999999.

Limiting NetWare account balances is useful when you want users to be aware of the amount of time they spend on a network. When a user's account reaches the low balance limit, they are asked to log out of the system. Users must log out at this time. If they do not log out, the system will do it for them. To prevent this inconvenience, set the Low Balance Limit to a negative number. If you set a user's balance to -1000, for example, the message `You have exceeded your credit limit for this server.` warns the user of a low account balance when the account reaches 0. The user now has 1000 units to use to finish and exit the network properly. The system tracks the way the user consumes certain network resources. As the user's account hits zero, the counter starts using negative numbers, which should not be confused with negative *units*.

Every time the user logs out of the system, NetWare accounting updates the account. You can use the PAUDIT file, illustrated in figure 7.8, to view login, logout, and system usage information for every user.

Figure 7.8:
An example of using the PAUDIT command.

```
    changed was SYS:DATA.
9/26/91 22:16:31  File Server CDI286
   NOTE: about User SUPERVISOR during File Server services.
   SUPERVISOR changed rights on object owned by USERAM to [ RWCEMF ].  Object
   changed was SYS:MAIL/90365.
9/26/91 22:23:47  File Server CDI286
   NOTE: about User CHRIS during File Server services.
   Logout from address 00000003:000000000070.
9/26/91 22:26:39  File Server CDI286
   NOTE: about User SUPERVISOR during File Server services.
   Logout from address 00000003:000000000051.
9/26/91 22:29:35  File Server CDI286
   NOTE: about Print Server PSCDI386 during File Server services.
   Logout from address 00000003:000000000016.
9/27/91 9:33:36  File Server CDI286
   CHARGE: 7 to User LORI for File Server services.
   Connected 822 min.; 360 requests; 000000000205067  bytes read;
   000000000000000 bytes written.
9/27/91 9:33:36  File Server CDI286
   NOTE: about User LORI during File Server services.
   Logout from address 00000003:0000000000A2.
9/27/91 12:33:01  File Server CDI286
   NOTE: about User SUPERVISOR during File Server services.
   Login from address 00000003:000000000051.
F:\SYSTEM>
```

The Change Current Server Option

The Change Current Server option in the Available Topics menu lists options for attaching to servers and logging out of servers. If you choose the Change Current Servers option, a menu appears that lists the file servers you are currently logged on to or attached to (see figure 7.9). Press Ins at this menu to list available servers that you can log on to. NetWare will ask you for a valid user name and a password before it attaches you to the new server.

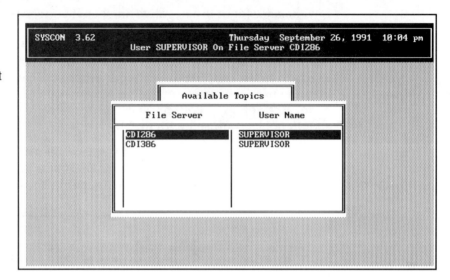

The File Server Information Option

The File Server Information option in the Available Topics menu enables you to view information about the operating system for each server on the network. To view information on a specific server, highlight the server name and press Enter in the Known NetWare Servers screen. This displays the File Server Information screen for the specified server (see fig. 7.10). You cannot change any information on this screen. If you are a supervisor or if you have supervisor privileges, the serial and application numbers for that server are displayed on this screen. Figure 7.10, for example, shows information about the file server named CDI that is important for the system administrator to know if it becomes necessary to contact an outside support person for assistance.

Figure 7.10:
An example of the
File Server
Information screen.

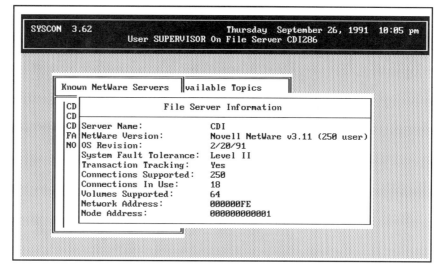

The Group Information Option

In NetWare, groups are designed to save you time and work when privileges are granted to users. If you choose the Group Information option in the Available Topics menu, a list of existing groups is displayed in the Group Names Screen (see fig. 7.11). When NetWare is installed, the only group created by the system is the group EVERYONE. Every user added to the system is automatically added to this group so that global rights can be issued.

You can modify a group in several ways by using the Group Information menu. To access this menu, use your arrow keys to highlight a group, then press Enter (see fig 7.12). The following sections discuss each option of the Group Information menu. To create a new group, press Ins and then name the group in the New Group Name screen (see fig. 7.13).

Full Name

If you select a group in the Group Names screen and press Enter, the Group Information menu appears. The Full Name option in this menu enables you to give a more descriptive name to the selected group.

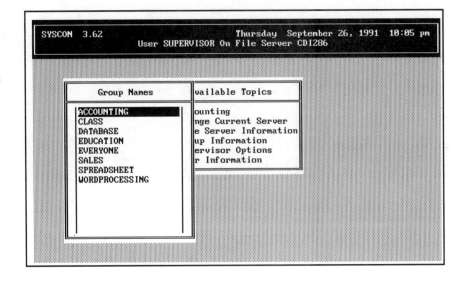

Figure 7.11:
The Group Names screen.

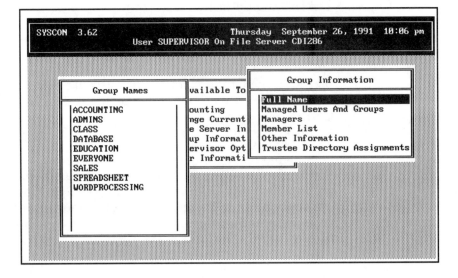

Figure 7.12:
The Group Information menu.

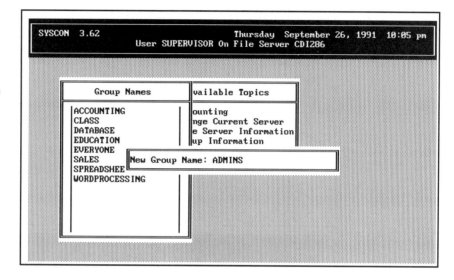

Figure 7.13:
Adding a new
group by using the
New Group Name
screen.

Managed Users and Groups

This option lists users and groups that can choose this option in the
Group Information menu to list the users and groups that the selected
group can grant and revoke rights. This does not give you rights over
the individual user accounts, but does enable you to modify member
list and trustee assignments.

Managers

Choose this option in the Group Information menu to list the managers of the group you selected in the Group Names screen. You cannot
modify this menu item unless you are a manager.

Member List

If you highlight this option and press Enter, members of the selected
group are listed in the Group Members screen. When a group is cre-

ated, it initially has no members (see fig. 7.14). To add users to a group, follow these steps:

1. Highlight the Member List option and press Enter.

2. Press Ins to list users that do not belong to the group.

3. For each user that you want to add to the new group, high-light the user in the Not Group Members screen and press F5. Use F5 to mark each of the users that you want to add to the group and press Enter.

   After you press Enter, the chosen users is added to the se-lected group.

Figure 7.14:
Choosing from the Not Group Members list.

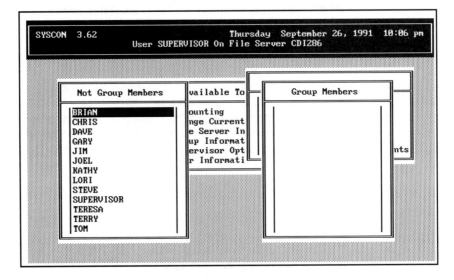

Trustee Directory Assignments

Choose this menu item to add rights to a group. If you highlight this item and press Enter, the currently assigned rights for the group are listed. As shown in figure 7.15, a new group has no assigned rights. To add rights, press Ins and type the full path name. If you are not sure of the directory structure, press Ins a second time to have the network prompt you for information about the path.

Figure 7.15:
Viewing the Trustee
Directory
Assignments menu.

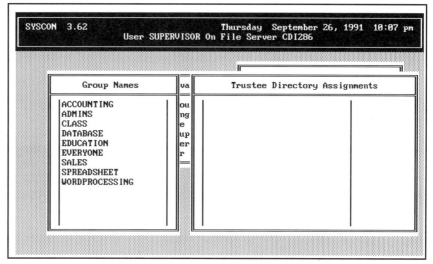

```
SYSCON  3.62                          Thursday  September 26, 1991  10:07 pm
                           User SUPERVISOR On File Server CDI286

              Group Names          va        Trustee Directory Assignments

          ACCOUNTING               ou
          ADMINS                   ng
          CLASS                    e
          DATABASE                 up
          EDUCATION                er
          EVERYONE                 r
          SALES
          SPREADSHEET
          WORDPROCESSING
```

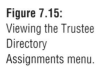 The following is the full set of rights for v2.2:

Read
Write
Create
Erase
File Scan
Modify
Access Control

The following is the full set of rights for v3.11:

Supervisor
Read
Write
Create
Erase
File Scan
Modify
Access Control

For more information about rights and the way they affect the network, refer to Chapter 3.

If you press Ins a second time, the File Servers menu appears. In this menu, NetWare prompts you to choose the server for which you want to assign rights (see fig 7.16). The server that you choose becomes the first part of the full path name.

After you choose a server and press Enter, the Volumes menu prompts you for the volume (see fig 7.17).

Figure 7.16:
Choosing a file server for the path.

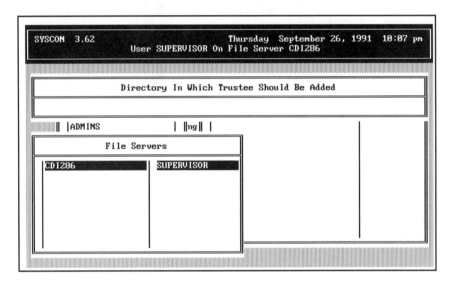

Figure 7.17:
Choosing a volume for the path.

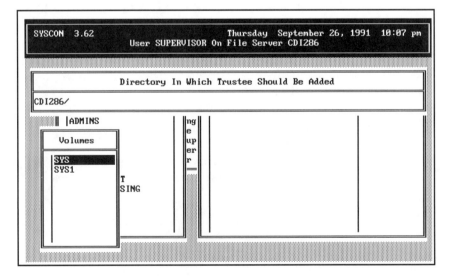

The last prompt for the path asks for the directory for which you want to grant rights (see fig 7.18). The NetWork Directories menu enables you to go as deep into the directory structure as needed. The double dot (..) prompt at the top backs up one directory. The path that you choose appears at the top of the screen in the Directory In Which Trustee Should Be Added screen. Press Esc to stop the selection process and to return to the top window. At this point, you can press Enter to accept the path or press Esc to erase the path you have chosen.

Figure 7.18:
Choosing a directory for the path.

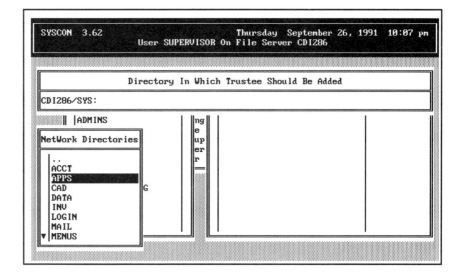

After you select a path, the Trustee Rights Granted screen appears. As shown in figure 7.19, File Scan and Read privileges are granted automatically to new groups.

To modify the rights assigned to a group, follow these steps:

1. Use the cursor keys to highlight the option that you want to change, then press Enter. A list appears displaying the right's full names.

   Figure 7.19 shows that the File Scan and Read rights have been granted for the SYS:APPS directory.

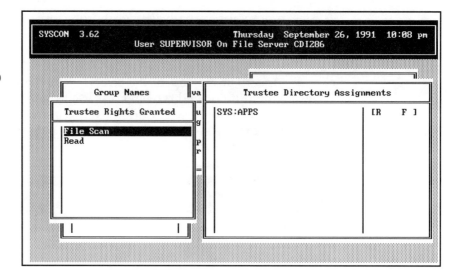

Figure 7.19:
Assigning rights to
a directory.

2. Press Ins to list rights that have not been granted in the
   Trustee Rights Not Granted screen. In figure 7.20, for example, a list of rights that have not been granted displays.

3. Use F5 to mark each right that you want to grant to the
   group, then press Enter.

   To delete rights in a group, mark the rights by using F5,
   and then press Del.

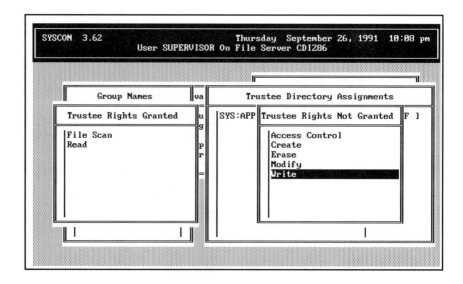

Figure 7.20:
Modifying the
rights assigned.

After you mark the rights you want to assign or delete, the new rights list is updated in the Trustee Directory Assignments screen (see fig. 7.21).

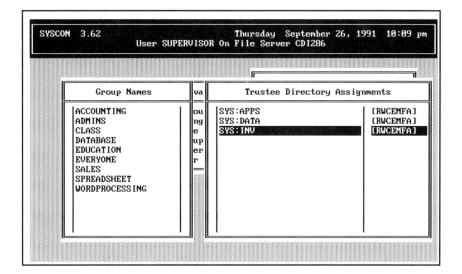

Figure 7.21:
Viewing the
modified rights.

Note

In v3.11, you also can grant rights to specific files. After you specify the path, NetWare prompts you for the file name. After you select a file, follow the previous steps for granting and revoking directory rights. If you try to specify the path and file in the first step, an error appears when it tries to find the path. If you become confused, read the titles to the screens and menus for help.

The Supervisor Options

The only users allowed to use the Supervisor Options menu of SYSCON are supervisor and supervisor equivalents. In this menu, supervisors can specify system defaults, set up FCONSOLE operators, manage server-configuration files, initiate intruder detection, manage the system login scripts, view the error log, and create workgroup managers (see fig. 7.22). Each of these options is outlined in the following sections.

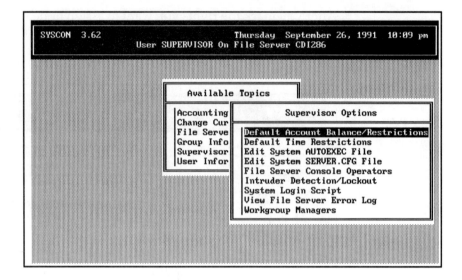

The Supervisor
Options menu in
SYSCON.

Default Account Balance/Restrictions and Default Time Restrictions

The first two items in the Supervisor Options menu affect only future users that are added to the system. These options are the same ones listed in individual user accounts. Default Account Balance/Restrictions and Default Time Restrictions have no effect on current users. As you add new users to the network, the parameters defined in these two options automatically are added to the new user's account.

Edit System AUTOEXEC File and Edit System SERVER.CFG File

The AUTOEXEC file is designed to define the printing processes. If you have core printing installed on the network and you want to save the configuration file to be processed when the server boots, you should place these commands in this file. See Chapter 8 for more information about core printing and the AUTOEXEC file.

The SERVER.CFG file, which is an option in NetWare v2.2, enables you to specify the value added process (VAP) wait time and uninterruptable power supply (UPS) information. Only the five following commands can be used in the SERVER.CFG file:

A *value added process* (VAP) is a process or program that runs on the file server to add functionality. The VAP WAIT command enables the file server to load VAPS automatically.

An *uninterruptable power supply* (UPS) is a battery backup power source. A Novell-approved UPS has the capability to communicate to the system the power status of the UPS. The UPS type statement informs the file server the type of port to which the UPS is attached.

VAP WAIT *xxx*

In the VAP WAIT *xxx* command, the *xxx* variable specifies the length of time in seconds that the network will wait before loading a VAP. You can enter a value of 10 to 300.

UPS TYPE=*x*

In the UPS TYPE=x command, the *x* variable is replaced by one of the following numbers, which correspond to the type of monitoring hardware used with NetWare:

Monitoring Hardware	Command
Stand-alone UPS monitor board	UPS TYPE=1
Host Bus Adapter	UPS TYPE=2
SS keycard	UPS TYPE=3
Mouse Port (PS/2)	UPS TYPE=4

UPS IO=*xxx*

In the UPS IO=*xxx* commands, the *xxx* variable is replaced by the input/output (I/O) address that was factory preset for a Novell Disk Coprocessor Board. The *I/O address* is the location where devices, such as a coprocessor board, are found. This information is used by the system to monitor the proper device.

Disk Controller Channel	I/O Address
Channel 1	UPS IO=346
Channel 2	UPS IO=34E
Channel 3	UPS IO=326
Channel 4	UPS IO=32E

UPS DOWN=*xxx*

The number you enter for the UPS DOWN command represents the number of minutes that the UPS will supply power to the server before it shuts down. The *xxx* variable is replaced with a value between 1 and 64,800.

UPS WAIT=*xxx*

The number you enter for the UPS WAIT command represents the amount of time in seconds that the UPS will wait before it tells users that the power is off. The *xxx* variable is replaced by a value between 15 and 300 seconds. The default is 15 seconds.

File Server Console Operators

In the File Server Console Operators Options menu, FCONSOLE operator status can be given to individual users or to groups. FCONSOLE is a menu utility that is used for monitoring the file server. Users that have supervisor privileges can use all the options in FCONSOLE. Regular users whose names appear in this screen cannot clear connections or down the server from FCONSOLE. Users whose names do not appear in this list can use FCONSOLE, but are severely limited as to what information they can see. For more information on FCONSOLE, see Chapter 10.

Intruder Detection/Lockout

Intruder detection is designed to alert the network when someone tries to log in to the system using an invalid password. The Intruder Detection/Lockout option has several configurable parameters because users often make a mistake when they type in a password.

The network enables you to track incorrect login attempts. An *incorrect login attempt* is considered to be the number of times a user can try to log in using an incorrect password in a specific number of minutes. In figure 7.23, for example, users can attempt to log in to the network seven times in fifty nine minutes before intruder detection locks them out. The length of lockout time also is configurable. The Length Of Account Lockout line in figure 7.23 shows the maximum allowable lockout time—40 days, 23 hours, and 59 minutes.

To unlock an account, you must select the User Information option in the Available Topics menu, and then choose the Intruder Lockout Status option under the name of the user that has been disabled.

Figure 7.23:
The Intruder
Detection/Lockout
option.

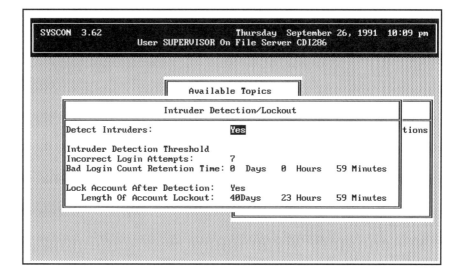

System Login Script

The System Login Script option is designed to configure the network environment for all users. This file is created and maintained by the system supervisor. For more information on the system login script, see Chapter 9.

View File Server Error Log

To view the file server error log file, press Enter on the View File Server Error Log entry in the Supervisor Options menu. Then use the arrow, PgUp, and PgDn keys to move around the File Server Error Log screen (see fig. 7.24). The information shown in the error log is stored in a file called NET$LOG.ERR. This file contains system errors and other information that is not serious enough to crash a file server, but still is important to the administrator. Press Esc to exit this screen. Before the error log exits, you are prompted to delete the current information.

Figure 7.24:
The File Server
Error Log screen.

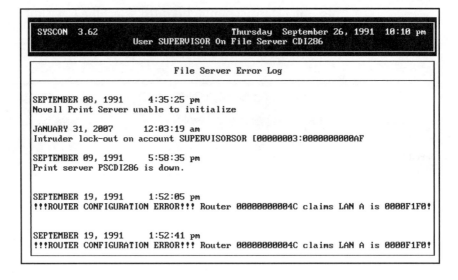

```
SYSCON  3.62                        Thursday  September 26, 1991  10:10 pm
                       User SUPERVISOR On File Server CDI286

                              File Server Error Log

SEPTEMBER 08, 1991      4:35:25 pm
Novell Print Server unable to initialize

JANUARY 31, 2007       12:03:19 am
Intruder lock-out on account SUPERVISORSOR [00000003:0000000000AF

SEPTEMBER 09, 1991      5:58:35 pm
Print server PSCDI286 is down.

SEPTEMBER 19, 1991      1:52:05 pm
!!!ROUTER CONFIGURATION ERROR!!! Router 00000000004C claims LAN A is 0000F1F0!

SEPTEMBER 19, 1991      1:52:41 pm
!!!ROUTER CONFIGURATION ERROR!!! Router 00000000004C claims LAN A is 0000F1F0!
```

Workgroup Managers

The Workgroup Managers option in the Supervisor Options menu enables you to define workgroup managers. As you saw earlier in this
chapter, *workgroup managers* are users or groups that can add, delete,
and manage other user accounts. Workgroup managers, however, cannot make other workgroup managers or use the Supervisor Options
in SYSCON. Press Enter to see the names of potential workgroup managers for users and groups on your network (see fig. 7.25). Press Ins to
choose other network users and groups to be workgroup managers.

The User Information Option

The User information option in the Available Topics menu enables you
to set up individual user accounts. Highlight this option and press
Enter to display every user that has an account on the network. Figure
7.26 shows the User Names screen that lists the names of users that
have been established on the network.

To create a new user, press Ins and use the User Name: window to
name the new user. Figure 7.27, for example, shows the user USERAM
being added to the network.

Figure 7.25:
The Workgroup
Managers screen.

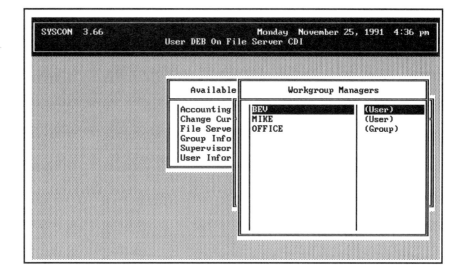

Figure 7.26:
The User Names
screen.

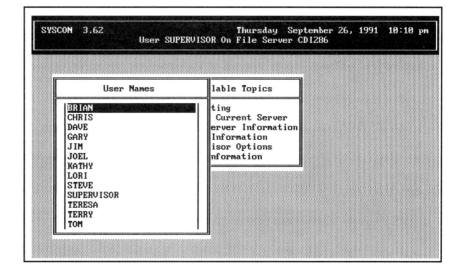

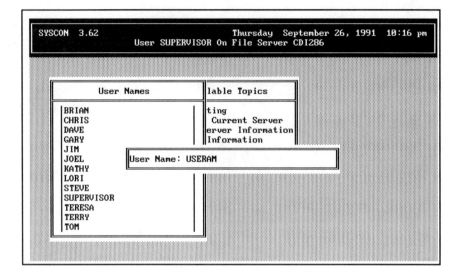

Figure 7.27:
Adding a user to
the network.

After you enter a name for a new user, the network prompts you to choose whether or not you want a home directory created for the new user on volume SYS:. Press Esc if you do not want to create a home directory for the user. If you want to give the new user a home directory, you also can modify the path. After you finish, NetWare creates the directory and assigns all rights to it for the new user. Figure 7.28, for example, displays the default path that the network creates for the user USERAM.

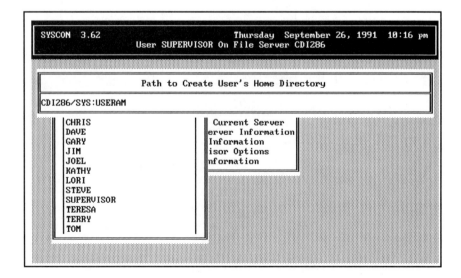

Figure 7.28:
Creating a home
directory.

After you create the new user, highlight the user's name and press Enter. The User Information screen appears and enables you to modify the user's account (see fig. 7.29). This screen displays the information that a system manager can modify for a specific user's account. Each option in the User Information menu is described in the following sections.

Figure 7.29:
The User
Information screen.

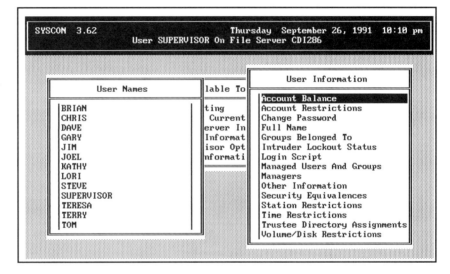

```
 SYSCON  3.62                         Thursday  September 26, 1991  10:10 pm
                       User SUPERVISOR On File Server CDI286

                                              User Information
            User Names              lable To
                                             Account Balance
      BRIAN                        ting       Account Restrictions
      CHRIS                         Current   Change Password
      DAVE                         erver In   Full Name
      GARY                         Informat   Groups Belonged To
      JIM                          isor Opt   Intruder Lockout Status
      JOEL                         nformati   Login Script
      KATHY                                   Managed Users And Groups
      LORI                                    Managers
      STEVE                                   Other Information
      SUPERVISOR                              Security Equivalences
      TERESA                                  Station Restrictions
      TERRY                                   Time Restrictions
      TOM                                     Trustee Directory Assignments
                                             Volume/Disk Restrictions
```

Account Balance

The Account Balance option in the User Information menu enables supervisors to set up and monitor the user's account balance. When you select this option, the Account Balance For User screen displays on-screen. If the Accounting option has not been installed on the network, the Account Balance option does not appear. In the example shown in figure 7.30, the user Steve has been given an account balance of 500,000. This amount decreases as Steve uses the accounting services.

Account Restrictions

Supervisors can use the Account Restrictions option of the User Information menu to set up the password and connection parameters for a user. Figure 7.31 lists the account restrictions for the user Steve. Each parameter in this menu is discussed in the following list.

Figure 7.30:
The Account
Balance For User
screen.

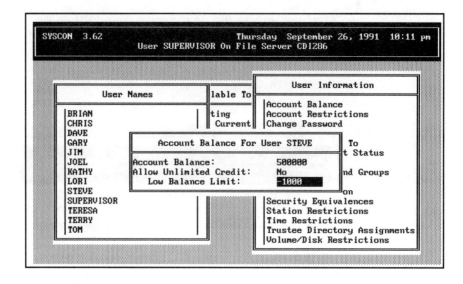

Figure 7.31:
The Account
Restrictions For
User screen.

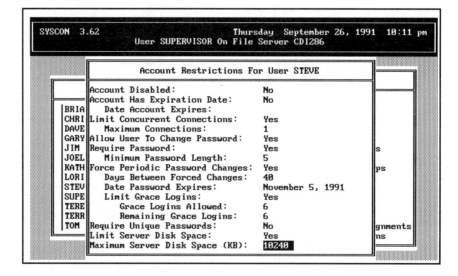

Supervisors can change the following items in the Account Restrictions For User screen to configure a new or existing user's account:

- **Account Disabled.** This line is set to Yes if any of the following conditions occur: if the user's expiration date has passed; if the grace logins have run out; or if a supervisor does not want this user logging into the network. If Account Disabled is set to No, the user can log in to the network.

- **Account Has Expiration Date.** If you want a new user to have only temporary access to the network, set an expiration date for his account. The user will not be able to log in to the network after the date that is set in this field. If you do not want to set an expiration date, set this line to No.

- **Limit Concurrent Connections.** The supervisor can use this field to specify the number of workstations a new user can log in to using the same login name. The default is all nodes on the network.

 It is a good idea to limit the number of allowable logins for supervisors and users with supervisor privileges. A limited number of connections prevents privileged users from leaving a trail of workstations that are logged in with supervisory rights.

- **Allow User To Change Password.** If this field is set to Yes, the user can change his password whenever he wants. If this field is set to No, only the system supervisor can change the user's password.

- **Require Password.** If you choose to require a password, set this field to Yes. You also need to specify the minimum length for the password. If you set this field to No, the user is not required to have a password. Even if Require Password is set to No, the user still can have a password.

- **Force Periodic Password Changes.** If you set this parameter to Yes, specify the number of days between forced changes and the next date that the password expires. The network default is 40 days.

One of Murphy's laws states that whenever something must be done immediately, it is always the worst possible time to do it. This "law" also applies to network users. For example, the morning a user logs in to the network to find that his password has expired probably will be the same morning that a record number of crises occur. This problem is the reason for *grace logins*, which involve telling the network that you are too busy at the moment to think of a new password, but to ask for a new password the next time you log in. The default for grace logins is six. In other words, you can answer no to a new password request six times before the network locks your account.

- **Require Unique Passwords.** This option for v2.2 requires each user to create up to eight new passwords before they can repeat the first password. In v3.11, users must create ten new passwords before they can repeat the first password. In addition, these passwords must be in effect for 24 hours.

- **Limit Server Disk Space.** If this option is set to Yes, you must specify the maximum amount of disk space in kilobytes that the user is allowed. When you limit a user's disk space, make sure the user knows that if he runs out of space while he saves or prints a file, he might lose the information. The network needs to store print files as temporary files on the network. If his memory space runs out while he prints a large job, the job will be lost.

 For the Limit Server Disk Space option to appear in v2.2, you must choose Limit Disk Space as an option during the installation of the NetWare operating system.

Change Password

The Change Password option in the User Information menu adds or changes passwords. The DOS command for this task is SETPASS. Users cannot see the password but are asked to repeat the new password to make sure that it was typed correctly. Supervisors do not need to know the old password, but regular users need to put in the old password before they are allowed to change it.

Full Name

The Full Name option in the User Information menu enables you to give a more descriptive name to the user. This is optional and is used with the identifier variable FULL_NAME.

Groups Belonged To

The Groups Belonged To option in the User Information menu provides an opposite view of the Group Information option in the Available Topics menu. In the Groups Belonged To option, you can view the groups to which the highlighted user belongs. Press Ins to view the groups that the user does not belong to (see fig. 7.32). The system manager can pick from this list the groups that he wants a user to belong to. To add a user to a group in this option, such as DATABASE, highlight the group and press Enter. The Groups Belonged To screen then shows the updated groups list (see fig. 7.33).

Intruder Lockout Status

The Intruder Lockout Status option in the User Information menu enables you to see whether a user has been locked out because of the Intruder Detection feature. Intruder Lockout Status displays the network and workstation address that a selected user is locked out of and the time remaining until the lockout is reset. If the user is not currently locked out, you can view only the system. If you are a system manager and the user is locked out, the border for this menu becomes a double line and you can unlock the account.

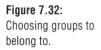

Figure 7.32:
Choosing groups to
belong to.

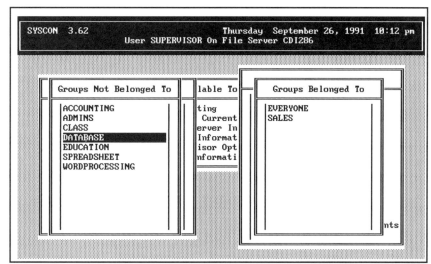

Figure 7.33:
The modified
groups list.

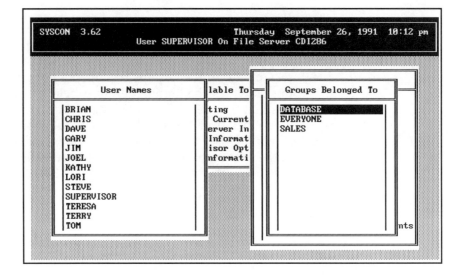

 Under the address portion of the Intruder Lockout Status screen, the first portion of the address is the network address. The second part is the workstation address, and the third number is a network socket number.

Login Script

The Login Script option in the User Information menu enables the user or a system manager to add or manage the login script for a selected user. In addition, login scripts can be copied from other users, but only if no existing login script exists for the current user. If a login script exists and you want to assign another user's login script, perform the following steps:

1. Highlight the existing login script by pressing F5 and use the arrow keys to mark it.

2. Press Del.

3. Press Esc to exit and then save the changes.

4. Press Enter to return to the login script screen.

   When you go back into this option, the system tells you that a login script does not exist. You now can read the login script from another user.

5. Replace the current user's name in the screen with the user's name that a login script is copied from. Figure 7.34, for example, shows that the user Steve does not have a login script. To copy one from the user Jim, use Backspace to delete "Steve" and then enter "Jim."

Figure 7.34:
An example of copying login scripts in SYSCON.

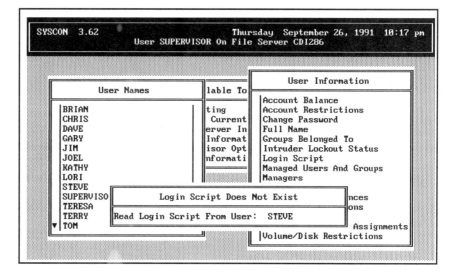

Managed Users and Groups

The Managed Users And Groups option in the User Information menu lists the users and groups that can be granted rights and have rights revoked by the selected user. In addition, this category designates the users whose accounts are managed by the selected user. You can use this option to modify member lists and trustee assignments.

In figure 7.35, the classification Direct means that the selected user is assigned specific users and groups to manage. Indirect-managed users and groups are assigned by the network so that the manager can change rights to the group EVERYONE. Although EVERYONE is created by NetWare, the system managers can add and delete rights for this group.

Figure 7.35:
Examples of managed users and groups.

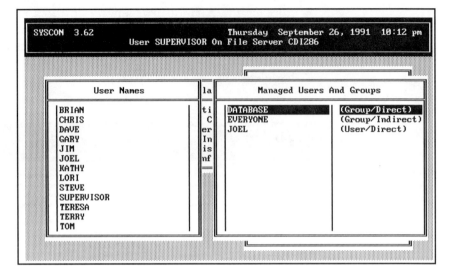

Managers

The Manager options in the User Information menu item lists the manager(s) of a selected user (see fig. 7.36). You can modify this opiton only if you are a manager.

Figure 7.36:
Account managers for the slected user.

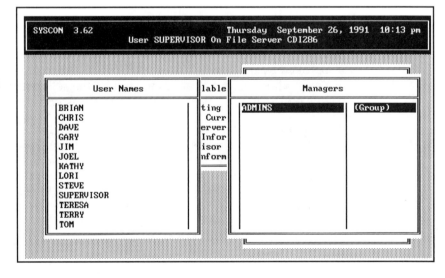

Other Information

The Other Information option in the User Information menu shows you when a selected user last logged in to the network. If this is a new user, the message Not known appears (see fig. 7.37). This screen also shows if this user is an FCONSOLE operator. The Maximum Server Disk Usage setting in the Account Restrictions option also appears here, including information about the amount of memory space the user currently is using on the network. The final field is the Users ID, which is the same as the directory under SYS:MAIL that belongs to this user.

Figure 7.37:
The Other
Information option.

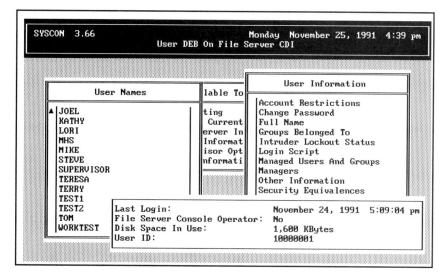

Security Equivalences

The Security Equivalences option in the User Information menu assigns the security rights of one user to another user. When you assign a new user to a group, that user automatically receives the equivalent privileges of every other user in that group. Figure 7.38 shows that the user Steve belongs to the groups DATABASE, EVERYONE, and SALES and has the same security rights as the groups listed.

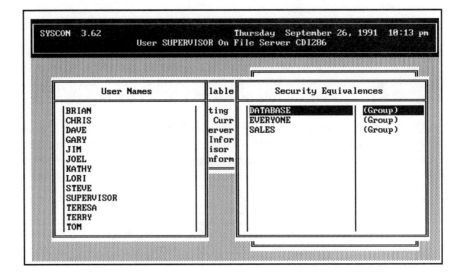

Figure 7.38:
The Security
Equivalences
option screen.

The following steps show you the way to assign supervisor privileges to a user. Figure 7.39 shows that SUPERVISOR has been added to the Security Equivalences option screen. This makes the new user Steve a supervisor equivalent user. To assign a user supervisor privileges, choose Security Equivalences in the User Information menu, and then perform the following steps:

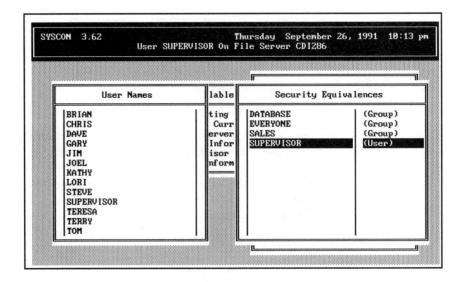

Figure 7.39:
Creating a
supervisor
equivalent user.

1. Press Ins at the Security Equivalences menu to display a list of options.

2. From the list, find the heading USER Supervisor.

3. Highlight SUPERVISOR and press Enter. The selected user now is a supervisor equivalent (see fig 7.39).

This process is the only way to make a supervisor equivalent user.

Station Restrictions

NetWare by default enables a user to log in to any workstation attached to the network. Through the Station Restrictions option in the User Information menu, the system administrator can create a list of networks and workstations that a user can log in to. The user cannot log in to any network or workstation whose address does not appear on this list. Figure 7.40 shows the list of node addresses and network addresses of the workstations from which a selected user is allowed to log in.

Figure 7.40:
A list of login addresses.

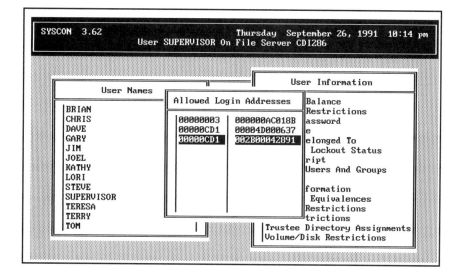

Time Restrictions

The Time Restrictions option in the User Information menu enables you to restrict individual users to network use at specific times. In figure 7.41, asterisks denote half-hour time increments that a user can be logged in to the network. Every empty space represents one half hour of time that a user is denied access. Press F5 and use the arrow keys to mark blocks of time. To delete or add asterisks, mark the desired block and press Enter.

Figure 7.41:
Setting time restrictions for a user.

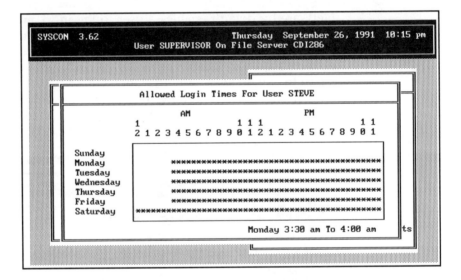

Trustee Directory Assignments and Trustee File Assignments

Choose this option in the User Information menu to view the rights assigned to a user and to add rights that a user needs. A new user automatically has rights to his home directory and to his SYS:MAIL/USER_ID directory. To add rights, press Ins and type in the full path name. See the section on adding rights to groups for more information about entering full path names.

NetWare grants the File Scan and Read privileges automatically. To modify the rights assignments, use the following steps:

1. Press Enter on the option that you want to change.

2. When a list of the right's full name appears, press Ins to list rights that have not been granted.

3. Press F5 to mark each right that you want to grant to the group, then press Enter.

To delete rights, press Del after you mark the rights by pressing F5.

The new rights list then is updated in the Trustee Directory Assignments window.

 In v3.11, you also can grant rights to specific files. Follow the same steps for granting and revoking directory rights, and then specify the file in the next screen that appears after you specify the path. If you type the path and the file appears in the Directory In Which Trustee Should Be Added screen, the system displays an error after it tries to find the path. Read the titles to the windows to help you follow the steps to typing the path.

Volume/Disk Restrictions

The User Volume/DISK Restrictions option in the User Information menu enables you to limit the disk space available to the user. This option displays in v2.2 only if the Limit Server Disk Space option was selected during installation. Figure 7.42 shows that the user can use 10240K or about 10M of space. The administrator can check this number to see the amount of space a user has taken up on the system. The Disk Space In Use field shown in figure 7.42, for example, shows that the user currently has not used any disk space.

Using Command Line Utilities

You have seen how NetWare's SYSCON menu utility helps administrators manipulate user accounts. This section discusses the command line utilities available in NetWare that administrators and managers can use to manipulate user accounts. Command line utilities are used from the DOS prompt.

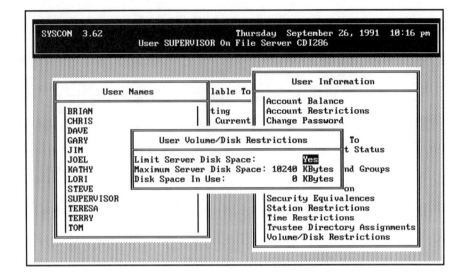

Figure 7.42:
The User/Volume Disk Restrictions option.

The RIGHTS Command

The RIGHTS command shows the user what rights they have in any given directory. If you seem to have more rights in one directory than you were granted originally, then rights have flowed down from a higher directory. This is referred to as flow through. *Flow through* automatically occurs to all subdirectories underneath the directory in which rights have been granted.

If you have fewer rights in a directory, the Inherited Rights Mask in v3.11 has blocked the flow of rights. In v2.2, the Maximum Rights Mask has prohibited certain rights from having any effect in a directory.

The syntax for the RIGHTS command is as follows:

```
RIGHTS path
```

In the example shown in figure 7.43, the RIGHTS command is entered from the O prompt to see the available rights in that directory.

Figure 7.43:
The RIGHTS command lists and explains each available right.

```
O:\OFFICE>rights
CDI\SYS:OFFICE
Your Effective Rights for this directory are [SRWCEMFA]
      You have Supervisor Rights to Directory.     (S)
    * May Read from File.                           (R)
    * May Write to File.                            (W)
      May Create Subdirectories and Files.          (C)
      May Erase Directory.                          (E)
      May Modify Directory.                         (M)
      May Scan for Files.                           (F)
      May Change Access Control.                    (A)

* Has no effect on directory.

      Entries in Directory May Inherit [SRWCEMFA] rights.
      You have ALL RIGHTS to Directory Entry.

O:\OFFICE>
```

The TLIST Command

The TLIST command displays which users have been given explicit rights in a given directory. Flow-through does not show up in TLIST. The TLIST command is typed as follows:

> **TLIST** *path*

In figure 7.44, the TLIST command shows that the user LORI and the group OFFICE have all rights except those of the supervisor.

The GRANT Command

The GRANT command is used to grant rights to users or groups. You also can use menu items in the User Information menu in SYSCON to grant rights. Any information changed by using the GRANT command is permanent and appears in the user's trustee information screens in SYSCON. The GRANT command is typed as follows:

> **GRANT** *rights list* **for** *file* or *path* **to** *user* or *group*

Figure 7.44:
TLIST displays the rights granted to users and groups.

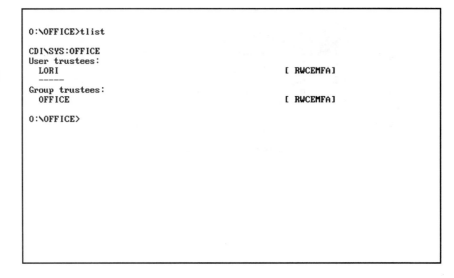

```
O:\OFFICE>tlist

CDI\SYS:OFFICE
User trustees:
  LORI                                                [ RWCEMFA]

Group trustees:
  OFFICE                                              [ RWCEMFA]

O:\OFFICE>
```

In figure 7.45, for example, the user Teresa requests Read and File Scan rights in the Office directory. The supervisor used the GRANT command and a shortcut to give her the rights. Instead of spelling out the full path name, the system needs only the drive letter that points to the proper path. The TLIST command was used after GRANT to verify that the rights were granted.

Figure 7.45:
The GRANT command gives rights to a user for a specific directory.

```
O:\OFFICE>grant r f for o: to teresa

CDI/SYS:OFFICE
OFFICE                           Rights set to [ R    F ]

O:\OFFICE>tlist

CDI\SYS:OFFICE
User trustees:
  LORI                                                [ RWCEMFA]
  TERESA                                              [ R    F ]

Group trustees:
  OFFICE                                              [ RWCEMFA]

O:\OFFICE>
```

The REVOKE Command

The REVOKE command is used to take away rights from a user in either a directory or a file. REVOKE uses the following syntax:

REVOKE *rights list* **for** *file* or *path* **from** *user* or *group*

Figure 7.46, for example, shows that the user Lori has more rights than necessary in the Office directory. The excess rights are removed by using the REVOKE command, and then the TLIST command is used to verify the process.

Figure 7.46:
The REVOKE command is used to deny rights from a user for a specific directory.

```
O:\OFFICE>revoke c e m a for o: from lori
CDI/SYS:OFFICE
Trustee's access rights set to [ RW   F ]

Rights for 1 directories were changed for LORI.


O:\OFFICE>tlist

CDI\SYS:OFFICE
User trustees:
    LORI                                        [ RW   F ]
    TERESA                                      [ R    F ]
    -----
Group trustees:
    OFFICE                                      [ RWCEMFA]

O:\OFFICE>
```

The REMOVE Command

The REMOVE command removes the user from the trustee list. REMOVE uses the following syntax:

REMOVE *user* or *group* **from** *path*

In figure 7.47, the user Teresa is removed from the O directory by using the REMOVE command. The TLIST command then is entered to confirm the results.

Figure 7.47:
The REMOVE command is used to remove a user from a trustee list.

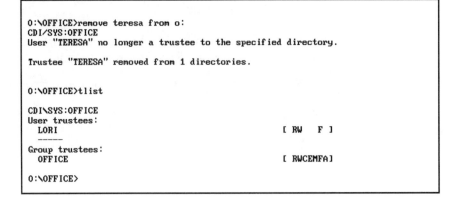

```
O:\OFFICE>remove teresa from o:
CDI/SYS:OFFICE
User "TERESA" no longer a trustee to the specified directory.

Trustee "TERESA" removed from 1 directories.


O:\OFFICE>tlist

CDI\SYS:OFFICE
User trustees:
  LORI                                          [ RW    F ]
  ────
Group trustees:
  OFFICE                                        [ RWCEMFA]

O:\OFFICE>
```

The ALLOW Command

The ALLOW command sets the Inherited Rights Mask for a directory or file. This command is available only in v3.11. The syntax is as follows:

ALLOW *file* or *path rights list*

The following example sets the Inherited Rights Mask to enable only Read and File Scan rights to flow through to the subdirectories::

ALLOW O:\OFFICE R F

The MAKEUSER Utility

MAKEUSER is a utility that you can use to create, edit, and process a script that adds users to the network (see fig. 7.48). For a list of commands that you can use in a MAKEUSER file, see the Command Reference.

The following rules will help you develop a MAKEUSER script:

- All keywords must be uppercase and must be preceded with a pound sign (#).
- If you want to use any keywords concerned with passwords, you must first type **#PASSWORD_REQUIRED**.
- The flow of events is always upward. The #CREATE statement always refers to the commands above it to determine the parameters the user will have.

Figure 7.48:
The MAKEUSER
utility options.

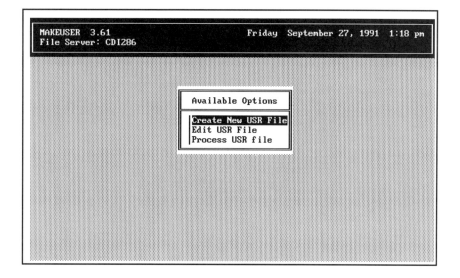

- Makeuser files are saved with a USR extension in the directory that the MAKEUSER utility is accessed.

- After the file is processed, MAKEUSER leaves a report file with the same file name, but with an RPT extension. This file shows if the users have been created.

You can use a MAKEUSER file as computerized notes for adding users to the network. All that is necessary for reprocessing this file is to change the name of the user on the CREATE statement.

Figure 7.49 shows an example of a MAKEUSER file. In this example, two users are created to use the system. Each user has several unique restrictions and shared parameters. Because of the way MAKEUSER interprets keywords, the user Diana is affected only by the keywords listed before the #CREATE DIANA statement. The user Henry, on the other hand, is affected by all the keywords in this file.

The USERDEF utility

The USERDEF utility enables you to add, create, and edit templates and then use those templates to process users. Figure 7.50 shows the Available Options menu for USERDEF. Instead of creating and managing several files from MAKEUSER, you can use templates available in USERDEF with different user parameters. Figure 7.51, for example, shows three templates that were created by the system administrator.

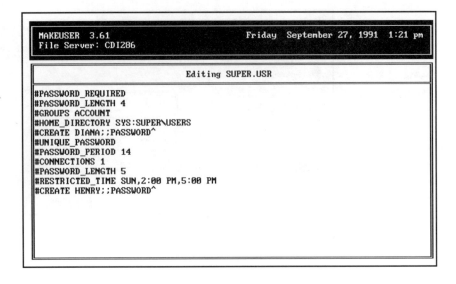

Figure 7.49:
An example of a
MAKEUSER script.

```
MAKEUSER  3.61                         Friday  September 27, 1991  1:21 pm
File Server: CDI286

                            Editing SUPER.USR

#PASSWORD_REQUIRED
#PASSWORD_LENGTH 4
#GROUPS ACCOUNT
#HOME_DIRECTORY SYS:SUPER\USERS
#CREATE DIANA;;PASSWORD^
#UNIQUE_PASSWORD
#PASSWORD_PERIOD 14
#CONNECTIONS 1
#PASSWORD_LENGTH 5
#RESTRICTED_TIME SUN,2:00 PM,5:00 PM
#CREATE HENRY;;PASSWORD^
```

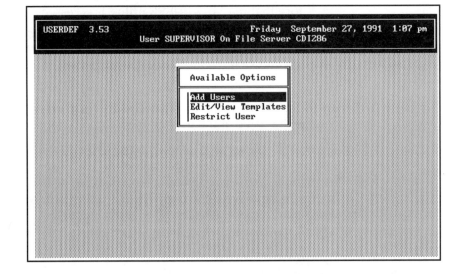

Figure 7.50:
The Available
Options menu in
the USERDEF
utility.

```
USERDEF  3.53                          Friday  September 27, 1991  1:07 pm
                    User SUPERVISOR On File Server CDI286


                              Available Options

                             Add Users
                             Edit/View Templates
                             Restrict User
```

Each template enables you to create or edit login scripts and other parameters (see fig. 7.52). The parameters you can use include setting up
default directories, copying printcon jobs from other users, determining which groups users should belong to, and creating account restrictions. Figure 7.53 displays all the available parameters for configuring
a template.

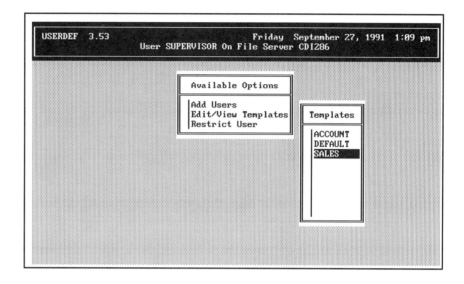

Figure 7.51:
Examples of
USERDEF
templates.

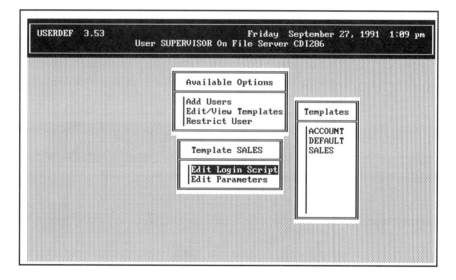

Figure 7.52:
USERDEF template
options.

When you add users, a list appears that displays users that already exist on the network and users that have not yet been added. If you press Ins, the USERDEF utility asks for the user's full name. In figure 7.54, for example, a new user named PM - Afternoon Shift is added to the list of users by using the Account template.

Figure 7.53:
USERDEF template
parameters.

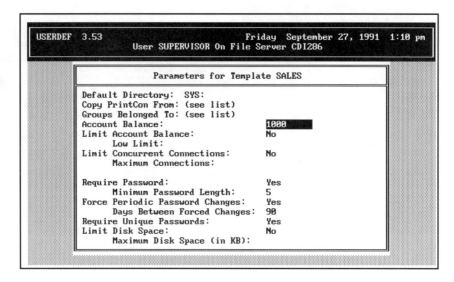

Figure 7.53 screen content:

```
USERDEF  3.53                          Friday  September 27, 1991  1:10 pm
                    User SUPERVISOR On File Server CDI286

                        Parameters for Template SALES

           Default Directory:  SYS:
           Copy PrintCon From: (see list)
           Groups Belonged To: (see list)
           Account Balance:                      1000
           Limit Account Balance:                No
                 Low Limit:
           Limit Concurrent Connections:         No
                 Maximum Connections:

           Require Password:                      Yes
                 Minimum Password Length:         5
           Force Periodic Password Changes:       Yes
                 Days Between Forced Changes:      90
           Require Unique Passwords:              Yes
           Limit Disk Space:                     No
                 Maximum Disk Space (in KB):
```

After you add the user, USERDEF uses the first name as the login name. If you press Esc, USERDEF asks if you want to create the user by using the specified template. Figure 7.55 shows the confirmation menu for the Sales template when you add a new user to the sales list. After you confirm that you want to create a new user using that template, NetWare compiles a USR file and processes it.

Figure 7.54:
Adding a new user
in the Account
template in
USERDEF.

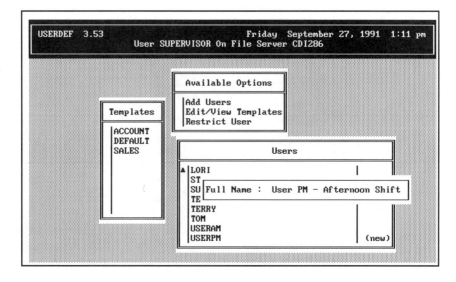

Figure 7.54 screen content:

```
USERDEF  3.53                          Friday  September 27, 1991  1:11 pm
                    User SUPERVISOR On File Server CDI286

                              Available Options

                              Add Users
           Templates          Edit/View Templates
                              Restrict User
           ACCOUNT
           DEFAULT                        Users
           SALES
                        LORI
                        ST
                        SU  Full Name :  User PM - Afternoon Shift
                        TE
                        TERRY
                        TOM
                        USERAM
                        USERPM                              (new)
```

Figure 7.55:
Confirming a new user in the Sales template.

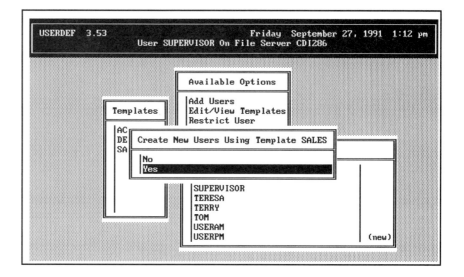

```
 USERDEF  3.53                         Friday  September 27, 1991  1:12 pm
                     User SUPERVISOR On File Server CDI286


                                    Available Options

                                    Add Users
                   Templates        Edit/View Templates
                                    Restrict User
              AC
              DE   Create New Users Using Template SALES
              SA
                   No
                   Yes


                                    SUPERVISOR
                                    TERESA
                                    TERRY
                                    TOM
                                    USERAM
                                    USERPM                          (new)
```

Summary

In this chapter, you were shown the many different methods of adding user accounts to the network. You also were shown the variety of configurable parameters users or group accounts can have set to give them rights and privileges on the network.

Novell supplies two ways of configuring user and group accounts: menu utilities and command line utilities. Command line utilities interact with menu utilities. That is, you can see the results of using the command line utilities in the menu utilities. System administrators can use either command line utilities or menu utilities to give users or groups rights.

In the next chapter, you are shown the way to configure printers on the network. As you will see, Novell gives the system administrator several ways to set up printing on a NetWare network.

8

Printing on a Novell Network

C hapters 6 and 7 showed you the way to set up directory structures, place attributes on application files, add users and groups to the network, and grant users and groups access to files and programs. The network users now should be able to use the applications that are on the file server. Many times, users need to print out hard copies of their work on a network, much as they do on stand-alone PCs. NetWare enables you to set up printing on your network so that any networked user can access the printer that he needs to get the job done.

In this chapter, you learn about the following:

- Using core print services vs print servers
- Setting up core printing in a v2.2 server
- Defining queues with PCONSOLE
- Installing print servers
- Directing the output

- Controlling the print server
- Customizing the printers with PRINTDEF
- Creating print jobs with PRINTCON
- Using related print commands

Understanding Network Printing

When you print from a stand-alone computer to an attached printer, the job goes through the cable to the printer's buffer. When the entire print job is in the printer's buffer, the computer is freed up to perform other tasks.

When you print on a network, however, the job is sent from your workstation out through the network cable to the file server. The job then is directed into a queue, which is assigned a hexadecimally named directory under SYS:SYSTEM. A *queue* assigns printer jobs in a specific order in which they are to be printed. Queues can have English names to help you remember them and are created at the file server console or through the PCONSOLE menu utility.

All print jobs are kept in the queues until the designated printer is available. The file server is in charge of polling the printers and queues to make sure that jobs are getting to the printers.

Novell provides four basic methods of printing in the network environment: core printing services, VAP or NLM print servers, dedicated print servers, and remote workstation printing.

Core printing services is the oldest method of network printing and was at one time the only method supplied by Novell. *Core printing services* enable you to connect printers directly to the file server. This means that printer jobs are handled directly by the operating system. This method is supported only on NetWare 286 and has both drawbacks and advantages. If your system simply requires one or two printers in a central location, then core printing may be all that you need. Although very basic, core printing can burden the file server with printing tasks that reduce file service performance. Core printing also requires downing the file server to make changes to printer port configurations. This method of printing usually must be scheduled for after hours to minimize any downtime inconvenience to other users. Core printing should be reserved for smaller, low-traffic situations that do not require extended control.

A second printing method involves the use of VAPs or NLMs as print servers. These systems can reside in the server as an extra process or in a Novell bridge or router. VAPs and NLMs provide you flexibility with utilities such as PSC, which will be discussed later, and provide remote control of all print server serviced printers. A print server also can support up to 16 devices both in the print server and remotely connected to a workstation.

About VAPs and NLMs...

Value added processes (VAPs) and *NetWare Loadable Modules* (NLMs) add functionality to the file server. VAPs are used on v2.2 file servers and NLMs are used on v3.11 file servers. One of the most common applications for VAPs and NLMs is extended printing capabilities, such as the PSERVER files discussed in this section.

A third printing method on NetWare requires the use of a dedicated workstation to be used as the print server. The PSERVER.EXE program supplies the same functionality as the VAP and NLM with the benefit of being dedicated to servicing printers. This solution is best for heavy production printing. The capability to use computers from the 8088 to the current 80486 computers enables you to tailor this configuration to your needs.

Novell also offers the capability to share a locally attached printer. To enable the RPRINTER.EXE command to function, you must set up a remote printer definition on a print server. The RPRINTER.EXE loads as a background task using approximately 9K of memory. Because of this background operation, you should not use this method for heavy printing use.

 The NetWare RPRINTER.EXE command is selective on the hardware it works with. If you experience problems with a particular computer port using this type of shared printing, you should use a different port.

Setting Up Core Printing in a v2.2 Server

Core Printing in a v2.2 server requires that you choose this option when you install NetWare. If you choose Basic Installation, core printing is initialized automatically for LPT1. Core printing enables you to attach up to five printers directly to the file server. To use these printers, the administrator should be aware of the following commands.

The P n CREATE port command assigns a printer number to a port on the file server. If you want LPT1 assigned as printer 0 and COM1 assigned as printer 2, type the following:

```
P 0 CREATE LPT1
P 1 CREATE COM1
```

If you are using a COM port that is set for anything other than the following parameters, you need to use the following command to reset parameters for the port: n CONFIG BAUD=a WORDSIZE=b STOPBIT=c PARITY=d XONXOFF=e. An example of this command follows:

```
BAUD = 9600
WORDSIZE = 8
STOPBIT = 1
PARITY = NONE
XONXOFF = No
```

The Q $name$ CREATE line enables the administrator to make a queue on the network. If you want to create a queue for a laser printer, for example, type **Q LASERQ CREATE.** A hexidecimally-named subdirectory is created automatically on the network for storing print jobs.

The P n ADD $queuename$ AT PRIORITY x statement hooks up the queue with the appropriate printer. You type the following command to attach printer 0 with the LASERQ queue:

```
P 0 ADD LASERQ
```

Normally, each printer has one queue. Other configurations are available, depending upon the needs of the users on your network. Queues also can have priorities. Priority 1 is the highest. No other queues are serviced until the queue with priority 1 is empty. Then the queue with priority 2 is serviced. To add a queue called DRAFTMODE to PrinterQ at priority 2, for example, use the following command:

```
PQ ADD DRATMODE AT PRIORITY 2
```

The S *n* TO *queuename* command enables the administrator to accomplish the following:

- Create a path for a default queue. This helps when a user issues a CAPTURE or NPRINT statement without any flags. If a default queue is not chosen with the spool statement, the user will receive an error message.

- Route jobs from applications that print to printer numbers. Many older applications are hard-coded to print to printer numbers. NetWare no longer enables the user to specify a printer number. To ensure the file printing, a spool statement also enables administrators to designate which queue a job will go to if the application sends it to a printer number.

- Print on a v2.2 system. The v2.0*a* NetWare program used the SPOOL statement instead of the CAPTURE statement. This option enables v2.0*a* system users to print on both v2.0*a* and v2.2 operating systems.

All of the preceding commands can be entered into the file server at the colon prompt. The best place, however, for these commands is the AUTOEXEC.SYS file that can be edited in the SYSCON Supervisor Options. When entered at the prompt, these commands are valid only while the file server remains running. Downing the file server loses all of the command's information except queue names. Putting these commands into the AUTOEXEC.SYS file ensures that they will be executed whenever the file server is rebooted.

One Printer Servicing Multiple Queues

Figure 8.1 shows an example of one printer that is serviced by three queues. Each queue in this example is set at a different priority. The DEFAULT queue is set at priority 3, RUSH is set at priority 2, and

NOW is set at priority 1. Users, by setting up system defaults, print to the DEFAULT queue. If a rush job comes in, it is sent to the RUSH queue. In the event of a super-high priority job coming in while there are jobs in the RUSH queue, that print job is sent to the NOW queue. Jobs currently printing are allowed to finish before priority queues are serviced.

Figure 8.1:
One printer
serviced by
multiple queues.

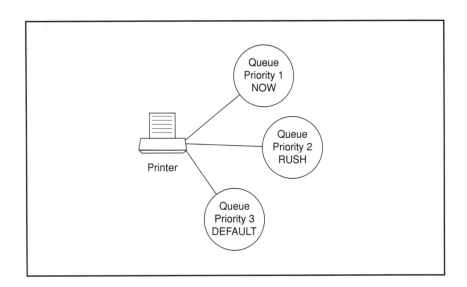

To implement this type of networked printing, type the following commands:

```
Q DEFAULT CREATE
Q RUSH CREATE
Q NOW CREATE
P 0 CREATE LPT1
P 0 ADD DEFAULT AT PRIORITY 3
P 0 ADD RUSH AT PRIORITY 2
P 0 ADD NOW AT PRIORITY 1
```

One Queue Using Identical Printers

In the example shown in figure 8.2, one queue is used to service three printers. This setup requires identical printers. Whenever a job enters the queue, the queue polls the printers to find the next available printer and sends the job there. Jobs are processed very quickly using this arrangement.

To implement this procedure, type the following commands:

```
Q  LASERQ  CREATE
P  0  CREATE  LPT1
P1 CREATE  LPT2
P2 CREATE  LPT3
P  0  ADD  LASERQ
P  1  ADD  LASERQ
P  2  ADD  LASERQ
```

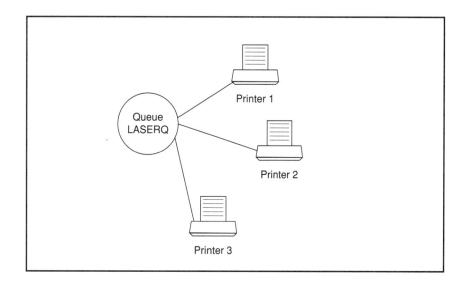

Figure 8.2:
An example of
using one printer
queue to service
multiple printers.

Defining Queues Using PCONSOLE

The PCONSOLE menu utility enables system supervisors to create and define queues and print servers. Queue operators and print server operators can manage queues and print servers from this menu. Users can place jobs into queues and manage their own print jobs from this menu.

The first PCONSOLE menu, the Available Options menu (see fig. 8.3), enables you to choose from the following three options: changing to another server, looking at print queue information, and looking at print server information.

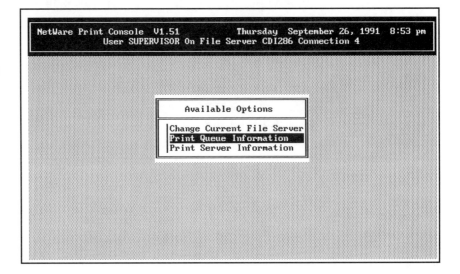

Figure 8.3:
PCONSOLE's main menu.

When you select the Print Queue Information option, a list of print queues display on-screen (see fig. 8.4). If you are a supervisor equivalent, you can create a new queue in this option by pressing Ins and entering the new queue.

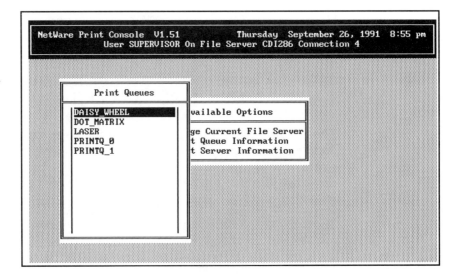

Figure 8.4:
PCONSOLE's print queue information.

When you press Enter on a queue, the Print Queue Information menu displays (see fig. 8.5). This menu has seven options, each of which is described in the following sections.

Figure 8.5:
PCONSOLE's specific queue information.

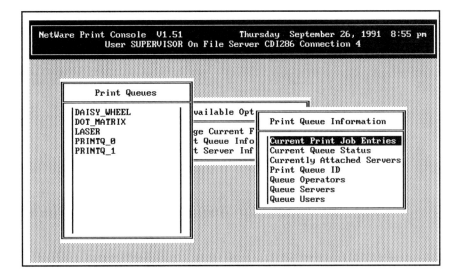

```
NetWare Print Console  V1.51              Thursday  September 26, 1991  8:55 pm
                   User SUPERVISOR On File Server CDI286 Connection 4

        Print Queues                 vailable Opt
                                                    Print Queue Information
   DAISY_WHEEL
   DOT_MATRIX                         ge Current F
   LASER                              t Queue Info   Current Print Job Entries
   PRINTQ_0                           t Server Inf   Current Queue Status
   PRINTQ_1                                          Currently Attached Servers
                                                     Print Queue ID
                                                     Queue Operators
                                                     Queue Servers
                                                     Queue Users
```

Current Print Job Entries

The Current Print Job Entries option in the Print Queue Information menu shows you all the jobs in a queue. The information is arranged, as illustrated in figure 8.6, in six columns. The first column, Seq, which stands for sequence, shows the order in which the jobs will be printed. The second column, Banner Name, is the name of the user sending the print job. Description, the third column, lists the file names. If the job is sent through a DOS command, such as PRINT, a print screen, or directed to a print device, then this column shows the logical port that the job was captured from and the word Catch, as shown in the third job in figure 8.6. The Form column shows which form has been mounted for this queue.

The fifth column, Status, displays one of five possible conditions: Active, Held, Adding, Waiting, and Ready.

The Active condition designates the job that is currently printing. No parameters can be changed for this job. If left alone, the job will print. You also can delete the job.

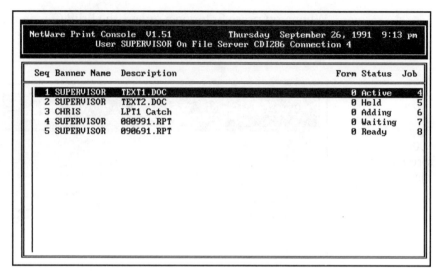

Figure 8.6:
An example of
PCONSOLE's active
jobs.

Any jobs marked with the Held condition are not printed until the
hold flag is removed. There are two different hold flags that can be
put on a job that has been queued to print. A User Hold can be placed
on the file by pressing Enter on the job and changing the User Hold to
Yes. The job owner and the queue operators can place and remove this
flag. The Operator Hold flag can be placed or removed only by the
queue operator. You can set this flag by pressing Enter on the job to be
held and setting the Operator Hold to Yes.

The Adding condition designates a job that is still in the process of
being sent by a user. If the user has exited an application and the job
still says ADDING, have the user type **ENDCAP,** which forces the job
into the Ready mode.

The Waiting condition is shown when a print job has been told to wait
for a specific date and time to occur before printing. Deferred printing
is set by pressing Enter on the queued job and setting Deferred Printing to Yes. You can define the Target Date and Time for that file to be
printed.

The Ready condition is put on any job that is available for printing.

The sixth column, Job, keeps track of the number of print jobs that
have gone through this queue since it was created.

Note All v3.x copies of NetWare currently do not show a valid number in the Job field.

You can press Enter on any queued job to display additional information about print jobs. Figure 8.7, for example, shows the information obtainable for each queued job and settable parameters after pressing Enter.

Figure 8.7:
Job entry
information in
PCONSOLE.

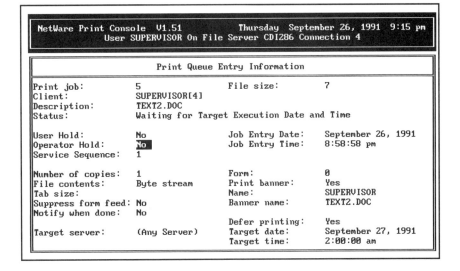

```
NetWare Print Console  V1.51              Thursday  September 26, 1991  9:15 pm
                   User SUPERVISOR On File Server CDI286 Connection 4


                          Print Queue Entry Information

Print job:          5                File size:          7
Client:             SUPERVISOR[4]
Description:        TEXT2.DOC
Status:             Waiting for Target Execution Date and Time

User Hold:          No               Job Entry Date:     September 26, 1991
Operator Hold:      No               Job Entry Time:     8:58:58 pm
Service Sequence:   1

Number of copies:   1                Form:               0
File contents:      Byte stream      Print banner:       Yes
Tab size:                            Name:               SUPERVISOR
Suppress form feed: No               Banner name:        TEXT2.DOC
Notify when done:   No
                                     Defer printing:     Yes
Target server:      (Any Server)     Target date:        September 27, 1991
                                     Target time:        2:00:00 am
```

Table 8.1 explains what some of the terms stand for in the Print Queue Entry Information screen.

You can add jobs at the Current Print Job Entries screen. Press Ins to bring up the current directory. Change to the directory containing the file to be printed and press Enter. The next screen is a list of all files in the directory (see fig. 8.8).

Once you highlight the file in this list to be printed, press Enter. If you wish to print several files, use F5 to mark each file, and then press Enter. The Print Job Configurations screen appears on-screen. This screen displays the list of printer configurations that you can use (see fig. 8.9). To select a configuration, highlight the configuration that you want to use, such as daisywheel, dotmatrix, laser, and then press Enter.

Table 8.1
Print Queue Entry Information

Item	Description
Print job	Specifies the job number in the queue.
File Size	Specifies the size of the print job.
Client	Specifies who sent the print job.
Description	Specifies the name of the job.
Status	Denotes the condition of the job.
User Hold	Denotes the print jobs that are placed or removed by the job owner or queue operator. Held jobs are not printed.
Operator Hold	Denotes the print jobs that are placed or removed by the queue operator. Held jobs are not printed.
Service Sequence	Specifies the order in which the job is printed. Reorganizes the order of print jobs.
Job Entry Data and Time	Shows the date and time that the queue received the job queue. These fields cannot be altered.
Number of copies	Specifies the number of copies of the file to be printed. This number can be set from 1 to 65,000.
File contents	Specifies text or byte stream print jobs. Text converts indents to spaces. Byte stream enables the application to determine the printer codes.
Tab size	Specifies the number of spaces to convert indents if File contents line is set to Text.
Suppress form feed	Turns form feed on or off.
Notify when done	Turns notification of job completion on or off.
Form	Sets the form number to use for the print job.
Print banner	Sets the banner to on or off.
Name	Displays the name printed on the banner. The sender's login name is the default.
Banner name	Displays the file name by default.

Table 8.1—continued

Target server	Displays the print servers that can service the current print job.
Defer Printing	Enables you to defer printing. Set to Yes or No.
Target date and time	Enables you to set the time and day. Default is set to the following day at 2:00 a.m.

Figure 8.8:
Selecting a file to print in PCONSOLE.

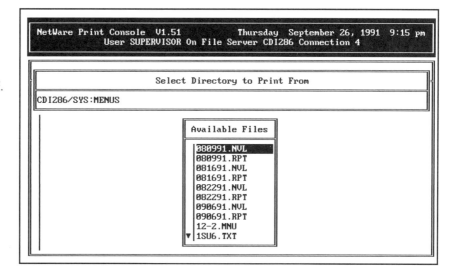

Figure 8.9:
The Print Job Configurations screen in PCONSOLE.

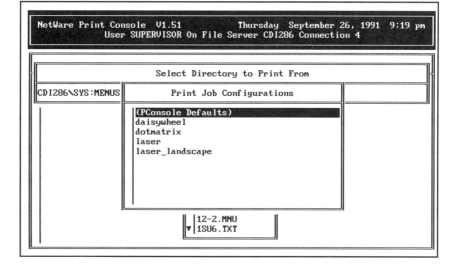

PCONSOLE then displays configuration options. After changing any necessary fields, press Esc and save the job. This job now appears in the queue to be printed.

Current Queue Status

The Current Queue Status option of the Print Queue Information menu has five items (see fig. 8.10). The Number of entries in queue: item shows you the number of print jobs currently in a queue. The Number of servers attached: item tells you the number of file servers that can use this queue. The Users can place entries in queue: item enables you to either put jobs (Yes) or not put jobs (No) into this queue. The Servers can service entries in queue: item enables you to have jobs printed (Yes) or not printed (No) in this queue. Like the preceding two choices, the New servers can attach to queue: item also has two options. Choosing Yes enables users on other file servers to use this queue. Choosing No denies users on other file servers access to this queue.

Figure 8.10:
PCONSOLE's Current Queue Status option.

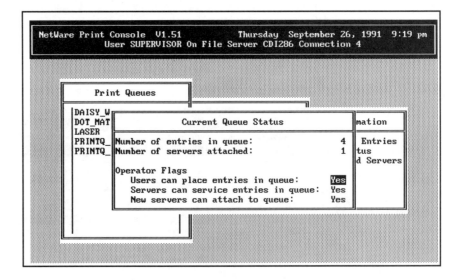

Currently Attached Servers

The Currently Attached Servers option of the Print Queue Information menu shows a list of all servers using this queue. This option can be used to see what file servers currently are putting jobs in to the queue.

Print Queue ID

The Print Queue ID option of the Print Queue Information menu indicates the name of the hexidecimally-named subdirectory under SYS:SYSTEM. Jobs printed to this queue are held in the subdirectory until printed.

Queue Operators

The Queue Operators option of the Print Queue Information menu lists all users who can manage the selected queue. *Queue operators* manage the queue and all jobs going through the queue. Supervisor equivalent users are automatically queue operators. Queue operators can rearrange the order in which the job will print. They also can mark print jobs as being held so that they do not print. To add users or groups to this list, press Ins and choose the users or groups that you want to manage this queue. Press Enter to accept your choices.

Queue Servers

The Queue Servers option of the Print Queue Information menu lists all the print servers that can service the selected queue. To add servers to this list, press Ins and choose the servers that you want to service this queue. Press Enter to accept your choices. After a printer is defined and attached to the selected queue, the print server that the printer was configured for appears on this list.

Queue Users

The Queue Users option of the Print Queue Information menu lists all the users and groups that can add jobs to this queue. The group labeled EVERYONE automatically becomes a queue user. To modify this list, delete the group EVERYONE. You then can add users or groups to this list by pressing Ins and choosing the users or groups that can use this queue. Press Enter to accept your choices.

Installing Print Servers

Print Servers can be either a file server or dedicated PC. PSERVER.VAP files are used on a router or v2.2 server, PSERVER.NLM files are used on a v3.11 server, and PSERVER.EXE files are loaded onto the PC that is the dedicated print server.

A NetWare print server can manage up to 16 printers. Five of those printers can be attached to the print server and the rest can be remote printers. A *remote printer* is any printer hooked up to a workstation that is attached to the network and can be used by other network users.

The following procedure shows the way to set up a basic print server that has two printers, one local and one remote. This setup can be modified to fit your networking needs.

1. Type **PCONSOLE**
2. Select the Print Queue Information option from the Available Options menu
3. Press Ins and add new queue names for every printer
4. Press Esc to return to the Available Options menu
5. Select the Print Server Information option
6. Press Ins to add new the print server name and press Enter (see fig. 8.11)
7. Select the Print Server Configuration option (see fig. 8.12)
8. Select the Printer Configuration option in the Print Server Configuration Menu (see fig. 8.13)

You now need to set up printers for local or remote ports. Choose a printer number that you want to configure and press Enter. Add a logical name for the printer and press Enter. Next, press Enter on the Type field. This displays the Printer types screen. The first seven options in this screen are for hooking up a printer to the print server (see fig 8.14). The next eight remote options in this screen are for remote printers.

Remote Other/Unknown enables the user running RPRINTER to define which LPT or COM port the printer is attached to. The last option on the Printer types screen, Defined elsewhere, assumes that another print server has this option defined.

Figure 8.11:
PCONSOLE's Print Server Information option.

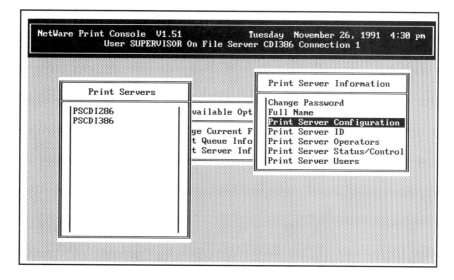

Figure 8.12:
PCONSOLE's Print Server Configuration option.

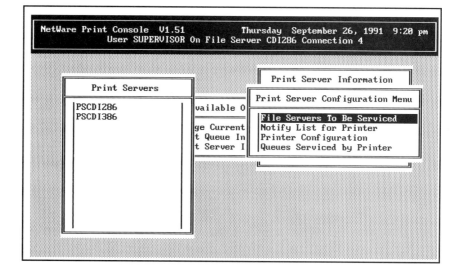

Figure 8.13:
Choosing
configured printers
in PCONSOLE.

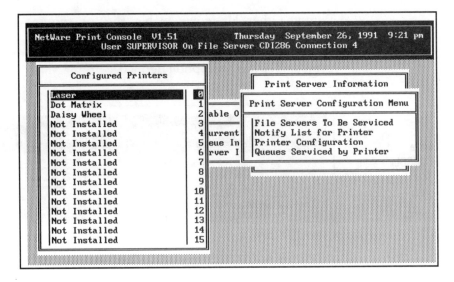

Figure 8.14:
Selecting printer
types in
PCONSOLE.

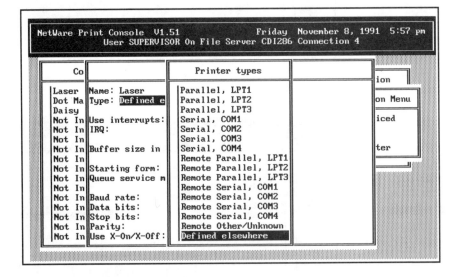

When you choose a printer type, NetWare displays several screens to
modify the printer setup (see fig. 8.15). When you are finished defining the printer options, press Esc. Then select Yes from the Save
Changes menu and press Esc.

Figure 8.15:
PCONSOLE's
Printer
Configuration
menu.

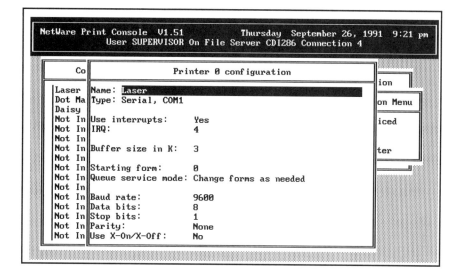

In the Print Server Configuration Menu, select the Queues Serviced by Printer option. Next, select the defined printer name in the Defined Printers screen (see fig. 8.16).

Figure 8.16:
Choosing a defined printer.

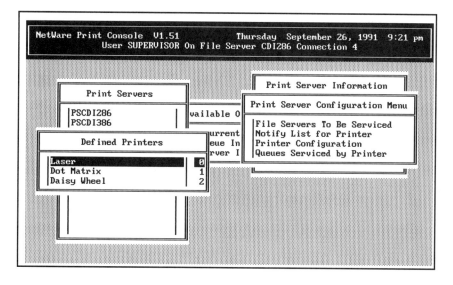

Press Ins to add a queue for each printer configured. Priority 1 is the highest queue that you can define, as shown in figure 8.17. Press Esc twice when finished.

Figure 8.17:
Adding a queue to a printer.

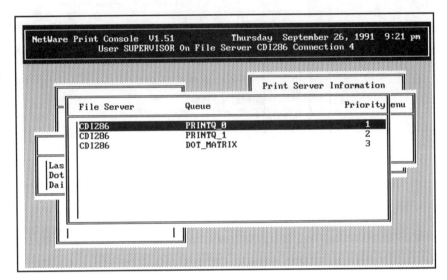

```
NetWare Print Console  V1.51              Thursday  September 26, 1991  9:21 pm
                   User SUPERVISOR On File Server CDI286 Connection 4

                                              ┌──────────────────────────────┐
                                              │  Print Server Information     │
               ┌────────────────────────────┐│                              │
              ┌┤ File Server      Queue                    Priority│enu      │
              │├CDI286            PRINTQ_0                       1  │         │
      ┌───────┤│CDI286            PRINTQ_1                       2            │
     │Las     ││CDI286            DOT_MATRIX                     3            │
     │Dot     │                                                 └────────────┘
     │Dai     │
              │
              │
              │
              └─────────────────────────┐
                │                      │
```

Next, select the Notify List for Printer option on the Print Server Configuration Menu. Then press Ins to add users or groups to notify if problems arise, such as if the printer is off-line or out of paper. At the top of the list of potential users and groups (see fig. 8.18), the option labeled (Job Owner) (Unknown Type) appears. This option reports any messages back to the job originator.

After choosing users or groups to be notified, the system prompts you for information about when they will be notified and how often. By default, the persons in the notify list are first told of printer problems in 30 seconds and again every 60 seconds until the problem is solved (see fig. 8.19). Press Esc three times when finished making your selections.

Select the Print Server Operators option in the Print Server Information menu. Then press Ins to add any users or groups that will need to support the print server. When finished making your selections, press Alt+F10 to return to DOS. At the file server, type the following to start the print server. You should spool printer 0:

```
SPOOL nn TO queue name
```

Figure 8.18:
The Notify
Candidates screen
for printer
problems.

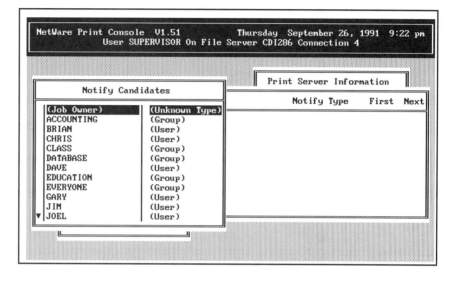

Figure 8.19:
The list of users to
be notified in case
of a printer
problem.

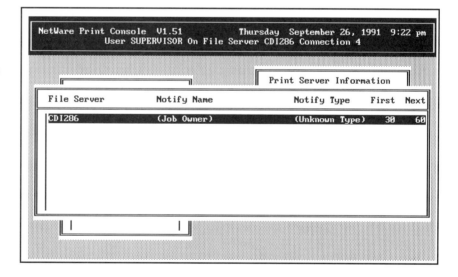

If you are at a workstation, type the following command to start the print server:

```
PSERVER printservername
```

Any workstation being used as a print server needs to have the number of sequenced packet exchange (SPX) connections increased. This can be done by creating a text file called SHELL.CFG. You need to place the line **SPX=60** in this file. This file needs to be in the directory from which IPX.COM is called when attaching to the file server (see fig. 8.20).

Figure 8.20:
The SHELL.CFG file and its contents.

```
A:\SHELLS>dir

 Volume in drive A is SYS
 Directory of   A:\SHELLS

SHELL    CFG          8  11-08-91   6:32p
TEMP     FIL          7   7-31-91   6:42p
IPX      COM      29919  10-10-91   6:38p
AUTOEXEC BAT         13   8-01-91   9:35a
NET3     COM      49198   2-06-91   4:44p
NET4     COM      49625   2-06-91   4:39p
NETBIOS  EXE      21506  11-15-90   3:48p
         7 File(s)   60473344 bytes free

A:\SHELLS>type shell.cfg
SPX=60

A:\SHELLS>
```

To start the print server at a v3.11 file server, type the following command. The file server then will prompt you for the name of the print server.

    LOAD PSERVER

To start the print server at a v2.2 file server, make sure that PSERVER.VAP is in the SYS:SYSTEM directory. Next, down the file server and reboot. As the file server boots, it will ask if you wish to load VAPs. Answer Yes and input the print server name.

No matter where the print server is activated, the main screen looks the same. Figure 8.21 shows a typical print server screen. When you press Spacebar, you can see the next group of printers—8 through 15.

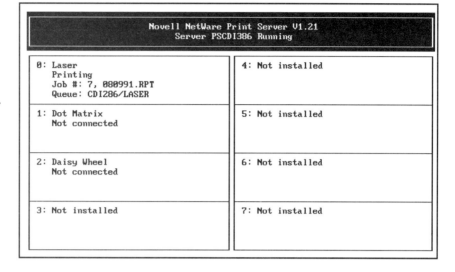

Figure 8.21:
An example of the print server information screen.

The final step in installing a print server is to type **RPRINTER** at each of the Remote Stations. A list of print servers then are displayed (see fig. 8.22). After choosing the print server, all available remote printer setups are displayed (see fig. 8.23). Select the workstation that you want and NetWare displays a message telling you that a successful installation of the 9K TSR (see fig. 8.24) has occurred.

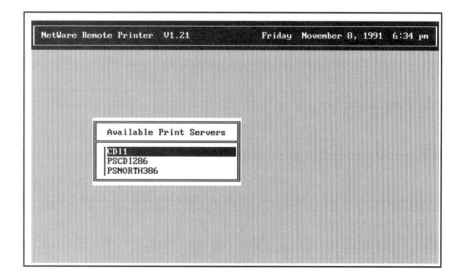

Figure 8.22:
RPRINTER's main menu selections.

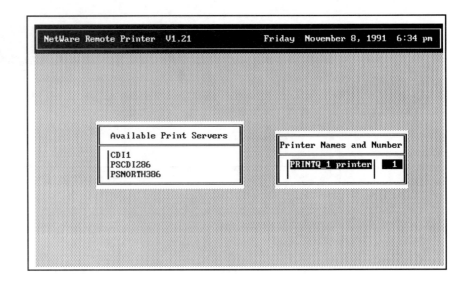

Figure 8.23:
RPRINTER's
remote printer
choices.

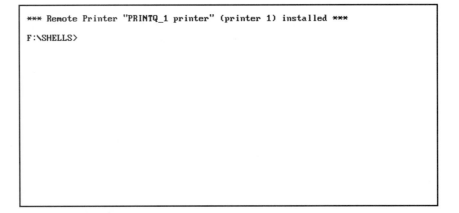

Figure 8.24:
RPRINTER's
installation
confirmation.

After the print server is installed, workstations can send jobs to net-work printers by indicating the queue name attached to those print-ers. The next section describes this process.

Novell's RPRINTER and Windows is at this time not a solid solu-tion. To get the best results, be sure to use the latest NetWare shells and add the following lines to your NET.CFG file:

```
SPX ABORT TIMEOUT = 4000
SPX LISTEN TIMOUT = 2500
```

Directing Printer Output

If you are using an application that was written to run on a Novell NetWare network, chances are that the program knows how to talk to a network printer. Many newer programs enable you to define a queue name as a print device. In these instances, the user will not be required to define the printing environment before entering the application.

A significant number of programs, however, still need help to print on a network. For these programs, the user must set up the printing environment before entering the program.

CAPTURE and NPRINT are two commands that enable you to print on the network. Figure 8.25 shows the way each command is filtered to the printer. CAPTURE sets up a printing environment for the user. This command dictates the way all print jobs sent by that user is directed, and does not change unless the user reissues a CAPTURE command or logs out. NPRINT is used outside of an application to send a file to a printer. This command is specific for a set of files and does not reset previous CAPTURE commands.

Figure 8.25:
Directing printer output by using the CAPTURE NPRINT commands.

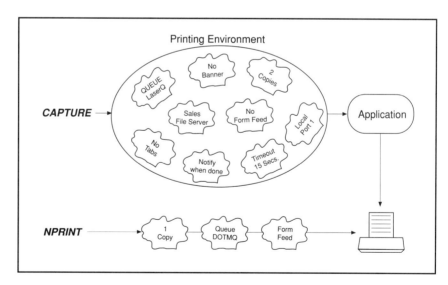

The CAPTURE Command

CAPTURE sets up the printing environment for a user. Before doing a print screen, the user must first do a CAPTURE statement.

Figure 8.26 shows an example of a CAPTURE statement that is directed to the queue called LASER, with no banners, no form feed, no tabs, and a timeout of 5 seconds.

Figure 8.26:
An example of using the CAPTURE command.

```
F:\DATA>capture q=laser nb nff ti=5 nt
Device LPT1: re-routed to queue LASER on server CDI286.

F:\DATA>
```

The CAPTURE command is not used to print existing files. CAPTURE is used to set up the way in which a file is printed. The generic form when using CAPTURE is the following:

CAPTURE *flags.*

The ENDCAP Command

If you use the CAPTURE command and it is set up for No Autoendcap, then ENDCAP must be specified at the DOS prompt before anything is printed. When you use the ENDCAP command by itself, it ends the CAPTURE statement to LPT1. ENDCAP also can be used to return the workstation ports to local use.

Table 8.2 lists the various flags that can be used to direct the ENDCAP statement.

Table 8.2
ENDCAP Flags

Flag	Description
ALL	Ends the CAPTURE statement on all ports, such as **ENDCAP ALL**
L=*n*	Stops the capture statement to a specified port. Replace *n* with the logical port number, such as **ENDCAP L=1**
C	Ends the CAPTURE statement to LPT1 and abandons any data without printing it, such as **ENDCAP C**
CL=n	Ends the CAPTURE statement for a specific port and discards the data to be printed, such as **ENDCAP CL=2**
C ALL	Ends the CAPTURE statement for all ports and abandons all data to be printed

The NPRINT Command

The NPRINT command is used to print data files or files that have been formatted for a specific printer. The syntax for NPRINT is the following:

```
NPRINT filenames flags
```

Wild cards are acceptable when indicating file names. A file name must be specified directly after the NPRINT statement and before indicating which flags to use.

Figure 8.27 shows an NPRINT statement that prints all files ending in RPT and sends the job to the LASER queue.

CAPTURE and NPRINT Flags

This section discusses each flag that you can use with the CAPTURE and NPRINT commands. See table 8.3 for a complete list and description of each flag.

Figure 8.27:
An example of
using the NPRINT
command.

```
F:\DATA>nprint *.rpt  j=laser
Queuing data to Server CDI286, Queue LASER.
CDI286\SYS:DATA
        Queuing file 092491.RPT
        Queuing file 092691.RPT
        Queuing file 092791.RPT
        Queuing file 092591.RPT

F:\DATA>
```

The following sections discuss the flags and tell you when you can use each with CAPTURE and NPRINT.

When you use the NOTI flag, NetWare notifies the user after the job is printed. When several jobs are buffered in the printer, you may want to know when the job is ready for the user to pick up. The normal default is not to notify the user when the job has been printed. Both NOTI and NNOTI work with CAPTURE and NPRINT. Use the following syntax lines for each flag:

```
CAPTURE NOTI
CAPTURE NNOTI
```

You can designate exactly where the job is to be printed by using the Print Server, Server, and Queue flags to specify the queue name, file server, and print server. If none of these is specified, the system relies on the SPOOL statement for printer 0 as the default. As mentioned earlier, you should spool printer 0. The S, PS, and Q flags work with both CAPTURE and NPRINT. Use the following syntax for these flags:

```
CAPTURE S=CDI386 PS=CDIPRINT Q=LASER
```

Table 8.3
CAPTURE and NPRINT Flags

Flag	Description
NOTI	NOTIfies when the job is done
NNOTI	Does not NOTIfy when the job is done
S	Specfies the Server
Q	Specifies the Queue
J	Specifies the Job configuration
F	Specifies the Form name
C	Specifies the number of Copies to print
T	Specifies the Tabs (TEXT)
NT	Specifies when No Tabs (BYTE STREAM) are used
B	Specifies when the Banner name is printed
NB	Specifies when No Banner is printed
NAM	Specifies the NAMe
FF	Specifies the Form Feed from the printer
NFF	Specifies No Form Feed from the printer
D	Deletes the file after it is printed
TI	Specifies the TImeout period before printing
AU	Denotes AUtoendcap
NA	Denotes No Autoendcap
L	Specifies the Local port
CR	CReates a file
K	Keeps the received portion of the job in the file server and prints it
SH	SHows the current CAPTURE settings
?	Lists the available flags

The PRINTCON menu utility enables the system administrator or user to create print jobs with parameters similar to the CAPTURE flags. The Job flag enables the user to call on one of the jobs that have been created. The J flag works with both CAPTURE and NPRINT. Use the following syntax with this flag:

```
CAPTURE J=LASER_LANDSCAPE
```

By using the PRINTDEF menu utility, the system supervisor can create forms. *Forms* in NetWare force a user to verify that the proper form is in the printer before printing starts. At the command line, the user can specify which form to use for a particular job. The default is form 0. The Form flag works with both CAPTURE and NPRINT. Use the following syntax with this flag:

```
CAPTURE F=14
```

At the DOS prompt, you can specify between 1 and 999 copies of a particular job. The system default is one copy. The Copies flag works with both CAPTURE and NPRINT. Use the following syntax with this flag:

```
CAPTURE C=3
```

When sending a print job to the printer as a text file, the Tabs flag is the fastest method of printing. Formatting codes are interpreted by the printer and text is printed. NetWare enables you to set the number of spaces between tabs at the command line. The default is 8.

When you use the No Tabs flag, all control characters are interpreted by the sending application. This also is called *byte stream printing*. This method is slightly slower than text.

If an application is sending simple text, such as a spreadsheet, send the job as Tabs. If the application sends fancy text, such as a desktop publisher, send the job as No Tabs.

A Note from the Author...

If the printer adds miscellaneous characters on the page, switch printing methods. If you print the file by using the Tabs flag (text), then resend the print job and use the Not Tabs flag (byte stream). The problem may occur when codes are being interpreted; the alternative method usually clears up any problems.

The T and NT flags work with both CAPTURE and NPRINT. Use the following syntax with these flags:

```
CAPTURE T=5
CAPTURE NT
```

The network, by default, sets up a banner page before each job is printed. This page contains information about who sent the job, the name of the file and when and where it was printed. The banner page is separated into three sections. The top section is information about the job and sender and cannot be modified. The second section is the name of the sender by default and can be changed by using NAM=n (up to 12 characters). The third section, by default, is the name of the file and can be changed by using B=n (up to 12 characters).

If you do not have a need for a banner page, use the No Banner flag after the CAPTURE statement.

The Banner, No Banner, and NAMe flags work with both CAPTURE and NPRINT. Use the following syntax with these flags:

```
CAPTURE NAM=GARY B=JUNERPT
CAPTURE NB
```

Sometimes printers give you more or less paper than what you really need. The Form Feed and No Form Feed flags are designed to help you tell the printer what you are expecting. Many laser printers kick out extra sheets of paper. Use the NFF switch to tell the printer not to send out the extra sheet after the job is done.

Dot Matrix printers often stop and reset the Top of Form if you send only a half page of data. To make sure that the printer returns to the true top of page use FF to issue a form feed after the print job.

The FF and NFF flags work with both CAPTURE and NPRINT. Use the following syntax with this flag:

```
CAPTURE NFF
```

The Delete flag only works with NPRINT. When the print job is finished, the file is automatically deleted from the system. Use the following syntax with this flag:

```
NPRINT SYS:DATA\*.RPT D
```

The system default requires you to exit, or *shell out*, to DOS before the job is printed. This is considered Autoendcap. Nothing prints until the user exits the program.

Most of the time, a user wants the job to print before exiting an application. The Timeout flag is designed to help the user print immediately and can be set from 0 to 1,000 seconds. This feature tells the system the amount of time to wait for new information to be sent to the printer before considering the job closed and it can start to print. 15 seconds is an average timeout period, but some applications may require more time.

Occasionally, you may find that neither the timeout flag nor the autoendcap flag produces the desired results. Some printers that contain down-loadable fonts, in combination with graphical interfaces, cannot work with an automatic endcap. In cases like this, you can use the No Autoendcap flag to enable the printer to work. Before the job prints, the user first must type **ENDCAP** at the DOS prompt. LOGIN, LOGOUT, NPRINT, and CAPTURE also force an ENDCAP statement.

The Autoendcap, No Autoendcap, and TImeout flags work only with CAPTURE. Use the following syntax with these flags:

```
CAPTURE TI=15
CAPTURE NA
```

NetWare enables the user to specify capture statements for up to three logical LPT ports. If you need two or three different capture statements, depending on the application you are using, CAPTURE can be run each time the user accesses the program. An alternative method is to issue different CAPTURE statements for each logical port and to tell the application which LPT port to use.

The Local Port flag works only with CAPTURE. Use the following syntax with this flag:

```
CAPTURE L=1 Q=LASER NFF
CAPTURE L=2 Q=LASER FF NT
CAPTURE L=3 Q=DOTMATRIX
```

Print jobs can be captured to a file instead of to a printer. This method imports screen captures to an editor or accumulates data from multiple programs. When using the Create flag, you must include the path and file name. By default, if you capture to a file that was previously used, the existing contents are overwritten with the new print job. To append information to a CAPTURE CR= file, use NA after the file name.

The CR flag works only with CAPTURE. Use the following syntax with this flag:

```
CAPTURE CR=SYS:DATA\SAVE.SCR NA
```

If there is a risk of your workstation hanging up or disconnecting during the printing process, use the Keep flag. This ensures that the server knows to accept as much of the job as possible and print it. The default environment permits the file server to discard print jobs if the sending workstation is disconnected during the print job.

The K flag works only with CAPTURE. Use the following syntax with this flag:

```
CAPTURE K
```

NetWare displays the current CAPTURE settings for a user. Figure 8.28 shows the capture statement that was issued and the result shown by using the SHow flag.

Figure 8.28:
Displaying current CAPTURE settings by using the SHow flag.

```
F:\DATA>capture q=laser nb nff ti=5 nt
Device LPT1: re-routed to queue LASER on server CDI286.

F:\DATA>capture sh

LPT1:   Capturing data to server CDI286 queue LASER.
        User will not be notified after the files are printed.
        Capture Defaults:Enabled        Automatic Endcap:Enabled
        Banner  :(None)                 Form Feed        :No
        Copies  :1                      Tabs             :No conversion
        Form    :0                      Timeout Count :5 seconds

LPT2:   Capturing Is Not Currently Active.

LPT3:   Capturing Is Not Currently Active.

F:\DATA>
```

The ? flag lists all of the available flags. SH and ? work only with CAP-TURE. Use the following syntax with these flags:

```
CAPTURE SH
CAPTURE ?
```

Controlling the Print Server

After you get the print server up and running, a new option displays in the Print Server Information menu (see fig. 8.29). This option, Print Server Status/Control, enables a print server operator to manage the print server (see fig. 8.30).

Under Printer Status, a print server operator can view information about the job currently being serviced. Figure 8.31 shows a job that has just entered the queue.

The Status: line shows that this job is being sent to the printer. The following service modes are available:

- **Change forms as needed.** Prompts the user to change forms each time a different form is encountered.

- **Minimize form changes across queues.** Specifies that the printer print all jobs with the same form number before proceeding to the next highest form number. This is done for all queues regardless of queue priorities.

Figure 8.29:
The Print Server
Information menu.

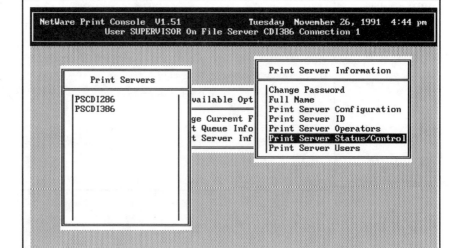

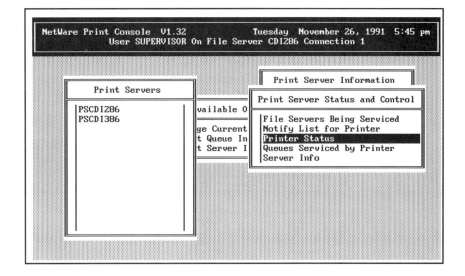

Figure 8.30:
The Print Server Status/Control menu.

- **Minimize form changes within queue.** Specifies that the printer print all jobs within a high-priority queue that share similar form numbers before servicing lower-priority queues.

- **Service only currently mounted form.** Prints only the jobs that have the current form number.

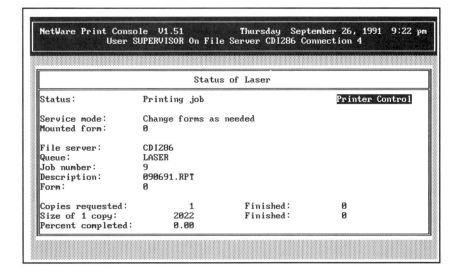

Figure 8.31:
An example of a print job status.

When the printer status screen displays, the Printer Control field is highlighted. Press Enter to display the next options menu (see fig. 8.32). The following options enable you to modify the print job that is currently printing. These options are not available from the Print Queue options, which enable you to modify only those print jobs that are not currently printing.

Figure 8.32:
The Printer Control menu.

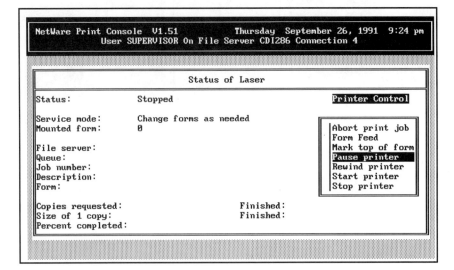

- **Abort a print job.** Enables the printer to abandon the current job. The job then is deleted from the queue.

- **Send a form feed.** Specifies that the printer advance to the top of the next page.

- **Mark the top of form.** Prints a row of asterisks (*) across the top of the page to check for form alignment.

- **Pause the printer.** Pauses the printer temporarily. To restart the printer, select the Start Printer option.

- **Rewind a printer.** Enables the printer to rewind a specific number of bytes or advance a specific number of bytes. This line also enables you to specify which copy to print if multiple copies are specified at the time of printing.

- **Start a printer.** Starts the printer if stopped or paused.

- **Stop a printer.** Stops the printer and returns the print job to the queue. Printing is stopped until the printer is started again by using the Start Printer option.

You now can select the Server Info item of the Print Server Status and Control menu. The Print Server Info/Status screen (see fig. 8.33) then displays the following information about the print server:

Figure 8.33:
An example of the Print Server Info/Status screen.

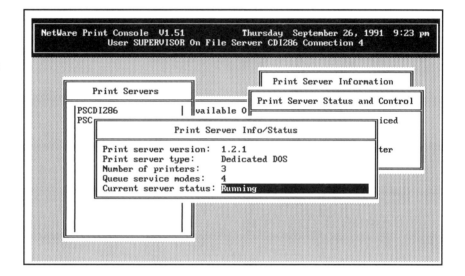

- **Print server version.** Specifies that the print server version is 1.2.1

- **Print server type.** Specifies that the print server is running on a dedicated DOS machine rather than on the file server

- **Number of printers.** Specifies that the print server is hosting three printers

- **Queue service modes.** Denotes the number of service modes available

- **Current server status.** Specifies that the print server is currently running

When you select the Current server status: option, a screen displays (see fig. 8.34) that enables the server operator to do the following three things: down the print server immediately, down the print server after the last job is printed, or enable the server to continue running.

Figure 8.34:
The Print Server
info/Status menu.

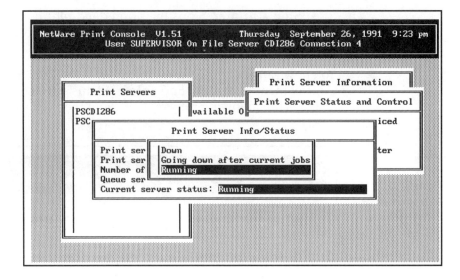

Customizing Printers Using PRINTDEF

NetWare's PRINTDEF menu utility enables a system administrator to
create forms and define printers (see fig. 8.35).

Figure 8.35:
PRINTDEF's main
menu.

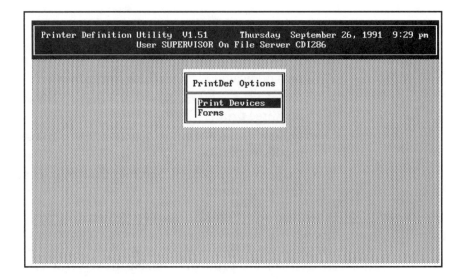

Print Devices

If you have a printer that is capable of advanced features and fonts, and you are using a program that does not know the way to make use of the printer's capabilities, then you can use PRINTDEF to solve this problem. A good example of this is when you want to print out a document sideways from a spreadsheet program using condensed print. This type of printing may be difficult to set up internally in the spreadsheet program. By using PRINTDEF, however, you can define a mode that has the functions necessary for the printer to print condensed and sideways.

To edit, import, or export print devices, select the Print Devices option in the PRINTDEF Options menu. The Print Device Options screen then displays on-screen (see fig. 8.36).

Figure 8.36:
PRINTDEF's Print Device Options menu.

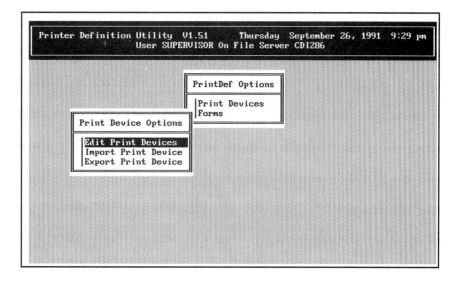

The PRINTDEF command contains a database of information about printers. Each printer has an entry in this database. If you had created a print device and wanted to let it be used on another network, you would choose the Export Print Device option. This option enables you to create a file with a PDF (printer definition file) extension that can be copied and imported into another network.

Importing is done when an administrator wants to use a PDF file that someone else has created. A large list of printer definition files are included with NetWare. These files are copied into the SYS:PUBLIC directory.

To see a list of PDF files in the SYS:PUBLIC directory (or whatever directory the files are stored in), select the Import Print Device option in the Print Device Options menu. Press Enter again and NetWare displays a list of PDF files (see fig. 8.37). To import a PDF file into the list of editable items, highlight the file and press Enter.

Figure 8.37:
PRINTDEF's
available files.

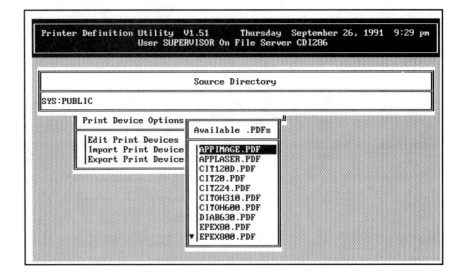

If you activate the Edit Print Devices option, a submenu appears that enables you to edit device modes or edit device functions (see fig. 8.38). A *device mode* is a list of functions that produce a desired output.

You must begin this editing process by first activating the Device Functions choice. When you press Enter after highlighting the Device Functions option, NetWare displays a screen that shows all of the escape sequences necessary for a specific printer (see fig 8.39). To add new functions, press Ins and input the escape codes. The codes can be input in either ASCII or hexadecimal format.

Figure 8.38:
PRINTDEF's Edit Device Options menu.

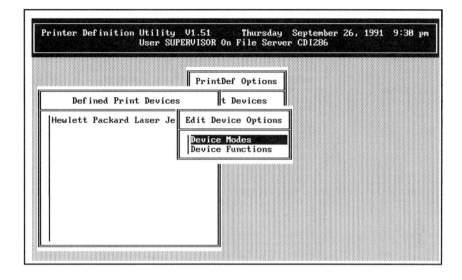

Figure 8.39:
PRINTDEF's printer escape codes.

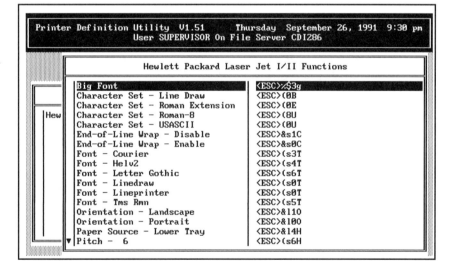

The other Edit Device Option, Device Modes, enables you to combine print functions to customize the printer output. As illustrated by figure 8.40, this example shows a Hewlett Packard LaserJet with the following possible settings: condensed, letter head, letter quality, spread sheet, memo, CAD drawings, sideways, and reinitialize.

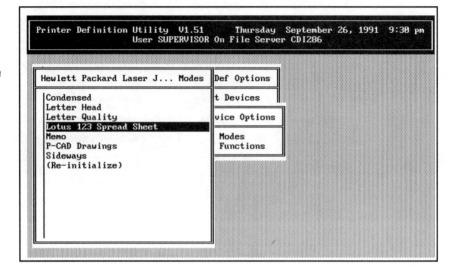

Figure 8.40:
PRINTDEF's Device Modes screen.

Figure 8.41 shows the suggested functions to print a Lotus 123 spreadsheet sideways.

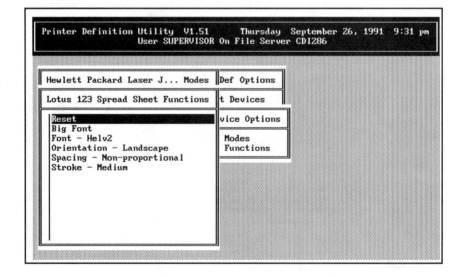

Figure 8.41:
The device mode for a spreadsheet.

To use the modes and devices defined here, you need to set up print job configurations in PRINTCON, which is discussed in the next section.

Forms

The second choice under the PRINTDEF Options menu is Forms. Some businesses need to share one printer for several different types of forms. By forcing different forms, you can attempt to control the use of the printer. Each time the printer encounters a change of form, it waits until either a statement is typed at the file server (such as PRINTER *printernumber* MOUNT *formnumber*) or the Print Server Command is issued (such as PSC PS=*printserver* P=*printer* MO=2). You can replace *formnumber* with *formname* when mounting a form with PSC.

After you select the Forms option, NetWare displays the Forms and Form Definition screen. Table 8.4 describes the four items that you need to fill in to define a form, as shown in figure 8.42.

Figure 8.42:
Defining a form in
PRINTDEF.

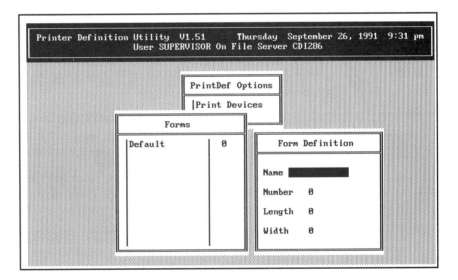

Table 8.4
Form Definitions

Item	Definition
Name	Specifies the name of the form, up to 12 characters
Number	Specifies the form number, from 0 to 255
Length	Indicates the number of lines in the form, between 1 and 255
Width	Indicates the number of columns in the form, between 1 and 999

The length and width of the form are there to help the administrator keep track of the use of that form. Neither the network nor the printer are affected by these numbers.

Creating Print Jobs Using PRINTCON

The PRINTCON command enables administrators and users to create print configurations. This means the difference between a user needing to know each of the CAPTURE flags or learning the name of a print job that uses all the same flags. Jobs work as shortcuts. You usually can remember job names easier than you can all of the flags that make up the job name.

The main menu in PRINTCON displays three options for supervisors (see fig. 8.43). Regular network users see only the first two options. Only supervisors can copy print job configurations.

To display a list of jobs, select the Edit Print Job Configuration option in the Available Options menu (see fig. 8.44). You then can add a new job by pressing Ins or modify a current job by pressing Enter.

Many of the flags available for CAPTURE and NPRINT can be set up in the Print Job Configuration screen, as shown in figure 8.45. The bottom half of the screen also enables you to use the Device and Modes that were set up in PRINTDEF.

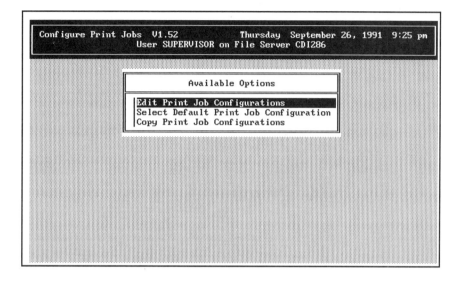

Figure 8.43:
PRINTCON's main menu.

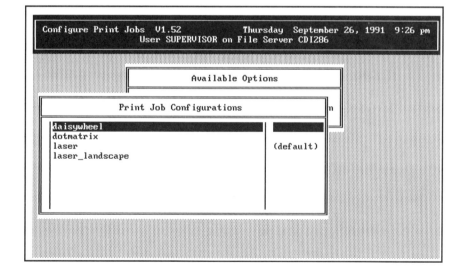

Figure 8.44:
An example of PRINTCON's available jobs.

In the example shown in figure 8.45, the print job named "laser" sends the printout to the queue named LASER. This queue is serviced by the print server PSCDI386, which is defined on the file server CDI386. To use this job, the user needs only type the following command:

```
CAPTURE J=LASER
```

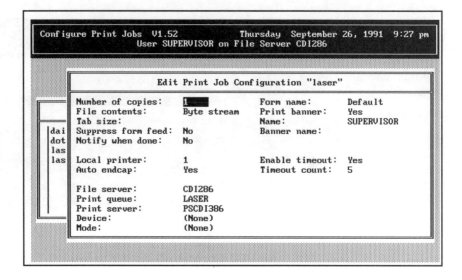

Figure 8.45:
PRINTCON's Edit
Print Job
Configuration
menu.

Without setting up this printer job to include all the parameters in figure 8.45, the user would need to type the following rather than typing the preceding syntax:

```
CAPTURE S=CDI386 PS=PSCDI386 Q=LASER C=1 NT F=0
FF NAM=SUPERVISOR NNOTI L=1 AU TI=5
```

As you can see, it is much easier to set up the print job once, then type in the short job name.

The Select Default Print Job Configuration option in the Available Options menu enables you to choose which job is the default. If you issue a CAPTURE or NPRINT command without specifying any commands, the parameters of the default job are used.

The Copy Print Job Configurations option in the Available Options menu enables supervisors to copy PRINTCON jobs to other users. The personalized PRINTCON file is called PRINTCON.DAT and is kept in the user's ID directory under SYS:MAIL.

When you select the Copy Print Job Configurations option, NetWare displays the Source User: prompt (see fig. 8.46). At this prompt, you need to enter the name of the user (the *source user*) whose job you want to copy. NetWare then asks you for the name of the user, called the *target user*, to copy the selected file to (see fig. 8.47). The

PRINTCON.DAT file then is copied from the source user to the target user. You must perform this procedure separately for each user needing the selected file.

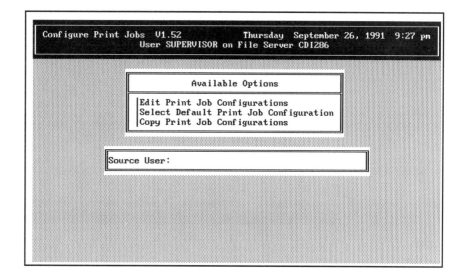

Figure 8.46:
The Source User prompt.

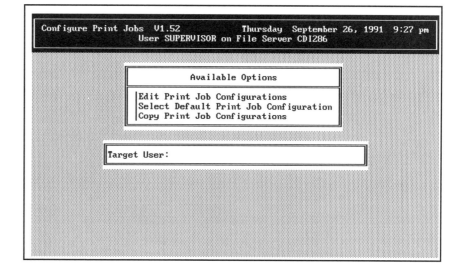

Figure 8.47:
The Target User prompt.

A Note from the Author...

The following steps enable you to make use of a common PRINTCON.DAT file that uses your files if defined or uses one kept in SYS:PUBLIC if undefined.

1. Copy the desired PRINTCON.DAT file into the SYS:PUBLIC directory.

2. Execute the following commands from the SYS:SYSTEM directory logged in as a supervisor and have Z: mapped to SYS:PUBLIC.

```
SMODE Z:PCONSOLE.EXE 5
SMODE Z:CAPTURE.EXE 5
SMODE Z:NPRINT.EXE 5
```

After you modify the search mode, the network uses this method to search for the specified file unless you issue another SMODE statement.

Using Related Print Commands

NetWare includes some commands for users and administrators to view and control print servers and print jobs. Although users have some control with these commands, unless they are supervisor equivalents, they may not have been granted the right to manipulate all parts of these utilities.

The PSTAT Command

The PSTAT command is effective only with core printing. PSTAT tells the user the following information:

- Which printers have been defined on the network
- Which printers are on-line or off-line
- Which printers are active or stopped
- Which form is currently mounted for a printer

Figure 8.48 shows an example of the PSTAT command.

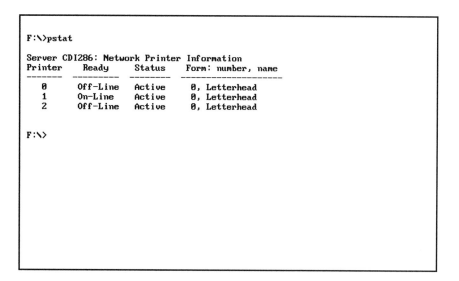

```
F:\>pstat

Server CDI286: Network Printer Information
Printer    Ready       Status     Form: number, name
-------    ---------   --------   --------------------
   0       Off-Line    Active     0, Letterhead
   1       On-Line     Active     0, Letterhead
   2       Off-Line    Active     0, Letterhead


F:\>
```

The PSC Command

The PSC command, which stands for Print Server Command, is used
to control and view the status of print servers. Many of the functions
that can be controlled with PSC also can be done from within
PCONSOLE. Sometimes, though, you may find that issuing a command at the DOS prompt is quicker than accessing a menu utility.
Table 8.5 lists the various flags available in the PSC command.

The following section discusses each PSC flag in more detail.

The ABort flag stops the current job from printing. The job is deleted
from the queue. The following command tells Print Server PS1 to abort
the job going to printer 2:

```
PSC PS=PS1 P=2 AB
```

The Cancel Down flag enables print server operators to override the
PCONSOLE command after the Going down after current jobs option
in PCONSOLE is selected to down the print server. Use the following
syntax when issuing this flag:

```
PSC PS=PS1 CD
```

Table 8.5
PSC Flags

Flag	Description
AB	ABorts the print job
CD	Cancels a Down server
FF	Advances (Form Feeds) the printer to the top of the next page
K	Keeps the received portion of the job in the file server and prints it
MA	MArks an asterisk (*) at the printer head
MO	Specifies a different MOunt form
PAU	PAUses the printer
PRI	Specifies that the printer is PRIvate
SH	Enables the printer to be SHared
STAR	STARts the print job
STAT	Shows the STATus of the connected printers
STO	STOps the print job

The Form Feed flag is used to advance the printer to the top of the next page. The user must stop or pause the printer before a form feed can be issued. Use the following syntax when issuing this flag:

```
PSC PS=PS1 FF
```

The MArk flag is used to position the form in the printer. The MArk flag places an asterisk (*) at the position of the printer head. The user can use any character to mark the form by placing that character after the MArk flag. When issuing this flag, use the following syntax:

```
PSC PS=PS1 MA ?
```

The MOunt Form flag is used if you choose a form number different than the one that is currently mounted. The correct syntax is MO=*formnumber*. Use the following example when issuing this flag:

```
PSC PS=PS1 P=0 MO=2
```

The PAUse flag temporarily pauses a printer. Use the STARt flag to resume printing. Use the following syntax when issuing the PAUse flag:

```
PSC PS=PS1 P=3 PAU
```

The PRIvate flag is used when you are at a remote printer and want to prevent others from using the attached printer. This flag removes the printer from the print server list. When issuing this flag, use the following syntax:

```
PSC PS=PS1 P=2 PRI
```

The SHared flag is used after issuing the PRIvate flag. This flag enables the remote printer to be used as a network printer again. Use the following syntax when using this flag:

```
PSC PS=PS1 P=2 SH
```

The STARt flag is used to resume printing if the STOp or PAUse flags are issued. The syntax for this flag is the following:

```
PSC PS=PS1 P=2 STAR
```

Use the STATus flag to show the status of printers connected to a specific print server (see fig. 8.49).

Figure 8.49:
An example of a
PSC status.

```
F:\>psc ps=pscdi286 stat
Printer 0: PRINTQ_0 Printer
Printing job
Off-line

Printer 1: PRINTQ_1 printer
Not connected

F:\>
```

STAT can display the following messages:

```
In private mode
Mark/Form feed
Mount Form n
Not Connected
Not installed
Off-line
Out of paper
Paused
Printing Job
Ready to go down
Stopped
Waiting for a job
```

The STOp flag is used to stop the printer. If the print job needs to be resubmitted from the beginning, then the Keep flag also should be used. Otherwise, the job is deleted from the queue. When issuing this flag, use the following syntax:

```
PSC PS=PS1 P=3 STO K
```

The SET Command

A user may need to use the PSC command on the same printer server and printer often enough to become frustrated by all the information that is necessary to remember. A default print server and printer can be specified either at the DOS prompt or from within a login script.

At the DOS prompt, type the following command:

```
SET PSC=PSprintserver Pprinternumber
```

A the login script, type the following command:

```
SET PSC="PSprintserver Pprinternumber"
```

Summary

In this chapter, you learned about the many different ways that you can set up printing on a NetWare network. Whatever your printing needs, NetWare has a method that will assist you in printing to any printer on your network. This chapter discussed the three menu utilities that you can use to set up printing—PCONSOLE, PRINTDEF, and PRINTCON. You also were shown the way command line utilities, such as PSC and CAPTURE, help you set up print jobs on NetWare.

Many applications are available for end users that can handle all printer options from within the application. The command line utilities discussed in this chapter are used if the application you are using does not recognize network printer queues.

In Chapter 9, you are shown methods for making printing automatically available to users by using login scripts and menus. You also learn about the options that are available to administrators to help them make networking easy and reliable for all users on the network.

9

Setting Up the NetWare Environment for Users

T he system administrator does the most work in setting up the network for end users so they can be more productive by using the network. The goal of networking with NetWare is to make the system as easy as possible to use for the people running applications.

Automating the system for users accomplishes this goal. The best automation system is a turn-key network. In a *turn-key* system, the user turns on the power for his or her workstation, and the process of booting into the network occurs through batch files. The process of setting up all paths to applications and environment variables is done through login scripts. Finally, the user is placed directly into an application, or if further choices are to be made, the user arrives at a menu that has customized choices available.

With this system, the user does not need to know the way the network functions. This system is common in large networks in which training every user on the details of networking is not practical. This method also helps to keep users out of trouble by setting up their work environments so that they are not hampered by entering lines of syntax.

This chapter examines the way to design the working environment for users. You examine drive mappings and why they are used, the three different kinds of login scripts and their uses, and customized menus. You can use each of these features alone or in any combination to fit your needs.

In this chapter, you learn about the following aspects of networking with NetWare:

- Mastering drive mappings
- Developing usable login scripts
- Creating custom menus
- Exploring the utilities for end users

This chapter also presents a list of network commands designed for the end user. These commands are simple utilities that end users can access when working on the network. With these utilities, users can send short messages to other users, attempt to retrieve accidentally deleted files, change their passwords, and list who is logged in to the network.

Before you attempt to use any of the utilities discussed in this chapter, you may want to list on paper all requirements for each user on the network. By grouping together similar types of users, you can make it easier to design a versatile environment.

Mastering Drive Mappings

NetWare uses *drive mappings* to enable users to quickly access commonly used directories. Drive mappings are necessary for all NetWare networks. This section discusses the following types of mappings that are available in NetWare and the ways you can use them to customize your network:

- Mappings to local drives
- Mappings to network data directories
- Search mappings to network program directories

You can think of drive mappings as *bookmarks* in NetWare. If you are reading a text book or reference manual, for example, the easiest way to access useful data quickly is to mark the pages with bookmarks. Then, whenever you need to access this information, you easily can flip to the pages by using the bookmarks. Drive mappings in NetWare enable the user to quickly find the directory that he needs.

Networks and Drive Mappings

Networks have 26 available mappings. By pointing these bookmarks to frequently used directories, you can move to any of these directories in three keystrokes. Suppose, for example, that the directory structure shown in figure 9.1 is on the hard drive of a PC shared by several part-time employees. The morning-shift user, USERAM, needs to access several directories, marked A, B, and C.

Figure 9.1:
A sample directory structure.

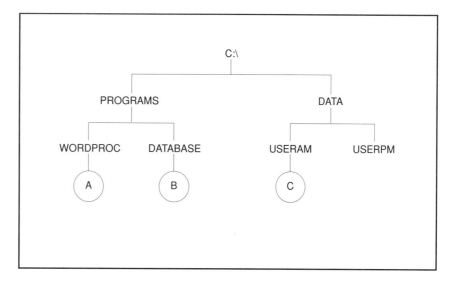

Now, suppose that USERAM boots the PC and begins the work day. First, USERAM needs to go to the word processing directory. At the C:\> prompt, the user types **CD PROGRAMS\WORDPROC**. When you include typing the space and pressing Enter, that is 21 keystrokes.

Next, USERAM needs to go to his home directory. From the C:\PROGRAMS\WORDPROC directory, USERAM needs to type

CD\DATA\USERAM to get to his home directory, which is a total of 15 keystrokes. USERAM'S manager now asks USERAM to print a database report, so USERAM must type **CD\PROGRAMS\ DATABASE**, which again is 21 keystrokes. These procedures can add up to a substantial number of keystrokes typed during the workday.

By using the same directory on a network, C:\ becomes the volume level. (Volumes are discussed in Chapter 6.) By assigning drive letters to each of these directories, USERAM can get to any of the directories in three keystrokes. Suppose, for example, that drive letter W: is assigned to the \PROGRAMS\WORDPROC directory, drive letter X: is assigned the \PROGRAMS\DATABASE directory, and drive letter H: is assigned to the \DATA\USERAM directory. To get to any of these directories, USERAM simply types **H:** and presses Enter, **W:** and presses Enter, or **X:** and presses Enter—just three keystrokes each time. Later in this chapter you are shown the requirements for setting up drive mappings on your network.

Networks and Search Drives

To make finding files in directories even easier, you can use *search drives*. These drive mappings enable you to place yourself in a directory created to store data and call the program from the searched drive. Most programs, unless otherwise configured, dump data into the same directory from which they were called. In NetWare, you can use search drives to help you locate certain files. NetWare performs the following basic steps whenever you ask for a file: first, the system searches for the file in the current directory. If the system fails to find the file in the current directory, the system searches each of the established search drives in order.

In NetWare, a maximum of 16 search drives are available out of a possible 26 drive mappings. The more search drives you use, the longer searches can take. Suppose, for example, that you have 16 search drives and are currently in a directory that is not set up as searchable. If you request a file that does not exist in any of these directories, the system searches through 17 directories before you receive a `File not found` error message. Another problem is that the system allocates file server RAM for search drives. The more search drives users have on the system, the more memory is taken away from the server.

Each user can create and use his or her own set of up to 26 drive mappings. The drive mappings that USERAM sets up, for example, have no effect on the mappings that USERPM creates. Figure 9.2 shows the way all 26 drive mappings can be mapped in NetWare. NetWare offers several options in assigning drive letters to a directory. These options are discussed later in this chapter.

Figure 9.2:
NetWare's default drive mappings.

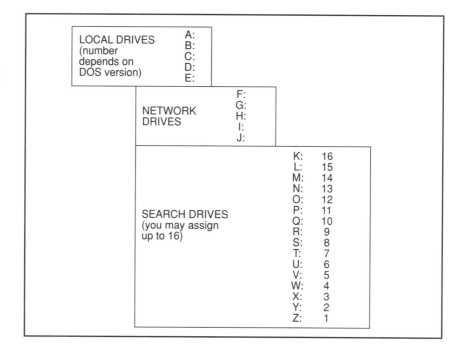

About Mappings and DOS Commands...

The DOS ASSIGN command fworks in a manner similar to network data directory mappings. Similarly, the DOS PATH statement is closely related to network search mappings. If you are not familiar with these DOS commands, try experimenting with them on a workstation with a hard drive. If you are comfortable with these commands in a DOS environment, you should be comfortable using the MAP command in NetWare.

Setting Up Drive Mappings

You can set up drive mappings in several places on the network. Two places are considered temporary, and three places are considered permanent. To set up drive mappings temporarily, you can type the command at the DOS prompt or from a menu called Session. Whenever you log out, these mappings are discarded. To set up drive mappings that are always available for use, use a system login script, user login script, or menu option.

With the exception of using SESSION, the syntax for defining drive mappings is the same. The syntax for drive mappings is discussed in the next few sections.

Using Local Drive Mappings

NetWare automatically allocates the letters A: through E: for local hardware. The drive letter A: refers to your first floppy drive, and B: refers to the second floppy drive. The drive letters C:, D:, and E: refer to local hard drives. Even if your workstations do not have all this local hardware, these drive letters are reserved. You can, however, redirect any of these drive letters to refer to a network drive. If a local drive is remapped to a network drive and then deleted, the drive letter reverts back to referring to the local drive. The following is an example of the way you can redirect the local drive E: to the network drive SYS:DATA:

```
MAP E:=SYS:DATA
```

Using Network Drive Mappings

You usually use network drive mappings with data directories. Several parameters are used when you map to a directory on the network. The following is the syntax for mapping network drives:

```
MAP options A-Z: = fileserver/volume:path
```

The following are the options that you can use in the preceding syntax:

- **NEXT.** This option enables you to map the next available drive letter. You can use this option when you are not sure which drive letters are not being used. End users using the DOS LAST DRIVE command can use this option to find the next open drive letter. When using this option, you do not specify a drive letter.

  This option also helps to prevent mapping over a drive letter that already has been mapped. When you map a drive letter that has been mapped previously, the original mapping is scrapped without an error message. By using the Next option, you preserve any existing mappings.

- ***#:.** This option is used only in login scripts and works in the same way as the NEXT option. *#: searches for the next unused drive letter and maps it to the directory.

- **ROOT.** Some older programs and many single-user programs require all rights in the root directory, which is an unacceptable request. To enable you to get around this requirement, NetWare enables you to specify a false root drive. A *false root drive* appears to be a real root directory to the user and the computer. A false root drive displays as a drive letter with a backslash, indicating that it is a root drive. When you use the CD\ command, you return to the false root, not the real root. To return to the real root, the user needs to type **CD *volume*:**, which returns the user to the true root of the volume.

  False root drives appear differently when you use the MAP command to display the drives. In figure 9.3, for example, S: is mapped to the false root of \APPS\SS. The user sees only part of the directory, in this case \DATA.

The choice of letters is up to you. Generally, a letter that mnemonically represents the directory path is chosen. This type of drive mapping should be done with directories holding data. Program directories should be search drives. You might, for example, map the drive letter M: to point to the \MENUS directory, as discussed in the following section. The following is an example syntax of this mapping:

```
MAP M:=SYS:MENUS
```

Figure 9.3:
An example of a
MAP screen.

```
S:\DATA>MAP

Drive  A:    maps to a local disk.
Drive  B:    maps to a local disk.
Drive  C:    maps to a local disk.
Drive  D:    maps to a local disk.
Drive  E:    maps to a local disk.
Drive  F: = CDI286\SYS:  \SHELLS
Drive  G: = CDI286\SYS:  \USERS\DAVE
Drive  S: = CDI286\SYS:APPS\SS  \DATA
       -----
SEARCH1:  = Z:. [CDI286\SYS:  \PUBLIC]
SEARCH2:  = Y:. [CDI286\SYS:  \PUBLIC\IBM_PC\MSDOS\V3.30]
SEARCH3:  = X:. [CDI286\SYS:  \APPS\SS]

S:\DATA>
```

If you are logged in to only one file server, you can skip the portion of the MAP command that refers to the file server name. Using the volume name always is recommended.

Using Search Drive Mappings

Search drive mappings are used with program directories to enable users to access programs while actually being at a DATA directory. The syntax for mapping regular drives follows:

MAP *options* **S***1-16***: = ** *fileserver*/*volume:path*

The following are the options that you can use in the preceding syntax:

- **INSERT.** This option puts a search mapping into a specific slot. INSERT ensures that an existing drive is not overwritten and that the new drive is put in the order specified.

About Path Statements...

If you require path statements to your local drives, always use INSERT for search drives. This procedure ensures that previous path statements to local drives are not overwritten.

By using this method, you can retain your DOS PATH statement when you log out of the network.

- **ROOT.** This option is the same as the ROOT option used for network data drive mappings. This option enables you to set false root directories. The command CD\ returns the user to the false root. To return to the real root, the user needs to type **CD** *volume:*, which returns the user to the true root of the volume.

When mapping a search drive, specify the drive letter and NetWare automatically assigns the next available drive letter starting at Z: and working backward through the alphabet.

Deleting Drive Mappings

Sometimes you may find that you are not using all of your current drive mappings. By eliminating these excess drive mappings, you can increase your file server performance by returning memory used for tracking search drives to the file server. Also, when a user exits an application and does not need access to a directory, you can maintain system security by deleting the drive mapping. This makes it more difficult to get to the directory through an existing mapping.

To delete a mapped data drive, use the following syntax:

    MAP DEL *drive letter:*

To delete a mapped search drive, use the following syntax:

    MAP DEL S *drive number:*

These commands take the mapping out of the list. You do not need to specify the full path to delete the drive mappings. NetWare is concerned only with the label, or drive letter.

Using the DOS CD Command on Drive Mappings

Drive mappings are *dynamic*, which means that they change. When you use the DOS CD command, drive mappings follow you around. As you learned in the previous sections, the MAP command establishes a drive letter and where that letter initially points. After the letter initially is set, you can determine where the letter points. To do this, use the CD command. This makes the mapping point to the new location. Drive mappings match the DOS prompt path; if it changes, the mapping reflects the change.

You might find that using the CD command can be a disadvantage if you issue it to a search drive. You may search a drive that does not need to be searched, as well as lose the path to a directory that is needed to run a program. If you find that you are lost, simply log in again. This procedure resets your mappings to the way they were set up in the login scripts.

Note

Figure 9.4 shows the screen that Windows provides for doing your mappings. Novell's Windows utilities follow the traditional *point-and-shoot* method of choosing a directory.

Figure 9.4:
The Windows
mapping screen.

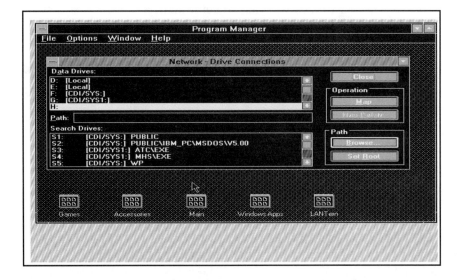

The following example shows what happens to search mappings when you use the DOS CD command:

1. Type **MAP F:=SYS:LOGIN**.

2. Check to see that Z: is the only drive mapped to SYS:PUBLIC.

3. Change to Z: and type **NDIR \MAP.* /SUB**. This command searches the network for the MAP.EXE command. You should see only one file, and it should be in the SYS:PUBLIC directory.

4. Change to F: and type **MAP**. This command shows you which drives currently are mapped.

5. Change back to Z: and type **CD**.

6. Change back to F: and type **MAP**. This time, you should receive an error message informing you that the file was not found.

   You receive the error message because the search drive to the PUBLIC directory created from the system login script was changed by the CD command in step 6. The drive now points to the root of SYS:, but MAP is still in the SYS:PUBLIC directory.

7. Type **\PUBLIC\MAP**. Notice where Z: is pointing. It should show you that you would be searching the route of this volume.

8. Change back to Z: and type **CD\PUBLIC**. This command resets your drive mapping to point to the PUBLIC directory. The MAP command now works from any drive letter.

As long as you know the results of using the CD command, you can use it on a network. Most of the time, creating more drive mappings can alleviate the problems created by accidentally using the CD command in the network.

Developing Usable Login Scripts

Login scripts enable system managers to customize the network environment for users. Map commands, as were discussed in the previous section, are used in login scripts to establish paths to commonly used directories. This section discusses many other command options that can you put into login scripts. NetWare has three types of login scripts: system, user, and default. These login scripts are discussed in the following sections.

System Login Scripts

The *system login script* is a text file called NET$LOG.DAT stored in the SYS:PUBLIC directory. This file is created and maintained by the system supervisor in the SYSCON menu utility, under supervisor options.

The system login script is designed to service all users on the network. Whenever a user logs in to the network, the system executes this login script. The system login script includes drive mappings intended for all system users, global DOS set variables, and greeting messages (see fig. 9.5). System login scripts contain commands that all users need, such as a search mapping to SYS:PUBLIC. For more information on these commands, see the login script commands section later in this chapter.

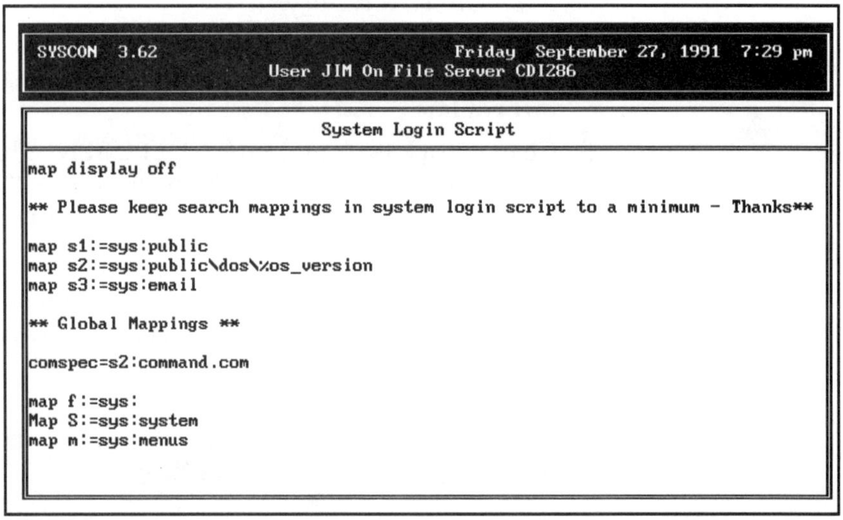

Figure 9.5:
An example of a system login script.

```
SYSCON  3.62                        Friday  September 27, 1991  7:29 pm
                      User JIM On File Server CDI286

                          System Login Script

map display off

** Please keep search mappings in system login script to a minimum - Thanks**

map s1:=sys:public
map s2:=sys:public\dos\%os_version
map s3:=sys:email

** Global Mappings **

comspec=s2:command.com

map f:=sys:
Map S:=sys:system
map m:=sys:menus
```

User Login Scripts

User login scripts are created and maintained by system administrators or by individual users for themselves. This log file, called LOGIN, is held in the user ID directory under SYS:MAIL. User login scripts contain commands that personalize the network environment for the user. The following section on login script commands discusses the commands that can be used with these scripts.

Default Login Scripts

Default login scripts set up basic mappings on the network if a user login script does not exist. The commands found in the default login script are established as part of the LOGIN.EXE file and cannot be altered. For more information about default login scripts, see the v2.2 *Concepts Manual* or the v3.11 *Installation Manual*.

Script Parameters

NetWare offers a variety of script parameters. One parameter is called *identifier variables*. Identifier variables force the network to return information, such as the time of day or a workstation address.

Identifier variables need to be presented in uppercase characters when enclosed in quotation marks. Although many commands are not case sensitive, less debugging is necessary if you present items in uppercase characters.

Each login script command requires its own line. The maximum is 150 characters per line; however, 78 characters per line is recommended. Make sure that the line wraps naturally when it is longer than the width of the screen. Hard returns are interpreted as new lines. Also, you can use blank lines. Blank lines have no effect on the execution of the script, but help to break up its appearance.

A cut-and-paste feature also is available in the login script screens. Use F5 to mark items and the arrow keys to highlight a block of data. By pressing Del, you can remove the block. You can return the information to the screen by pressing Ins; you can use Ins as many times as needed as long as you do not exit SYSCON. Each time you use the blocking and deleting process, you replace previous data.

Login Script Commands

You can use all the login script commands in system login scripts or user login scripts. Keep in mind that everyone needs to go through the system login script; personalization can be done through variables or user login scripts. The following commands show you a variety of ways to make a login script "personal."

The MAP Command

The MAP command can be placed in login scripts. In regular drive mappings, the syntax is as follows:

MAP *options A-Z:* **=** *fileserver/volume:path*

The options you can use are ROOT and *#:.

In search drive mappings, the syntax is as follows:

MAP *options* **S***1-16:* **=** *fileserver/volume:path*

The options you can use are ROOT and INSERT.

NetWare also enables you to turn on and off what users see when they log in to the network. The DISPLAY statement functions like the DOS ECHO OFF command. MAP DISPLAY ON, which is the default, enables the user to see all commands as they are executed. MAP DISPLAY OFF does not display the login commands. The syntax for each follows:

```
MAP DISPLAY ON
MAP DISPLAY OFF
```

NetWare also provides many *identifier variables*, variables for which the file server automatically knows the values. You can use identifier variables in several ways in the login scripts. When you use them with the MAP command, a corresponding directory that matches the result of the variable must exist. See the section on Identifier Variables for a complete list of these variables.

 When you use identifier variables in a MAP statement, the variable must be in uppercase characters and be preceded by a percent sign (%).

Some examples of the MAP command and identifier variables follow:

- When mapping a home directory that changes depending on who logs in, NetWare assumes that a directory that matches the user's login name is on the system. The following syntax shows you the way to map H: to a user's home directory:

    ```
    MAP H:=SYS:USERS\%LOGIN_NAME
    ```

- If you want a mapping to a directory based on the current year and month, use the following map statement to check the file server for dates:

  `MAP G:=SYS:%YEAR\%MONTH`

- You should have a mapping for each different COMMAND.COM your workstations use to boot. Depending on the number of different versions you have, the MAP statements that follow ensure that workstations find the appropriate files.

  The following MAP statement assumes that the only differences are the DOS version numbers:

  `MAP S2:=SYS:PUBLIC\DOS\%OS_VERSION`

  The following MAP statement assumes that you may have different DOS types, such as DR DOS, MS-DOS, and PC DOS, as well as different version numbers:

  `MAP S2:=SYS:PUBLIC\%OS\%OS_VERSION`

  Occasionally, DOS versions may be recognized as other types, due to similarities in size, dates, and signatures. In these cases, two different COMMAND.COMs may register as the same version, which means that some users may receive an `Invalid Command.com` or `Command.com Not Found` message. The following MAP statement solves this problem. (See the section on required commands later in this chapter for more information on this procedure.)

  `MAP S2:=SYS:PUBLIC\%MACHINE\%OS\%OS_VERSION`

The WRITE Command

The WRITE command enables you to print information to the screen. To use this statement, you must observe the following conditions:

- Enclose in quotation marks the text to be written to the screen

- Type variables inside of quotation marks in uppercase characters

- Precede the variables with a percent sign (%)

Figure 9.6 shows three statements in a user's login script. Figure 9.7 shows the results if the user, James Weyand, logs in to the network at 4:30 p.m. with the login name JIM.

Figure 9.6:
Examples of login script commands.

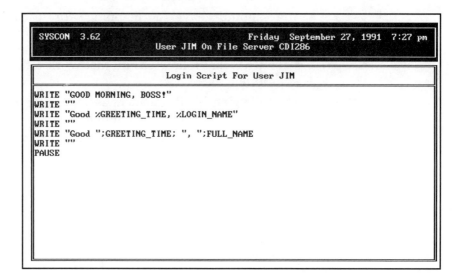

```
SYSCON  3.62                        Friday  September 27, 1991  7:27 pm
                          User JIM On File Server CDI286

                          Login Script For User JIM

WRITE "GOOD MORNING, BOSS!"
WRITE ""
WRITE "Good %GREETING_TIME, %LOGIN_NAME"
WRITE ""
WRITE "Good ";GREETING_TIME; ", ";FULL_NAME
WRITE ""
PAUSE
```

Figure 9.7:
The results of the login script statements.

```
F:\>LOGIN JIM
GOOD MORNING, BOSS!

Good evening, JIM

Good evening, James T. Weyand

Strike any key when ready . . .
```

The PAUSE Command

The PAUSE command, when placed in a login script, issues the message `Press any key when ready`. The system waits until the user presses a key before continuing.

The FIRE PHASERS Command

The FIRE PHASERS command produces a "bloop" noise for every number placed after the command. The resultant noise was designed to draw the user's attention to the screen without startling the user. This command is useful if you want to display a message to the user. Use the following syntax for FIRE PHASERS:

    FIRE PHASERS *nn*

The IF..THEN..ELSE Statement

IF..THEN..ELSE are conditional statements that enable a parameter to be issued if a condition exists. In an IF..THEN..ELSE statement, the basic idea is "If the condition is true, then do something."

If you want the system to do only one thing, you can specify the command on one line (see fig. 9.8). On the first line in figure 9.8, the system is checking whether today is Friday. If today is Friday, then the system writes `TGIF!!!!` on-screen. If today is any other day of the week, the system skips over this conditional statement.

If you need more than one thing to happen, BEGIN and END statements are necessary. Examples of both conditions are shown in figure 9.8. BEGIN appears before any executable statements, and END completes the entire statement.

In the second IF..THEN statement, shown in figure 9.8, the condition is true if the time is between 9:00 a.m. and 9:59 a.m. If the file server time is in this range when a user logs in, then the workstation issues an attention-getting sound. The FIRE 9 command tells the user by name that he or she is late, and then pauses, as shown in figure 9.9 . If the condition is not true, then the ELSE statement is executed; in this example, the statement is about the user being on time again (see fig. 9.10).

In this example, hours before or after 9 a.m., such as 8 a.m. and 10 a.m., force the statement about being on time, which may not be the intended result. You cannot embed IF..THEN statements, so the best solution is to use two separate statements—one for hours before 9 a.m. and one as shown in figure 9.8.

Figure 9.8:
An example of an
IF..THEN statement.

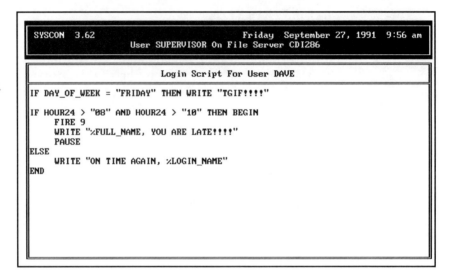

```
SYSCON  3.62                          Friday  September 27, 1991  9:56 am
              User SUPERVISOR On File Server CDI286

                         Login Script For User DAVE

IF DAY_OF_WEEK = "FRIDAY" THEN WRITE "TGIF!!!!"

IF HOUR24 > "08" AND HOUR24 > "10" THEN BEGIN
    FIRE 9
    WRITE "%FULL_NAME, YOU ARE LATE!!!!"
    PAUSE
ELSE
    WRITE "ON TIME AGAIN, %LOGIN_NAME"
END
```

Figure 9.9:
The result if both
conditional
statements are
true.

```
F:\>LOGIN CHRIS
TGIF!!!!
Christopher Winslow Bell, YOU ARE LATE!!!!
Strike any key when ready . . .
```

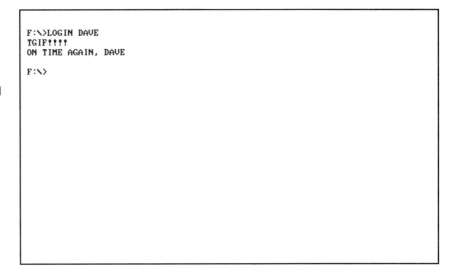

Figure 9.10:
The result if only
the first conditional
statement is true.

```
F:\>LOGIN DAVE
TGIF!!!!
ON TIME AGAIN, DAVE

F:\>
```

The BREAK ON/OFF Command

The BREAK ON/OFF command determines whether you can interrupt the login script by using Ctrl-Break or Ctrl-C.

The DISPLAY and FDISPLAY Commands

The DISPLAY and FDISPLAY commands enable you to display a text file on the user's screen as he or she logs in. If the file is an ASCII file, the DISPLAY command presents the file's contents. If the file was created through another program and extra characters are displayed, FDISPLAY filters out all control characters and displays only text. Use the following syntax for the DISPLAY command:

DISPLAY *volume:path/filename*

In figure 9.11, the system is looking for the date to be July 4. If the date is July 4, the screen shown in figure 9.12 is displayed.

Figure 9.11:
A DISPLAY command in a login script.

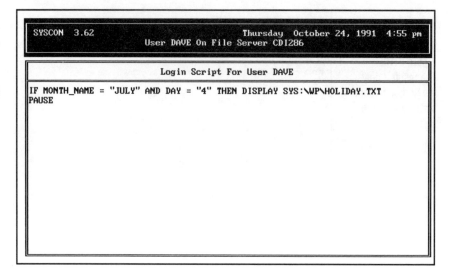

Figure 9.12:
The result if the date is July 4.

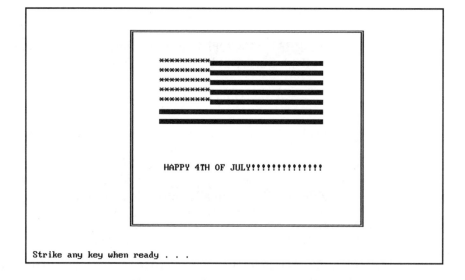

The INCLUDE Command

The INCLUDE command enables the system administrator to control changes to the login scripts from a common text file. INCLUDE works like a subroutine in a login script. This text file can be created by any text editor and should contain only valid login script commands. All the commands listed in this section qualify. INCLUDE's syntax is as follows:

INCLUDE *volume:path/filename*

 If you have several users who share common scripts, placing an INCLUDE statement into their existing login scripts is convenient. Then any changes can be made to the text file.

DOS Commands

DOS BREAK determines whether you can use Ctrl-Break or Ctrl-C at the DOS prompt to interrupt programs.

DOS SET enables you to set DOS variables to a specified value. The syntax is as follows:

DOS SET *variable name* **=** *"value"*

DOS VERIFY enables you to verify that files are copied correctly to a local drive.

The COMSPEC Command

COMSPEC stands for *COM*mand *SPEC*ifier. You can use this command to specify the search drive that a workstation is to use to find the appropriate COMMAND.COM. The syntax is as follows:

COMSPEC = *search drive:***COMMAND.COM**

The DRIVE Command

The DRIVE command specifies exiting to a previously mapped drive letter from a login script. The syntax is as follows:

DRIVE *drive letter:*

The GOTO Command

You use the GOTO command in the same way as you do from a DOS batch file. Do not use GOTO within a BEGIN..END conditional statement. For easy debugging, you also should use the BREAK ON command. For more information on this command, see your DOS manuals.

Exit Commands

This section discusses the various ways in which a login script can be exited. When you use the EXIT command by itself in the system login script, NetWare exits to DOS without going to the user login script.

In a user login script, EXIT takes the user to the DOS prompt, which usually is the default drive. To execute a DOS command, use the following syntax:

EXIT *"filename"*

The file name can be any file ending in EXE, COM, or BAT. The system takes you to DOS, closes the login script, and executes the command. You are limited to 14 characters inside the quotation marks.

If no EXIT statement is called in the system login script, the user login script is executed. If no EXIT statement is called in the user login script, the user is taken to the default directory DOS prompt.

If you type the following syntax, for example, you can execute a command at the DOS prompt, then return to the login script to complete further commands.

#*filename*

This command only works with files that end in EXE or COM.

If you have an internal DOS command, such as CLS, or you want to execute a batch file, you must use the following syntax:

#COMMAND /C *command*

This command loads an additional DOS environment to execute the command. If you want to clear a screen from the login script, for example, type the following:

#COMMAND /C CLS

If workstations run out of memory frequently with the programs you use, using # in login scripts is not advisable. The memory that it takes to execute the command at the workstation is not released back to the workstation until it is rebooted.

Remark Statements

Remark statements are used to leave notes for the administrator. Remark statements enable you to document what you have done in a login script and do not get executed. Three ways are available for creating a remark statement in a login script. REM, *, and ; are all valid remark parameters, and they must be the first characters on a line.

Command Line Parameters

NetWare also enables you to use parameters in the login statement to customize your login even further. The available parameters are %0 through %9, in which %0 is the file server name, %1 is the user name, and %2 through %9 are user-definable parameters.

The example that follows enables a user named Diana to exit to DOS if she types **OUT** after her name on the login line.

First, the following line must be placed in the login script:

```
IF "%2" = "OUT" THEN EXIT
```

Then, at the DOS prompt, Diana can type the following in order to exit to DOS:

```
LOGIN DIANA OUT
```

In the preceding syntax, **OUT** is considered to be the %2 variable.

The ATTACH Command

By using the ATTACH command, users can attach to other file servers from within the login script. The syntax is as follows:

```
ATTACH fileserver/user name;password
```

Note A password that is placed in the login script file can be a security breach. NetWare prompts you for all information if you choose not to include the password, user name, or file server.

Required Commands of Login Scripts

Novell requires the following three statements in the system login script:

```
MAP S1:=SYS:PUBLIC
MAP S2:=SYS:PUBLIC\%MACHINE\%OS\%OS_VERSION
COMSPEC=S2:COMMAND.COM
```

By placing the search mapping to PUBLIC first, you ensure that all commands kept there are executed with priority. You can alter the mapping to the DOS path to match your directory structure. In figure 9.13, you see a small network with five workstations that all use a different COMMAND.COM.

Figure 9.13:
An example of automatic mapping to the proper COMMAND.COM.

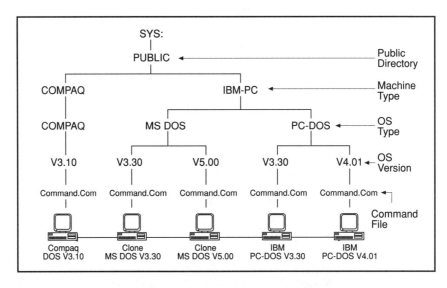

The network queries the workstation at bootup to fill in the variable values. By default, NetWare recognizes all workstations as IBM PCs. If you need to use another directory at this level, you must create a SHELL.CFG text file wherever you call your IPX.COM. In that file is one line that should read as follows:

LONG MACHINE NAME = *directoryname*

Standards help you to regulate the way systems are set up. Standards also help you to avoid conflicts. These three lines attempt to standardize the operating system environment. You can use other options, but these lines guarantee that you will not get invalid or missing COMMAND.COM statements that lock workstations when you are exiting programs.

Identifier Variables

Table 9.1 lists the identifier variables and their definitions. You can use these variables in login scripts.

Table 9.1
Identifier Variables

Conditional Items	Screen Display
ACCESS_SERVER	Displays TRUE if access server is functional; displays FALSE if not functional
ERROR_LEVEL	Displays the number of errors; if 0, no errors are found
MEMBER OF *group*	Displays TRUE if the user is a member of a specified group; displays FALSE if the user is not member of a specified group
Date	
DAY	Displays the day from 01 to 31
DAY_OF_WEEK	Displays the day of the week
MONTH	Displays the month from 01 to 12
MONTH_NAME	Displays the name of the month
NDAY_OF_WEEK	Displays the number of the weekday
SHORT_YEAR	Displays the year in short format, such as 90, 91, and so on
YEAR	Displays the year in full format, such as 1990, 1991, and so on
DOS Environment	
<>	Use any DOS environment variable as a string

Table 9.1—continued

Conditional Items	Screen Display
Network	
NETWORK_ADDRESS	Displays the network number of the cabling system in eight hex digits
FILE_SERVER	Displays the name of the file server
Time	
AM_PM	Displays the time as day or night, by using a.m. or p.m
GREETING_TIME	Displays the time of day as morning, afternoon, or evening
HOUR	Displays the time of day in hours, from 1 to 12
HOUR24	Displays the hour in 24-hour time, from 00 to 23
MINUTE	Displays the minutes from 00 to 59
SECOND	Displays the seconds from 00 to 59
User	
FULL_NAME	Displays the full name of the user by using SYSCON information
LOGIN_NAME	Displays the user's login name
USER_ID	Displays the ID number of each user
Workstation	
MACHINE	Displays the machine for which the shell was written, such as IBMPC
OS	Displays the workstation's operating system, such as MSDOS
OS_VERSION	Displays the DOS version of the workstation
P_STATION	Displays the station address or node address in 12 hex digits
SMACHINE	Displays the name of the machine in short format, such as IBM
STATION	Displays the connection number

Creating Custom Menus

Menus make accessing applications easy for end users. By using menus, users never have to learn what drives a program. Instead, they can focus their efforts in more productive areas. Many third-party menu programs are available, but few have the simplicity and network compatibility that the menus in NetWare offer. One of the most appealing features of NetWare menus is the cost; they are free with the NetWare operating system.

If you know how to write DOS batch files, you have an excellent background for writing a menu in NetWare. Almost anything that you can accomplish from a batch file can be done—with the same syntax—from a menu script. These files are DOS text files with the extension MNU. All the files displayed in figure 9.14 are menus.

Figure 9.14:
Examples of menu files.

```
F:\MENUS>dir *.mnu

    Volume in drive F is SYS
    Directory of  F:\MENUS

12-2      MNU      557   7-31-91   2:40p
ADMINS    MNU      494  10-04-90   6:23p
SALES     MNU     1314   8-07-89   4:44p
BACKUP    MNU      425   8-13-90   1:21p
ACCOUNT   MNU     5171   4-15-91   1:05p
WORK      MNU     2072   7-25-90   1:36p
        6 File(s)   32436224 bytes free

F:\MENUS>
```

 Note
By calling a batch file from within a menu, you may experience unreliable results. You should replicate all commands within a batch file in the menu script for smooth execution.

Understanding the Menu Format

This section discusses the format that can be used to create a menu. In NetWare, you can create menus by using any text editor. The following shows the format of a menu file:

- Precede menu and submenu names with a percent sign (%) and line them up with the left margin.

- Left-align the options you want to use as items that users can choose from a menu.

- Make sure that all executable statements appear on their own lines and are indented at least one space.

- Indent and use a percent sign (%) when calling a submenu.

- Make sure that no spaces exist between the percent sign (%) and a menu name.

- When defining a submenu, make sure that the menu name is identical to the way it is called. If you call a submenu %UTILITIES, for example, you must match the name when defining it later.

You can place menus and submenus anywhere on-screen and use one of eight colors as defined in NetWare's COLORPAL utility. After you name the menu, you must define three fields, which are separated with commas. The order is *row* (which is from 1-24), *column* (which is from 1-80), and *color*. The row and column fields make up the size of the computer screen.

In NetWare, the on-screen coordinates 12,40 are the default coordinates of menus. This is the middle of a typical screen. You can place menus at any location on-screen, and they will not wrap if you do not give the menu enough room. The coordinates 1,1 place the menu in the upper left corner, 1,80 in the upper right corner, 24,1 in the lower left corner, and 24,80 in the lower right corner.

To determine where you want to place your menu on-screen, you need to plan around a screen that has coordinates of 24 rows and 80 columns. You calculate menu positions by specifying the point at which the center of the menu should be placed.

You then need to determine the size of the menu. To do this, figure the number of lines you want above the menu. This is done by making a rough sketch of the menu on lined paper. Your menu should be large enough to accommodate the desired text for the menu. The size of the menu is determined by the length of the menu option and the quantity of options in the menu. You need to determine where the middle of the menu needs to be placed.

You now need to decide the number of blank lines on the monitor you want above the menu. Next, count the number of lines you want in the menu and divide that number by two. This locates the starting point of the menu at the middle of the screen. Add these two numbers together to determine the placement of the menu on the vertical axis, known as the *vertical placement*, as follows:

# of lines above menu + (# of menu lines / 2) = r ow

If you want a menu that is six lines above the menu and has six lines in the menu, for example, the vertical placement is 9.

Next, determine the number of columns you want before a menu. Count the number of characters in the longest menu item and divide by two. Add these two numbers together to determine the placement of the menu on the horizontal axis, known as the *horizontal placement*, as follows:

# of columns before menu + (# of columns in longest menu option / 2) = column

The following is the syntax of a menu in NetWare:

```
%main menu name,row,column,color
option
  %submenu
option
  executable
%submenu,row,column,color
option
  executable
```

In the preceding syntax, the `%main menu name,row,column,Color` line specifies the name of the menu. This also specifies the placement of the menu on-screen and the color of the menu. The `option` line specifies the names of the available options that you want to display on the menu. The `%submenu` line calls a submenu option where an additional menu is defined. The **executable** line specifies the commands that can call the menu option.

Using Required Rights

NetWare requires you to have Read and File Scan rights in the directory that holds the menu (MNU) files. In addition, you need Read, Write, Create, Erase, Modify, and File Scan rights in the directory in which you call a menu.

In the optimum condition, MNU files are flagged as Read-only, and Read, Write, Create, Erase, Modify, and File Scan are the user's trustee rights in that directory.

Using the GO*.BAT and RESTART*.BAT Files

GO*.BAT and RESTART*.BAT files are pointer files used when you call programs from a menu. The system creates one of each file for each user running the menu. These files tell the system where you are when you call a program and the way to get back when you are done.

These files are *recyclable*, in that you never have more on your system than you have users using the menus. When a user exits the menu properly by pressing Esc and selecting Yes, or by selecting the logout option, these files are erased. Limiting where a user can call a menu is a good idea; otherwise, you may find these files scattered throughout the network. To limit a user to one directory for calling menus, make sure that the user is aware of the acceptable location (directory) if the user calls a menu from a DOS prompt. Another way to make sure a user is in the proper directory is to place him there in a login script and call the menu from the login script. This method is discussed in the section on menu calling procedures.

NetWare enables you to exit from a menu by using the LOGOUT command. The network knows the way to close all open files, including the GO*.BAT and RESTART*.BAT files. When you exit in this manner, however, you are disconnecting yourself from the place where these files are kept. The result is that the menu program that was brought into the workstation's memory gives two error messages. The message `Batch File Missing` is displayed twice. The program is looking for the GO*.BAT and RESTART*.BAT files, but now you are logged out of the network.

Because users often are frightened by error messages, NetWare enables you to use the !LOGOUT command from a menu. The exclamation point (!) simply blocks the error messages from the screen.

Understanding Menu Calling Procedures

Now that the menu is created and the rights are established, you need to bring the menu up on-screen. This enables you to use the menu on your network. To call a menu from the DOS prompt, use the MENU command and type the name of the menu file name. The extension, MNU, is optional, as follows:

MENU *filename*

The extension is optional, because MENU knows to look for a file with an MNU extension. In figure 9.15, for example, the menu SALES is called from the menu subdirectory. This is done by issuing the following command:

MENU SALES

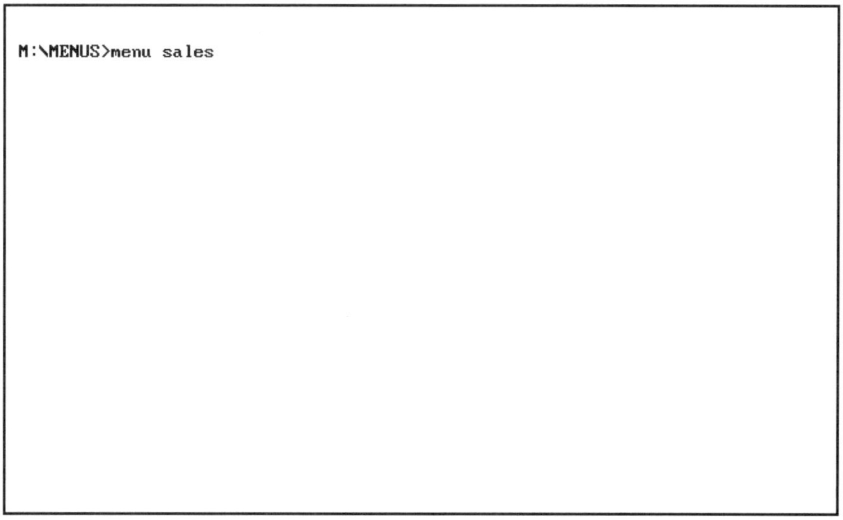

Figure 9.15:
Calling a menu
from the DOS
prompt.

```
M:\MENUS>menu sales
```

NetWare offers several ways to call up a menu from a login script. The best method is to create a batch file that calls the menu. You then should call the batch file from the EXIT statement, as follows:

```
EXIT "NETMENU"
```

In this example, the file NETMENU.BAT is in a directory mapped earlier in the menu and contains the following command:

```
MENU NETMENU
```

Another method to call up a menu is to use the # call. This method enables you to return to the login script when you exit from the menu. The following is an example of calling up a menu using the # call:

```
#MENU NETMENU
```

This method does require more workstation memory. For more information, see the previous section on login commands.

Using Techniques for Setting Up Menus

Many methods are available for setting up menu options. In this section, you examine a menu with a few hints for creating a clean, smooth-working menu environment. In the following example, you examine a menu created for the SALES department. The following file is called SALES.MNU:

```
%Sales Dept Main Menu
Applications
  %Application Menu
Utilities
  %Utilities Menu
Logout
  !LOGOUT
%Application Menu,1,1,3
Data Base
  map insert s3:=sys:apps\db
  map f:=sys:data\sales\db
  f:
  datab
  m:
  map del s3:
```

```
      map del f:
Spread Sheet
   map insert s3:=sys:apps\s2
   map f:=sys:data\sales\ss
   f:
   ssheet
   m:
   map del s3:
   map del f:
%Utilities Menu,24,80,5
Send a Message
   Send " @1"Type a message" " @2"Send it to?"
Capture Settings
   Capture q=@1"Type Queue Name" c=@2"# of Cop-
ies?" @3"FF  or NFF?"
Ncopy a File
   NCOPY @1"Source path/file" @2"Destination"
```

After creating this menu as a text file, type **MENU SALES** at the DOS prompt. The screen that appears is shown in figure 9.16. Notice that NetWare put the options in alphabetical order. If you want options listed in a different order, you must place numbers in front of the options. This then puts the items in numerical order.

Figure 9.16:
The Sales Dept
Main Menu screen.

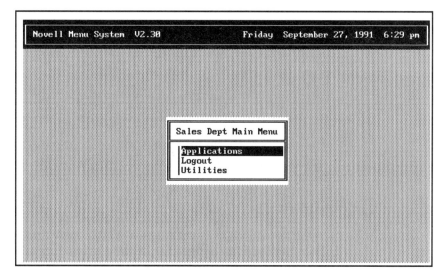

Note If you number the menu options, you need to remember the way a computer counts. Numbering the options 1, 2, 3, and so on, works fine as long as you do not use the number 10. When a computer reads the number 10, 10 falls between 1 and 2. Use two-digit numbers, such as 01, 02, 03, and so on, if you need more options.

When you press Enter while the Applications option is highlighted, NetWare calls up the Application menu (see fig. 9.17). In this menu, two options are available—Data Base and Spread Sheet. You now can choose the Spread Sheet option or Data Base option by highlighting the desired option and pressing Enter. This executes the commands contained under that option you select.

Figure 9.17:
The Application Menu.

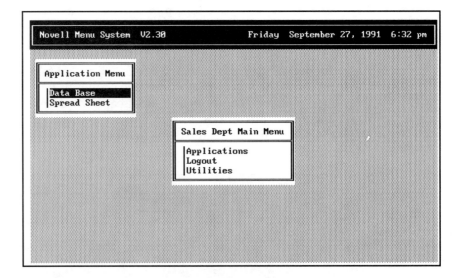

The idea behind the mappings in this example is to keep the system running as lean as possible. Search mappings take up file server memory. By leaving drives mapped, users can get at them from DOS more easily. Keeping the mappings in menus instead of the login script works well.

In figure 9.18, the system maps a search drive and maps a data drive. Then the system changes to the data drive and calls the program. At this point the application, such as the Spread Sheet option, starts. You then exit the spreadsheet program after you finish working in it. As figure 9.19 shows, when exiting from the application, the system returns to the default directory, which ensures that the GO*.BAT and RESTART*.BAT files are deleted properly. Then the network deletes the search drive and the data drive. The last step takes the user back to the menu.

Figure 9.18:
Choosing the
Spread Sheet
option.

```
M:\MENUS>map insert s3:=sys:apps\ss

SEARCH3:  = X:. [CDI286\SYS:  \APPS\SS]

M:\MENUS>map f:=sys:data\sales\ss

Drive  F: = CDI286\SYS:  \DATA\SALES\SS

M:\MENUS>f:
```

Figure 9.19:
Exiting the
application to
display the
remaining
executables.

```
F:\DATA\SALES\SS>m:

M:\MENUS>map del s3:

The search mapping for drive X: was deleted

M:\MENUS>map del f:

The mapping for drive F: has been deleted.

M:\MENUS>
```

Press Esc to close the option menu and to return to the Sales Dept Main Menu. The next choice is the Utilities option (see fig. 9.20). Under this option, several commands have been added that need user input. To get the user to answer questions, the menu utility allows input variables designated as @1 through @9.

About Input Variables...

Input variables enable the user to type information into a window from the menu. This information is sent to the DOS prompt for execution. This is helpful if users have different needs for calling programs. A good example is printing by using the CAPTURE command. Different users might need to print to different queue names. The following option enables the users to input the appropriate queue name:

```
CAPTURE Q=@1"ENTER QUEUENAME"
```

You can use up to nine windows for each command, such as @1, @2, ... @9. Enter the prompt that the user sees on-screen between the quotation marks in the preceding syntax.

Figure 9.20:
The Utilities Menu.

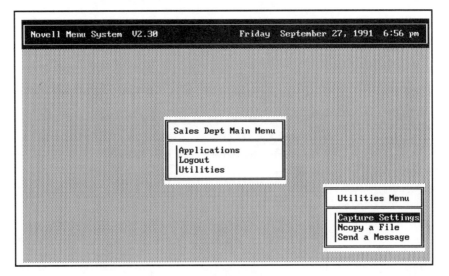

The next item that you can choose is the Capture Settings option, which enables you to see the Type Queue Name: prompt (see fig. 9.21). This prompt asks you for the name of the printer queue you want to use. When you created the menu, you placed the input question within quotation marks. No space exists between the input variable and the quotation marks. For the prompt to work, you need to make sure that you do not insert spaces between the input question and the quotation marks. Spaces cause the window to fail to appear and the command is issued with an error.

Figure 9.21:
The Type Queue Name input box.

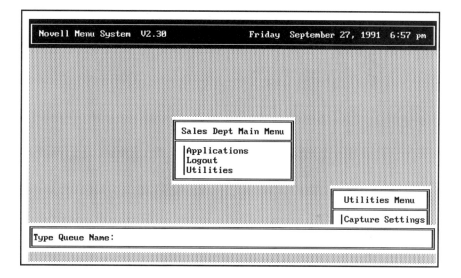

As you answer each prompt that appears on-screen, NetWare stores the information until you answer all the questions. Then, NetWare sends the information to the DOS prompt.

In figures 9.22 through 9.25, for example, NetWare prompts you for the printer queue name, number of copies, and whether you want form feed or not. After you answer the last question, NetWare returns you to the DOS prompt. You now can print by using the CAPTURE options.

The user can answer the questions as they appear. The information is stored temporarily until all questions are answered; then the input information is sent to the DOS prompt and executed (see figs. 9.22 through 9.25).

Figure 9.22:
Inputting the name
of the queue.

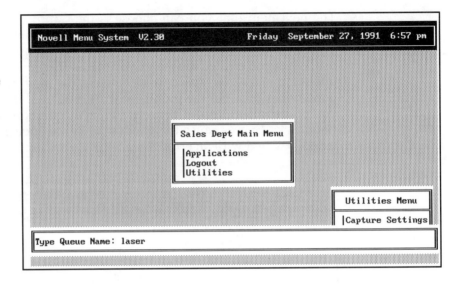

Figure 9.23:
Inputting the
number of copies
for the printer.

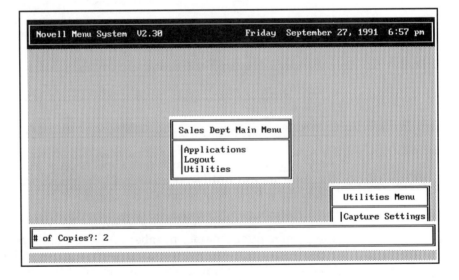

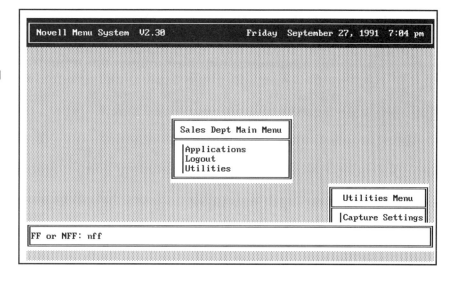

Figure 9.24:
Selecting form feed
or no form feed.

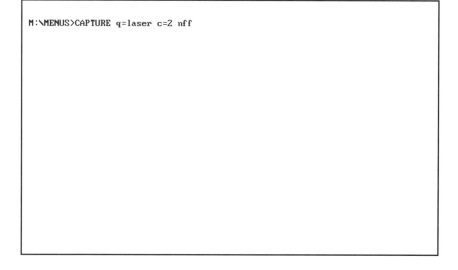

Figure 9.25:
The result of the
CAPTURE
statement.

This example showed you the way to create a menu that enables you set up a CAPTURE statement. This type of statement helps you automate NetWare for you as well as all end users on the network. To take full advantage of NetWare's utilities, you should look for ways to automate every task that is repetitive or time-consuming. Let yourself get creative with menus. The interface truly helps users become comfortable with using network utilities.

Exploring the Utilities for End Users

NetWare provides several utilities that can be used by both supervisors and end users. These utilities enable users to set up their own user environment. The following utilities can be used by all network users.

The SESSION Utility

The SESSION menu utility enables users to change to another server, map drives, and send messages (see fig. 9.26). Changing file servers is like using the ATTACH command at the DOS prompt. Everything that you do while you are using the SESSION utility is temporary and is forgotten when you log out of the network.

Figure 9.26:
The Available
Topics menu.

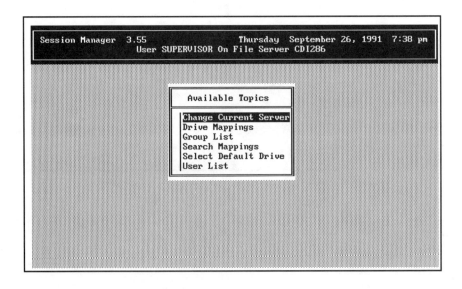

The Current Drive Mappings option displays the current mappings for that user (see fig. 9.27). To add a drive mapping, first press Ins. NetWare displays the next available drive letter as an option (see fig. 9.28). You can use any other unused drive letter instead of the one displayed.

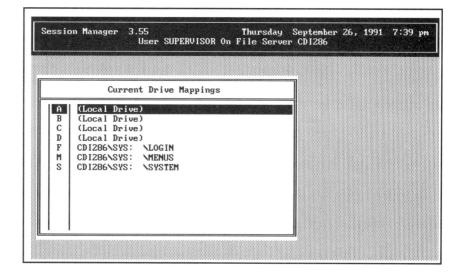

Figure 9.27:
The Current Drive
Mappings screen.

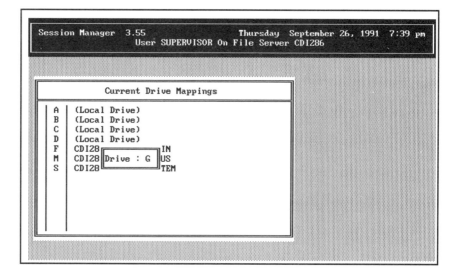

Figure 9.28:
Inserting a drive
mapping into
SESSION.

The next input box asks you which directory you want mapped (see fig. 9.29). You now need to enter the drive mapping that you want; in this case, **DATA**. After you specify the drive you want mapped, NetWare displays a box that asks you whether you want the drive mapped as a root drive (see fig. 9.30). The new mapping then is added to the Current Drive Mappings screen (see fig. 9.31).

Figure 9.29:
Specifying the directory.

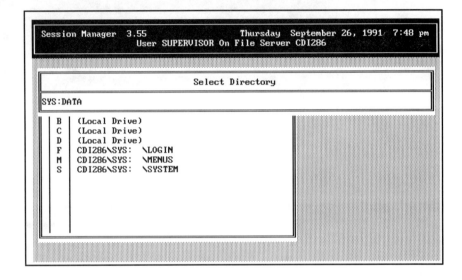

Figure 9.30:
Deciding whether the drive is to be mapped as a root.

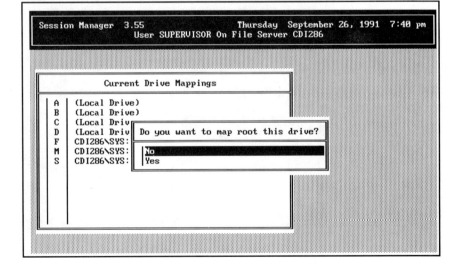

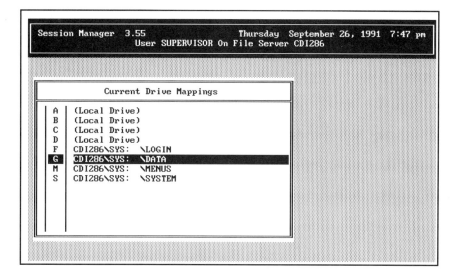

Figure 9.31:
The new drive mapping added to the Current Drive Mappings screen.

Similar screens appear under the Current Search Mappings screen (see fig. 9.32). The major difference occurs when the user presses Ins (see fig. 9.33). The next available search drive number is displayed.

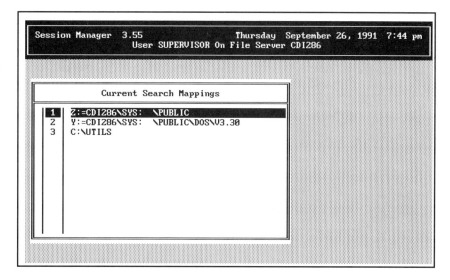

Figure 9.32:
The Current Search Mappings screen.

Figure 9.33:
The Search Drive
Number box.

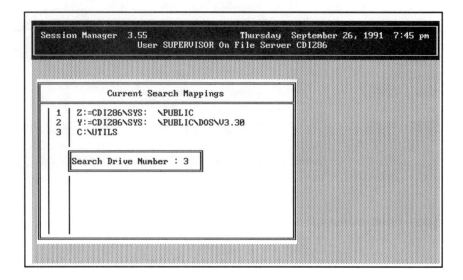

```
Session Manager   3.55                    Thursday  September 26, 1991  7:45 pm
                        User SUPERVISOR On File Server CDI286



                        Current Search Mappings

               1   Z:=CDI286\SYS:   \PUBLIC
               2   Y:=CDI286\SYS:   \PUBLIC\DOS\V3.30
               3   C:\UTILS

               Search Drive Number : 3
```

The Group List option in the Available Topics menu enables the user to send a message to any member of the chosen group who is currently logged in to the network.

By selecting the User List option, NetWare takes you to the Available Options menu, which enables you to view information about a specific user or send users a message (see fig. 9.34). If you select the Display user information option, you see a box that lists the user's full name, when the user logged in to the network, and the user's network and node address (see fig. 9.35). Notice that this box is surrounded by a single-line border. This type of border indicates that you can view the information only; you cannot make any changes to this type of box.

If you choose the Send Message option from the Available Options menu, you always see a list of users' names and their network connection numbers. To send a message, make sure that the entire message fits within the length of the input box that appears on-screen (see fig. 9.36).

The Windows screen for sending messages is more graphically oriented. Figures 9.37 and 9.38 show the screens for sending a message as a command and from within the Windows SESSION menu.

Figure 9.34:
The Available
Options menu.

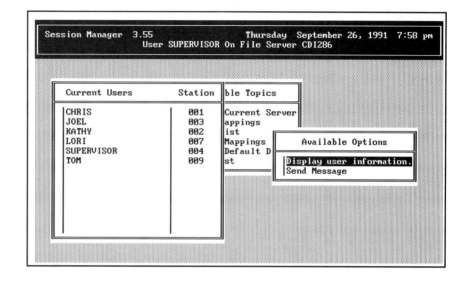

Figure 9.35:
The result of
selecting the
Display user
information option.

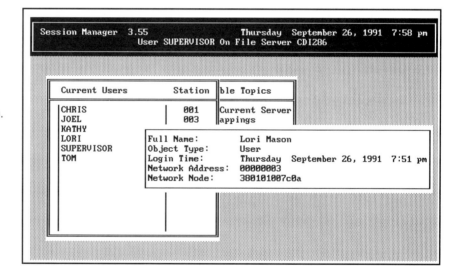

Figure 9.36:
Sending a
message.

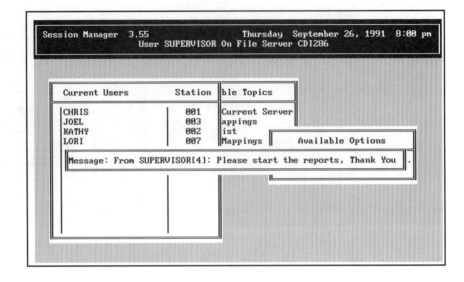

Figure 9.37:
The Windows Send
screen, for sending
a message as a
command.

Figure 9.38:
The Windows Send
Message screen,
for sending a
message from
within SESSION.

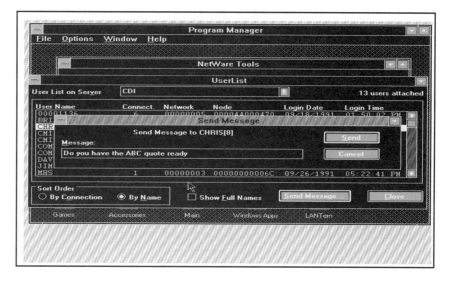

As you have seen, the SESSION utility makes it easy for the user to set up mappings, send messages to users and groups, and change to a mapped drive. SESSION is convenient and accessible without being as intimidating as the DOS prompt.

The USERLIST Utility

The USERLIST utility displays all users currently logged in to the network. The syntax is as follows:

USERLIST *fileserver*/*username* /*option*

The following are the options you can use with **USERLIST**:

- **/A.** Lists the network and node address
- **/C.** Turns on a continuous display
- **/O.** Lists all objects attached to the network

Figure 9.39 shows a list of users and their addresses.

Note

In Windows, you can view the currently logged-in users to the network. This displays a screen similar to one when you use the USERLIST command at the DOS prompt (see fig. 9.40).

```
F:\DATA>userlist cdi/ /a

User Information for Server CDI
Connection  User Name        Network       Node Address    Login Time
----------  ---------        -------       ------------    ----------
    1       MHS             [    3] [            6C]   9-26-1991   5:22 pm
    2       DAVE            [    3] [             3]   9-26-1991   9:58 pm
    3       SUPERVISOR      [    3] [            C6]   9-27-1991   9:34 am
    5       LORI            [    3] [            3F]   9-27-1991   9:07 am
    6       00001136        [    5] [      44000470]   9-18-1991   1:50 pm
    7       JOEL            [    3] [            11]   9-27-1991   9:29 am
    8       CHRIS           [    3] [            DB]   9-18-1991   5:43 pm
    9     * SUPERVISOR      [    3] [            51]   9-27-1991  12:39 am
   10       CMI             [    3] [            42]   9-27-1991  10:41 am
   11       COMM            [    3] [            3A]   9-27-1991  12:38 am
   12       COMM            [    3] [            FA]   9-27-1991  11:49 am
   13       CMI             [    3] [            1D]   9-20-1991  12:21 am
   14       TERRY           [    3] [            EC]   9-24-1991   3:25 pm
   17       SUPERVISOR      [    3] [            B0]   9-27-1991  10:44 am

F:\DATA>
```

Figure 9.39:
An example of a USERLIST display.

Figure 9.40:
The Windows UserList screen.

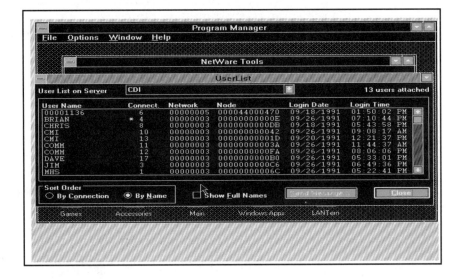

The SEND Command

The SEND command works at the DOS prompt. SEND enables a network user to send a one-line message to another user or group of users who are currently logged in. Only two messages can be buffered on a user's screen. Messages are temporary and are not stored permanently on the network. The syntax of SEND is as follows:

```
SEND "message" destination
```

In the preceding syntax, destination can be a user name, group, or connection. The name of the connection can be found by using the USERLIST command of FCONSOLE.

When you use the SEND command to send a message, NetWare limits you to the size of the message. To calculate the size of the message that you can send, use the following formula. This formula uses the length of your login name to calculate the message size:

```
45 - (length of your login name)
```

If your login name is Joe_M, for example, you have five characters in your login name. Subtract this sum from 45. This gives you 40 characters that can be in your message. Anything over this number is truncated.

When a message appears on a workstation, all processing on that workstation is halted. This does not affect most programs. After the user removes the message from the screen, the local application resumes any processing. (See the following sections on CASTOFF and CASTON to prevent messages from being received.) When a message appears, the screen displays instructions for eliminating the display on the right side of the message. Pressing Ctrl-Enter releases your screen.

Some programs that use a graphical user interface (GUI) tend to have problems with the SEND command. You probably will want to use CASTOFF before executing these programs.

The CASTOFF and CASTON Commands

The CASTON command enables messages to be received by a workstation. The CASTOFF command prevents messages from being sent to a workstation. Use CASTOFF if you notice that the SEND command causes screen problems or if you are processing an unattended program. Because CASTON is the system default, you must use the following syntax to activate CASTOFF:

    CASTOFF

If you use the A parameter in the preceding syntax, you turn off all messages, including those sent from the file server.

The SALVAGE Command

In NetWare v2.2, the SALVAGE command enables you to attempt to retrieve a file that recently has been deleted (see fig. 9.41). If the memory in the file server's hard drives has been updated, however, you probably will not get the file back.

Figure 9.41:
The v2.2 SALVAGE Main Menu Options screen.

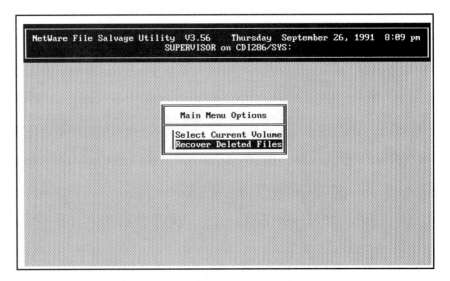

In v3.11, SALVAGE is much more sophisticated. From the main menu, users can view or recover files, choose a directory, or set the viewing options (see fig. 9.42). Users must have the Create right before they can retrieve a file by using SALVAGE.

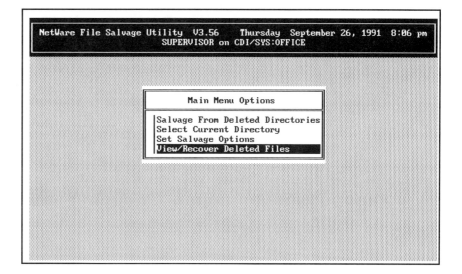

Figure 9.42:
The v3.11 SALVAGE Main Menu Options screen.

Files retrieved by using SALVAGE are put back into the directory from which they were deleted. If a file with the same name already exists, the system prompts you to rename the file being salvaged. Files are tracked by date and time, so several versions of the same file name may accumulate. NetWare does not keep track of directories that have been deleted, but the program does track the files in deleted directories. When you are salvaging files from a deleted directory, the files are restored to a hidden directory called DELETED.SAV. Although you do not see this directory, one exists on every volume. Supervisors can use the DOS CD command to make DELETED.SAV the current directory.

SALVAGE also enables the user to choose specific file names to view (see fig. 9.43). Each file displayed in the resultant list has been deleted, but the directories are still there. The directories display so you can change directories from this screen. If you press Enter with a file highlighted, NetWare shows you when that file was deleted, when it was modified prior to deletion, who owned it, and who deleted it. At this time, you can restore the file by answering Yes at the Recover This File menu (see fig. 9.44).

Figure 9.43:
Specifying the files to view.

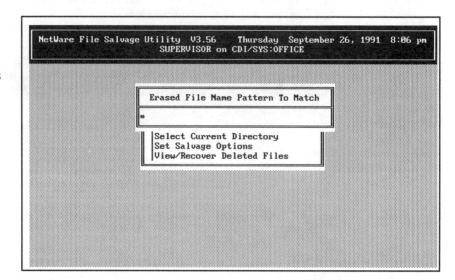

Figure 9.44:
Preparing to restore a deleted file.

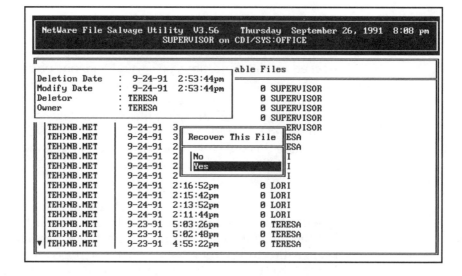

You can use F5, F6, F7, and F8 to mark and unmark patterns of files for restoring or purging. When you press Del with a file highlighted, NetWare purges the file from the list (see fig. 9.45). When you purge a file, it cannot be retrieved under any circumstances.

When preparing to view a list of files that can be salvaged, you can sort by deletion date, deletor, file size, or file name (the default). These options are on the Salvage Options menu (see fig. 9.46).

Figure 9.45:
Purging a deleted file.

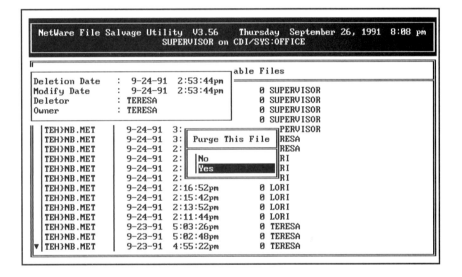

Figure 9.46:
The Salvage Options menu.

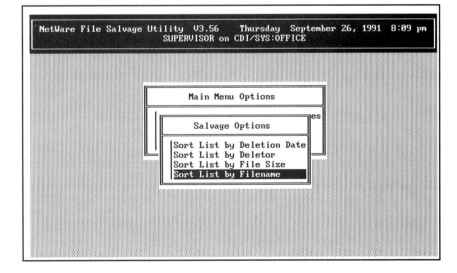

Files can be salvaged as long as the files are not marked with a P (for Purge), the directory is not marked with a P, and the system has enough room. As room is needed on the server's hard drive, the oldest files are removed from SALVAGE.

The PURGE /ALL command from the DOS prompt also clears out all files that are salvageable from a volume.

The SETPASS Command

The SETPASS command enables users to change their passwords from the DOS prompt. Unless the user is a supervisor or manager, the user is prompted to enter his or her old password before changing to a new password. The syntax is as follows:

SETPASS

Windows enables you to change your password from the SetPass screen (see fig. 9.47).

Figure 9.47:
The Windows
SetPass screen.

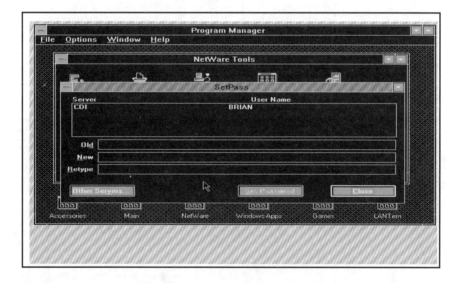

The SYSTIME Command

You can run SYSTIME on a user's workstation to view the file server's date and time. This command also synchronizes the workstation's time and date to that of the file server. The syntax is as follows:

```
SYSTIME
```

The WHOAMI Command

The WHOAMI command displays information about the user that is logged in. Figure 9.48 shows a WHOAMI statement that lists all available information on a user.

Figure 9.48:
An example of a WHOAMI statement.

```
F:\>whoami/a
You are user KATHY attached to server CDI286, connection 4.
Server CDI286 is running Dedicated NetWare V2.2(100) Rev. A.
You are a workgroup manager.
You are Object Supervisor over LORI.
You are Object Supervisor over ACCOUNTING.
Login time: Thursday  September  26, 1991  8:45 pm
You are security equivalent to the following:
     EVERYONE (Group)
     ACCOUNTING (Group)
     SPREADSHEET (Group)
     SUPERVISOR (user)
You are a member of the following groups:
     EVERYONE
     ACCOUNTING
     SPREADSHEET
[RWCEMFA]  SYS:
[RWCEMFA]  SYS1:
Server CDI286 is not in a Domain.


F:\>
```

The syntax of WHOAMI is as follows:

```
WHOAMI /options
```

The options you can use follow:

- **/S.** Returns security equivalences
- **/G.** Returns the groups the user belongs to

- **/R.** Returns effective rights
- **/O.** Returns object supervisor information
- **/W.** Returns workgroup manager information
- **/SY.** Returns general system information
- **/A.** Returns all available information
- **/C.** Returns a continuous display

Summary

The system administrator does the most work in setting up the network for end users so they can be more productive by using the network. The goal of networking with NetWare is to make the system as easy as possible to use for the people running applications.

This chapter showed you the way to create your own menus to customize the NetWare environment for all users. This chapter also showed you the way to write different scripts to help your networked users use NetWare in the most efficient manner. Finally, the chapter discussed the various utilities and commands that are available to all users on the network.

The next chapter discusses the various tools that help you monitor the file server on the network. You are shown ways to limit users' disk space, check the network by using diagnostic tools, and monitor disk space usage.

System Administration and Troubleshooting

M ost NetWare networks experience a substantial growth of new users shortly after the initial installation. This is due primarily to the new system's reliable operation. But with this growth comes performance degradation and potential problems. NetWare provides many features for the adjustment of the operating system. When tuned and configured properly, a Novell NetWare file server can provide service for many users. One of the most common causes of problems is not file server failure, but improper file server configuration. Whether it was configured improperly initially or by user growth, the results can be the same—a poor level of performance.

In this chapter you learn about the following:

- Using FCONSOLE for management operations of a 2.2 file server
- Using MONITOR to track NetWare 3.11 operations
- Monitoring disk space usage

351

- Checking the network by using simple diagnostic tools
- Limiting user disk space

In this section, you are shown some of the simple tools and methods used to monitor your file server. Careful monitoring of and knowing about your file server enables you to prevent many problems before they happen. Except for hardware failures, most file server problems are visible through monitoring utilities long before the critical stage.

The network administrator's main responsibility is to monitor and record any file server problems. In most cases, if the administrator does not watch out for these problems, no one will. System monitoring and troubleshooting is enhanced by a wide range of Novell NetWare diagnostic and monitoring utilities. These utilities can give both users and system administrators the data required to maintain an efficient operating file server. By monitoring a few of the system's resource statistics, you can make adjustments to the file server that can prevent system failure and increase performance.

The administrator can easily monitor and change NetWare's active parameters to maintain a properly operating file server. With a simple understanding of the following parameters, many system problems can be prevented.

- File service processes
- Disk cache performance
- File server utilization
- Communications buffers
- Dynamic memory dgroups

Using FCONSOLE for Management Operations

The File Server Console, or FCONSOLE menu utility, enables the system administrator to maintain and fine-tune the file server. This command finds and places in a list all file servers. FCONSOLE enables you to view user connections, memory management statistics, and LAN I/O statistics. FCONSOLE also can provide advanced diagnostics information that can assist debugging procedures.

User limitations depend on the user's security level. All functions and submenus are open for use by the system supervisor or equivalent. Selected functions and submenus are locked and not functional if you are a normal system user. Users designated as FCONSOLE Operators in the SYSCON supervisor options have limited use of FCONSOLE, but have more options than the normal end user.

Being aware of FCONSOLE's specific tools for management operations should help filter out the screens of detailed technical information that are not as important to day-to-day administrative concerns. After executing the FCONSOLE command, you are presented with the opening menu (see fig. 10.1).

Figure 10.1:
FCONSOLE's main menu.

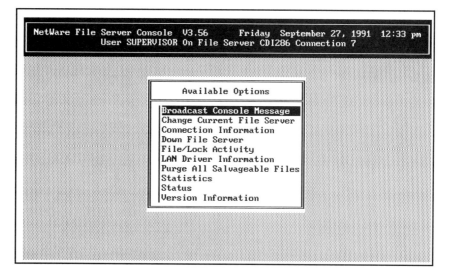

```
NetWare File Server Console   V3.56      Friday  September 27, 1991  12:33 pm
                  User SUPERVISOR On File Server CDI286 Connection 7

                        ┌──────────────────────────┐
                        │     Available Options     │
                        ├──────────────────────────┤
                        │ Broadcast Console Message │
                        │ Change Current File Server │
                        │ Connection Information    │
                        │ Down File Server          │
                        │ File/Lock Activity        │
                        │ LAN Driver Information     │
                        │ Purge All Salvageable Files │
                        │ Statistics                │
                        │ Status                    │
                        │ Version Information        │
                        └──────────────────────────┘
```

The first main menu option, Broadcast Console Message, enables you to send a message to every user currently logged in to the file server. This is a useful function when informing users of a scheduled downtime or other global announcement.

The second option is used in a multi-server environment. It enables the FCONSOLE user to attach to other file servers from within the FCONSOLE utility. This enables you to use FCONSOLE to examine multiple file servers. The interface follows the NetWare utility standard by making use of Ins to add other file servers to the pick list. After choosing a file server from the list, you are then required to supply both a login name and password.

The Connection Information option provides a submenu that enables operations on that particular connection. The Connections Information Menu, illustrated in figure 10.2, shows the Current Connections submenu which lists the options provided.

When entering this menu, the Current Connections window displays all users currently logged in to the file server. After selecting a user by highlighting that user's name, press Enter and the Connection Information window appears.

Figure 10.2:
The Connection Information menu.

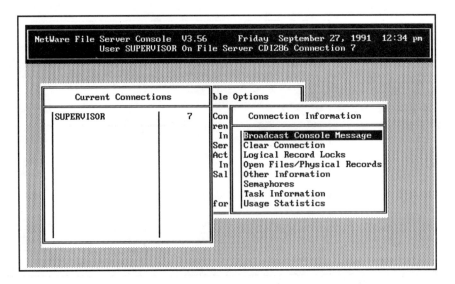

The options listed here can be useful when attempting to inspect connections on the system. From here, you can broadcast messages, clear connections, and inspect a user's open files.

The most commonly used options might be Broadcast Console Message, Clear Connection, and Open Files/Physical Records. These options are often used while requesting users to log off the system for maintenance. For example, you can broadcast a message asking that users please log off the system. After a reasonable period of time, you can then check the Open Files option to determine if they are still in an application. You can decide whether their connections should be cleared by using the Clear Connection option.

 If a user does not log out properly, files may be left open on the system. If a user's workstation is turned off, that person's workstation still shows on the FCONSOLE and an improper logout procedure has probably occurred. In this case, clearing the connection is the proper solution to the problem.

Not all applications show up as an open file on the system. A user, for example, can use Lotus 1-2-3 and show no files open. This is due to the nature of the program and should be considered when deciding to clear a connection.

The other Connection Information options are used by advanced system developers when troubleshooting problems related to file sharing and the proper operation on a network. This specialized information is generally useful to programmers and applications development people. A brief description of these other options follows.

The Logical Record Locks option displays the logical record locks which the connection has logged to the file server. This information can be useful when debugging a network application sharing data files.

The Open Files/Physical Records option displays the open files a connection has opened. This option also displays tasks and file status information. By highlighting a particular file and pressing Enter, various status messages are displayed, depending on the open state the file is in. More detailed information about this option can be found in the NetWare manuals.

The Other Information option shows additional information about the connection, including login name, full name, login time, and network address.

The Semaphores option enables you to get a list of semaphores that can be used. A *semaphore* is used by system tasks to limit how many tasks can use a resource at a time and to limit the number of workstations that can run a program at the same time.

The Task Information option shows which tasks are active at the selected workstation.

The Usage Statistics option shows the total disk usage and packet requests since the selected user logged in. This option can determine the activity of a workstation.

Some older technology application programs may be more sensitive to clearing a connection than others. It is a good practice to test or confirm this process with the software developers to prevent having to rebuild data files if damaged.

Choosing the Statistics option from FCONSOLE's main menu calls up the File Server Statistics menu (see fig. 10.3). This menu has several useful choices for getting information about network performance and system integrity. In particular, the Cache Statistics, Disk Statistics, and Summary options are important monitoring and diagnostic tools.

Figure 10.3:
FCONSOLE's File Server Statistics menu.

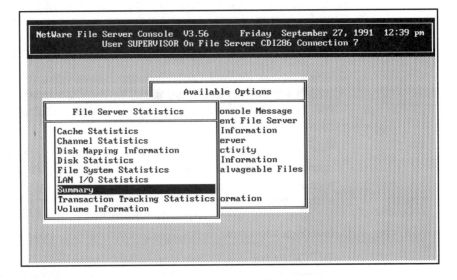

Cache Statistics

The Cache Statistics screen deals almost exclusively with memory usage. This screen tells you about NetWare file caching in the current server. Several of the screen parameters help you evaluate if there is enough memory in your file server. An example of the Cache Statistics screen is shown in figure 10.4.

Figure 10.4:
A typical Cache
Statistics screen.

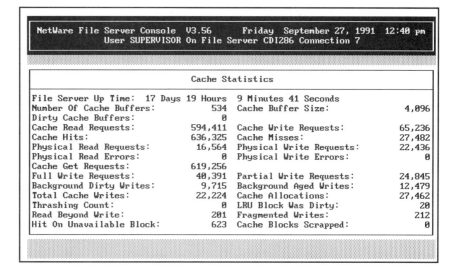

```
NetWare File Server Console   V3.56      Friday  September 27, 1991  12:40 pm
                 User SUPERVISOR On File Server CDI286 Connection 7
```

```
                              Cache Statistics

File Server Up Time:   17 Days 19 Hours  9 Minutes 41 Seconds
Number Of Cache Buffers:          534   Cache Buffer Size:           4,096
Dirty Cache Buffers:                0
Cache Read Requests:          594,411   Cache Write Requests:       65,236
Cache Hits:                   636,325   Cache Misses:               27,482
Physical Read Requests:        16,564   Physical Write Requests:    22,436
Physical Read Errors:               0   Physical Write Errors:           0
Cache Get Requests:           619,256
Full Write Requests:           40,391   Partial Write Requests:     24,845
Background Dirty Writes:         9,715   Background Aged Writes:     12,479
Total Cache Writes:            22,224   Cache Allocations:          27,462
Thrashing Count:                    0   LRU Block Was Dirty:            20
Read Beyond Write:                201   Fragmented Writes:             212
Hit On Unavailable Block:         623   Cache Blocks Scrapped:           0
```

The Cache Hits: and Cache Misses: parameters show you how many times a memory cache handled a read-write request and how many times the hard disk had to be accessed instead. In other words, a *cache hit* happens when the requested information is found in memory, and a *cache miss* happens when the information has to be taken from the hard disk. Because the minimum requirements for the network is 80% or more serviced from cache, the amount of misses should never be more than 20% of the total. Make sure that you have allotted enough memory for cache buffers in the server.

The Physical Read Errors and Physical Write Errors parameter values should always be low, if not zero. As these numbers increase, it is an indication that there are communication problems with the hard disk when cache is requesting a read or write.

Note

Physical read and write errors, along with Hot Fix Blocks discussed in the next section, should be zero in a healthy system.

An occasional error or Hot Fix Block may happen with normal equipment wear, but continual errors or hot fix blocks used weekly and daily indicate possible future failure. Errors can occur over a period of time and then stop. This generally indicates a media failure that NetWare handled properly. However, when errors continue and do not stop, you should be concerned.

The Thrashing Count parameter number should always be near zero. *Thrashing* occurs when a cache block is needed, but none is available. File server performance is seriously degraded when this happens. Adding memory until this number goes to zero is the first strategy. If at 12M of memory the problem does not go away, the only alternative is to upgrade to v3.11 to take advantage of dynamic memory allocation.

Dynamic memory allocation is the process used by NetWare 3.11 to allocate or assign memory according to needs and availability. When the 3.11 file server starts, all free memory is assigned to file caching. As the demand increases, memory is allocated as needed. NetWare 2.2 allocates memory in a static manner. All memory must be allocated upon startup and cannot be changed during operation.

Disk Statistics

Two important parameters in the Disk Statistics screen are IO Error Count and Hot Fix Table Size/Hot Fix Remaining. Figure 10.5 shows the information available for a typical physical disk.

Figure 10.5:
FCONSOLE's
Physical Disk 0.

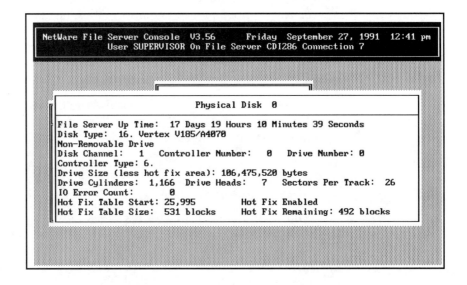

```
NetWare File Server Console  V3.56      Friday  September 27, 1991  12:41 pm
                 User SUPERVISOR On File Server CDI286 Connection 7


                            Physical Disk  0

File Server Up Time:  17 Days 19 Hours 10 Minutes 39 Seconds
Disk Type:  16. Vertex V185/A4070
Non-Removable Drive
Disk Channel:   1    Controller Number:   0    Drive Number: 0
Controller Type: 6.
Drive Size (less hot fix area): 106,475,520 bytes
Drive Cylinders:  1,166  Drive Heads:   7   Sectors Per Track:  26
IO Error Count:       0
Hot Fix Table Start: 25,995       Hot Fix Enabled
Hot Fix Table Size:   531 blocks      Hot Fix Remaining: 492 blocks
```

The IO Error Count parameter figure indicates the number of problems encountered when trying to read or write to the hard disk. A separate information screen is displayed for each drive.

The Hot Fix Table Size parameter tells you exactly how many Hot Fix blocks were allocated when the system was generated. The Hot Fix Remaining parameter tells you how many of those blocks are still left. Every time a bad block is encountered on the hard disk, the Hot Fix Remaining decreases.

 As part of a normal maintenance schedule, system administrators should check Hot Fix Remaining once a month. If the number goes down by more than five blocks, check the Hot Fix numbers once a week. The nature of hard disks is that they will accrue an occasional bad block, but if there is a problem, they usually accumulate bad blocks quickly. If you see a steady decrease in the number of blocks remaining, be prepared to repair or replace the drive.

File Server Statistics Summary

Choose the Summary option from the File Server Statistics menu to get to the File Server Statistics Summary screen. As figure 10.6 shows, this summary screen provides the technical summary data that has been gathered since the file server has been up and is, therefore, very informative when monitoring the operation and reliability of your server.

The File Server Up Time parameter shows the amount of time the file server has been running. This time resets if the server is downed or shut off.

The Number of File Service Processes parameter, also known as FSP, tells you the number of processes the file server has. A file server should have at least three processes, but four is recommended and is the average. NetWare v2.2 has a maximum of 10 FSPs. Although three processes enable your file server to operate, a slow CPU, a single heavily-used disk controller, or a low amount of cache memory may require more. This number can be manipulated by adjusting devices that used memory from dgroup one.

Figure 10.6:
The File Server
Statistics Summary
menu.

```
NetWare File Server Console  V3.56      Friday  September 27, 1991  12:39 pm
              User SUPERVISOR On File Server CDI286 Connection 7

                         File Server Statistics Summary

File Server Up Time:  17 Days 19 Hours  8 Minutes 59 Seconds
Number Of File Service Processes:     6  Current Server Utilization:      6%
Disk Requests Serviced From Cache:  96%  Packets Routed:                  0
Total Packets Received:        527,763  File Service Packets:            6
Total Number Of Cache Buffers:    534  Dirty Cache Buffers:             0
Total Server Memory:         4,194,304  Unused Server Memory:        3,072

                        Maximum      Peak Used    Currently In Use
Communication Buffers      150          13             0
Open Files:                240          41            21
Indexed Files:               5           0             0
Bindery Objects:           500          69            41
Connections:               116          10             1
Dynamic Memory 1:       12,232       2,374           994
Dynamic Memory 2:       26,576       6,124         5,264
Dynamic Memory 3:       59,500       1,130           694
Dynamic Memory 4:       63,646         944           144
```

If your file server appears to have a problem with File Service Process, a system reconfiguration is generally required. Consult a Novell engineer who is familiar with this problem if reconfiguring the system does not correct the situation.

The following factors can decrease the number of FSPs available on a network:

- Network board packet size is too large
- Network boards using DMA
- An overabundance of directory entries

Be cautious about reducing directory entries. You can lose files, directories, and trustee rights if this number is reduced drastically.

The most complete reference about all of the factors that affect FSPs is the September 1991 NetWare Application Notes. The Notes may be purchased from the Novell Research Order Desk. For more information call 1-800-453-1267, extension 5380.

The Disk Request Serviced from Cache parameter is the disk cache performance indicator. This number shows the amount of requests received at the file server that are taken from the cache memory. The remainder of the requests received have to go to the hard disk. Accessing information from cache is 100 times faster than going to the hard disk. The more the file server can get from memory, the faster the network functions. If disk cache performance drops below 93%, memory should be added. According to Novell recommendations, this number should never fall below 80%. The actual number of cache buffers your system needs depends on your applications and the load created by the users. If users request more data than their cache buffers can handle, the file server performance suffers.

 A good rule of thumb is to have between 800 and 1000 cache buffers. You may need to adjust this number after monitoring system statistics.

In some cases, it is possible to have too much memory. In a NetWare 2.2 file server, more than 10M of memory can be almost as slow as direct disk I/O, but is normally not a problem.

The Current Server Utilization parameter shows the percentage of use of the file server processor. A utilization that continually reaches a high percentage may require hardware changes or splitting the network load.

The Communication Buffers parameter is also an important area to watch. These numbers tell how many buffer areas have been set aside to hold incoming packets while currently held packets are being processed. These buffers are necessary to handle both incoming and outgoing packets. If no buffer is available, that packet is lost and a retransmit is required, which can greatly decrease performance.

You should have at least 100 communication buffers, plus one for each workstation. If the Peak Used is equal to the Maximum, increase the number of buffers. An overabundance of these buffers is a waste of cache memory.

About the Number of Buffers...

Novell's rule of thumb is to either use a 100 buffers or use the following formula to determine the number of buffers, and then to use the number which is larger.

$$10 * \text{\# of directly connected nets}$$
$$+ 3 * \text{\# of concurrent workstations}$$
$$+ 1 * \text{\# of directly connected workstations}$$
$$\overline{\text{Total number of buffers}}$$

The suggested number of buffers can be adjusted down after the system runs for awhile, but cutting the Novell default number of 100 communication buffers on the initial INSTALL is not recommended.

The Open Files parameter tells you how many open files the server can track. As the Peak Used reaches the maximum allowed, users are not able to run applications.

There are four Dynamic Memory pools at the bottom of the File Server Statistics Summary screen. The dynamic memory pools are important to monitor, but in most cases, they are difficult to adjust. Make sure that the Peak Used number is always at least 2K below the Maximum number.

Dynamic memory pools are 64K memory segments defined by NetWare 2.2. These segments hold information such as drive pointers, file handles, print queue pointers, and other system housekeeping information.

Dynamic Memory Pool 1, considered the all-purpose memory pool, is used for global allocated data, process stacks, packet buffers, volume tables, and general purpose work space. This number is not user-configurable.

About Monitoring Memory Pools...

When monitoring the Dynamic Memory Pool 1 information, keep in mind that the peak should never be more than the maximum—2K. This can prevent possible problems caused by system activity peaks.

Dynamic Memory Pool 2 is used for file and record locking. This number can be modified by reducing the maximum number of open files.

Dynamic Memory Pool 3 contains Router and Server Tables. This number is not user-configurable.

Dynamic Memory pool 4 is used for Drive handles. Each mapping you create uses 16 bytes of memory. This number is not user-configurable, but if you decrease the number of mappings you keep, you can reduce this number.

Using MONITOR NLM for Management Operations

MONITOR is the replacement for v2.2 FCONSOLE's Statistics option. To view the MONITOR screen, type **LOAD MONITOR** at the file server. The NLM (NetWare Loadable Module) MONITOR program runs on the NetWare 3.11 file server only and provides menus with most of the same statistics as provided by the NetWare 2.2 FCONSOLE command. MONITOR.NLM also provides a full set of statistics used with advanced diagnostics procedures. Notice that MONITOR's main menu, as seen in figure 10.7, displays many of FCONSOLE's statistics summary parameters. Although the information displayed here has much of the same meaning as the 2.2 version, the information is dynamically configurable in place of the NetWare 2.2 static configuration.

The information available in FCONSOLE is drastically decreased in v3.11. The information is now available in the MONITOR command that is run from the file server.

Connection Information

The first item on the Available Options menu is the Connection Information option (see fig 10.8). This screen shows everyone who is currently logged into the network, as well as any workstations that have IPX and the shell loaded but are not logged in. This option is comparable to the Connection Information option in FCONSOLE. Workstation connections can be cleared by highlighting the connection and pressing Del.

Figure 10.7:
The MONITOR.NLM
main menu.

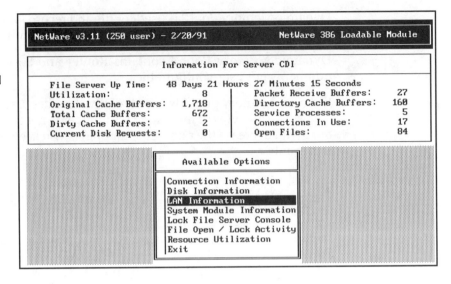

Figure 10.8:
MONITOR's
Connection
Information screen.

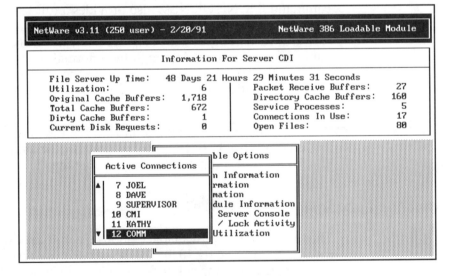

Disk Information

The next option, Disk Information, displays a Drive Status screen for all drives (see fig. 10.9). The Drive Status screen includes Hot Fix Status information.

Figure 10.9:
System disk drive information.

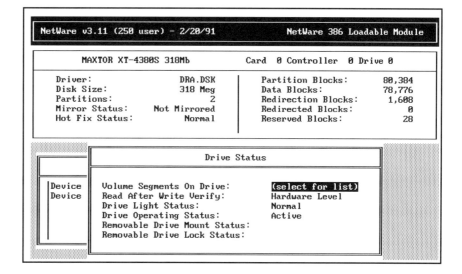

```
NetWare v3.11 (250 user) - 2/20/91           NetWare 386 Loadable Module

        MAXTOR XT-4380S 318Mb           Card  0 Controller  0 Drive 0

    Driver:              DRA.DSK        Partition Blocks:      80,384
    Disk Size:           318 Meg        Data Blocks:           78,776
    Partitions:              2          Redirection Blocks:     1,608
    Mirror Status:    Not Mirrored      Redirected Blocks:          0
    Hot Fix Status:      Normal         Reserved Blocks:           28


                              Drive Status

    Device    Volume Segments On Drive:     (select for list)
    Device    Read After Write Verify:      Hardware Level
              Drive Light Status:           Normal
              Drive Operating Status:       Active
              Removable Drive Mount Status:
              Removable Drive Lock Status:
```

LAN Driver Information

Each LAN driver that was loaded at the file server is displayed after accessing the LAN Information option (see fig. 10.10). LAN Driver information shows packet information, addresses, and protocol information. Figures 10.11 and 10.12 show the information that is available for each of the system's LAN drivers. Notice that figure 10.12 shows an abnormally high number of collisions. Further investigation is recommended.

Figure 10.10:
LAN Driver
Information's main
screen.

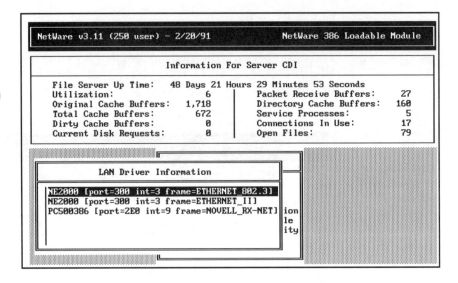

Figure 10.10:
LAN Driver
Information's main
screen.

Figure 10.11:
LAN Driver
Information,
page 1.

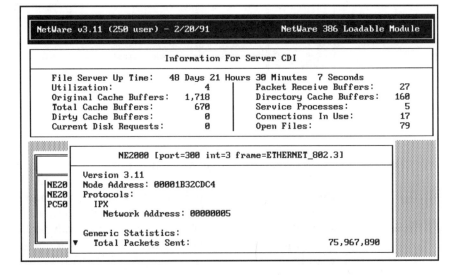

Another important screen to watch is the Resource Utilization option. This MONITOR.NLM window provides information on system memory. The statistics shown in figure 10.13 summarize the memory usage. A detailed explanation of each item can be found in the NetWare 3.11 *System Administration* reference. As illustrated, 38% of server memory is currently free as cache buffers. When this number drops below 20%, memory should be added to the file server. The amount of memory needed depends on the circumstances, but should be added in increments of one to two megabytes.

Figure 10.12:
LAN Driver
Information,
page 2.

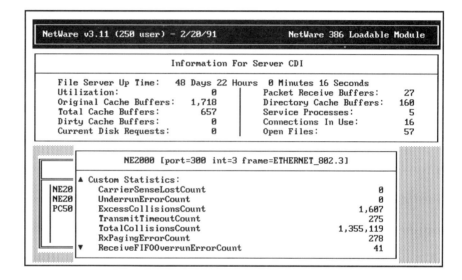

Figure 10.13:
The Resource
Utilization menu.

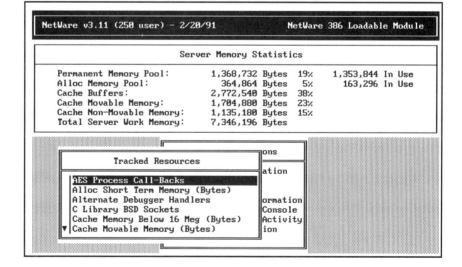

Using Other Commands To Monitor the Network

Other related commands that should be checked from time to time enable administrators to monitor the amount of disk space used, oversee the amount of free space, and provide control over how much disk space a user may use. In a network environment, the amount of disk space can be critical. For instance, if a network volume fills to capacity, all network printing may stop, menu systems may fail, and applications may generate errors. It is not simply a problem with disk space. The following utilities are intended to provide the system administrator and users with information that should help to prevent a disk drive from filling up.

Many other programs are available on the market. The following NetWare commands are a great place to start looking for solutions to network problems. If these commands do not fix the problem, it may be a hardware-specific problem. If this is the case, test the equipment and look for specialized diagnostic programs.

Using RCONSOLE To Make the Connection

Although much of the familiar FCONSOLE functions are no longer available when used on the 3.11 file server, Novell has provided a workstation connection through RCONSOLE that enables system administrators to access the MONITOR and other console utilities. RCONSOLE enables system utilities and CONSOLE operations that normally require direct console access from the workstation.

The RCONSOLE utility requires two NLMs to be loaded at the file server. Both REMOTE.NLM and RSPX.NLM must be loaded on any 3.11 file server that requires access by the RCONSOLE utility. After selecting the file server from the list provided and typing in your password, you are presented with a connection to the file server console.

Checking the Directory Using CHKDIR

CHKDIR is used to view information about a volume or directory. CHKDIR displays space limitations for the file server, volume, and directory you may be checking.

This command displays the maximum storage capacity of a volume or directory if a space limitation has been placed on it. CHKDIR is a very useful utility for all users to determine the amount of free space their directory may have.

If space limitations have been placed on users, the CHKDIR utility enables users to keep track of the amount of space they have left. CHKDIR is used by simply entering the command by itself or by entering the command plus the path of the directory you are checking on.

Checking Volume Space Using CHKVOL

The CHKVOL utility displays total volume space. This space includes total space used by files, deleted files, FATs, and directories. All CHKVOL information is presented in kilobytes and is useful when complete volume information is required.

The information provided by CHKVOL is presented in a simple, two-column format. CHKVOL displays the following information:

- File server name
- Volume name
- Total volume space
- Total space used by files, FATS, and directory tables
- Space in use by deleted files
- Space available from deleted files
- Space remaining on volume
- Space available to user

As with CHKDIR, CHKVOL can be used with or without a directory path. CHKVOL also permits the use of the standard DOS wild card characters (* and ?). CHKVOL *, for example, displays information for all volumes, and CHKVOL */* displays information for all volumes on all the file servers you are attached to.

Administering VOLINFO

The VOLINFO (Volume Information) utility is probably the administrator's most commonly used command. The VOLINFO utility presents in table form the total space, free space, and directory entries on all volumes (see fig. 10.14). Issuing the VOLINFO command is the simplest way to view volume free space.

Figure 10.14:
Volume Information main screen.

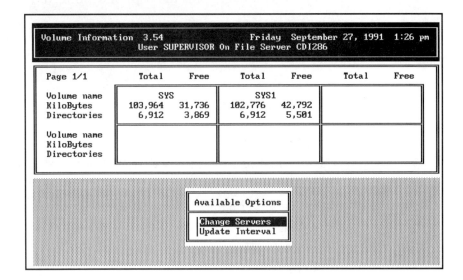

Novell also has made available a Windows version of VOLINFO. Figure 10.15 is an example of VOLINFO for Windows. This is part of the NetWare tools programs provided by Novell. This utility provides a standard Microsoft Windows interface and enables space to be presented in megabytes or kilobytes.

Using NVER

The NVER command is useful when the LAN driver version and configuration and file server versions are needed. This utility is a common tool when performing telephone support.

Figure 10.15:
Windows 3.0
Volume
Information screen.

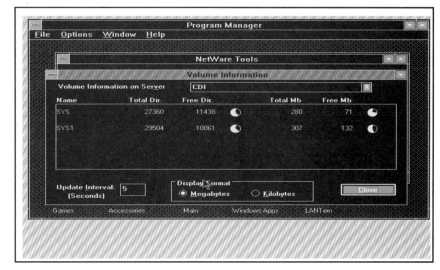

NVER supplies version information for the following:

NETBIOS

IPX

SPX

LAN driver

SHELL

DOS

File server name

The NVER command is very convenient when checking version numbers and updating LAN drivers.

Checking Connections with COMCHECK

Comcheck enables the administrator to check workstation communication and node addresses without being logged in to the network. Figure 10.16 shows the main screen as each workstation calls up COMCHECK.

Figure 10.16:
COMCHECK's main
screen.

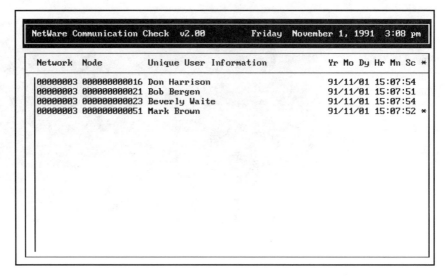

Before using COMCHECK, each workstation that you want to test must have IPX loaded. COMCHECK asks for unique user information so that each workstation can be tracked as it is attached.

Esc brings up an optional menu from which the administrator can modify the Broadcast Delay Period and the Dead Timeout Period. Figure 10.17 shows that the default Broadcast Delay Period is 15 seconds, which is how often this workstation broadcasts its capability to talk on the cable.

The Dead Timeout Period, as shown in Figure 10.18, by default is 60 seconds. The Dead Timeout Period shows how long a workstation waits for another workstation to broadcast. If no new broadcasts are received, the workstation is considered "dead" or unable to respond.

Changing NET$OS.EXE or ROUTER.EXE with DCONFIG

DCONFIG can be used to discover the current settings for a v2.2 operating system or for the router. To view the settings, type **DCONFIG**, and then **NET$OS.EXE** or **ROUTER.EXE**.

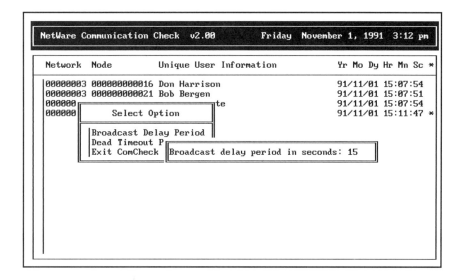

Figure 10.17:
Comcheck's
Broadcast Delay
Period.

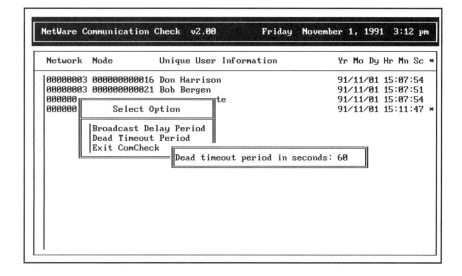

Figure 10.18:
Comcheck's Dead
Timeout Period.

DCONFIG displays the amount of buffers allocated, network address, hardware configuration, and channel information (see fig 10.19). The standard DCONFIG display shows all the possible hardware configuration options. The option highlighted by the * is the currently selected option. All of this information can be changed on the command line without regenerating the program.

```
Buffers: 40
LAN A Configuration:
  Network Address: 00000003
  Node address is determined automatically.
  Hardware Type: NetWare RX-Net  V1.00 (881010)
* 0:  IRQ = 2,  I/O Base = 2E0h,  RAM Buffer at D000:0
  1:  IRQ = 2,  I/O Base = 350h,  RAM Buffer at C000:0
  2:  IRQ = 2,  I/O Base = 300h,  RAM Buffer at CC00:0
  3:  IRQ = 2,  I/O Base = 2F0h,  RAM Buffer at DC00:0
  4:  IRQ = 3,  I/O Base = 2E0h,  RAM Buffer at D000:0
  5:  IRQ = 3,  I/O Base = 350h,  RAM Buffer at C000:0
  6:  IRQ = 3,  I/O Base = 300h,  RAM Buffer at CC00:0
  7:  IRQ = 3,  I/O Base = 2F0h,  RAM Buffer at DC00:0
  8:  IRQ = 4,  I/O Base = 2E0h,  RAM Buffer at D000:0
  9:  IRQ = 4,  I/O Base = 350h,  RAM Buffer at C000:0
 10:  IRQ = 4,  I/O Base = 300h,  RAM Buffer at CC00:0
 11:  IRQ = 4,  I/O Base = 2F0h,  RAM Buffer at DC00:0
 12:  IRQ = 7,  I/O Base = 2E0h,  RAM Buffer at D000:0
 13:  IRQ = 7,  I/O Base = 350h,  RAM Buffer at C000:0
 14:  IRQ = 7,  I/O Base = 300h,  RAM Buffer at CC00:0
 15:  IRQ = 7,  I/O Base = 2F0h,  RAM Buffer at DC00:0
Disk Driver: Industry Standard ISA or AT Comp. Disk Cont. V2.01 (890810)
  Channel 0 Configuration:
* 0: ISADISK       PRIMARY        Verify=ON       I/O=1F0h    IRQ=14
-- More --
```

Figure 10.20 shows the command line options available. Using DCONFIG is a convenient way to make minor modifications to the operating system. To change the file on the file server, flag the file as Read/Write first. Remember to flag the file as Read Only after the change has been made, and then reboot the machine.

The DCONFIG utility is helpful when you need to change the network LAN address and LAN driver configuration options or when you need to adjust communications buffers. Each of these parameters was discussed earlier in the chapter.

Requiring LAN addresses to be changed is common when a multi-server network is moved or reconfigured.

Troubleshooting Utilities

Included with NetWare are several utilities that enable system administrators to diagnose and repair network problems. These utilities are designed to be used in the event of specific difficulties. In this section, you learn about repairing the binderies with BINDFIX, limiting disk space with DSPACE, and fixing Volumes with VREPAIR.

Figure 10.20:
DCONFIG Options.

```
O:\NETWARE\SYSTEM-2>dconfig
Usage:  dconfig [volume:]file [parameter list]
           or
         dconfig -i[volume:]file   (Take input from specified file.)

Where [parameter list] is zero or more of:
  A-E: [net address], [node address], [configuration #];
  C0-7: [driver type], [configuration #];
  OTHER: [signature], [Configuration #];
  SHELL: [node address], [configuration #];
  BUFFERS: [number of buffers];

O:\NETWARE\SYSTEM-2>
```

As a system supervisor, you need to be aware of the items in a network that frequently have problems. Even more important, you need to know where to check for information in order to prevent system downtime and performance problems.

Repairing the Binderies Using BINDFIX

Bindery files contain all the security information about users and groups on the system. Password requirements, station and time restrictions, and security equivalences are all kept in these files which are flagged as Hidden and System files residing in the SYS:SYSTEM directory.

The two bindery files in v2.2 are NET$BIND.SYS and NET$BVAL.SYS. NET$BIND.SYS contains all the user and group names as well as all the account restriction parameters. NET$BVAL.SYS contains all the values that apply to the account restrictions. All users access the bindery files through the file server to make use of network facilities.

NetWare v3.11 provides three bindery files: NET$OBJ.SYS, NET$PROP.SYS, and NET$VAL.SYS. When a user logs into the network, the system first checks the NET$OBJ.SYS file to see if the login name is recognized by the file server. After verifying that the login name is valid, the system looks into the NET$PROP.SYS file to see if any account restrictions are on the login ID. If there are any restrictions, the final step is to check the NET$VAL.SYS file to find the actual value of the restrictions.

One of the system supervisor's responsibilities is to change the rights for a user. As a manager, you normally make the modification to a user's account from the SYSCON menu or the GRANT command line utility, and then exit. Outside of SYSCON, you might notice that it appears that the change did not take place, and upon re-entering SYSCON, you find that the modification has disappeared. This scenario indicates a possible corruption of the bindery files. The BINDFIX utility is designed to examine the bindery files and to mend defects.

The rules for running BINDFIX are simple, but should be followed exactly for the most accurate results.

1. Make sure that you are the only user logged in to the system, as the user supervisor.

2. Secure the file server with the command DISABLE LOGIN, so that no one can log in while you are performing the BINDFIX operation.

3. Place yourself in the SYS:SYSTEM directory and type BINDFIX.

 Note BINDFIX is one of the supervisory commands found in the SYS:SYSTEM directory. By default, only supervisor equivalents have rights to this directory.

The program asks two questions: would you like to delete mail directories for users that no longer exist? Would you like to delete trustee assignments for users that no longer exist? BINDFIX attempts to repair the binderies so that users no longer on the system are no longer part of the current security setup.

BINDFIX attempts to match common network elements on the system. For example, it checks to see that if a user is a member of a group, that the group really exists. Likewise, if a user is a member of a group, BINDFIX attempts to verify the existence of that user on the system (see fig. 10.21).

Figure 10.21:
The BINDFIX utility.

```
F:\SYSTEM>bindfix
Rebuilding Bindery.  Please Wait.
Checking for invalid nodes
Checking object's property lists.
Checking properties to see if they are in an object property list.
Checking objects for back-link property.
Checking set consistency and compacting sets.
Building avail lists and new hash tables.
There are 271 Object nodes and 64 Property Nodes free.
Checking user objects for standard properties.
Checking group objects for standard properties.
Checking links between users and groups for consistency.
Delete mail directories of users that no longer exist? (y/n): Y
Checking for mail directories of users that no longer exist.
Checking for users that do not have mail directories.
Delete trustee rights for users that no longer exist? (y/n): Y
Checking volume SYS.  Please wait.
Checking volume SYS1.  Please wait.

Bindery check successfully completed.
Please delete the files NET$BIND.OLD and NET$BVAL.OLD after you have verified
the reconstructed bindery.

F:\SYSTEM>
```

When BINDFIX is complete, it returns a message that it was successful or unsuccessful. If unsuccessful, you might have to rely on a version of the binderies that was previously backed up before the corruption occurred.

If BINDFIX is successful, the next step is to verify that the problem is gone. In this example, go back into SYSCON and try to modify the trustee assignments. BINDFIX creates new bindery files and renames the previous files with OLD extensions. If the problem is gone, the OLD files can be deleted.

NetWare also provides a utility called BINDREST. This utility is intended to restore the "old" bindery files if a problem occurs. To run BINDREST, follow the rules used with BINDFIX and run the BINDREST command. BINDREST replaces the binderies with the OLD extension.

The only time to use BINDFIX, when no problems are evident, is if you have deleted a large number of users from the system. BINDFIX makes sure that the binderies are purged of any information pertaining to the deleted users.

Limiting Disk Space Using DSPACE

NetWare's DSPACE utility enables system administrators to place limits on the amount of disk space a particular user can use. DSPACE is designed to limit a user's personal use of disk space. Many network users assume that the file server has unlimited storage capacity. A knowledgeable computer user can easily use a large amount of disk space. When used properly, DSPACE can limit a user's available space without jeopardizing normal network operations. Figure 10.22 shows the opening screen of the DSPACE utility.

The DSPACE utility provides the following options:

- Limit users' disk space
- Limit disk and directory space
- Change current file server

Figure 10.22:
The DSPACE main
menu.

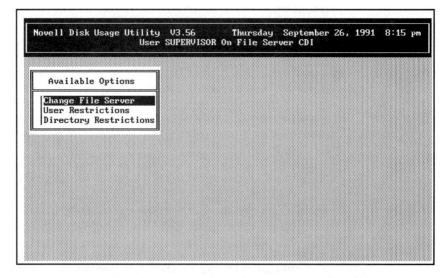

To limit disk space in a volume directory, select the Directory Restrictions option from the menu. Then select a directory and modify the field presented in the Directory Disk Space Limitation Information data entry box (see fig. 10.23). If you do not have rights to modify this directory area, the DSPACE utility does not provide you with modifiable fields.

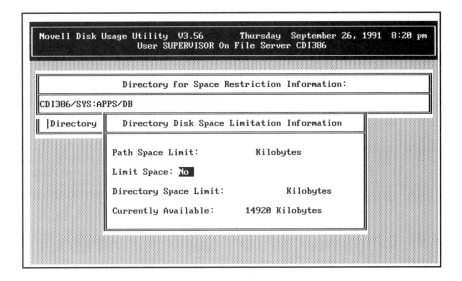

Figure 10.23:
Directory Disk
Space Limitation
Information.

To limit a user's space on a disk drive, select the User Restrictions option from the DSPACE main menu (see fig. 10.22). After selecting a user, a list of available volumes appears. You are presented with the User Disk Space Limitation Information screen (see fig. 10.24) if you have the proper rights.

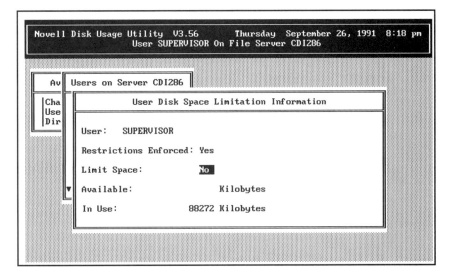

Figure 10.24:
User Disk Space
Limitation
Information screen.

In both figures 10.23 and 10.24 the user SUPERVISOR has no restrictions. To limit disk space, you must answer Yes to Limit Space and then fill in the memory limit.

Fixing Volumes Using VREPAIR

VREPAIR enables an administrator to attempt a software repair of a volume that appears to have problems. The most common use of VREPAIR is when the power to the file server has been cut off, causing Data Mirror Mismatches or FAT table errors that prevent the server from booting.

From a v2.2 server, boot the file server with DOS and run the version of VREPAIR configured on the OSEXE disk when the system was generated. From v3.11, you type **LOAD VREPAIR** and repair the dismounted volume.

 Use VREPAIR with discretion and always make sure that you have a current backup. When run on a good disk that is having FAT table errors, VREPAIR is effective. If, however, there are defects with the disk that are hard to detect, VREPAIR may destroy data.

The VREPAIR NLM enables you to choose a volume to repair or set the VREPAIR options (see fig. 10.25). The options that you can set are as follows:

- Remove Name Space support
- Write the DET and FAT tables to disk
- Write changes at once to disk

VREPAIR checks the volume and attempts to repair file discrepancies with a valid File Allocation Table. Figure 10.26 shows the VREPAIR prompts. VREPAIR takes a considerable length of time if there are problems with the files. It is best to avoid interrupting the VREPAIR process, so allow sufficient time for the utility to complete the repair procedure.

Figure 10.25:
The VREPAIR
options screen.

```
Current Vrepair Configuration:

    Quit If A Required VRepair Name Space Support NLM Is Not Loaded

    Write Only Changed Directory And FAT Entries Out To Disk

    Keep Changes In Memory For Later Update

Options:

    1. Remove Name Space support from the volume

    2. Write All Directory And FAT Entries Out To Disk

    3. Write Changes Immediately To Disk

    0. Return To Main Menu

    Enter your choice:
```

Figure 10.26:
VREPAIR on VOL1.

```
Total errors: 0
Current settings:
  Pause after each error
  Do not log errors to a file
Press F1 to change settings

Start 5:08:33 pm
Checking volume VOL1

FAT blocks>...................................................................<
Counting directory blocks and checking directory FAT entries
Mirror mismatches>...........................................................<
Directories>.................................................................<
Files>.......................................................................<
Trustees>....................................................................<
Free blocks>.................................................................<

Done checking volume
Total Time 0:00:10
<Press any key to continue>
```

Troubleshooting and Optimizing Your File Server

The process of optimizing a Novell 2.x or 3.x file server has always been, and probably always will be the source of debate among LAN engineers and technicians. Some argue that adjusting memory settings, upgrading to new high performance drivers, and adding exotic new file server devices is simply unnecessary, while others willingly go to great lengths in search of improved performance. As with the automobile, some are satisfied with a simple, functional Chevrolet; others require an exotic sports car. But whether your file server is a Chevy, or a Ferrari, it requires a tune-up now and then.

As new hardware technology continues to develop and programming engineers devise new methods of communicating with them, optimization methods also will continue to evolve. In this chapter, you learn some of the tips, tricks, and facts used by LAN engineers who live and breath networks.

The information given in this chapter is not for everyone. Each file server and each network operates in a different set of circumstances. Each environment requires a different set of system adjustments. In this section, you are given an explanation of each of the SET commands supplied to NetWare 3.x users. You also are shown when and where to adjust some of these settings. Users of NetWare 2.x are given some suggestions on how to make sure that their servers are operating as best they can. Again, each environment and each file server requires a separate set of rules and instructions to properly make use of the facilities available.

To optimize a LAN file server or workstation for that matter, is an art, not an exact procedure. The process is made up of carefully thought out and documented steps, with each step having a goal. Although NetWare 3.1x is a self-tuning operating system, many issues may require manual changes. The following paragraphs give you an overview of the file server components and explain how they can be adjusted.

Workstation Notes

Before you spend a large amount of time in search of file server performance, always be sure that you are using the most current version of workstation software. Novell has gone through many versions of IPX and NETx. The dedicated IPX.COM program previously created with Novell's WSGEN or SHGEN programs is at this time version 3.10. Novell intends to phase out the dedicated IPX, so this should be the last version.

Currently, with Novell's ODI drivers you should use at least LSL version 1.21 and IPXODI version 1.20. The MLID drive varies with each manufacturer. Novell's NETX, BNETX, EMSNETX, and XMSNETX DOS requesters are at this time version 3.26. Every release of these programs includes programming fixes and enhancements. To obtain the current version of all workstation software is a good way to start the optimizing process. This can save you many hours of searching for something someone else has already found.

DOS Memory Optimizing

When you optimize your local workstation's memory, you must prevent conflicts with other components using these memory areas. Many network cards use memory areas that conflict with software memory managers. These managers are designed to administer and reclaim unused memory for program use, but sometimes the managers reclaim memory needed by other applications.

Figure 10.27 displays some commonly used—or misused—memory areas that you should be aware of. These areas are commonly used, but are not indisputably what your computer may be using. The only absolute way to tell what your computer uses is to check with the documentation that comes with each installed adapter card.

A common problem that causes workstation lockup or network errors is memory manager software stepping on the memory buffer area of your network card. For example, if your network interface uses a memory segment from D000h to DFFFh, then this area should be excluded from your memory manager software. This informs the memory manager software that the area will be used at a later time by another device.

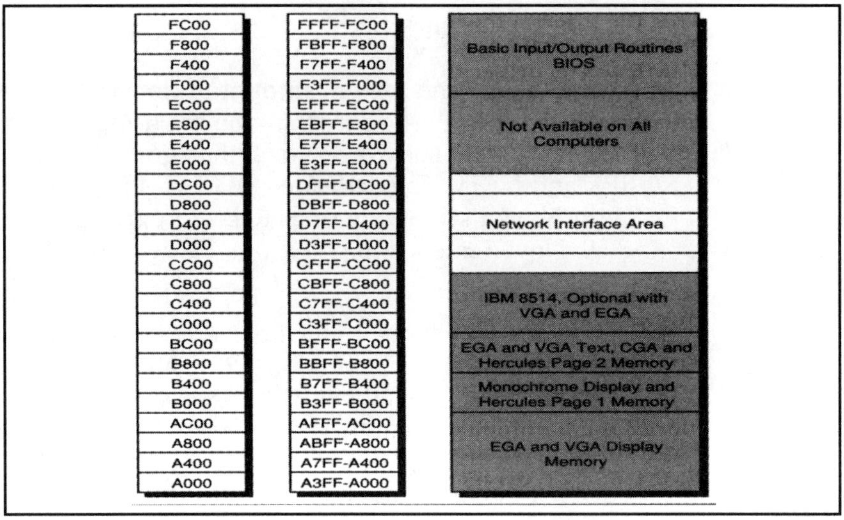

Figure 10.27:
Common memory
usage areas.

FC00	FFFF-FC00	
F800	FBFF-F800	Basic Input/Output Routines
F400	F7FF-F400	BIOS
F000	F3FF-F000	
EC00	EFFF-EC00	
E800	EBFF-E800	Not Available on All
E400	E7FF-E400	Computers
E000	E3FF-E000	
DC00	DFFF-DC00	
D800	DBFF-D800	
D400	D7FF-D400	Network Interface Area
D000	D3FF-D000	
CC00	CFFF-CC00	
C800	CBFF-C800	
C400	C7FF-C400	IBM 8514, Optional with
C000	C3FF-C000	VGA and EGA
BC00	BFFF-BC00	EGA and VGA Text, CGA and
B800	BBFF-B800	Hercules Page 2 Memory
B400	B7FF-B400	Monochrome Display and
B000	B3FF-B000	Hercules Page 1 Memory
AC00	AFFF-AC00	
A800	ABFF-A800	EGA and VGA Display
A400	A7FF-A400	Memory
A000	A3FF-A000	

NetWare 3.1x Server Components

To properly understand how or why your server needs optimizing requires a basic knowledge of the different components that make up
the Novell NetWare file server.

Both NetWare 2.x and 3.x contain the following four basic components:

- **Memory.** Novell NetWare greatly depends on memory for
  much of its performance and normal operation. Memory is
  not only used for the disk caching most of you are familiar
  with, but also for communications buffers and the maintenance of many memory resident tables and buffer areas of
  the individual modules that are part of your file server.

- **Communications.** All LAN I/O is controlled in the communications component. Things like packet size, buffers,
  protocols, and communications to other network cards are
  performed by these processes.

- **File System.** The NetWare file system includes not only direct control of the storage devices, but also reading and
  writing of cache. This cache technology enables NetWare
  to supply the performance it is known for.

- **Main Processor.** This is the Intel CPU and bus architecture of the file server itself. Intel currently produces a wide range of popular processors, such as the 80286, 80386 and 80486. These are used in computers designed with ISA, MCA and EISA bus technologies.

Novell provides the tools to monitor most of these functions in both the 2.x and 3.x product line. NetWare 3.x provides SET commands to make manual fine adjustments, whereas NetWare 2.x generally requires some system reconfiguration to adjust these options. In the NetWare 286 product line, you do not have SET commands to tune the environment. A full reference to these SET commands is presented at the end of this chapter.

NetWare Memory

In NetWare 2.x, Novell used the Intel 80286 processor chip and its protected mode memory model. Because of this, NetWare 2.x requires everything to be configured when loading. This prevents the capability to optimize or fine-tune while the system is operational.

NetWare 3.x takes advantage of the Intel 80386 enhanced addressing capability. This enables the processor to access a continuous segment of memory by the use of 32-bit registers. NetWare 3.x makes use of memory pools—memory groupings that have similar characteristics—to manage its memory requirements. These memory pools require optimizing, whether automatically or manually through the SET commands. These memory pools each supply resources to particular file server functions. A summary of each of the memory pools follows:

- **File Cache Buffers.** This is the main memory pool. This pool is primarily used for disk cache reads and writes and acts as the main resource for memory when needed. Memory taken from this pool can be returned when no longer needed. The pool also contains two sub-pools.

    The Cache Non-movable Pool provides memory to NLMs that require it. Both MONITOR and INSTALL pull memory from this pool.

The Cache Moveable Pool is a special pool that cannot be accessed by NLMs. This pool is used for tables such as FAT and Directory tables that expand or shrink.

- **Permanent Memory Pool.** The permanent memory pool is primarily used for Directory Cache Buffers and Communications Buffers. This memory is allocated when needed and not returned after use. One of the issues discussed in this section is how to efficiently allocate this memory to prevent the waste of these precious resources.

- **Semi-Permanent Pool.** The semi-permanent pool is a sub-pool used for LAN and disk drivers. This memory pool allows the return of memory when no longer needed.

- **Alloc Short Term Memory Pool.** This memory pool is for small, short term uses. Memory allocations from this pool are less than 4KB and are generally returned very quickly. This pool normally does not grow much, but allocates memory from the Permanent Memory Pool if needed. If additional memory is taken from the Permanent Memory Pool, it will not be returned until the file server is rebooted.

Communications

The Novell communications processes provide services that include Packet Sizes, Communications Buffers, Burst Mode, SAP filtering and Network cards.

In the Communications section you can manually control the default file server packet size. The standard default size is 1KB, which may or may not be properly set for your installation. This can be adjusted by placing the appropriate SET command in your STARTUP.NCF file. The SET commands that deal with communications should be set properly to provide memory efficiently.

 To maintain the flow of Novell's current technology, the Communications buffers may also be referred to as *LSL (Link Support Layer)* Buffers.

As Packet Receive Buffers are needed, they are allocated as memory blocks equal to the default packet size. A *Packet Receive Buffer* is a block of memory used to hold data temporarily during times of heavy traffic. For example, if you are using Ethernet which communicates using a packet size of 1KB, and you have your default packet size set to 4K, the amount of wasted memory can be substantial. Buffers will be allocated at a size of 4KB each, which is not returned to the pool. This greatly reduces the amount of available memory to be used elsewhere.

Set the Maximum Physical Receive Packet Size to the proper size used on the server without going larger than necessary. This ensures that precious memory can be used for other processes that need it.

A short list of standard packet sizes that can be used when the actual size is unknown is shown below:

Arcnet	618
Ethernet	1130
4Mbps Token Ring	2154
16Mbps Token Ring	4202

NetWare 2.x does not enable you to adjust the Packet Receive Buffer size. This is determined by the network interface driver.

After efficiently configuring your packet size, evaluate the number of buffers allocated on startup. These Communications buffers are allocated as needed. You can pre-allocate these buffers and set a maximum on startup. This can prevent initially slow response time after you reboot your server.

The following commands are contained in the end of this section as well as an explanation on how to properly use them.

```
SET MINIMUM PACKET RECEIVE BUFFERS=

SET MAXIMUM PACKET RECEIVE BUFFERS=

SET NEW PACKET RECEIVE BUFFER WAIT TIME=
```

These commands complement each other and should be adjusted with a balance of performance and memory usage in mind.

For example, when you install the Novell EISA NE3200 ethernet adapter, you should set up a minimum of 200 Communications Buffers. When using the proper packet size, this is a memory requirement of 226KB. If the file server is set up with a maximum packet size of 4202, it requires 840.4KB. This is a memory waste of 614.4KB.

NetWare 2.x does not allocate Communications Buffers dynamically. Communications buffers, as with all other memory requirements must be allocated upon startup.

To adjust the number of Communications Buffers allocated by NetWare 2.2, you must use the Novell DCONFIG utility or make changes through the INSTALL utility under the File Server Definition Screen. You also can make this change to an existing 2.2 file server by using the INSTALL -f.

Server Network Cards

The network interface card can be one of the most difficult items to diagnose. Statistics on the LAN drivers can be viewed by using the FCONSOLE utility on NetWare 2.x and the MONITOR utility on NetWare 3.x. Network interface saturation can result in a bottleneck that can greatly reduce LAN read and write performance.

With both NetWare 2.x and NetWare 3.x, no adjustments affect the performance of your network cards. The methods of optimization used here are proper selection and configuration of the hardware. Novell instructs network card manufacturers to make use of approximately 15 statistics monitored by way of the FCONSOLE or MONITOR utilities. About 20 optional statistics can be implemented if the manufacturers so desire.

Statistics to watch vary from one manufacturer to another and are difficult to discuss without explaining each and every popular network card.

For example, when you use NetWare 3.x and the Novell NE2000 16-bit ethernet interface card, the statistic EnqueuedSendsCount must not be over 2% of the total packets transmitted. This indicates the number of packets placed into a buffer because the network interface was too busy to service it. This is an indication of a saturated network card. The only solution is to lower the load on the interface or install a 32-bit interface.

Name Space

When name space OS/2, MAC, or NFS is added to a NetWare 3.x volume, you must consider whether to reinitialize the volume. When you add name space to a volume during initial creation, the DOS FAT table and Name Space are created within the same Directory Block. This allows the non-DOS workstation to, in most cases, only require a single block to be cached when searching for a file.

If Name Space is added at a later date, after thousands of disk reads and writes, it is virtually impossible for these directory tables to be written to the same Directory Block. This requires the non-DOS client to cache more Directory Blocks to access the same data. On a busy network, this can be a significant performance degradation.

 In a NetWare 2.x environment, Macintosh space support is handled by the VAPs and is not controllable as in NetWare 3.x.

File System

NetWare's High Performance File System depends greatly on memory cache. The process of optimizing the NetWare file system requires adjusting the block and buffer size, FATs, Directory Entry Tables, and NCP reads and writes.

Because NetWare relies so heavily on memory for the many processes running on the file server, memory should never be reduced for budget reasons. This is comparable to leaving out the spare tire on your new car to reduce the cost. It runs OK until you need it; then things get a little slower.

NetWare 3.x requires much more memory than a 2.x file server. A properly performing 3.x file server will attempt to allocate memory when needed by the many processes. Communications Buffers, Directory Entry Tables, and other processes may require additional RAM depending on your system's load.

 The rule of thumb in NetWare 3.x is the sky is the limit. NetWare 3.x does not have a limit on the practical maximum of memory you can add to the file server. It is to your advantage to have memory available if needed.

Many of the SET parameters used to adjust the file system are unnecessary if you simply install enough memory.

NetWare 2.x has a point of diminishing return when it comes to memory and cache blocks. In a 2.x file server the rule of thumb is to have between 800 and 1000 cache blocks. More than this provides little improvement and in some cases can cause a performance loss because of system overhead.

When you create a NetWare volume, you have the capability to select the Disk Block Size. Unless you have a special application that suggests larger block sizes, use the default of 4KB. NetWare enables you to configure the block size by volume. If you think you may need larger disk blocks, keep in mind the number of standard DOS files you also may have. The tradeoffs of giving large blocks to a few large applications may be a performance degradation for the remainder of the network unless you segregate your applications on different volumes.

 In v3.11, when adding Novell NFS to a volume, consider installing the volume with 8K blocks. This increases the NFS performance because the NFS transmits data in 8K blocks.

Also, large amounts of cache memory greatly increase NFS performance.

An optimized NetWare NFS server should have 8K Disk Blocks and 8K Cache Blocks.

NetWare 3.x also enables you to configure the cache block size. Highest performance is achieved when the cache block and disk block size match. This may not be possible as you must maintain a cache block size that matches the smallest disk block used on the file server.

NetWare 3.x provides SET commands that enable you to fine-tune some of these performance features. The cache and disk blocks described above do affect disk performance, but basically set up the system's static configuration. The following are a few settings that enable you to modify some of the dynamic settings.

 In terms of advanced system optimizing, NetWare 2.x falls behind. Because all NetWare 2.x settings are static, you are limited greatly. Here is where NetWare 3.x shows its superiority.

When you optimize your NetWare 3.x file server, determine whether you should optimize for read performance or write performance. Most systems perform many more reads than writes. All the NetWare SET commands are detailed at the end of this section, but a few of the most common are highlighted here.

- MAXIMUM CONCURRENT DISK CACHE WRITES. This setting determines how many disk writes are put into the NetWare elevator for actual disk I/O. In a write intensive file server, if you increase this value, you increase disk write performance. If you decrease this value, read performance increases.

Here again, memory is important. The more memory your server has, the better the performance is.

 In NetWare 3.x, no more than 75% of total cache can be considered Dirty Cache Blocks—or a block in need of service, or one that needs to be written to the disk.

- IMMEDIATE PURGE OF DELETED FILES. NetWare 3.x as a default maintains a table of deleted files. This table is used by the SALVAGE command when searching for deleted files. Although this service is nice at times, it does require substantial overhead and requires the disk system to perform extra operations to keep the list current.

  If you change this option from the default of OFF to ON, you can greatly improve the response time of disk access on a busy file server. This does, however, have the drawback of disabling the salvage capability.

- DISK READ AFTER WRITE VERIFY. This function controls NetWare's read after write services. This service is critical to the integrity of your data, but may be redundant depending on your hardware. This SET command controls the option of providing this service with software. Some higher level disk controllers, such as SCSI controllers, provide disk read after write verification at the hardware level which makes this NetWare option redundant. In this case, when you set DISK READ AFTER WRITE VERIFY=*OFF*, you increase your disk I/O responsiveness.

 The option of DISK READ AFTER WRITE VERIFY should not be modified on an operating server. Some controllers report unpredictable results when they attempt to make this change while the file server is running. You can make the change either in the STARTUP.NCF or with the drive dismounted.

In NetWare 2.x, the capability to modify the DISK READ AF-
TER WRITE VERIFY option is determined by the 2.x VADD
(Value Added Disk Driver). If implemented, this option must
be selected while generating the system.

Be careful when controlling this option. If you turn off this option
when not supplied by the hardware, you will effectively disable
NetWare's HOT FIX functionality.

Main Processor

The main system processor is normally the least likely source of any
file server's problems. Items such as memory and intelligent adapter
cards can generally be installed to lessen the support required by the
main processor. Loading the 3.x console MONITOR utility with the
command line switch of -p, as in the following example, provides information you can use to aid in determining this fact.

Load monitor -p <enter>

Figure 10.28 shows the screen after loading MONITOR with a -p option. The -p option provides the added menu choice of Processor Utilization which can be used to monitor each of the processes requiring
CPU service time. This option enables you to monitor processes and
hardware items by watching their hardware interrupt service time.

Figure 10.28
Load MONITOR -p.

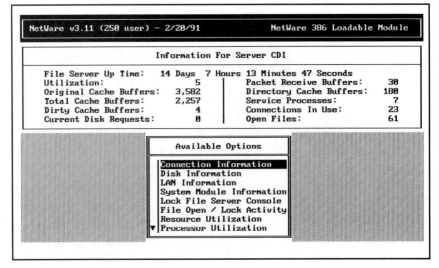

Note When you press <F3> after selecting the Processor Utilization option, all file server processes display. When you press <F5> on each item, you can tag and monitor select items for viewing.

While you are monitoring the file server processes, be aware of items that require a high level of support time. When you observe the Processor Utilization screen, the Polling Process should make up the majority of the CPU's time. See the example in figure 10.29. Notice both the Polling Process and the Remote Process. In many cases, it may be showing levels in the 90s. This is completely normal; the polling process is using what other processes are not in search of a process to service.

Figure 10.29:
MONITOR -p with <F3>.

```
NetWare v3.11 (250 user) - 2/20/91          NetWare 386 Loadable Module

         Name                    Time      Count     Load
Fi ▲  Polling Process         1,064,523       76    92.47 %
Ut    PRODRA-I/O 0 Process        1,489        5     0.12 %      30
Or    PRODRA-IOCTL 0 Process          0        0     0.00 %      80
To    REMIRR Process                 0        0     0.00 %       7
Di    Remote Process            55,966       33     4.86 %      23
Cu    RSPX Process                   0        0     0.00 %      61
      Server 01 Process         11,553       17     1.00 %
      Server 02 Process              0        0     0.00 %
      Server 03 Process              0        0     0.00 %
      Server 04 Process              0        0     0.00 %
      Server 05 Process              0        0     0.00 %
      Server 06 Process              0        0     0.00 %
      Server 07 Process              0        0     0.00 %
      STREAMS Q Runner Process       0        0     0.00 %
      TCP Test Server Process        0        0     0.00 %
      TCP Timing Loop Process      403       18     0.03 %
      TCP/IP Packet Process          0        0     0.00 %
   ▼  TCP/IP Utility Process         0        0     0.00 %
```

By using the AUTOEXEC.NCF and STARTUP.NCF files as documentation, you can determine which hardware device is attached to which interrupt. Figure 10.30 shows a file server with a disk controller at interrupt 10 and network cards at interrupts 3 and 9. This enables you to determine what part of your file server may require upgrading or adjustments.

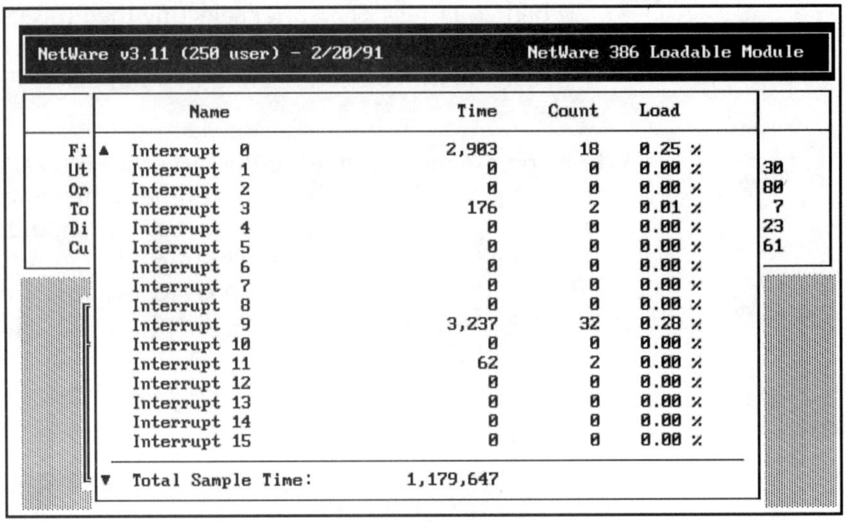

Figure 10.30:
Hardware
interrupts.

```
┌──────────────────────────────────────────────────────────────────┐
│ NetWare v3.11 (250 user) - 2/20/91        NetWare 386 Loadable Module │
├──────────────────────────────────────────────────────────────────┤
│          Name                    Time      Count    Load            │
│ Fi ▲  Interrupt  0              2,903       18     0.25 %           │
│ Ut    Interrupt  1                  0        0     0.00 %      30   │
│ Or    Interrupt  2                  0        0     0.00 %      80   │
│ To    Interrupt  3                176        2     0.01 %       7   │
│ Di    Interrupt  4                  0        0     0.00 %      23   │
│ Cu    Interrupt  5                  0        0     0.00 %      61   │
│       Interrupt  6                  0        0     0.00 %           │
│       Interrupt  7                  0        0     0.00 %           │
│       Interrupt  8                  0        0     0.00 %           │
│       Interrupt  9              3,237       32     0.28 %           │
│       Interrupt 10                  0        0     0.00 %           │
│       Interrupt 11                 62        2     0.00 %           │
│       Interrupt 12                  0        0     0.00 %           │
│       Interrupt 13                  0        0     0.00 %           │
│       Interrupt 14                  0        0     0.00 %           │
│       Interrupt 15                  0        0     0.00 %           │
│    ▼  Total Sample Time:      1,179,647                            │
└──────────────────────────────────────────────────────────────────┘
```

Using NetWare's SET Options

This section breaks the SET options down into nine different areas. Each area includes a chart of the available options and their ranges and default settings. After the charts, each option is explained in detail.

Communications Options

Communications buffers can be controlled through several parameters that deal with the packet receive buffers and the watchdog. The packet receive buffers are areas in the file server's memory used to hold data packets while the server attempts to process the data.

The watchdog is a service provided by the network to determine whether connections are valid. When the server notices that a workstation has not sent a packet in a preset amount of time, a watchdog packet is sent to the workstation. If the workstation does not respond in a given amount of time, another watchdog packet is sent. This continues for a preset number of retries, after which the server assumes that the workstation is no longer connected and the connection is cleared. Each of these variable parameters can be configured at the file server.

Table 10.1 lists the Communications Parameters for the file server configuration files and their defaults and option ranges. Each parameter is discussed in detail after the chart.

Table 10.1
Communications Options

Options	Default	Range
Console Display Watchdog Logouts	Off	On/Off
Delay Before First Watchdog Packet	4 Min 56.6 Sec	15.7 Seconds to 20 minutes 52.3 seconds
Delay between Watchdog Packets	59.3	1 Second to 10 Minutes 26.2 Seconds
Maximum Packet Receive Buffers	100	50 to 2000
Maximum Physical Receive Packet Size	1130	618 to 4202
Minimum Packet Receive Buffers	10	10 to 1000
New Packet Receive Buffer Wait Time	.1 Seconds	0.1 to 20 Seconds
Number of Watchdog Packets	10	5 to 100

Console Display Watchdog Logouts determines if a message is displayed on the file server monitor when the watchdog clears a workstation's connection. Use this option if you need to see which stations are being cleared through the watchdog. This option can be saved in the AUTOEXEC.NCF file or typed at the console prompt.

Delay Before First Watchdog Packet enables you to set the amount of time the server waits without hearing from a workstation before it sends out the first watchdog packet. Increase this option if your workstations load processor-intensive programs after loading the shell. You can place this option in the AUTOEXEC.NCF or type it at the console prompt.

Delay between Watchdog Packets enables you to set the amount of time between sending the watchdog packets. Use this option if the connections are being cleared too quickly. This option can be placed in the AUTOEXEC.NCF or typed at the console prompt.

Maximum Packet Receive Buffers enables you to configure the maximum number of packet receive buffers that the server can allocate. If the current number of packet receive buffers is at the maximum, increase this number until you have one buffer per workstation. Increase this number in multiples of 10.

If you are using EISA or microchannel bus master boards in the file server, increase this number for at least 5 buffers per board. If you are receiving `No ECB available count` errors, increase this number for at least 10 buffers per board. You can place this option in the AUTOEXEC.NCF or type it in at the console prompt.

Maximum Physical Receive Packet Size sets the maximum packet size for any packet transmitted on the internetwork. If you have network boards capable of transmitting more than 512 bytes of data per packet, set this parameter to the largest packet size. This option must be set in the STARTUP.NCF file.

Minimum Packet Receive Buffers is the minimum number of buffers that the server immediately allocates upon booting. Increase this number if the server is slow to respond immediately after booting. If you are using EISA or microchannel bus master boards in the file server, and you are receiving `No ECB available count` errors, increase this number for at least 5 buffers per board. This option must be set in the STARTUP.NCF file.

New Packet Receive Buffer Wait Time enables you to set the amount of time the server waits before it creates a buffer after receiving a buffer request. This option can prevent the operating system from creating too many packet receive buffers during sudden peak usage times. This option can be placed in the AUTOEXEC.NCF or typed at the console prompt.

 If you have an EISA bus master board in the file server, you should not change this parameter.

Number of Watchdog Packets sets the number of watchdog packets that will be sent out without receiving a reply from the workstation before terminating the connection. Increase this number if the watchdog is terminating sessions too quickly. This option can be placed into the AUTOEXEC.NCF or typed at the console prompt.

Directory Caching

This section discusses the parameters involved in fine-tuning Directory Caching on the file server. *Directory caching* is the method used to store frequently accessed files for instant access. These files are kept in a buffered memory area. As the file server receives requests for additional buffers, the server is is required to wait a certain amount of time before allocating the buffers. These variables can be changed and are defined below.

Table 10.2 lists the Directory Caching Parameters for the file server configuration files and their defaults and option ranges. Each parameter is discussed in detail after the table.

Table 10.2
Directory Caching Parameters

Options	Default	Range
Directory Cache Allocation Wait Time	2.2 Sec	.5 to 2 minutes
Directory Cache Buffer NonReferenced Delay	5.5 Sec	1 Second to 5 Minutes
Dirty Directory Cache Delay Time	0.5 Sec	0 to 10 seconds
Maximum Concurrent Directory Cache Writes	10	5 to 50
Maximum Directory Cache Buffers	500	20 to 4000
Minimum Directory Cache Buffers	20	10 to 2000

Directory Cache Allocation Wait Time enables you to set the amount of time the operating system must wait after allocating a new cache buffer before it can allocate another directory cache buffer. If you increase this number too much, the server may perform slowly. If the server is slow performing searches even after it has been running for 20 minutes, decrease this number. If you decrease this number too much, too many buffers are created and memory is wasted. Place this option in the AUTOEXEC.NCF or type it in at the console prompt.

Directory Cache Buffer NonReferenced Delay sets the amount of time an entry must be cached before it can be overwritten by another directory entry. If you increase this time, you increase the chance of a file being found in memory. If you decrease this time, you lessen the need for more cache buffers. This option can be placed in the AUTOEXEC.NCF or typed at the console prompt.

 File caching and directory caching are directly related. If you increase the number of directory buffers too much, the number of available file buffers decreases. These parameters must be balanced to achieve maximum performance.

Dirty Directory Cache Delay Time enables you to set the amount of time a directory table write request stays in memory before the server writes it to the disk. An increase in this time gives you somewhat quicker performance, but the risk of corrupting the directory tables increases. A decrease in this time lessens the probability of corrupting the directory table, but increases the number of writes, thereby decreasing the server's overall performance. This option can be placed in the AUTOEXEC.NCF or typed at the console prompt.

Maximum Concurrent Directory Cache Writes enables you to configure how many write requests will be buffered before the server initiates elevator seeking. *Elevator seeking* is the process by which the server accepts a number of requests to read or write information. The server then finds or writes the information in one pass, instead of making several passes.

An increase in this option makes writing to the disk more efficient; a decrease in this option makes reading from the disk more efficient. This option can be placed in the AUTOEXEC.NCF or typed at the console prompt.

Maximum Directory Cache Buffers sets the maximum number of directory cache buffers that the operating system can create. Directory cache buffers are allocated permanently until the server is rebooted. This option helps to keep the number of unnecessary blocks down.

Increase this number if the file server is responding slowly when doing directory searches. Decrease this number if you receive messages that the server is low on memory, or if too much memory is being allocated to directory caching. This option can be placed in the AUTOEXEC.NCF or typed at the console prompt.

Minimum Directory Cache Buffers enables a minimum number of directory cache buffers to be allocated for directory searches. Increase this number slightly when directory searches are slow immediately after booting the server. You need to have enough buffers to quickly do searches, however, you do not want to over-allocate these buffers because they do not go back into the memory pool. Unused directory cache buffers simply remain unused. This option can be set in the AUTOEXEC.NCF or STARTUP.NCF file, as well as at the console prompt.

Disk Options

This section contains only one configurable option for the hard drive: enabling the verification of Read After Write. This option controls one part of the Dynamic Bad Block Remapping, or Hot Fix. Hot Fix compares what was just written to what is still in memory. If the information that was written matches what came from memory, then the block is considered good. If the information does not match, then Hot Fix marks the block as bad and writes the information to the redirection area.

Table 10.3 lists the Disk Parameters for the file server configuration files and their defaults and option ranges. Each parameter is discussed in detail after the table.

Table 10.3
Disk Parameters

Options	Default	Range
Enable Disk Read After Write Verify	ON	ON or OFF

Enable Disk Read After Write Verify can be set to disable the read after write verification that NetWare's Hot Fix uses. This option is normally enabled if you have reliable hard drives that perform their own read after write verification. If you turn this option off, you can increase the performance of your disk writes. This option can be placed in the AUTOEXEC.NCF or typed at the console prompt.

File System

This section deals with file system options, such as warnings about almost full volumes, file purging, and reusing turbo FAT tables. Table 10.4 lists the File System Parameters for the file server configuration files and their defaults and option ranges. Each parameter is discussed in detail after the table.

Table 10.4
File System Parameters

Options	Default	Range
File Delete Wait Time	5 Minutes 29.6 Seconds	Seconds to 7 Days
Immediate Purge of Deleted Files	OFF	ON or OFF
Maximum Extended Attributes per File or Path	32	4 to 512
Maximum Percent of Volume Used By Directory	13	5 to 50
Maximum Percent of Volume Space Allowed for Extended Attributes	10	5 to 50
Maximum Subdirectory Tree Depth	25	10 to 100
Volume Low Warn All Users	ON	ON or OFF
Minimum File Delete Wait Time	1 Minute 5.9 Seconds	0 Seconds to 7 Days
NCP File Commit	ON	ON or OFF
Turbo FAT Re-Use Wait Time	5 Min 29.6 Sec	.3 seconds to 1 Hour 5 Minutes 54.6 Seconds
Volume Low Warning Threshold	256	0 to 1000000
Volume Low Warning Reset Threshold	256	0 to 100000

File Delete Wait Time enables you to set the amount of time the operating system attempts to keep a deleted file in a salvageable state. Remember that the operating system requires 1/32 of the entire volume size to be made available to users creating new files. Any file that has exceeded the time limit set by this parameter is set to be purged if the space is needed for new files.

Set this limit to any range acceptable to users that potentially need erased files. This limit has no effect if the volume is filled. When the volume is full and new files are created, the operating system starts purging the oldest deleted files in an attempt to open space for the new files. This option can be placed in the AUTOEXEC.NCF or typed at the console prompt.

Immediate Purge of Deleted Files enables you to decide if you want to keep deleted files for salvage. To improve system performance, set this option to ON. To maintain the capability to recover deleted files, leave this option set to OFF. You can place this option in the AUTOEXEC.NCF or enter it at the console prompt.

Maximum Extended Attributes per File or Path limits the number of extended attributes that can be assigned to the file or subdirectory on all volumes. Increase this number if you are using a large number of extended attributes. This option can be placed in the AUTOEXEC.NCF or typed at the console prompt.

Maximum Percent of Volume Used By Directory enables you to set the amount of volume space allocated for the directory tables. Adjust this number if you need to allow more room for or limit the size of the Directory Entry Tables. This option can be placed in the AUTOEXEC.NCF or typed at the console prompt.

Maximum Percent of Volume Space Allowed for Extended Attributes enables you to set the amount of the volume space to be used for extended attributes. This option takes effect only when the volume is being mounted. Adjust this number to allow adequate space for extended attributes. This option can be placed in the AUTOEXEC.NCF.

Maximum Subdirectory Tree Depth enables you to configure the number of subdirectory levels that the operating system can support. Increase this number if your applications can support directory levels greater than 25. Some DOS applications can only support 10 subdirectories. Decrease this option if your applications cannot support 25 subdirectories. This option must be set in the STARTUP.NCF file.

Volume Low Warn All Users enables you to determine whether users are warned when a volume is getting low on available space. If a volume becomes low on space often or if the message that is sent causes problems with an application turn this option OFF. This option can be placed in the AUTOEXEC.NCF or typed at the console prompt.

 If this option is turned off, make sure that you check the space on the volume frequently. Many applications crash if they do not have enough space to make temporary files. Novell's Message Handling Service (MHS) is an example of an application that has problems when the volume space is too low.

Minimum File Delete Wait Time enables you to set the amount of time a file must remain in the salvageable state before being flagged as purgeable. Increase this option if you want to make certain that files are kept salvageable even if the volume is full. This option can be placed in the AUTOEXEC.NCF or typed at the console prompt.

NCP File Commit allows an application to flag files for an immediate write to the hard drive. If you have applications that force an immediate write to the hard drive, set this option to ON to ensure that the write request does not sit in cache. Place this option in the AUTOEXEC.NCF or enter it at the console prompt.

Turbo FAT Re-Use Wait Time enables you to specify how long the Turbo FAT buffer will remain in memory after the file has been closed. (NetWare 3.x automatically indexes files that have 64 entries in the File Allocation Table. Because these indexes— called Turbo FATs—take some time to build, the system does not immediately delete the index when the file is closed.) Increase this option if you frequently reopen the same file. Decrease this option if you want the memory immediately added back for other files to use. This option can be placed into the AUTOEXEC.NCF or typed at the console prompt.

Volume Low Warning Threshold enables you to define how much space needs to be free on the volume before a volume low warning is sent. Increase this option if low volumes are not a problem for your applications; decrease it if you want early warnings about low volumes. This option can be placed in the AUTOEXEC.NCF or typed at the console prompt.

Volume Low Warning Reset Threshold sets the threshold at which the system sends another Volume Low warning to users. The volume's free space can teeter at the threshold set by Volume Low Warning Threshold. When this happens, users are creating and deleting enough files to cause the system to dip below the threshold and then rise above it. The system can send a warning for each dip below the threshold, but this may inundate users with messages. Use this option to set the reset level to an acceptable state so that the users get fewer messages for dipping below the threshold. This option can be placed in the AUTOEXEC.NCF or typed at the console prompt.

File Caching

This section defines the options that can be set to fine-tune how the file server can best access frequently used files. Accessed files often are stored in file cache buffers. The amount of buffers and the time that files are stored in the buffers is discussed below.

Table 10.5 lists the File Caching Parameters for the file server configuration files and their defaults and option ranges. Each parameter is discussed in detail after the table.

Table 10.5
File Caching Parameters

Option	Default	Range
Dirty Disk cache Delay Time	3.3 Sec	.1 to 10 seconds
Maximum Concurrent Disk Cache Writes	50	10 to 100
Minimum File Cache Buffers	20	20 to 1000
Minimum File Cache Report Threshold	20	0 to 1000

Dirty Disk Cache Delay Time sets the amount of time the file server keeps a write request that does not fill up an entire cache buffer in memory before writing it to disk. Increase this number if your users make many small write requests. This makes disk writing more efficient. A decrease in this number can reduce performance. This option can be placed in the AUTOEXEC.NCF or typed at the console prompt.

Maximum Concurrent Disk Cache Writes enables you to set the number of write requests that will be buffered in the elevator before the disk heads start to make a sweep of the drive. An increase in this number makes writing to the disk more efficient; a decrease makes the reading of the disk more efficient. Place this option in the AUTOEXEC.NCF or enter it at the console prompt.

Minimum File Cache Buffers enables you to set the minimum number of file cache buffers needed on your system, thereby limiting the amount of memory that can be given to requesting services. If this number is set too high, you may have trouble loading additional NLMs into memory. Increase this value only when you need more memory for file caching. This option can be placed in the AUTOEXEC.NCF or typed at the console prompt.

Minimum File Cache Report Threshold can warn you when all but the specified number of buffers, greater than the minimum file cache buffers, have been allocated to other resources. Use this option to alert yourself when the file cache buffers are getting low. This option generates the message `Number of cache buffers is getting too low.` The message `Cache memory allocator exceeded minimum cache buffer left limit` appears when you reach the minimum number of buffers. This message appears regardless how this option is set. This option can be placed in the AUTOEXEC.NCF or typed at the console prompt.

Locks

This section defines the configurable parameters for the Lock mechanism. These parameters include options for how many record locks can be used, how many files a workstation can open, and how many open files the server can handle at one time.

The three types of locks are File, Physical, and Logical. A *File lock* ensures that the entire file cannot be accessed by another user while it is open. A *Physical lock* manages several users opening a file at one time. This type of locking ensures that a range of bytes within the file are kept from being changed by more than one user. The operating system enforces this type of lock. A *Logical lock* is like a Physical lock, except that the application enforces the lock by assigning a name to the section of data that needs to be protected.

Table 10.6 lists the Lock Parameters for the file server configuration files and their defaults and option ranges. Each parameter is discussed in detail after the table.

Table 10.6
Lock Parameters

Options	Default	Range
Maximum File Locks	10000	100 to 100000
Maximum File Locks Per Connection	250	10 to 1000
Maximum Record Locks Per Connection	500	10 to 10000
Maximum Record Locks	20000	100 to 200000

Maximum File Locks determines the total number of opened and locked files that the file server can handle. Increase this amount when the number of opened files approaches the default. Decrease this amount when users are taking up too many file server resources. This option can be placed in the AUTOEXEC.NCF or typed at the console prompt.

Maximum File Locks Per Connection is the total number of opened and locked files a station can use at one time. Increase the number of file locks when an application tries and fails to open several files. Decrease this number if too many file server resources are being used. This option can be placed in the AUTOEXEC.NCF or typed at the console prompt.

 A workstation using OS/2 may need a default much higher than 250.

Maximum Record Locks Per Connection is the total number of record locks that a station may use at one time. Increase the number of record locks when an application tries and fails to lock several records; decrease this number if too many file server resources are being used.

Place this option in the AUTOEXEC.NCF or enter it at the console prompt.

Maximum Record Locks is the maximum amount of record locks that the file server can handle. Increase this amount when users receive error messages indicating that not enough record locks are available. Decrease this amount when the users are using too many file server resources. This option can be placed in the AUTOEXEC.NCF or typed at the console prompt.

Memory

This section defines the parameters that enable you to manage the size of the dynamic memory pool and cache buffers. You also can use one of these parameters to register the memory on an EISA bus computer.

Table 10.7 lists the Memory Parameters for the file server configuration files and their defaults and option ranges. Each parameter is discussed in detail after the table.

Table 10.7

Memory Parameters

Options	Default	Range
Auto Register Memory Above 16 Megabytes	On	ON or OFF
Cache Buffer Size	4096	4096, 8192 or 16384
Maximum Alloc Short Term Memory	2098152	50000 to 16777216

Auto Register Memory Above 16 Megabytes can be set to automatically see memory above 16 MB (megabytes) on an EISA bus machine. Leave this option set to ON if you want the server to find memory above 16 MB. Set this option to OFF if you have a network board that uses DMA or AT bus mastering. This option set to ON under these conditions corrupts file server memory. You must set this option in the STARTUP.NCF file.

Cache Buffer Size sets the size of the cache buffers. If you are using block sizes greater than 4KB, increase the cache buffer size to improve performance. If your volumes vary in size, set the cache buffer so that it is no larger than the smallest block size. You must set this option in the STARTUP.NCF file.

 The file server will not mount any volumes where the block allocation size is smaller than the cache buffer size.

Maximum Alloc Short Term Memory enables you to set the amount of memory given to Alloc Short Term Memory. Alloc Short Term Memory is responsible for drive mappings, NLM tables, user connection information, request buffers, open and locked files, and messages waiting to be broadcast.

Decrease this value if the server is allowing too much memory to be allocated due to some temporary condition. Increase this value if you receive error messages indicating that operations are not completed because this memory pool has reached its maximum. This option can be placed in the AUTOEXEC.NCF or typed at the console prompt.

Miscellaneous

This section contains the options that do not fit into any of the other categories. These options include encrypted passwords, Alerts, Server Processes, and NCP searches.

Table 10.8 lists the miscellaneous options for the file server configuration files and their defaults and option ranges. Each parameter is discussed in detail after the table.

Table 10.8
Miscellaneous

Options	Default	Range
Allow Unencrypted Passwords	OFF	ON or OFF
Display Disk Device Alerts	OFF	ON or OFF
Display Lost Interrupt Alerts	ON	ON or OFF
Display Old API Names	OFF	ON or OFF

continues

Table 10.8—continued

Options	Default	Range
Display Relinquish Control Alerts	OFF	ON or OFF
Display Spurious Interrupt Alerts	ON	ON or OFF
Maximum Outstanding NCP Searches	51	10 to 1000
Maximum Service Processes	20	5 to 40
New Service Process Wait Time	2.2 Seconds	.3 to 2.2 Seconds
Pseudo Preemption Time	2000	1000 to 10000

Allow Unencrypted Passwords enables you to set whether to use unencrypted passwords to access the network. Versions of NetWare older than v3.1 used passwords encrypted at the server. Newer versions of NetWare encrypt the password at the workstation. Set this option to ON if you have users logging in to or attaching to the network from older NetWare servers. This option can be placed in the AUTOEXEC.NCF or typed at the console prompt.

 If you do not have v2.0a servers, you can copy the NetWare v3.1x utilities onto the v2.1x or above servers and leave this option turned OFF.

Display Disk Device Alerts displays disk information at the file server console. Use this option to troubleshoot problems with the hard drives when turned ON. This option can be set in the AUTOEXEC.NCF or STARTUP.NCF file, as well as at the console prompt.

Display Lost Interrupt Alerts enables you to set whether the Lost Interrupt error message appears on the file server console. The error message `interrupt controller detected a lost hardware interrupt` occurs when a device requests an interrupt and then drops the request before the server can reply. After you find the offending piece of hardware, contact the vendor for a solution. In the mean time, set this option to OFF. The system continues to work, but performance can be considerably slower. This option can be set in the AUTOEXEC.NCF or STARTUP.NCF file, as well as at the console prompt.

Display Old API Names displays the name of the old APIs on the file server console. (NetWare v3.1 renamed some of the API calls.) Use this option if you are writing your own NLMs or if you are upgrading to new NLMs. The old APIs are slower than the new ones. This option can be set in the AUTOEXEC.NCF or STARTUP.NCF file, as well as at the console prompt.

Display Relinquish Control Alerts enables you to see messages about CPU control on the file server console. This option should be set to ON if you are writing you own NLMs. Set this option in the AUTOEXEC.NCF or STARTUP.NCF file, or at the console prompt.

Display Spurious Interrupt Alerts enables you to turn off the error message `Spurious hardware interrupt <number> detected`, which occurs when the file server detects an interrupt defined and reserved for another device. This error message appears when a hardware conflict needs to be resolved. Turn this error message OFF when waiting for a resolution from the vendor when the offending piece of hardware is discovered. This option can be set in the AUTOEXEC.NCF or STARTUP.NCF file, as well as at the console prompt.

 Some file servers can generate this message if their processor speed is set too high for the network boards. Set this parameter to OFF in cases such as this.

Maximum Outstanding NCP Searches enables you to set the maximum number of NetWare Core Protocol (NCP) directory searches that can be processed. This number should only be increased if you have applications that support multiple outstanding search operations. This option can be placed in the AUTOEXEC.NCF or typed at the console prompt.

Maximum Service Processes enables you to set the maximum number of service processes that the operating system can create. Increase this number only if more than 20 requests are being delayed. This option can be placed in the AUTOEXEC.NCF or typed at the console prompt.

New Service Process Wait Time enables you to set the amount of time the file server waits before allocating new service processes. Increase this option when you have a temporary condition that requires more service processes. Place this option in the AUTOEXEC.NCF or enter it at the console prompt.

Pseudo Preemption Time can be set to manage the CPU time certain NLMs use. Use this option only when the NLM documentation requests a change. This option can be placed in the AUTOEXEC.NCF or typed at the console prompt.

Transaction Tracking

This section defines the parameters used with Transaction Tracking Services (TTS). TTS ensures database integrity by making certain that a transaction is either completed without error or, if an error occurs, that the file is rolled back to a known state.

Table 10.9 lists the Transaction Tracking Parameters for the file server configuration files and their defaults and option ranges. Each parameter is discussed in detail after the table

Table 10.9
Transaction Tracking Parameters

Options	Default	Range
Auto TTS Backout Flag	OFF	ON or OFF
Maximum Transactions	10000	100 to 10000
TTS Abort Dump Flag	OFF	ON or OFF
TTS Backout File Truncation Wait Time	59 Minutes 19.2 Seconds	1 minute 5.9 Seconds to 1 Day 2 Hours 21 Minutes 51.3 Seconds
TTS Unwritten Cache Wait Time	1 Minute 5.9 Seconds	11 Seconds to 10 Minutes 59.1 Seconds

Auto TTS Backout Flag sets whether a file server can roll back incomplete TTS files when recovering from a crash. If you want the file server to automatically roll back any TTS files upon reboot after a crash, turn this option ON. When this option is turned OFF, you must answer the following question upon rebooting the crashed server: `Incomplete transaction(s) found. Do you wish to back them out?` This option must be set in the STARTUP.NCF file.

Maximum Transactions enables you to specify how many TTS transactions can occur simultaneously. Decrease this value if you are only using TTS on very few files. You can place this option in the AUTOEXEC.NCF or type it at the console prompt.

TTS Abort Dump Flag enables you to save the backed out information in a file. If you turn this option to ON, the operating system will write the backed out information to a file called TTS$LOG.ERR. This is an ASCII text file. This option can be placed in the AUTOEXEC.NCF or typed at the console prompt.

TTS Backout File Truncation Wait Time sets the length of time an allocated block remains available for the TTS backout file. Modify this parameter if you need more or less time for TTS to use. Set this option in the AUTOEXEC.NCF or enter it at the console prompt.

TTS Unwritten Cache Wait Time enables you to set the length of time a block of TTS data can be held in memory. Increase this time if the TTS blocks are reaching the maximum time limit. Other requests are waiting for the block to be written and will slow the process down. You can set this option in the AUTOEXEC.NCF or enter it at the console prompt.

Using Advanced Troubleshooting Methods

This section is for the advanced administrator who wants to know more about the technical details that make up a NetWare file server. The information was presented in such a way as to help you weed out insignificant details and focus on the ones most often needed. The SET commands introduced to you in the text are parameters that can be adjusted without harm to your data. These commands are presented with the goal of increasing your file server's overall performance while enabling you to understand why things happen.

As mentioned earlier, no one set of parameters will supply an optimized environment to every file server. Novell's NetWare 2.x provides a general well-balanced networking platform for the office that does not require anything but the average) while NetWare 3.x is designed to grow and change with your company's growth. Normally, NetWare 3.x will administer itself as loads and demands change. But in some unwieldy environments these manual changes can help to maintain a smoothly running system.

Summary

In this chapter, you were shown some basic troubleshooting methods and important items to monitor. An important part of managing a file server is to monitor system functions. NetWare provides many features and utilities that show information that can be used to predict a problem.

A simple method that you can use to provide a basic level of monitoring is to record all statistics of the file server. This record should be made when the system is in a known stable condition. With this information as a baseline, any changes can be investigated for possible concerns. Statistics will vary greatly from one file server to another, making a single standard almost impossible to recognize.

In the next chapter, you will be presented with management and performance issues involved in maintaining a reliable file server. Whether your file server is a single part of a large corporate LAN, or it represents the center of a small workgroup solution, a properly administered file server can provide a firm foundation for your data processing needs.

11

Management Concerns

Properly evaluating and selecting a backup device that fits your needs requires some background information about the technology available today. This chapter explains the utilities included with NetWare and gives an overview of where technology is today and where it is heading. You will be able, as a result of this information, to implement a recovery plan that fits your needs.

In this chapter, you will be shown two utilities supplied by Novell, and you will learn about the main components of a backup system. You will walk through NBACKUP and SBACKUP and learn about the following topics:

- Interface adapters
- Media and drive types
- Software
- Backup plans and strategies
- Support issues

This information will provide the basic data required to understand the different backup systems available and will enable you to choose the system that best suits your needs.

413

When it comes to protecting your network data, most companies feel an occasional backup is all that they need. After all, they say to themselves, our system runs fine, so why should it crash? Its hard to believe how many companies, large and small, do not own a reliable backup device or maintain a reliable backup schedule. If the same data was located on a computer such as a minicomputer or a mainframe, a reliable system of backing up data would be a requirement.

To effectively determine a data-protection system, you first need to evaluate the importance of your data in relation to the impact of losing it. Can your company or department operate without your system data for 1 hour, 4 hours, 8 hours, 24 hours or longer? Can you continue to operate with the total loss of your system data? These are all possibilities that most companies can't afford to experience. There is a study performed by the University of Texas that reports some alarming statistics. The study showed that 43 percent of all companies that didn't plan for a total failure never reopened. And 90 percent of those unprepared companies that did reopen went out of business within 2 years.

Data backup on a shared data storage device is critical. Yet this seems to be the first area where the budget is cut. Data can be lost or damaged in many ways. A user can cause accidental damage, and although this type of data loss can be controlled by system security, it is still one of the most common. Software bugs or improper setups can cause data loss. Hardware failures can vary from drive or controller failure to a workstation hanging or the file server itself failing. The computer virus is becoming more common in the workplace and also should be a concern when designing a protection plan. Sooner or later, all computer equipment fails. Data loss or data corruption may require files to be restored from a earlier copy. It is the investment in the backup system that minimizes the inconvenience and cost of downtime.

It is difficult to choose from among all the backup devices on the market today the one device that is right for you. It requires both hardware and software to create a complete backup system. But keep in mind that it requires a motivated individual to make the backup system work.

Using File Server Backup Utilities

NetWare's NBACKUP and SBACKUP utilities supply the minimum requirements needed to provide an adequate level of protection. These programs are very useful when used within the boundaries of their limitations.

NBACKUP

The NetWare NBACKUP utility is used to back up and restore files on a NetWare file server and local hard drives.

 A user does not require full or supervisory rights to properly back up files. Any user with the minimum rights of filescan and read can use NBACKUP to back up personal files.

NBACKUP allows the following devices to be used as backup media:

- Floppy drives
- Tape drives that use DOS device drivers
- Optical drives that use DOS device drivers
- Local hard drives
- Network drives
- Novell DIBI devices (Novell Wangtek Tape Drive)

To back up the complete file server, the user must have supervisor privileges to access the system security information. The first screen displayed enables the backup device type to be selected. Select the device required and continue.

 If a NON DOS device is not available, this menu selection can be removed by deleting the DIBI$DRV.DAT file from the SYS:PUBLIC directory.

Select Backup Options from the NBACKUP main menu. Then choose the Select Working Directory option as shown in figure 11.1. This directory is where the session and error log files are held. These files are important to determine the integrity of the backup session and to restore the session. Insert the path of the directory you wish to use.

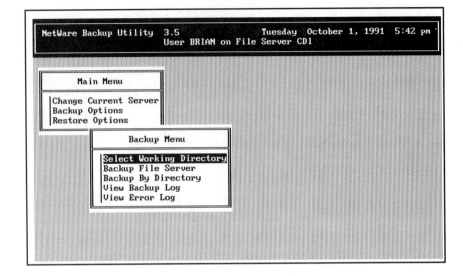

Figure 11.1:
Backup Menu.

After selecting your working directory, choose the Backup File Server option, and you are presented with a Backup Options window that enables you to customize the backup session (see fig. 11.2). The session parameters are configured here.

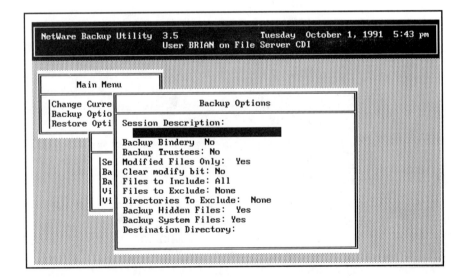

Figure 11.2:
Session
Configuration.

NBACKUP will not back up hidden and system files on a NetWare 2.x file server. Volumes with additional name space support also are not supported in NBACKUP.

You tell NBACKUP what task you wish it to perform by responding to the following options:

- **Session Description.** Provides a means to place a label on each session making them unique.

- **Backup Bindery.** Determines if the bindery is to be backed up.

- **Backup Trustees.** Determines if the trustees are to be included in the session.

- **Modified Files Only.** Checks the modify bit and if set to Yes, backs up the files that have been modified since the last backup.

- **Clear Modify Bit.** Enables you to select whether the Modify bit will be cleared or not.

- **Files to Include.** Enables you to back up selected files. The default is All.

- **Files to Exclude.** Used to prevent specific files from being backed up. The default here is None.

- **Directories to Exclude.** Operates the same as the Files to Exclude option but at the directory level.

- **Backup Hidden Files.** Backs up hidden files.

- **Backup System Files.** Backs up system files.

- **Source Directory.** Locates where you have chosen to back up whether it is a file server, volume, or directory.

- **Destination Directory.** Locates the DOS device to which you wish to archive data. It can be any DOS device to which you have access and security privileges.

When selecting from the Backup Menu to back up a file server or a directory structure, the Backup Options window changes since options that do not pertain to that operation are not made available.

As with most NetWare utilities, the data entry fields pertaining to volumes and directory provide a point-and-shoot menu choice when Ins is pressed, as figures 11.3 and 11.4 illustrate.

Figure 11.3:
Select destination.

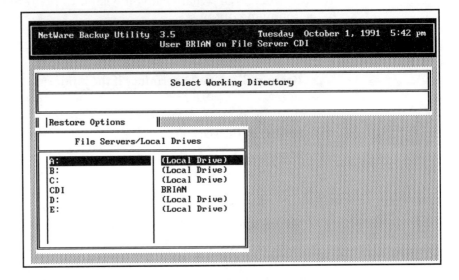

Figure 11.4:
Select volume.

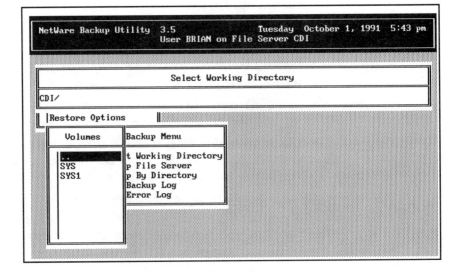

After completing the options window, the backup process is started by pressing Esc. You are then prompted to start the backup now or to start it later. If you choose to start it later, you are prompted for the start date and time. At this point, the workstation remains at that prompt until the desired time and date. The workstation can be interrupted simply by pressing the Esc key.

After the backup begins, the status screen displays the current activity, errors encountered, and total files and directories backed up (see fig. 11.5). This screen remains active until the session is completed.

Figure 11.5:
Status screen.

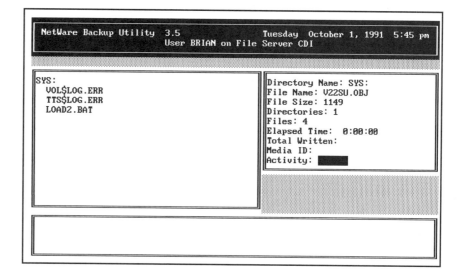

Always examine the error log after the session is complete. One of the most common problems encountered with backup systems is failure to check the log file. Most operators just assume everything is fine, and it is not until later when the backup is needed that they find out otherwise.

The error log is very simple to inspect. After the backup or restore session is finished, simply highlight the View Error Log option of the Backup Menu and select the current entry from a list that will be displayed. A sample error login is shown in figure 11.6.

Figure 11.6:
Session error log.

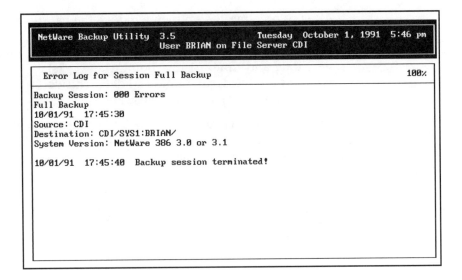

```
┌─────────────────────────────────────────────────────────────────────┐
│  NetWare Backup Utility  3.5               Tuesday  October 1, 1991  5:46 pm │
│                          User BRIAN on File Server CDI                │
├─────────────────────────────────────────────────────────────────────┤
│   Error Log for Session Full Backup                            100%   │
│                                                                       │
│  Backup Session: 000 Errors                                           │
│  Full Backup                                                          │
│  10/01/91  17:45:30                                                   │
│  Source: CDI                                                          │
│  Destination: CDI/SYS1:BRIAN/                                         │
│  System Version: NetWare 386 3.0 or 3.1                               │
│                                                                       │
│  10/01/91  17:45:40  Backup session terminated!                       │
│                                                                       │
│                                                                       │
└─────────────────────────────────────────────────────────────────────┘
```

SBACKUP

The SBACKUP utility is actually a 3.11 NetWare Loadable Module (NLM) that enables a tape drive to be attached directly to the file server. The SBACKUP system implements a technology that uses a host and a target. The target technology allows multiple file servers located on the LAN to be selected for backup as long as the target file server is running the TSA.NLM.

SB ACKUP uses Novell's new SMS or Storage Management Services that provide the required components to third party developers. The SMS services are to be standardized across all current and future NetWare releases.

Understanding the following terms will help you appreciate this system.

A *host* is a file server that has a backup device attached. A *target* is a file server that is being backed up.

The SBACKUP system is made up of the five modules, three host modules, and two target modules. These modules are provided by Novell and are included with NetWare 3.11.

The host modules include the following:

- SBACKUP.NLM The main user interface.
- SIDR.NLM The data requester. This module passes data to and from the host and target NLM using Novell's Storage Management Services Protocol (SMSP).
- *driver*.NLM The actual device driver required for interface. The module name varies for different interface cards.

The target modules include the following:

- TSA.NLM The link between the data requester and the target.
- TSA-311.NLM The target module for NetWare 3.11.

The host file server requires, in addition to the minimum memory required to operate NetWare, approximately 3M to operate the backup device properly.

Together the five SBACKUP modules make up a system that allows data to be backed up from any target on the network to the host. Figure 11.7 depicts a network of four file servers, all using the SBACKUP system with one acting as host and three acting as targets.

Figure 11.7:
Host/Target
communications.

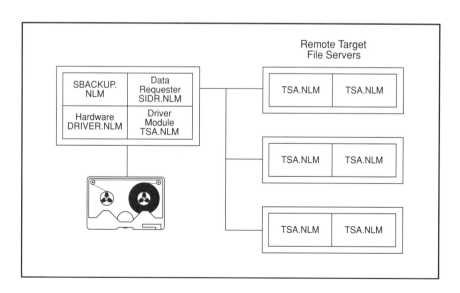

Note Novell has licensed the use of ArcServe from Cheyenne Software to enable SBACKUP to support a reasonable range of devices. This is only at the hardware device driver level. SBACKUP and Cheyenne's ArcServe product are not the same.

Novell supplies drivers that support approximately 50 tape drives currently being sold by various manufacturers. These drives, with a SCSI controller, enable you to back up the complete file server at speeds generally not possible on the workstation.

The SBACKUP system is made up of a hardware NLM, a target NLM, and the SBACKUP NLM itself. The Adaptec driver pictured in figure 11.8 is included with NetWare 3.11. This driver supports the common 16-bit 154x series SCSI controller that supports many popular SCSI tape drives.

 Note The Adaptec 154x controller also is a popular NetWare SCSI disk controller but cannot be used for both disk drives and tape drives simultaneously. Configuring the Adaptec controller should be done by a certified engineer because an incorrectly installed interface can cause problems with other installed devices.

Figure 11.8:
Adaptec driver.

```
              ADAPTEC DIBI-2 SCSI Tape Driver  Version 3.0A
          Copyright (C) Cheyenne Software, Inc. 1990. All rights reserved.


        I) Initialize                    T) Test
        E) Erase
        R) Retension                     U) Unload NLM



  Choose a function: [R]



                      Waiting for Connection Request

   Tape: [None                    ]
   User: [None                    ]

   Configuration:  I/O Port = 0330h   IRQ = 12   DMA = 5   BUS = ISA
          Buffers:  6
       Drive Type:  EMERALD  TDC 3600       R06:
```

Because the tape drive is installed directly in the file server, the data transfer rate is determined by the throughput rate of the file server's bus and to the tape and hard drive interface cards. This arrangement provides very high performance when backing up the locally attached server. When backing up a remote target file server located on the LAN, however, the data throughput drops drastically due to the network cable and possible bridge hops to reach the data.

The operation of SBACKUP is very similar to NetWare's NBACKUP. After loading the hardware driver with the console LOAD command, your hardware operation can be checked directly with the driver, which provides the erase, initialize, and retention options. At this point, you may load the TSA.NLM and SBACKUP. Because you are not normally logged in at the file server, SBACKUP prompts for a login name and password as figure 11.9 illustrates.

Figure 11.9:
SBACKUP user login prompt.

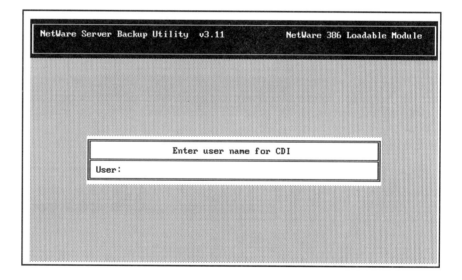

The main menu option Select Target to Backup/Restore displays a menu of all file servers currently running the TSA target NLM. After selecting a target, you are prompted to again log in to the selected file server. After your target selection, you return to select the backup or restore option. At this time, you see a Backup Menu similar to the one in the NBACKUP utility. The screens in SBACKUP have been altered slightly from those in NBACKUP but still provide the necessary session configuration options. Figures 11.10 and 11.11 show the additional submenus that make up the SBACKUP configuration screens.

In figure 11.10, you are presented with a menu that asks what you want to back up and if any special configuration options are to be used. The first item asks what to back up—the file server, a directory, or a list of files. By making use of the available options under the exclude and include selections, as shown in figure 11.11, you can customize the backup session. These options generally default to the most commonly-used settings. Changing these parameters requires an understanding of how your system is structured and in most cases, the defaults are safe to use.

The SBACKUP utility provides a high-speed solution to data backup but can be cumbersome and a heavy load on the file server. The SBACKUP system is a limited version of some of the full backup systems available.

Figure 11.10:
Backup Options
main menu.

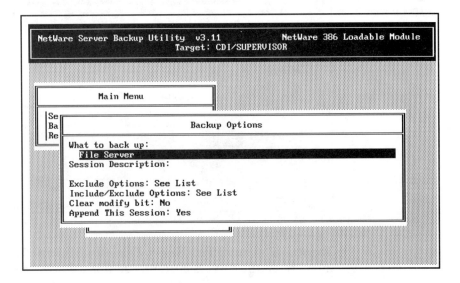

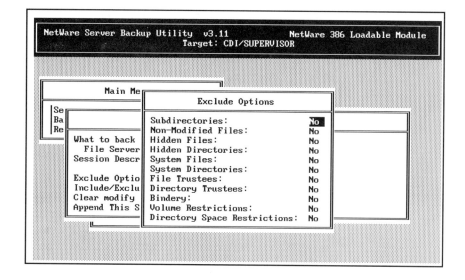

Figure 11.11:
Backup Options submenu.

Note

The tape cartridge data format used by SBACKUP is not the same as that used by NBACKUP. Data sets, therefore, cannot be read from one utility to the other.

Backup Hardware

The only thing constant about computer technology is change. Hardware and software are evolving faster than most companies can keep up with. Rather than try to keep up with technology, what you need to do is take advantage of it. Not all new products are right for everyone. As technology makes advances, it provides the user with a wider range of products. If selected carefully, new products can provide a solution that is efficient and economical.

The most commonly used backup devices utilize floppy disks, hard drives, tapes, and optical drives. Floppy drives do not provide a means of efficiently backing up a file server because of their media size. There are some systems that use nonremovable disk drives as the backup media. These devices should only be considered as temporary or secondary backup devices because they are susceptible to the same defects as the original hard drive. Also, hard drives are generally not kept off site to protect against hazards such as fire, so they are a poor choice as a primary backup device. This section discusses the technology available in tape and optical drives.

Interface Adapters

Any backup device, whether a tape drive or a disk drive, requires an interface card. Currently, there are three popular interface standards: the floppy controller, SCSI Host Adapter, and QIC interfaces. All of these interfaces can provide adequate data throughput in the right environment.

The floppy interface is used by a lot of popular personal tape systems and provides an acceptable level of data transfer on small systems and personal computers. This interface, however, generally cannot handle the data transfer of a larger company's file server. The floppy controller can supply throughput from 250kbps on an XT class computer to 500kbps on the AT class computer. The floppy controller also is limited to a single tape drive and is not expandable beyond the initial installation.

The Quarter Inch Cartridge (QIC) interface was developed primarily for the DC6xxx tape systems providing 60M and larger capacity. This interface provides up to 5M-per-minute in a properly designed system. This standard, although early technology, can still provide an adequate backup system with a properly designed software system. The QIC standard at this time consists of many variations that provide standards for the DC6xxx and DC2xxx series of data cartridges.

 For any corporation with a wide variety of computer equipment and needs, standards may be the key to a successful future. And when multi-vendor communication is important, following standards is almost a requirement. Without standards in a complex system, you cannot ensure functionality and support in the future.

Although support of industry standards always should be a concern when you design a system, many good networking solutions are not necessarily a standard. Most network hardware manufacturers support Novell NetWare, and many manufacturers provide small companies with low-cost, highly reliable solutions that may or may not follow a standard.

Using standards is not always the best approach when you implement a system. In some cases, in which connectivity to larger systems is required, standards may offer the highest degree of reliability and serviceability, but not the performance of alternative methods. In these cases, you must weigh the values of performance, reliability, and serviceability before making a decision.

The Small Computer System Interface (SCSI) was designed as a general purpose interface for mass storage devices. The SCSI interface is a standard maintained by the American National Standards Institute (ANSI). The SCSI standard allows up to eight devices to be placed on the interface. This design, which provides expendability for future system growth and the interface's ability to transfer data at much higher speeds than either a floppy controller or the QIC interface, makes SCSI the interface of choice for current and future technology.

 The SCSI adapter is actually a Host Bus Adapter (HBA). SCSI is a bus system standard just as the Industry Standard Architecture (ISA) and Micro Channel Adapter (MCA) are IBM bus standards. The SCSI interface is a converter enabling the different busses to communicate.

Media and Drive Types

Manufacturers supply many different media and recording methods. The most common methods are explained here to give you some general knowledge of the different types available.

QIC and cassette tapes are recorded in a back and forth manner. This method, as illustrated in figure 11.12, is called the *serpentine recording method* and enables multiple tracks to be recorded on the tape by moving the tape across a stationary recording head. These tapes can provide from 15M to 320M storage on a single tape depending on the tape type.

Helical scan technology is probably the most commonly used recording method today. This technology has been used in video equipment since the mid-1950s and is used in the common VCR. Helical scan tapes are available in 4mm and 8mm tapes providing from 1.3G to 5G on a single tape cartridge. In this recording method, both the tape and the recording head move. The recording head is constructed as a drum and is placed at a 5 to 6 degree angle to the tape surface (see fig. 11.13). This positioning allows the recording head to write diagonal stripes on the tape.

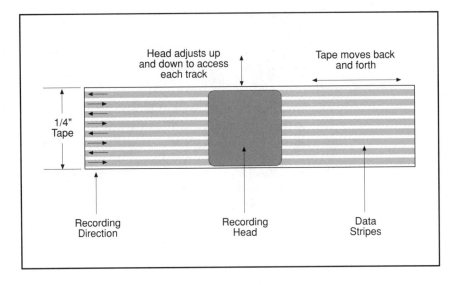

Figure 11.12: Serpentine recording method.

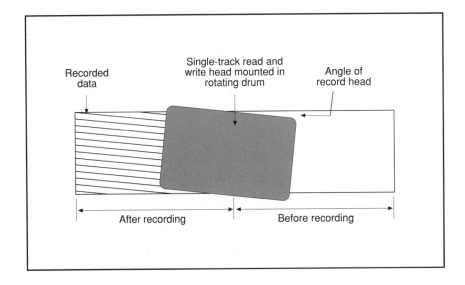

Figure 11.13: Helical scan technology.

The 8mm tape cartridges are similar to those used in today's video 8mm camcorders, but with an important difference. The recording surface of videotape normally has some flaking of the oxide. In the video environment, this may show up as a single speck of snow on the screen which may not even be visible to the viewer. But in the data environment, a single flake of oxide can represent extensive loss of data. To prevent oxide flaking, the data-specific tapes are manufactured to higher specifications, and the cost of these tapes generally reflects this higher quality. Currently, this technology is supplied by the Exabyte Corporation and offers a 2.2G and 5G version.

The 4mm or Digital Audio Tape (DAT), offering 1.2G and 2.0G storage, also is making its way into the technologically sophisticated tape drive market. This tape format is similar to the 8mm technology. Both the 4mm and the 8mm tape systems provide high throughput and reliability along with a very convenient compact tape size.

Optical Drives

The family of optical disk drives includes the Compact Disk-Read Only Media (CD-ROM), Write Once Read Many (WORM), and Magnetic Optical (MO), that is, erasable optical disks. These removable drives provide very fast data access in a reliable format, if implemented properly.

Although the CD-ROM is a read-only device and is, therefore, not a backup device, this device is rapidly becoming popular for fixed data storage. This technology is very reliable and is used as a storage device for large databases that do not change, but are often used as reference. CD-ROMs use a solid-state laser beam to read the surface.

WORM is very similar to CD-ROM technology except that, whereas the CD-ROM information is written on the surface by the manufacturer, the WORM drive can write data to the disk. Once this data has been added, however, it cannot be erased. The WORM disk is not susceptible to mechanical head crashes experienced by normal hard drives because WORM disks have no read/write heads that come in contact with the surface. These disks also are not magnetic and, therefore, do not suffer from degradation due to electrical, magnetic disturbances. Figure 11.14 illustrates the CD-ROM and WORM technology.

The MO disk is actually two technologies working together to provide an optically-erasable disk that gives the performance of a low-end hard drive. As illustrated by figure 11.15, the magnetic optical disk operates by using a solid-state laser beam to heat the surface of the disk to allow a magnetic field to change the phase of the metallic structure of the coating on the disk's surface. The phase changes are then interpreted as digital 1s and 0s.

Figure 11.14:
CD-ROM and
WORM technology.

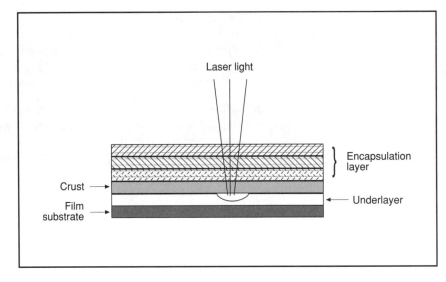

Figure 11.15:
Magnetic optical
technology.

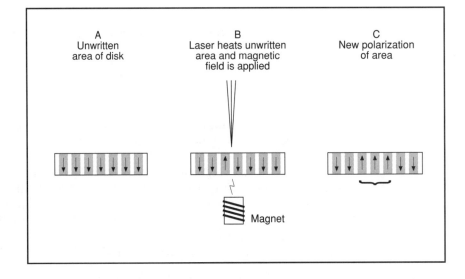

Optical drives also are available in automatic disk changers referred to as *jukeboxes*. These jukeboxes can provide many gigabytes of data but require special software to manage the robotic movements needed to perform the disk change operations.

Software

There are many high-quality tape and optical drives currently available, but without good software, these drives are basically worthless; it is the software, not the hardware, that directs the backup and manages the data. Ask the following questions when putting together the backup system that is right for you:

- Does it back up *all* NetWare security information?
- Does it allow password protection on the backup media?
- How does it handle a selective backup and restore?
- Can I redirect the data on a restore?
- Can it back up open files?
- What type of backup media management does it provide?
- How does the system handle backup media or tape spanning?
- How does it handle automatic or nonattended backups?
- What method of reporting is used?

All of these questions are important when selecting a backup system. It also is important to add any questions that may be required to service your company's special needs.

When considering a backup system for a NetWare network, be sure that the system can back up all the NetWare bindery files and trustee information. Smaller software systems may not be able to do this because it requires the ability to close, back up, and reopen special invisible system files located on the file server.

Novell provides special API function calls to the programmer. The following calls back up the bindery files:

    CloseBindery
    OpenBindery

To back up Novell directory trustees, the function calls include:

    ScanDirectoryForTrustees
    AddTrusteeToDirectory

To maintain file attributes, the function calls include:

ScanFileInformation
SetFileInformation

All the Novell API programing function call information is available from Novell vendors in both OS/2, NLM, and DOS assembly and C libraries.

Security should be considered. If your system has sensitive information, a nonprotected tape could be a security hole. Some tape software systems have the capability of adding a password to the tape, which disarms the restore function without the proper password. The password, if used, is very important because most tape software packages cannot read the tape without it.

Also, you should consider the method used to back up files. Some tape software programs provide image, file-by-file, or both methods of backing up data. The image method is fast and can provide a very efficient means of restoring the system in the event of a total failure. But the image method generally is very cumbersome, and it is sometimes impossible to restore a single file when needed. Most systems today back up using the file-by-file method. This method reads each and every file separately while performing the backup, unlike the image method of reading the disk partition from beginning to end.

The capability to redirect data during a restore is a very convenient feature when needed. Redirecting data can save many hours of time when replacing data to a different drive. Although most systems provide this feature, it may be worth confirming.

Open files have always been a problem with tape software because files open during backup did not get backed up. The normal way of dealing with this problem was to skip the file, add an entry into the error log, and proceed. Some systems make use of the error report and attempt to back up open files after the main backup has finished. This feature works in some cases, as long as the files are not open due to an improperly logged out workstation. A software package has come on the market recently that backs up open files. This software makes a "best attempt" service and is dependent on how the file was opened. The integrity of these files is uncertain.

The ability to span tape is no longer as great a concern as it used to be. *Spanning* allows a backup to fill one tape and to continue on another.

Many of the older technology systems did not provide this service. Current technology does provide spanning, but "don't leave the store without it."

Currently, some backup software programs have trouble backing up large files or traversing large directory structures. If your system maintains a large database, avoid backup software that cannot back up large files. Traversing large directory structures also can be a problem but may be handled by restructuring the directories. Large directory structures can cause a performance problem whereas large files sometimes can prevent correct operation.

 There is a little known problem with DOS that can occur on file servers or very large DOS drives. DOS starts to experience performance problems with more than 500 files or directories at a single level. This problem is due to the sequential manner in which DOS starts at the top of the file allocation table (FAT) and scans to the end in search of a file. More than 500 files in a subdirectory, or more than 500 subdirectories under a single directory, will cause the problem. If this limit reaches 1000, the problem becomes visible to the user; and when the limit reaches 2000 or more, serious performance problems occur when backing up these files or directories.

If the backup software builds a temporary table in memory, a large directory structure also can cause problems by running out of memory.

Another area of concern should be documentation and the user interface. Any well-written program should include properly written user and administrator manuals. Both manual and user interface should be clear and easy to understand. The interface should have a system of double checks and confirmations to prevent accidental damage to files. A functional on-line help system can be a great time saver and, over time, is worth every dollar spent.

Although a well-written user interface with on-line help makes a system easy to use and understand, the capability to execute the backup from a command line also is very important in some cases. The command line capability can provide an inventive system administrator the ability to implement various methods of starting and automating the backup procedure.

Some systems provide batch or macro functionality in place of command line utilities. This also can be very beneficial if the macro system is not overly complicated. You also should confirm that both the command line and macro options provide a full set of functions that would be available through the normal user interface.

Most backup software provides a scheme of starting the backup at a later time. These scheduling schemes vary greatly in their functionality; however, you should make sure that whatever system you use maintains a level of security while waiting for the scheduled time to perform the backup. Some systems simply sit at the DOS prompt, logged in with supervisor rights, until backup time. Sitting at the DOS prompt could be a major security problem in some environments.

Some server-based backup systems are currently available. These systems enable the backup device to be connected directly to the file server and run as a Valued Added Process (VAP) or NetWare Loadable Module (NLM). Evaluate these systems just as critically as you would any standard workstation-based software.

Most server-based systems can provide backup services without the use of a workstation and can supply very high data throughput because the data is not required to travel through the network cable. These functions are not automatic. One server-based system, for instance, requires a Windows application running on a workstation to perform a backup. This system transmits the data from the server to the workstation and back to the server effectively eliminating most of the advantages of a server-based system because it doubles network traffic instead of reducing it.

All backup software should use some kind of reporting method. It is very common for errors to occur during an unattended backup. Without a status report, these problems could go undetected and cause problems later on.

Most backup software written today includes the capability to generate status reports. These reports vary in the level of detail recorded, but most are more than adequate for tracking errors.

 Not all NetWare 3.11 third party backups provide support for added NAME SPACE. These special NAME SPACE FAT areas are not backed up unless the backup system specifically addresses this issue. Without this additional information, the MAC, OS/2, or UNIX files are not restorable even if they appear to be on the backup media.

Novell provides a certification program for manufacturers who wish to have their products tested as Novell-approved. This testing procedure confirms that products provide an adequate level of performance and are compatible with the Novell NetWare environment.

Copies of the Independent Product Testing (IPT) bulletins are available from any Novell vendor or CompuServe NetWire.

Backup Plans

After locating a suitable backup software and hardware system, you must develop a plan that effectively uses the equipment to obtain the level of protection required. This plan should at least answer the following questions:

- Who will be responsible?
- When and how often do you back up?
- What method of rotating the backup media should be used?
- When and which backup media should be taken off site?
- When and how often should backup media be tested?
- What type of plan do you need for a disaster?

An adequate backup system should account for these questions, and although each item may vary slightly in importance depending on your situation, none should be bypassed.

Your company also may require additional steps to be taken to ensure total protection. There is no one set plan that fits everyone. Each company has different priorities and resources. A properly-designed plan should provide a standard procedure and an alternative that will not allow the level of required protection to fail.

Responsibility

The person chosen to be responsible for maintaining the backup system must be sufficiently motivated to back up when planned.

Inconsistent backups allow periods of time when files may not be re-trievable and can prove costly under the wrong circumstances.

Frequency

Because most backup software requires users to be logged out of the system, the most common time to perform backup is after business hours. This generally requires an unattended backup system that provides adequate error reporting.

The frequency of the backup should be determined by the amount of data changed and the cost to reconstruct the data if lost. Most companies find that a backup once a day is adequate. Those companies that require more frequent backups usually do so because they have large systems requiring many hours of data entry if rebuilt. The cost of this reconstruction should be calculated on a worst-case basis to determine if backups are required more often or if a dedicated backup device may be required.

Rotating Method

Rotating the backup media is extremely important to provide proper protection. Rotating the media provides multiple copies of data in the event of a natural disaster such as a fire or in the case of a physical backup media failure. The term *tape set* is used in the following discussion and refers to a set of tapes required to perform a backup. There are many ways to rotate tapes. The following examples are the most commonly used and proven methods.

Grandfather Methods

The grandfather method is fairly simple and provides an adequate level of protection to a small- to mid-size file server. This method requires 19 tape sets and is simple to control if the total disk volumes can fit on a single tape and if the backup system can transfer all the data in an acceptable amount of time.

In the grandfather system, four daily tapes (or other media) are labeled Monday through Thursday, four Friday tapes are labeled to be used on Friday, and twelve monthly tapes are labeled January through

December. The four daily tapes are used on the designated day with the weekly Friday1, Friday2, Friday3, or Friday4 tape being used on that week. The twelve monthly tapes are used on the last day of each month as labeled. This method provides current files Monday through Thursday and a weekly and monthly archive tape set.

If the file server to be backed up is larger than the maximum tape capacity, the number of tapes and the need to exchange tapes halfway through the backup becomes difficult to manage.

Ten Tape Rotation

The ten-tape method rotates all tapes evenly and provides a backup history of about twelve weeks. This system also becomes cumbersome if the data requires more than one tape to perform the backup.

 Many companies use a method of only backing up modified files on a daily basis to overcome the problem of the tape drive being too small. Most tape software can check the DOS Modified Attribute (the +A parameter sets the archive bit) to determine if the file has been changed since the last backup. This greatly reduces the number of files that require backup on a daily basis.

Managing this type of rotation can be very complicated and possibly hazardous if a mistake occurs. This method of backup also can greatly increase the time required to restore a system in the case of a failure. To restore more than a single file from this type of rotation may require *all* tapes to be restored. This can take many hours using some software systems.

This method uses a series of four-week cycles during a forty week period. During a four-week cycle the same four tapes are used Monday through Thursday. This technique starts out very much like the grandfather method but with the next series of weeks incrementing the tape sets.

The chart below shows the different tape sets as they would be used during the complete forty-week period. As you can see, this method can become confusing if multiple tapes are required for each backup session.

```
1-2-3-4-5-1-2-3-4-6-1-2-3-4-7-1-2-3-4-8
2-3-4-5-6-2-3-4-5-7-2-3-4-5-8-2-3-4-5-9
3-4-5-6-7-3-4-5-6-8-3-4-5-6-9-3-4-5-6-10
4-5-6-7-8-4-5-6-7-9-4-5-6-7-10-4-5-6-7-1
5-6-7-8-9-5-6-7-8-10-5-6-7-8-1-5-6-7-8-2
6-7-8-9-10-6-7-8-9-1-6-7-8-9-2-6-7-8-9-3
7-8-9-10-1-7-8-9-10-2-7-8-9-10-3-7-8-9-10-4
8-9-10-1-2-8-9-10-1-3-8-9-10-1-4-8-9-10-1-5
9-10-1-2-3-9-10-1-2-4-9-10-1-2-5-9-10-1-2-6
10-1-2-3-4-10-1-2-3-5-10-1-2-3-6-10-1-2-3-7
```

Tower of Hanoi Method

This method is named after a mathematical game in which the player must move a stack of different size rings in the proper order.

The tape sets are labeled A, B, C, and so on. A tape set generally has between 5 to 8 tapes. The chart below shows a typical rotation. The bold letters show the first use of a tape set.

```
A-B-A-C-A-B-A-D-A-B-A-C-A-B-A-E
A-B-A-C-A-B-A-D-A-B-A-C-A-B-A-F
A-B-A-C-A-B-A-D-A-B-A-C-A-B-A-E
A-B-A-C-A-B-A-D-A-B-A-C-A-B-A-G
```

This rotation method is one of the most difficult to maintain manually but can offer a wide range of file histories. The window of available files doubles each time a new tape set is introduced. A set of five tapes, for example, provides files up to 16 days old, 6 tapes 32 days, and 7 tapes 64 days. This system also can be implemented to use a single for a whole week, which extends the window to 16 weeks, 32 weeks, and 64 weeks respectively.

This rotation method has recently been implemented in a backup system that maintains a full database and handles the task of rotating tapes when needed. This system is one of the few that provides a full archive of file histories and enables the system administrator to restore from a list of versions in the archive. This particular system enables a spreadsheet or database to be restored as it was weeks or months ago.

Off-Site Backups

When examining the backup systems and rotation methods available, you should allow for multiple-tape sets so that a complete set can be stored off site. Having a moderately current data set off-site protects you in the event of a building disaster, such as a fire or flood. A log book should be set so that others know where you last were in the rotation. Knowing this helps to keep the backup as consistent as possible. Tape sets should be scheduled to be stored off-site with plenty of time provided to retrieve them before needed. These off-site sets also should be second- or third-level copies which enable the most recent sets to remain on-site for immediate access if needed. Generally, sets are moved on- and off-site every one to two weeks. This may be done more frequently on a large system.

As networks become more complex and require a higher level of protection, backup systems will need to be more versatile. Automatic Expert systems are already starting to appear, providing full, intelligent solutions. One current system is not just a tape backup but a fully automated storage-management product. Providing fully automatic on- and off-site tape rotation schedules, these systems require a high level of knowledge to totally understand their flow of events.

Testing

It is critical that a backup system be tested from time to time. Many systems have experienced permanent data loss simply because the backup system was never tested. What good is a backup if it is not restorable?

A simple testing method is to create a dummy test directory containing a few executable programs that are backed up at all times. This approach enables you to delete the directory structure and to restore from the backup media without the danger of losing important data. This restore test should be done after the initial system install and after any system change that can affect the operation of the backup device. Workstation hardware changes or DOS upgrades can very easily cause a backup system to malfunction.

Disaster Recovery

A disaster recovery plan should be a complete solution. This solution should include a backup system and a company plan to follow in the event of a total system failure. In most cases, disaster recovery is simply an afterthought, something that would have been handy. A backup system is required to maintain a complete set of data, as complete and current as possible. This data will sometimes be required to re-create the system as it was after a major hardware problem.

But a backup device is only a single part of what is generally needed to be properly protected. The following is not a complete or absolute list to follow but is intended as a guide to aid you in planning the proper system that fits your needs. Disaster-recovery systems or plans should be taken seriously if your company's data has any value. A written list of procedures, a list of support personnel, or a tape backup can make an adequate disaster recovery plan if it covers all your needs. Although most plans include some or all of these items, the key is to create a plan that provides your company with the necessary insurance.

Proper Pre-Planning

Proper pre-planning of a recovery system is a subject that could easily become overly complicated if allowed to. The best plan is one that can be followed, fits the needs of your company, and provides an acceptable end result. A well-designed plan should have a backup schedule or log, a documented list of steps to take in the event of a problem, and include more than one responsible person.

Needed Equipment

Novell provides safety mechanisms for a first level of protection if implemented. NetWare's disk mirroring or disk duplexing can greatly reduce the cost of downtime in the event of a hard drive failure. NetWare does this by providing a *hot* backup drive or complete disk channel that takes over in the event of a primary drive failure.

Many companies do not take advantage of this feature simple because of the cost of an additional hard drive. In most cases the mere cost of a second hard drive is much less than the cost of downtime that may be experienced during a drive failure.

 If implemented properly, Novell NetWare's disk duplexing can add as much as 50 percent to the disk read performance. This additional performance alone can offset the cost of the extra hard drive and controller required.

By using disk mirroring or duplexing, a hard disk failure can be scheduled for repair after normal business hours, eliminating user downtime completely.

Power Protection

A major source of file server data corruption is power related. NetWare increases its performance by reading large amounts of data into a special portion of memory called a *cache*. The cache allows data to be read many times faster than if it were being read directly from the hard disk. But the cache is very vulnerable to poor power conditions. If a power line spike or surge is allowed to pass through the file server, data reliability is effected.

 Many NetWare administrators are familiar with the General Protection Interrupt (GPI) or Non-Maskable Interrupt (NMI) errors at the file server console. These errors are displayed by an operating system task that is constantly checking the integrity of the system memory. Both of these errors are generally traced to power or memory problems. And in most cases, it is a power-related problem that makes the memory appear bad.

Power protection is very important to the integrity of data on a file server. The minimum protection would be a good surge strip to guard against spikes and surges.

A good quality uninterruptable power supply should be installed to prevent any unnecessary problems. An uninterruptable power supply that has Novell communications capability can save many hours by making it unnecessary to repair data in the event of a power failure. Many vendors offer an interface that informs the file server that commercial power has been lost. When properly installed, these units can shut down the file server correctly, minimizing damaged data.

Available Utilities

The computer *virus* (Vital Information Resources Under Siege) appears to be a growing problem. The first virus-like programs started out as a game, a battlefield between a few young geniuses writing self-repairing, roaming code. These programs had a mission to seek out and destroy the opponent. From these first amazing programs, the virus has developed into a special program designed to interfere with the normal operations of a computer. This interference varies from a simple message informing the user of its presence to the destruction of as much data as possible. Currently, over 400 virus programs are known to exist, and more are being added to the list daily.

 Most viruses found today multiply by attaching to executable (.EXE and .COM) files and becoming memory-resident.

This spread of infectious programs prompted the growth of vaccine or virus detection and repair software. The capability of these programs to seek out and destroy the virus can allow the system administrator to breathe more easily.

Although anti-virus software has proven very useful in the battle against viruses, do not think of it as an alternative to a properly-designed network security system. Currently, no well-designed and properly-administered Novell security system has been infected. The most dangerous and most common access point of a virus is through the user supervisor.

 The special user supervisor and supervisor equivalents should be reserved for administrative tasks only. There should be no reason for a user to have the rights of the system supervisor to execute normal applications.

If a user has the right to change the read-only flag that is on all executable files, most new virus programs will attack those files. If the user does not have the right to modify the flag, the file is protected.

Currently, the quality and methods of anti-virus programs varies from one system to another. The best means of selecting a detection system is to follow the trade magazines software reviews or to contact a reputable software retailer.

Support Issues

An experienced and knowledgeable network service person is difficult to find although network service persons are everywhere.

A good, reputable service organization that can provide quality service and support is probably the one most important key to a successful operation. Whether you are self sufficient or totally dependent, you will need replacement parts and occasional assistance.

As part of your plan, a carefully thought-out service contract or agreement should be set up to supply the level of support your company may need in the event of a system failure. Include in the contract such items as on-site service, software, and hardware. The amount of on-hand parts and a reasonable time period should be specified as well. The service organization should be able to supply suitable replacement parts within the agreed time period and handle the problem with a suitable level of knowledge.

If your network is large, it may require an internal support staff. If this is the case, Novell offers a Network Support Encyclopedia that can supply answers to a majority of your technical questions. This extensive database is available on both floppy and CD-ROM formats. Novell provides yearly subscription services that supply updates.

Each main menu option offers submenus that enable administrators to narrow the search field or perform global searches on the complete database. The NSE database provides very useful information that can be obtained quickly and is a practical addition to the NetWare toolbag.

Novell's Netwire special interest group (located on CompuServe) also is a very good source of information. Through Netwire, you can communicate with other users, system administrators, and Novell technical persons. It is not uncommon to post a question in the evening and have a suggested solution waiting for you in the morning.

Training

As demonstrated in the industry, successful Novell networks are administered and run by highly competent people using Novell NetWare. The most cost-effective way to become familiar with the system is to receive professional training from an organization that can supply a working hands-on environment. An experienced instructor can help you with both application and procedural issues. You will compensate for the cost of this training many times over by your improved ability to handle normal administrative issues internally.

Today's NetWare networks are not just an office of personal computers sharing printers. These networks have replaced many large expensive corporate systems and have proven their ability to supply office automation.

Many common problems are most often created by untrained employees and administrators. A simple, time-consuming problem like "my data was there before lunch" can very easily be avoided by a knowledgeable administrator. A well-designed security system with a functional menu can prevent most accidental problems. In most cases, missing data files and programs are products of untrained users allowed to roam the system. These accidents usually stem from good intentions and could have been prevented with proper user and administrator training.

Consultants

The network industry can supply professional consultants for any technical and administrative area needed. There are many consultants that are extremely good at what they do, and there are some that are not. Just as with selecting a service organization, selecting a consultant should be based on his or her experience and knowledge. You can train your staff to operate and administrate your network. You should not be required to train your consultant to obtain the level of service you require.

Summary

This chapter reviewed the concerns and basics that a system administrator should consider. Backing up data is the simplest and most basic of management concerns. The implementation of a disaster recovery plan, the proper training of personnel, and the recognition of future service needs were also addressed. The information presented in this chapter was not intended to be followed lock-step as your master plan, but was presented in the hope that it would assist you in determining what concerns are important to the survival of your company's data processing system.

12

Network E-mail

E-mail is one of the many new buzz words circulating in PC-based networks; everyone is talking about it. E-mail has long been a standard feature in most mainframe environments. Now today's PC- based e-mail provides a vast quantity of functions and features and improves user productivity. Whether you use e-mail as simply a way to enable your staff to communicate effectively or as a method of controlling and scheduling your company's resources, e-mail is a valuable utility and a growing industry.

In this chapter, you are given an overview of e-mail as it is commonly installed on a Novell network. E-mail not only provides a means of sending and receiving messages, but also an effective method in which to distribute data between applications. For example, a software company can use e-mail to distribute updates automatically; a company's inventory can be distributed to branch offices twice daily; or a main warehouse can distribute price changes to every retail store in a chain automatically. All of these examples and personal messages can be performed painlessly with an automated e-mail system.

Understanding E-mail Transports

As with everything else in the networking world, e-mail has many standards. The UNIX world has SMTP (Simple Mail Transfer Protocol), Microsoft has implemented MAPI (Mail Application Programming Interface), Lotus has VIM (Vendor Independent Messaging), OSI has X.400 or XAPI, and Novell has MHS (Message Handling System). Each of these currently popular interfaces has many features to offer. Although all are used in the industry, this chapter focuses on Novell's MHS. MHS has been optimized for the NetWare environment and is Novell's method of transporting e-mail between NetWare file servers and remote sites.

Introducing Novell's MHS (Message Handling System)

Novell's MHS is becoming popular in the NetWare market and is supported by many of the leading software vendors. Novell's MHS is not to be confused with the MHS standard of the ODI's X.400 interface. MHS currently supplies a major part of the NetWare e-mail market and continues to mature. New functionality is added with each release. At this time, almost all major PC-based e-mail applications developers offer a version of their software for the MHS system.

Overview

Novell's MHS (Message Handling Service) is a software product that provides message handling services for applications written to make use of the MHS applications programming interface. MHS handles the collection, routing, and delivery of information presented to it in a designated format.

MHS uses store-and-forward technology to transfer both messages and files between sites that use the MHS system. This can be established by asynchronous communications lines, gateways, or internetwork paths. MHS is an application-independent system that provides transport services to many front-end applications.

MHS is comprised of three distinct layers or sections: the Directory Manager, the Connectivity Manager, and the Transport Server. Each of these components handles a particular task required to provide transparent communications services to the front-end applications. The Connectivity Manager and Transport Server provide the actual communications, while the Directory Manager provides and maintains the routing services.

The Connectivity Manager picks up messages and places them in queues depending on the routes maintained by the Directory Manager. This information, held in queues, is then delivered or picked up by the Transport Server by making a connection to other MHS servers. This connection is done by directly connecting through a network link or through an asynchronous line established directly or through a dial-up type modem.

If this data is targeted for a local user, then the MHS Connectivity Manager delivers it to a local mailbox. If a message is destined for a user reached by a gateway, then the message is delivered to the gateway which in turn provides the delivery services.

Figure 12.1 is an example of the many methods an MHS message may travel. In this example, four NetWare file servers are located at four different locations. As you can see, company A and B are connected with a T-1 LAN-to-LAN Router. You also can see that company C and D are connected by a 56Kbps LAN-to-LAN Router. Each of these corporations has the capability to communicate through e-mail even though company A and D have no active MHS host or modem connection to the outside world. In these cases both companies B and C are acting as the Routing Host for the other attached network.

For example, if a user located on the company D network needs to send a message to a user located on company B's network, he or she can address the message to "user @ companyB." The e-mail application being operated by the user on the company D network places the message in company D's MHS outbound directory. Next, the active MHS Routing Host running on a dedicated workstation on company C's network attaches to the remote file server and provides both pickup and delivery services. This happens at a predetermined interval set up by the MHS administrator. After picking up the messages, company C's MHS host then provides the remote connection to company B's destination by way of an asynchronous modem connection.

Figure 12.1:
MHS E-mail
Network.

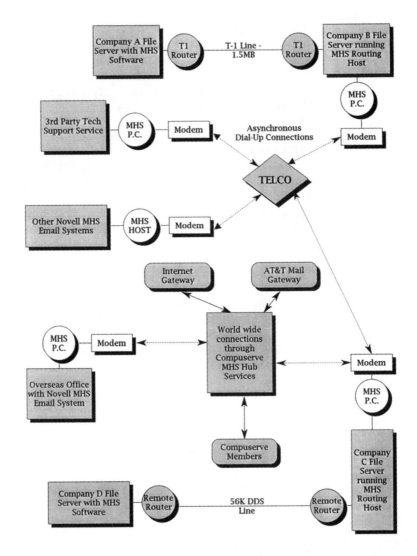

Figure 12.1: MHS E-mail Network.

In configurations like these, every connected file server does not need to operate an active MHS Routing Host. Although every NetWare file server requires that MHS services must be loaded and administered, a dedicated PC that provides routing services is not always needed. As seen in figure 12.1, you also can connect to many other mail services. These can be other NetWare MHS sites or other e-mail services by connecting to a large routing hub such as that supplied by CompuServe.

Each of these features is discussed in greater detail later on in this chapter.

Workgroups

MHS can be set up in many different configurations. Workgroups are the most common. Workgroups enable a number of hosts to be configured into a workgroup with each workgroup being serviced by a single active MHS ROUTING HOST. Workgroups are normally set up at the corporate level with one MHS host acting as the "workgroup-wide router," while each workgroup host provides the services for local delivery. Routing hosts provide the services required to deliver messages to both remote hosts and other local non-routing hosts. This configuration enables users to direct messages to a single location and to have the MHS Directory Manager of the routing host handle the details.

Addresses

MHS addresses use the following syntax:

```
name . application @ target {extended address-
ing}
```

The *name* is the name designated to you as an MHS e-mail user. The *application* field informs or controls which particular application this message is targeted for. As an MHS user, you can operate more than one program that makes use of the MHS delivery services. The *target* is either the HOST name given to your MHS server or a workgroup maintained on a MHS ROUTING HOST. *Extended addressing* is an area defined for applications to use to pass information that may not normally be used. This field varies greatly from application to application because of its custom nature. A common use of this field is to pass secondary addressing to a gateway device as in the following example:

```
brian @ fax {p=1-313-544-7155 n=Brian-
Chaffins}
```

This example passes both a phone number and a name to a FAX GATEWAY running on the MHS host. In this case, the message will be faxed to Brian Chaffins at the fax machine located at 313-544-7155.

It is also through the use of the extended MHS addresses that an MHS user can reach users of non-MHS systems, as in the following example:

```
mail @ cserve{INTERNET:bchaffin @
umcc.ais.org}
```

This example sends an MHS message to the user bchaffin located on the host umcc.ais.org which is located on the Internet. This message is directed to the Compuserve MHS HUB with the address syntax of mail @ cserve, and is directed to the Internet with INTERNET. Gateways are discussed in detail in the following section.

MHS Gateways

The Novell MHS system enables optional gateways to be defined and run on the MHS host PC. These gateways are special software applications written to conform to the rules set up to operate as an MHS gateway. MHS provides a timer, or scheduler that enables the administrator to automatically cycle the MHS host at predetermined periods. In this cycle, many functions are performed. MHS scans all users, looks for both incoming and outgoing messages, and runs the defined gateways. A few common gateways are described in the following paragraphs.

Gateways allow access to other mail services. Whether a gateway delivers messages to MCI Mail, AT&T Mail, or a UNIX host, it should perform these tasks transparently to the user. Many MHS gateway products are appearing on the PC market. A few of the more productive gateways are described below to give you an idea of what is available.

E-mail Forwarding

Infinite Technologies produces a gateway that you may find beneficial. ForwardIT!, is an MHS gateway product that enables MHS users to forward e-mail. Each user can manually turn this capability on or off and keep a copy if desired. This product works well when sales persons are out of town and want their mail sent to a remote location or to the person handling their calls. This product also can provide a generic name in which support messages can be sent.

Discussion Groups

Discussion groups have been common for years among UNIX and dial-up services. These are now provided to Novell MHS users by way of a specialized gateway. Again, Infinite Technologies makes one of the gateways that can supply this service. A *Discussion Group* is an automatically maintained mailing list to which users can subscribe. When a message is posted to the discussion group, each member of the group receives a copy of it. The same holds true when a member replies to the message. These discussion groups can be very productive if rules are followed. A common drawback of discussion groups is that they can sometimes get out of hand if left unmonitored.

Library Services

Libraries or file services are another UNIX-world derivative. These gateways enable users to request files from a manually maintained library. These files can be public access or can require passwords. Libraries also can be a productive method of file distribution. The Library Gateway can provide software updates and other data files retrievable without the time- consuming manual operator reply.

Routing Services

Routing services encompass a broad range of commercial services available today. Many large services provide routing services to MHS users and hosts. These services such as that supplied by CompuServe's Mail Hub provide world-wide access to both MHS users and other mail services. With CompuServe's member list now over one million and connections to the Internet communities, this becomes one of the most powerful portals into the e-mail world. Novell's NHUB is another routing service that can provide a connection to other MHS hosts through the United States. NHUB has been around since the early days of NetWare and many MHS sites use their services to gain access to many other MNJ users with a single phone connection.

Exploring E-mail Applications

E-mail applications cover a wide range of products. User-to-user messages, file transfers via e-mail enclosures, and application acknowledgment are all popular e-mail features. A few DOS command line utilities also provide the capability to send messages from DOS batch files.

Infinite Technologies ExpressIT!

Included with this book is an evaluation copy of the Infinite Technologies ExpressIT! e-mail application. This program is supplied in both DOS and Microsoft Windows versions. ExpressIT! is a good example of a truly functional e-mail product.

Figure 12.2 is an example of the opening screen presented by the DOS version of ExpressIT!. The ExpressIT! product provides an intuitive interface and minimizes the need for expensive user training.

Figure 12.2:
ExpressIT! for
DOS.

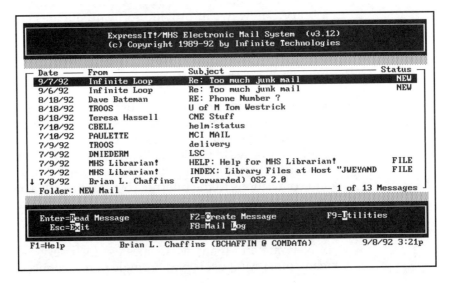

Figure 12.3 is an example of ExpressIT! for Windows. This version displays the same basic information, but takes advantage of the added

Windows capabilities. Both the DOS and Windows opening screens are similar enough to enable users to perform normal daily operations without retraining.

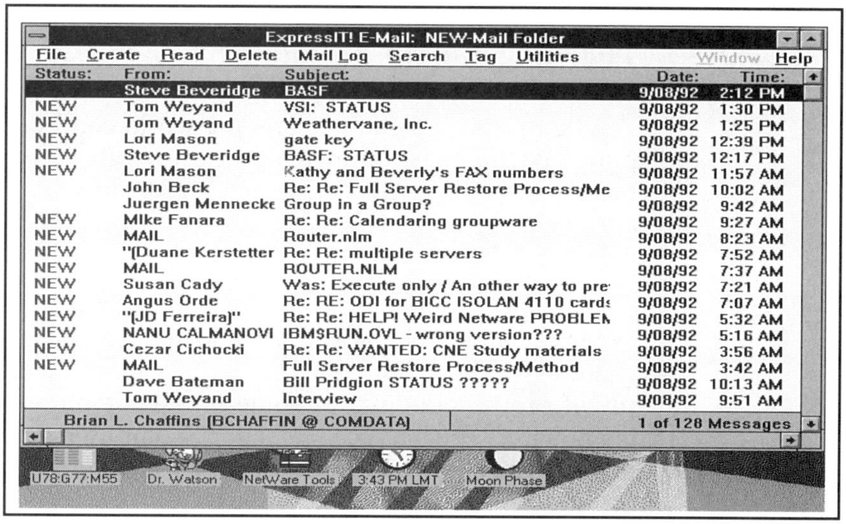

Figure 12.3:
ExpressIT! for
Windows.

ExpressIT!, as with many other applications, provides a mixed variety of features. Public and private phone books, as well as distribution lists are all features most applications supply. The extended features make the difference, in both price per user and functionality.

Using the Internet

The Internet or "capital I" network is a world-wide network that was brought about by the 1960's research project headed by the Department of Defense. This network (ARPANET) was the first packet-switching network. It started with an experimental four node network which has now grown into over 800,000 Hosts. The Internet has become the prime method of connecting both government agencies and major education campuses.

Currently, Novell and many other commercial companies are providing hosts to the Internet communities, which are providing both software files and e-mail services to the mass number of users.

Learning E-mail Etiquette

Yes, there is e-mail etiquette. As the world continues to become computerized, humans continue to lose the ability to express emotion. Expressions are key to conveying thoughts. Angry, happy, and frustrated, are all emotions most people express daily in both the work place and at home. Yet most e-mail is plain and unexpressive, often in all uppercase or all lowercase letters.

When e-mail is used as a communications media between persons, it should contain a certain level of expression. Whether it consists simply of proper grammar or some of the common abbreviations now being used, e-mail is a conversation. Computers must not remove the qualities that make us human.

Some of the common abbreviations and pictograms currently used in the PC e-mail arena are listed below:

- IMO   **In My O**pinion
- IMHO   **In My H**umble **O**pinion
- BTW   **By The W**ay
- IOW   **In O**ther **W**ords
- \<g\>   Grin
- \<G\>   Big Grin
- OTG,L&R   **On The Ground, Laughing and Rolling** about

Computer versions of the smiley face are as follows:

- :-)   Happy Face
- ;-)   Wink, Wink, Nudge, Nudge
- :-(Sad Face
- :-| Don't do it again
- :-*   Oh!

E-mail is a functional and productive communications media that can be used with or with out expression. The choice is yours. Proper, polite communications between people can make all the difference <G>.

Summary

This chapter was not intended to be a tutorial on e-mail or Novell's MHS. E-mail can easily take up a complete book of its own. But this chapter did attempt to inform those not currently using e-mail of its availability and value. E-mail can, if implemented correctly, add both productiveness and enjoyment to the workplace.

E-mail and Novell's MHS are two distinctly different services. MHS is a message handling service used by e-mail, but not all messages are required to be e-mail. The MHS service not only provides a means of e-mail delivery, it also can be used to transfer data files, or send acknowledgments to selected persons on the status of a program. Novell's MHS has many uses and is currently still in the early implementation stages. While many applications use MHS, others are just starting to recognize its capability to transfer and maintain data files.

Installing NetWare v2.2

etWare v2.2 is the newest Novell 286-based operating system product and requires a completely new installation method. The software interface now being used is very different from the previous 2.1x NETGEN system. If this is your first NetWare installation, this is not a concern to you. If, however, you have installed NetWare in the past, you are in for a change. After some initial confusion looking for the old utilities, you will find this new user interface to be friendly and functional.

Preparing the Hardware

To prepare for the installation of NetWare v2.2, you should first select components that are certified by Novell and reliable.

 It is very important to check that the hardware you use has been re-certified for NetWare v2.2. Most previously-certified equipment works well in the v2.2 environment. Several disk controllers and LAN cards, however, may require new driver versions.

Hardware Requirements

The hardware requirements for NetWare v2.2 depend on the level of service required. Disk controllers, LAN cards, and memory requirements must be chosen with reliability and functionality as the main objectives.

In general, the minimum hardware requirements are an 80286, 386, or 486 machine with at least a 10M hard disk and a minimum of 2.5M of RAM. Note that the RAM requirements increase with the amount of hard disk space in your particular configuration. The NetWare v2.2 OS and utilities take up approximately 7M of hard disk space.

The level of performance varies, depending on the components used. It is highly recommended that low-cost components be evaluated with the value of your file server's data in mind. Reliability and integrity should be your primary concerns when choosing your company's file server.

Before you continue with the installation, you should make a list of all I/O addresses, interrupts, memory addresses, and DMA channels used by your hardware. This list should include serial ports, parallel ports, video adapters, and all other known settings used by your system. Writing this list enables you to install the required network adapters and disk drive controllers.

You should be able to determine this information from the documentation provided with your hardware components and actual switch and jumper settings. If this information is not available, you may want to use a utility program, such as CHECKIT, that provides memory and I/O addresses, interrupts, and DMA channels for the installed components. You also may consult a guide such as Novell's *Hardware Ready Reference* which lists this information for many common hardware components.

Knowing the hardware settings for all of your server components is vital to the installation process. You need to know the disk controller and LAN card settings to make appropriate selections from installation menus, and it is impossible to achieve a properly functioning file server if conflicts exist between hardware components within the server itself.

Note   Watch for I/O and memory overlaps. Not all hardware devices operate true to the published specifications (this may not be apparent from the documentation). A problem can occur, for example, when two cards are installed at adjoining I/O addresses, as in the following:

Card A installed at I/O 300h
Card B installed at I/O 308h

This example appears correct. Card A, however, uses 10 bytes of memory, placing it two bytes into card B's space. Such problems can be difficult to locate.

Memory Requirements

NetWare v2.2 has both a minimum and a maximum memory requirement. If the file server operates in the nondedicated mode, the system must be configured to use a minimum of 2.5M or a maximum of 8M of memory. The server may contain more memory than Novell's published maximums, but the operating system can only utilize the memory up to those maximums. Any excess RAM remains unused by NetWare and, therefore, serves no practical purpose.

If configured as a dedicated file server, the minimum requirement remains 2.5M of memory, but the maximum is now 12M. Remember that the minimum of 2.5M is to be used with a 80M hard drive. If your disk drive is larger, it requires more memory to operate properly.

A simple rule of thumb is to multiply *0.005 x disk storage in M + 2M*, providing that you do not run any value-added processes (VAPs). Suppose, for example, that you have a 650M disk drive and do not load any VAPs. You can compute the memory required to operate a bare v2.2 file server as follows:

$$0.005 \times 650 = 3.25 + 2 = 5.25M$$

This number should be rounded up to the nearest standard memory configuration. In this example, you should consider installing 8M of memory to allow for expansion, print services, and VAPs. Actual memory requirements for VAPs depend on which VAPs you are loading. You should generally add an average of 2M to your memory requirement if you plan to run any VAPs.

Most file servers that report poor performance are configured with the minimum (or less than the minimum) amount of memory. It is not good practice to limit the file server's memory because of budget constraints. You wouldn't, for example, consider buying an 8-cylinder car and ask the dealer to install only 4 park plugs.

Software Requirements

You need working copies of the NetWare v2.2 disks for the installation process. The DOS DISKCOPY command copies all files and subdirectories from the original disks and also transfers the appropriate volume labels, which the INSTALL utility checks for. You also need to have the disks containing any necessary drivers that are not included as part of NetWare.

Installation Methods

Novell NetWare v2.2 provides options other than the floppy-drive, hard-drive, or network-drive methods of installation. The install program assists you without regard for your level of experience.

Floppy-Drive Method

The floppy-drive method of generation is done on high-density floppy disks and requires fewer disk swaps than the previous 2.1x versions. To use this method, create disk copies of four disks (labeled SYSTEM-1, SYSTEM-2, OSEXE, and OSOBJ) by using the DOS DISKCOPY command. This maintains complete compatibility with the originals.

This method of installation is most effective when you need to complete the preliminary steps of the installation at another machine or location. You can then run the INSTALL utility on the actual file server to transfer the configured operating system and utilities.

Hard-Drive Method

NetWare v2.2 also can be generated on a local hard disk. To prepare the disk for this method, you need to run the NetWare UPLOAD program, which creates all proper subdirectories and copies the correct files to the appropriate locations.

After completing the operating-system generation, use the DOWN-LOAD program to copy the generated files back to floppy disks to prepare for the file-server installation.

This installation method enables you to configure the operating system and utilities at a machine other than the server more efficiently than the floppy-drive method. You then transfer the configured files to the server, again using the INSTALL utility.

Network-Drive Method

To install by using the network-drive method, you also run the UP-LOAD program. There are, however, additional advantages when the generation is complete.

Use the new file server as your generation workstation. After the generation process is complete, the installation is performed by downloading the system files directly to the new file server. This method is convenient if more then one file server is required.

 If you boot your dedicated 2.2 file server on DOS 5.0, you may experience lockup problems. The current solution is to boot on a version of DOS other than 5.0 or to obtain the patch 22DOS5.ZIP from Novell.

The Four Install Modules

The NetWare v2.2 installation system is made up of four modules, as shown in figure A.1.

- **Module 1—Operating System Generation**

  This module enables you to choose the mode of operation (dedicated or nondedicated), communications buffers, network interface card, options, and disk controller information.

- **Module 2—Linking and Configuring**

  This module performs the linking process to be completed on the object files selected from your answers to the questions.

- **Module 3—Track Zero Test (ZTEST)**

  This module performs the track zero integrity check on the file server's hard drive.

- **Module 4—File Server Definition**

  This module enables you to choose the file server name and whether to limit disk space. It also provides the options for configuring the volume tables, mirroring information, and specifying the Macintosh VAP installation.

Figure A.1:
Installation
modules.

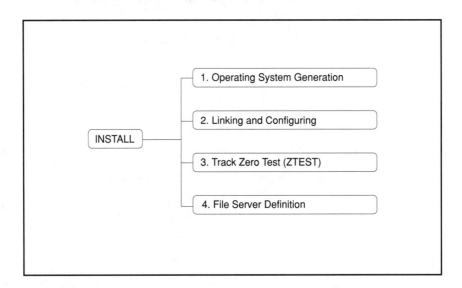

All four modules are handled and operated by the main INSTALL program, which provides the required user interface and passes control to each module.

Basic Installation Option

The basic installation procedure is only for first-time installations that do not require special options. This configuration supports an arrangement with one internal hard drive, one network interface card, one parallel printer, and no internal routers. All other settings take predefined defaults, and the network interface must be set to option 0.

The basic installation procedure asks the following three questions:

1. Type of file server (dedicated or nondedicated)?
2. File server name?
3. Type of network interface card?

Advanced Installation Option

The advanced installation procedure is used for a first-time installation in which special options and configurations are required. During the advanced generation, you must fill in two screens of information about the operating system you are creating. This information includes the file server mode, name, and network card information. In addition, you are required to select the disk driver, network card configuration option, and other options related to the system configuration.

In the advanced installation procedure, you have the control to select and customize the system as needed. This requires some knowledge about the requirements of your system.

Maintenance Installation Option

The maintenance installation option enables you to modify a system that was created with either the basic or advanced installation options. By using the maintenance installation option, you have the ability to do the following:

- Change the file server operating mode.
- Change the number of communications buffers.
- Remove or install core printing.
- Create an internal router.
- Change the file server name.
- Change the number of open files.

The maintenance option maintains all previously-configured options, unless you run the ZTEST program. ZTEST is provided in the maintenance option to enable additional drives to be installed. Many manufacturers now produce NetWare-ready disks which do not require the use of ZTEST. Consult the documentation or manufacturer in regard to your specific drive.

The ZTEST module executes a surface test of track zero on the selected drive, performing both writes and reads. Alteration of track zero causes the loss of all data on the disk, so be certain you have a reliable backup before executing this module. Track zero holds critical system information and must be completely error-free in a NetWare environment.

Upgrade Installation Option

The upgrade installation option is required if you upgrade from an earlier version of NetWare. The upgrade option works with NetWare 2.0a and newer (not including NetWare 2.0) versions of NetWare.

 If a version of NetWare older than version 2.0a must be upgraded, you *must* upgrade to version 2.0a or 2.1x first. The NetWare v2.2 upgrade module does not support these older versions—the loss of data is possible.

If an upgrade to a newer NetWare version is not possible, you can back up all data and restore after NetWare v2.2 is installed. Do not back up any NetWare security. All users and security information have to be re-created manually after the data is restored.

The upgrade procedure is very similar to that of the advanced option. You are presented with the file server definition screen and required to select the proper options.

Novell writes configuration information into the very beginning of a hard drive (track zero). The upgrade installation option checks your existing volume and printer configuration. The information is supplied to Module 4 and installed during the upgrade process. The upgrade routine reads this information from the older routine, supplying it to module 4. You then have the choice of modifying this information. Information retained from NetWare v2.1x includes file server name, number of open files, disk space limits, and hard disk information.

Using the Command Line Options

Novell supplies a series of advanced command line options that come with the NetWare v2.2 installation system. These options give the advanced installer control over the steps completed by the install program and offer the advanced installer a great deal of flexibility to customize the installation process or add additional drivers.

The Command Line Options

The command line for the INSTALL utility enables you to choose from nine options or combinations of options. You may choose to perform part or all of the installation process, skip over informational steps, or configure the operating system on a machine other than the file server.

- **INSTALL—E (Expert Installation).** Selects the advanced installation option by bypassing the welcome screen. The –E option completes modules 1 and 2, or modules 1 through 4, depending on how you answer the question "Is this the file server?"

- **INSTALL—L (Linking Complete).** Completes modules 3 and 4. This option is used after the -E option if you answered no to the question "Is this the file server?" and executed modules 1 and 2 on a machine other than a file server.

 The INSTALL—L option destroys all data on the hard drive and should not be used for maintenance.

- **INSTALL—N (No Linking).** Completes module 1. The -N option creates the LNK and CFG files placed on the SYSTEM-2 disk. This option is generally used by consultants and engineers who want to change or upgrade object files before completing the system generation.

- **INSTALL—C (Configuration Complete).** Completes modules 2 through 4 and is used after running INSTALL—N.

 INSTALL—N and INSTALL—C must be used sequentially because of their direct association.

- **INSTALL—M (Maintenance).** Bypasses the welcome screen and starts with module 1 and ends with 2 or 4. The maintenance option enables changes to the system configuration without losing data—provided that you do not run ZTEST.

- **INSTALL—M —L (Maintenance, Linking Complete).** Completes the maintenance operation if the initial process was performed on a workstation. This option must be run on the downed file server.

- **INSTALL—F (File Server Definition).** Starts at module 4 and enables changes to the File Server Definition screen. This option retains all system information and data.

- **INSTALL—U (Upgrade).** Upgrades a file server from version 2.x to version v2.2. This option bypasses the welcome screen and offers the same functionality as the upgrade option located on the main menu. It uses modules 1 through 4, depending on whether you are on the file server or not.

- **INSTALL—U —L Upgrade, Linking Complete).** This option starts with module 3 and ends with module 4; it completes the upgrade process if the -U option was not run on the file server.

Filling in the Blanks

This section guides you through a basic and advanced installation of a new file server. You must complete your hardware installation and resolve any conflicts before proceeding.

Basic Installation Demonstration

After you prepare your installation method, whether it is the floppy-drive, hard-drive, or network-disk method, you can start the install programs. The main install menu displays, as shown in figure A.2.

After you select the Basic installation option, you see the introduction screen, as shown in figure A.3. This screen has a welcome and a warning message that confirms your choice.

After confirming that you want to continue (by pressing Enter), you are asked to select the file server mode (see fig. A.4), either dedicated or nondedicated. A *dedicated* file server is dedicated to the task of being a file server. Unless the system you are installing is very small (up to five users) and has lightly-used disk access, you should install in the dedicated mode. The option of using the file server as a worksta-tion can sometimes be a problem instead of an advantage. To choose, simply highlight your choice and press Enter.

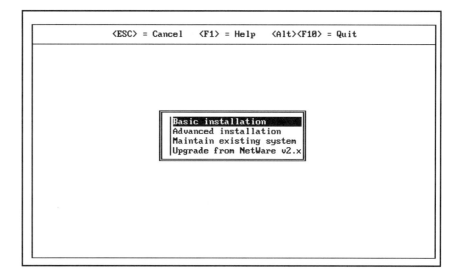

Figure A.2:
Install menu.

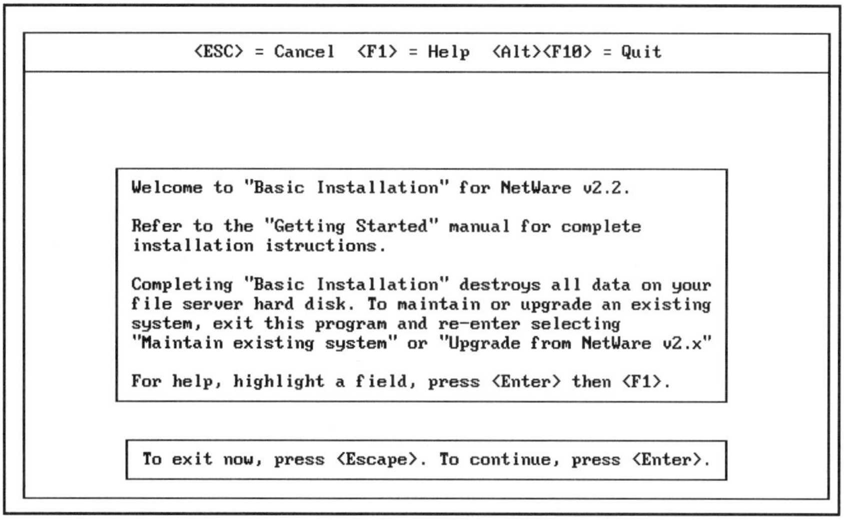

Figure A.3:
Introduction screen.

Figure A.4:
File server mode
menu.

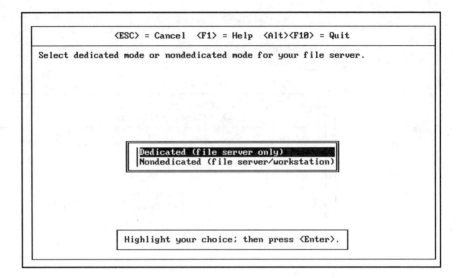

```
          <ESC> = Cancel   <F1> = Help   <Alt><F10> = Quit

  Select dedicated mode or nondedicated mode for your file server.




                 Dedicated (file server only)
                 Nondedicated (file server/workstation)




                Highlight your choice; then press <Enter>.
```

Many system administrators do not realize the critical importance of operating a nondedicated file server. A nondedicated file server's processing power as a file server is greatly reduced by switching between the workstation and file server modes.

With a nondedicated file server, the system runs a much higher risk of system failure and data corruption. The single workstation user that operates programs on the file server has the ability to disrupt all other users if program execution "hangs."

After you select the file server mode of operation, you must now give the file server a name. Each file server located on the LAN must have a unique name. If you have only a single file server, the name is simply a label and is not used by the users (as in a multiple-server environment).

The file server name screen, as shown in figure A.5, is self-explanatory. The name given to your file server is not limited to any particular words. The name can be as simple as your company's name or the name of a department the file server is servicing. You may use any name containing 2 to 45 characters. No spaces or periods are permitted as part of the server name.

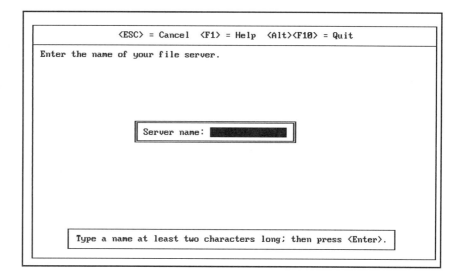

Figure A.5:
File server name
screen.

```
          <ESC> = Cancel   <F1> = Help   <Alt><F10> = Quit
Enter the name of your file server.




                    Server name: ███████████

             Type a name at least two characters long; then press <Enter>.
```

Next, you need to select the network interface card installed in your
file server. The NetWare install program presents you with a list of
drivers supplied with NetWare, as in figure A.6. If the driver you need
is not shown, press Ins and provide the required driver from the disk
supplied by the manufacturer or Novell.

Figure A.6:
Network card driver
selection.

```
          <ESC> = Cancel   <F1> = Help   <Alt><F10> = Quit
Select the driver for the network board in your file server.

     3Com 3C501 EtherLink  V2.45EC (881005)
     3Com 3C503 EtherLink II w/AT 1  v4.11EC (900817)
     3Com 3C503 EtherLink II w/AT 2  v4.12EC (900817)
     3Com 3C505 EtherLink Plus (Assy 2012) w/AT 1  v4.33EC (910110)
     3Com 3C505 EtherLink Plus (Assy 2012) w/AT 2  v4.33EC (910110)
     IBM PCN II & Baseband  v1.18 (910111)
     IBM PCN II & Baseband LAN Support Prog Compatible  v1.18 (910111)
     IBM Token-Ring w/AT 2  v2.60 (900720)
     NetWare Ethernet NE1000  V3.00EC (891204)
   ▼ NetWare Ethernet NE2000  V1.00EC (881004)

        Highlight your choice; then press <Enter>. If the
        driver you need is not listed, press <Insert>.
```

After you complete the network card selection, you see the linking and configuration information display on the screen as each process is performed.

After module 2 or the Link and Configure processes finish, you are prompted, as illustrated by figure A.7 with the ZTEST screen. This screen warns you about data loss that occurs if you proceed.

Figure A.7:
ZTEST warning screen.

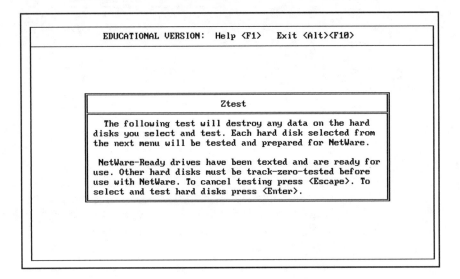

```
        EDUCATIONAL VERSION:  Help <F1>    Exit <Alt><F10>



                                  Ztest

             The following test will destroy any data on the hard
        disks you select and test. Each hard disk selected from
        the next menu will be tested and prepared for NetWare.

             NetWare-Ready drives have been texted and are ready for
        use. Other hard disks must be track-zero-tested before
        use with NetWare. To cancel testing press <Escape>. To
        select and test hard disks press <Enter>.
```

At this point, you have completed modules 1 through 3, and you are ready for the module 4 installation process. By using the Basic option, the file server definition screen defaults to a generic configuration, and the loading of all files begins automatically.

Advanced Installation Demonstration

The Advanced installation method is the most commonly used of the installation options. You need to understand file server hardware and your system requirements to complete the information on-screen.

To start, run the install program again and select the Advanced installation option, as shown in figure A.8.

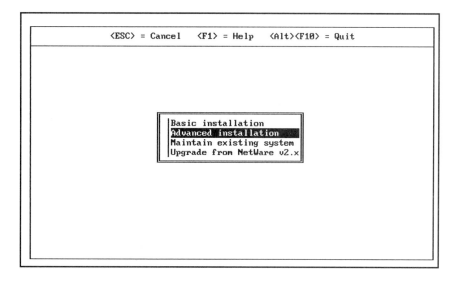

Figure A.8:
Advanced
installation screen.

After selecting this option, you see the familiar welcome screen that informs you of your choice. Press Enter, the welcome screen clears, and the main Operating System Generation screen appears. This screen, as shown in figure A.9, supplies hardware level configuration options.

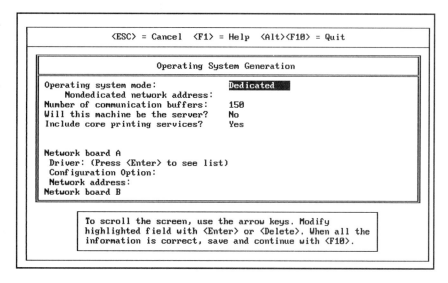

Figure A.9:
Operating System
Generation window.

The Operating System Generation screen contains the following options:

- `Operating system mode:` (Dedicated or Nondedicated)
- `Nondedicated network address:`
- `Number of communication buffers:`
- `Will this machine be the server?`
- `Include core printing services?`

This screen also has options for disk controllers, network card drivers, addresses, and hardware. Note the set of instructions at the bottom of the screen.

First, select the operating system mode (as with the Basic option, discussed previously). If you choose a nondedicated server, you also must supply a network address for this process. This address must be different from any other you use.

Next, configure the communication buffers. The number of buffers varies, depending on the equipment used and the number of users and their work load.

It is important for the integrity of your data to have sufficient communications buffers. If your system runs out of buffers during normal operation, data will be lost. The default of 150 buffers is sufficient for most installations.

You can estimate the number of required buffers by using two buffers for each user and ten buffers for each file server network card. If this number is fewer than 150, use the default.

NetWare 2.2 gives you the option of generating the operating system on a machine other than the file server and then transferring the linked and configured files to the server. If you have chosen this method of OS generation, you will answer No when prompted as to whether this machine will be the server. If you are performing the installation on the server itself, respond Yes to the question.

You are asked if you wish to include core printing. If you only need a couple of printers connected to a file server, core printing may be the best solution. If your printing requirements are more involved, and you need printers distributed throughout the office, you can use the server VAP, rather than core printing.

It is important to know the hardware configuration of your network and disk controllers because you must insert a network-interface driver for each of the four LAN cards you may have installed. To select a network driver, highlight the Network board A field and press Enter. The driver option window is displayed (see fig. A.10).

Figure A.10:
Network board driver selection window.

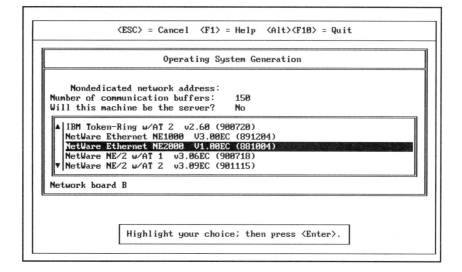

```
            <ESC> = Cancel   <F1> = Help   <Alt><F10> = Quit

    ┌─────────────────────────────────────────────────────────┐
    │                Operating System Generation                │
    │                                                           │
    │    Nondedicated network address:                          │
    │  Number of communication buffers:     150                 │
    │  Will this machine be the server?      No                 │
    │  ┌──────────────────────────────────────────────────────┐ │
    │  ▲│IBM Token-Ring w/AT 2  v2.60 (900720)                │ │
    │   │NetWare Ethernet NE1000  V3.00EC (891204)            │ │
    │   │NetWare Ethernet NE2000  V1.00EC (881004)            │ │
    │   │NetWare NE/2 w/AT 1  v3.06EC (900718)                │ │
    │  ▼│NetWare NE/2 w/AT 2  v3.09EC (901115)                │ │
    │  └──────────────────────────────────────────────────────┘ │
    │  Network board B                                          │
    └─────────────────────────────────────────────────────────┘

            ┌─────────────────────────────────────────────┐
            │ Highlight your choice; then press <Enter>.  │
            └─────────────────────────────────────────────┘
```

This window enables you to scan through the Novell-supplied drivers and choose the one required. If your driver is not listed in this window, you can press Ins and supply the install program with the appropriate LAN_DRV_??? disk.

In this example, the Novell NetWare Ethernet NE2000 driver (see fig. A.10) and the first configuration option (0) are chosen (see fig. A.11).

In the Network address field, enter an address that is unique to any other network segments your system may be connected to. This process is repeated for network boards B, C, and D, if needed.

Next, enter configuration information for disk channels 0 through 4. Because you are selecting an ISA standard disk controller in this instance, choose channel 0.

Figure A.11:
Hardware options.

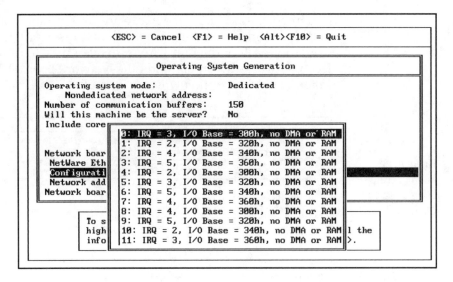

 Novell provides support for four concurrent disk channels. Channel 0 is generally reserved for an ISA disk controller, but other devices can use it if permitted by the driver software.

Channels 1 through 4 are designed for high-performance controllers. These controllers normally are not intended for use on DOS-based computers. The Novell DCB was the first to make use of channels 1 through 4 and does not support channel 0.

Press Enter and the disk driver selection window displays. For this example, select the Industry Standard ISA controller choice, as shown in figure A.12.

After selecting your disk controller type, you need to configure hardware options. For an ISA disk controller, the selected option is 0, as shown in figure A.13.

 The ISA controller also provides options 1 through 9, but these options may not be supported on all controllers. Currently, the only ISA disk controller that is certified to use all options is the standard Compaq controller.

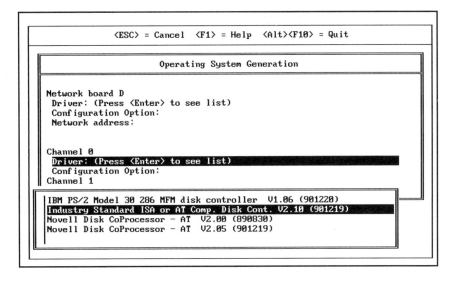

Figure A.12:
Disk driver
selection window.

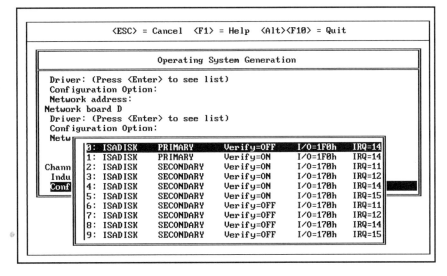

Figure A.13:
Disk driver options.

After you complete the disk controller information fields, press F10 to save the selections and continue with module 2. You see the link and configuration information scroll as the different steps take place. If you selected the option that identifies the machine you are working on as the file server, you see the same ZTEST screen that appeared in the basic installation method. If you selected the option that your machine is not the file server, advanced installation is almost complete.

The remaining portion of the Installing NetWare v2.2 directions is explained in the next module under changing hardware. The last step performed by module 4 is the actual file server definition screen and is used in both maintenance and installation.

B

Installing NetWare v3.11

NetWare 3.11 installation involves several basic steps. Begin by assembling the hardware for your server, keeping in mind that you need to keep track of all interrupt, I/O address, DMA, and base memory address settings. Proceed by booting the server with DOS, creating a DOS partition on your hard disk (or creating a bootable floppy), and copying necessary system files to your boot disk. Run the SERVER.EXE utility to load the NetWare operating system and define the server. Load the required disk drivers, load the INSTALL module to create and mount volumes, and copy the SYSTEM and PUBLIC files onto the server. Finally, load the LAN drivers and other necessary modules, bind protocols to the LAN drivers, and create the server boot files.

Installation and loading procedures for NetWare 3.11 have changed substantially from previous NetWare versions. NetWare 386 no longer requires the linking process that was needed to create the NetWare 286 OS executable file. NetWare 386 is totally dynamic and relies on NetWare loadable modules (NLM) to supply the software modules and drivers needed.

The installation of NetWare 286 required that all hardware settings, LAN drivers, and other configuration options be specified during in-

477

stallation. These specifications were then "linked" during the OS generation, thus becoming hard-coded into the 286 operating system. Any changes in configuration required that a new OS be generated. NetWare 3.11 enables drivers and other modules to be unloaded and reloaded with new configurations without having to down the server.

This appendix not only guides you through a typical 3.11 installation, but also offers suggestions and warns you of potential problems. The installation of NetWare 3.11 generally is trouble free if the hardware selected is "standard," meaning that all necessary drivers are included with NetWare. Generally, more basic hardware configurations may not offer the highest performance levels; this should be a consideration if you want increased performance. Note, however, that the more basic the file server configuration is, the less complex the NetWare installation will be.

Selecting components that are certified and proven should be your first concern; performance should be second. A high-performance system that is down much of the time is less productive than a reliable, lower-performance system. The following sections assume that you have a properly-configured file server that can deliver the expected level of performance and reliability. Proper configuration of the server involves all aspects of the hardware—from the amount of installed RAM to the types of disk drives, controllers, and the switch settings on the cards installed in the server.

Preparing the Hardware

Before you begin the installation process, make a list of all the I/O addresses, interrupts, memory addresses, and DMA channels used by your hardware. This list should include serial ports, parallel ports, video adapters, and all other known settings used by your system. You must know this information so that you can determine where you can install the required network hardware. Each network interface card and other required hardware should supply documentation that describes the supported settings. Using the supplied documentation and the list you created, you should be able to determine where each hardware card can reside. If documentation is not available for system components, you can use a utility such as CHECKIT to determine I/O addresses, interrupts, memory addresses, and DMA channels for the installed hardware on your server. You also can consult a guide such as Novell's *Hardware Ready Reference*, which lists address and interrupt information for many common hardware components.

 Watch out for I/O and memory overlap. Although the documentation may not mention memory overlap, not all hardware devices operate true to the published specifications.

You may experience problems if two cards are installed at adjoining I/O addresses. Suppose that card A is installed at I/O 300h, and card B is installed at I/O 308h. These settings may appear to work properly, but card A needs 10 bytes of memory, which places it two bytes into card B's space. This type of problem is sometimes difficult to locate because the network may appear to function properly at first. List all known information in the list you create.

You can accomplish an installation with address overlaps present in your configuration. Be sure to carefully examine your list of hardware settings. If you find any potential conflicts, reconfigure one of the components if possible. This is better than having to isolate the cause of transient network problems after the network is operational.

You should test the equipment for proper DOS operation. Start by booting DOS from drive A to confirm that the computer is operating and then check the amount of installed extended memory. NetWare 286 and 386 both require a certain amount of extended memory to operate properly.

To determine the approximate amount of memory required for NetWare 3.11, use the following formula:

$$\frac{\text{drive size} \times .023}{\text{block size}} + 4M = \text{memory required}$$

If the volume has added name space, use the following formula:

$$\frac{\text{drive size} \times .032}{\text{block size}} + 4M = \text{memory required}$$

Drive size is stated in megabytes and block size is the size chosen in the installation program (4 is the default for 4K). The following example illustrates this formula:

$$\frac{650 \times .023}{4} + 4 = 7.7375 \text{ or } 8M$$

After you boot the system on DOS, you can create a DOS or drive C partition on the system disk. This partition is used for the initial booting and loading of the NetWare operating system. You can follow the procedure you use to partition a standard DOS drive, with one exception: you designate a different partition size. For the proper operation of a 3.11 system, you need a 3M to 5M partition size. A 5M partition is suggested because it allows extra space for PC diagnostics utilities that can save time in the event of a problem.

The remaining disk space can be used for a NetWare partition on which network volumes can be created. If you do not create a DOS partition, you must create a bootable floppy from which to start your server. Be aware, however, that booting your server from a floppy disk adds considerable time to the process of bringing up the network from a cold start.

The disk that you are preparing should be low-level formatted by either the original manufacturer's DOS utility or the NetWare INSTALL utility before you proceed any further. The manufacturer's DOS utility is suggested because it can prevent problems with some nonstandard controllers and drives. Some manufacturers now ship their drives preformatted and NetWare-ready. Before you try a low-level format, check the documentation or contact the manufacturer to see if the procedure is recommended or necessary.

Any hardware cache memory should be disabled during the format and installation procedure so that you eliminate any possible problems with incompatible devices during the initial installation. Note that if NetWare 286 has been installed previously on the drive, this step is a requirement.

After the DOS FDISK utility creates the partition, the partition is formatted as a bootable drive with the command **FORMAT C:** **/S**. If the FDISK or the FORMAT command fails, a hardware problem is evident and must be solved before you proceed with the installation.

After you successfully create a bootable DOS drive C, you can copy both the SYSTEM-1 and SYSTEM-2 floppy disks to this drive. These two system disks provide the minimum files required to create and load the NetWare volume. If any nonstandard disk drivers are being used, they also must be copied to drive C.

If you did not create a DOS partition on the server hard drive, you should copy the following files to your bootable floppy disk: SERVER.EXE, VREPAIR.NLM, all INSTALL files (regardless of extensions), all files with a NAM extension, and the appropriate disk driver files (with a DSK extension).

 Novell suggests that you use DOS versions 3.1, 3.3x, or 5.0 to create the DOS partition. Both V3.2 and V4.0x may cause problems in the Network environment.

Loading SERVER.EXE

You now can load the main SERVER.EXE program. This program is the heart of NetWare 3.11 and must be loaded to launch the NetWare operating system and make the server operational. Type **SERVER** and press Enter. The screen displays LOADING . . . and the calculated performance speed of your file server.

 NetWare 386 calculates your file server performance speed by setting up a speed counter and watching the CPU time (ticks) as it increments the counter. After three CPU ticks, the counter is divided by 1,000 and the result is used as the speed indicator.

The *speed indicator* determines the relative speed difference between computers that run as 3.11 file servers. Table B.1. offers some common examples.

Table B.1
Common Speed Measurements

CPU	Clock Speed	Wait State	Novell Speed Rating
Compaq 386/25	25MHz	0	242
Novell 386AE	16MHz	1	121
Everex 386/33	33MHz	0	342
Everex 486/33	33MHz	0	914

You next are prompted for a file server name. Type in a name (two to 47 characters long with no periods or spaces) and press Enter. When prompted for the internal network number, type any hexadecimal (one to eight digits in length) and press Enter. Note that this number must be unique—different from all other numbers of connected networks or servers.

 Novell NetWare 386 uses an internal network structure that enables NLMs to communicate. This internal network requires that the "NET" numbers and "Net" numbers be different.

After the Server command loads, a header or banner appears, which displays the NetWare version and user count. The user count confirms the number of user connections this particular version allows.

 The Server command can be used with command line parameters. Use the following parameters to troubleshoot suspected problems with file server boot files or to change buffer size:

- -NA prevents AUTOEXEC.NCF file execution.
- -NS prevents STARTUP.NCF file execution.
- -C enables you to modify the cache buffer size from the default of 4K per block.

After the banner is displayed, you should see a colon (:) prompt, which is the normal prompt for the NetWare console. You can load the appropriate disk driver and continue to create a Novell volume.

Disk Drivers

Novell supplies five standard driver files: ISADISK, DCB, PS2ESDI, PS2MFM, and PS2SCSI. Use the DCB (Disk Coprocessor Board) driver with the original Novell disk coprocessor board or any DCB-compatible, such as the Adaptec 4000 series disk controllers. The PS2 drivers are for IBM Micro Channel (MCA) computers. Other disk drivers are supplied by the controller manufacture or distributor. Note that Novell must certify any drivers. The reliability of the disk driver is critical to the operation of your file structure.

The disk driver you need depends on the disk controller you have installed in your file server. The standard MFM or ESDI controllers that are shipped with most AT computers use the ISADISK.DSK driver. If you are using a non-IBM SCSI controller, you must load the appropriate driver supplied by the manufacturer.

 Currently, Compaq is the only AT-type ESDI controller that is certified to allow duplexing with the standard ISADISK driver.

A few cases have been reported in which the new 3.11 ISADISK driver failed to operate properly. Novell says that the driver was optimized for higher performance, and therefore may not operate with some less compatible controllers. The solution is to use the ISADISK driver from the earlier NetWare V3.10.

The following example illustrates the procedure you follow to load the driver name. Suppose, for example, that you want to load a custom driver written by Procomp for its SCSI disk coprocessor controller. Copy the DRA driver to the DOS drive C. To load the driver, type the following and press Enter:

    LOAD DRA

After the driver is loaded, you are prompted for any hardware configurations needed. In this case, you are asked for the PORT number and the INTERRUPT number, which you have to determine from your own hardware settings and documentation. For this example, a port of 340h and a interrupt of B or 11 are used.

Duplexing versus Mirroring

If you plan on using a second controller to implement the duplexing feature or second disk channel, you must load the driver a second time by following the preceding instructions, with the exception of the port and interrupt settings. A message should appear to inform you that the drivers have been loaded. The second driver is not really loaded twice. Novell simply tells the system to use the driver twice, which is defined as *re-entrantly* loading the driver.

Duplexing with a second disk channel adds disk read performance because the system can read from each disk concurrently. Mirroring uses only a single controller and provides no
added read performance and disk write performance loss.
Both options provide a redundant disk drive for data protection, but with a cost-versus-performance trade-off. Only
duplexing provides for data protection in case of a disk-channel failure.

Performance Issues

If a file server must support a large number of users and uses more
than one volume, you may want to install a second or even a third
disk channel to support the disk I/O traffic. Many file servers are installed today with a single disk controller and loaded with disk drives.
This configuration is generally due to system expansion without
proper planning. Splitting up disk traffic to multiple controllers often
can relieve the file server disk load by allowing a wider bandwidth for
data to flow.

The Install Program

You now are ready to load the installation program and start the actual installation process. To load the Install program from the DOS
drive C, type the following and press Enter:

```
LOAD INSTALL
```

You should see the main Installation Options screen (see fig. B.1).

Novell walks you through the installation process, starting with the
Disk Options and continuing with Volume Options, System Options,
and Product Options.

Disk Options

After the main screen appears, select Disk Options by highlighting it
on the Installation Options menu and pressing Enter. You see a screen
like the one in figure B.2. The Available Disk Options menu includes
the following options:

- Format
- Surface Test
- Mirroring
- Partition Tables
- Return To Main Menu

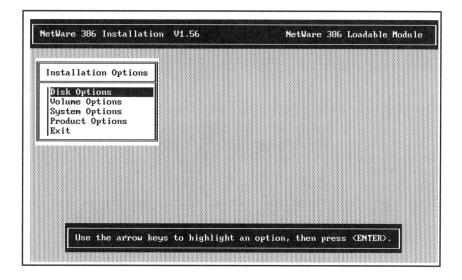

Figure B.1:
The Installation
Options menu.

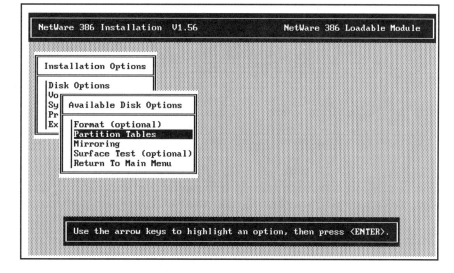

Figure B.2:
The Available Disk
Options menu.

Select the Partition Tables option to create the NetWare volume by highlighting the option and pressing Enter. You should see a list of the drives that are attached to the controller. The example in figure B.3 shows two devices that are attached to a SCSI controller.

If no drives or the wrong drive type appear in this window, do not proceed! If the Available Disk Drives window is empty, check all connections to the drive and confirm the driver software options you are loading. If the wrong drive type appears in the window, *do not proceed with the install process*. You could write to the disk incorrectly. Back up by pressing Esc, follow the instructions at the bottom of the screen, and then confirm all hardware and software steps performed previously.

Figure B.3:
The Available Disk Drives window.

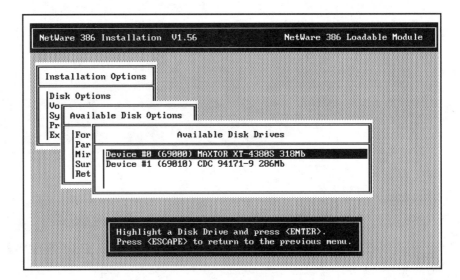

If the disk drive or drives shown are correct, select the first device and press Enter. You should see the Partition Type screen that contains the options to create and modify the partitions.

Figure B.4 shows the Partition Type screen after the NetWare partition has been created. When you first enter this option, you see only the DOS partition you created with the DOS FDISK utility. If the DOS partition does not appear correctly on this screen, do not proceed until the problem is solved.

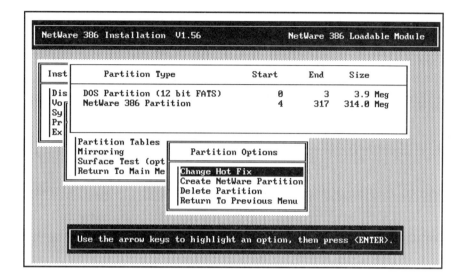

Figure B.4:
The Partition
Options menu.

 The Change Hot Fix option, which is located on the Partition Options menu, enables you to modify the size of the Hot Fix Redirection Area. Novell suggests that you do not make the Hot Fix Area any smaller than the default.

You also can use the Change Hot Fix option to match drives of different physical sizes, making them appear to be the same size, when mirroring or duplexing is desired.

After you create the Novell partition, return to the Installation Options menu (each time you press Esc you back up one menu level). Select the Volume Options option and press Enter.

Volume Options

The Volume Information screen (see fig. B.5) enables you to choose the volume configuration. The window is opened by highlighting a volume name on the Volumes menu and pressing Enter. You can select the block size and create spanned volumes. *Spanned volumes* occupy NetWare partitions on more than one physical disk drive. The Volume Information window also enables you to rename volumes later without the chance of losing data.

Figure B.5:
The Volume
Information
window.

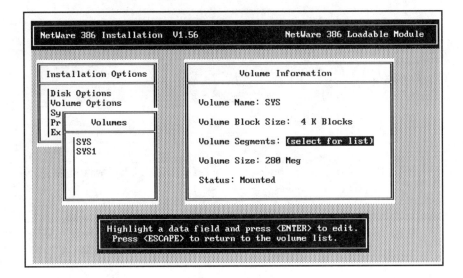

The first NetWare volume must have the name SYS: but the following volume names can be of your choice. To create this first volume using the entire disk space (as in the previous figure), press Esc to return to the volume list. Any volume option modifications must be completed at this time. To make changes later, you must delete the volume, which causes you to lose all data on that volume.

If you want to create a volume that does not use the entire disk space, you can calculate the segment size by multiplying the desired size of the volume (in megabytes) by 1024, and then dividing by block size. The sum is the number of blocks equal to the desired segment size. If you want to create a 50M volume on a 100M drive and the volume block size is the default value of 4K, for example, the number following are the of blocks in the segment:

(50 x 1024)/4 = 12800 blocks

Therefore, 12800 blocks equals a 50M volume. This information is entered into the Initial Segment Size field.

 Volume spanning can provide very high performance, but not without cost. The rule of thumb is that for every drive you span, your disk access time is divided by the number of drives. But note that the possibility of failure is multiplied by the same number.

Novell suggests that you implement duplexing whenever a volume is spanned. This technique also adds to the performance by allowing the same split reads available with normal duplexing.

Volume spanning is a feature of NetWare 3.11 that enables multiple drives to be logically linked into a single volume. This feature increases performance because the drives operate in a parallel manner, thereby enabling them to access more data with less mechanical movement. To create a spanned volume, you add volume segments to obtain the desired size.

The individual block size of a volume can be modified from the 4K default. You can select sizes of 4K, 8K, 16K, 32K, or 64K. Unless you have a special application that can benefit from a large block size, it is recommended that you use the default. A larger block degrades the performance of most applications. This feature is intended for very large database systems with large data blocks. Note that any calculations made with formulas listed previously have to be revised if block size is changed.

System Options

After you create the NetWare volume or volumes, you go to the System Options menu to complete the initial installation. Press Esc to back up to the Installation Options menu, highlight System Options, and then press Enter. The System Options menu (see fig. B.6) enables you to load the remaining software and create the files required to automatically boot as a file server.

You first must copy all System and Public utilities. Select the Copy System and Public Files option by highlighting that choice on the Available System Options menu, press Enter, and then follow the prompts. Because you did not mount the volume, you are prompted to do so now. After mounting volume SYS:, a window appears, and you are asked to insert the System-2 disk and press Esc. Continue this process until finished.

After you load all the software, select the Create STARTUP.NCF File option. This option enables you to create the file needed to automatically load the disk driver and set particular operating environment features as seen in figure B.7.

Figure B.6:
The Available
System Options
menu.

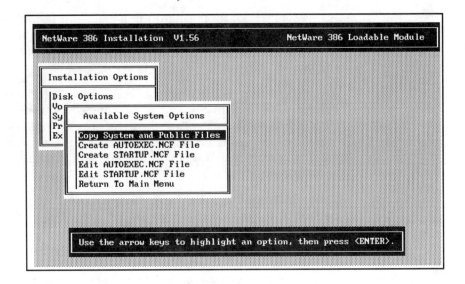

```
NetWare 386 Installation  V1.56          NetWare 386 Loadable Module

  Installation Options
  Disk Options
  Vo
  Sy      Available System Options
  Pr
  Ex    Copy System and Public Files
        Create AUTOEXEC.NCF File
        Create STARTUP.NCF File
        Edit AUTOEXEC.NCF File
        Edit STARTUP.NCF File
        Return To Main Menu




      Use the arrow keys to highlight an option, then press <ENTER>.
```

Figure B.7:
The STARTUP.NCF
setup screen.

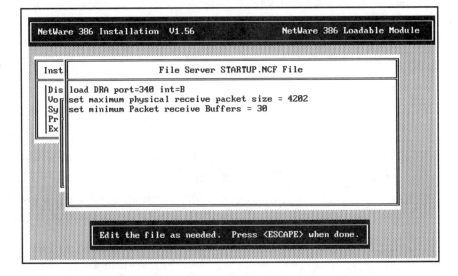

```
NetWare 386 Installation  V1.56          NetWare 386 Loadable Module

  Inst              File Server STARTUP.NCF File

  Dis  load DRA port=340 int=B
  Vo   set maximum physical receive packet size = 4202
  Sy   set minimum Packet receive Buffers = 30
  Pr
  Ex






      Edit the file as needed.  Press <ESCAPE> when done.
```

The STARTUP.NCF file contains the commands to load the disk driver
and the special SET commands. You can set the maximum and minimum packet size. Figure B.7 shows that the maximum size for any
transmitted packet on the network is 4202 bytes and the minimum
number of receive buffers on the server is 30. The packet size is to allow proper operation of the Arcnet TURBO-II standard and the buff-

ers of 30 are to help in heavy traffic situations. To leave the editing screen for the STARTUP.NCF file, press Esc and answer Yes to save the file; press Esc again until you return to the Installation Options menu.

Product Options

You now are ready to load the additional software options to the 3.11 operating system. To install software, such as the Macintosh NLM, select Product Options from the Installation Options menu and press Enter. Press Ins to see a list of available options to install (see fig. B.8). To install an option, highlight it on the menu and press Enter.

Figure B.8:
The Installed
Products window.

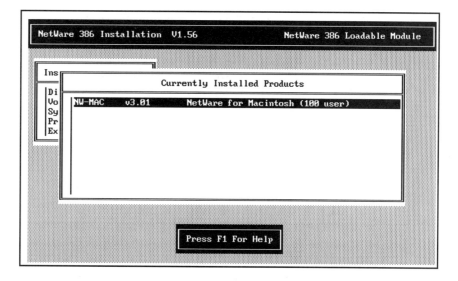

Press Alt-Esc to switch out of the INSTALL utility without leaving the program, or press Ctrl-Esc to choose from a list of options. You return to the colon prompt so that you can load your LAN drivers.

LAN Drivers

LAN drivers for NetWare 3.11 are NLMs that must be loaded to make the network function as a network. These modules drive the LAN cards in the server, enabling communication between the server and the nodes of the network.

Loading LAN Drivers

The next step in the installation process is to load the LAN or network interface drivers. This explanation assumes that you have installed and tested the network cabling.

Suppose, for example, that you have a setup that is a little more complicated than the average setup. This system has both a Standard Microsystems 16-bit ARCNET interface and a Novell NE2000 16-bit ethernet interface. This example illustrates the way in which you can load a second frame type so that one network card operates as two cards. This example uses a second ethernet frame type to communicate with a TCP/IP system.

Miscellaneous problems have been encountered with the installation of 8-bit network interface cards in the file server. Novell suggests that you use no fewer than 16-bit cards in the file server to prevent problems. Do not be tempted to install a high-performance file server system, such as NetWare 3.11, and attempt to use a low cost workstation interface card.

The ARCNET driver used in this example is not included with NetWare 3.11, but was previously copied to the DOS C: partition.

Use the LOAD command to install the ARCNET driver by entering **LOAD C:\PC500386**. PC500386 is simply the file name of the driver and for now it is only located on drive C. After you load the driver, you are prompted for the hardware settings of PORT and INTERRUPT, which you have to determine from your own hardware settings and documentation. In this example, use a port of 2E0h and int 9.

If the LOAD command fails, check all the hardware switch and jumper settings. Improper settings and conflicts with other devices are the most common problems.

Check that you do not have a switch setting reversed. It is quite common to have the "on" and "off" or "1" and "0" settings in a mirror image.

Use the BIND command to bind the proper protocol to the LAN driver. Type **BIND IPX TO PC500386** and press Enter. You are prompted for a Network number:, which is the network number assigned to the cable segment to which you are connected. For this example, use three (3). You now are connected to the network, and communications packets are being transmitted and received.

Next, you must load the NE2000 driver (see fig. B.9) that is included with NetWare. It was copied to the SYS: volume during installation and does not have to be loaded from the C drive.

Figure B.9:
Loading the
NE2000 driver.

```
:load ne2000
Loading module NE2000.LAN
    NetWare NE2000   v3.11 (910131)
    Version 3.11     January 31, 1991
Supported I/O port values are 300, 320, 360
I/O port: 300
Supported interrupt number values are 3, 4, 5
Interrupt number: 3
:
```

You are prompted for port and interrupt option settings. This particular interface requires port 300h and interrupt 3 (your settings depend on your particular hardware configuration). Because both drivers were loaded with no command line parameters, use the default FRAME type. Use the BIND command (see fig. B.10) to bind the proper protocol to the driver, which is IPX in this case.

Now you can load a different frame type to support the IP packet protocol to enable the routing of TCP/IP packets. Following the preceding method, load the NE2000 driver a second time (see fig. B 11).

Figure B.10:
Binding the proper
protocol to the
driver.

```
:bind ipx to ne2000
Network number: 5
IPX LAN protocol bound to NetWare NE2000  v3.11 (910131)
:
```

Figure B.11:
Loading the
Ethernet II frame.

```
:load ne2000
Loading module NE2000.LAN
Do you want to add another frame type for a previously loaded board? y
Supported frame types for NE2000 using I/O Port 300h to 31Fh, Interrupt 3h are:
     1. ETHERNET_II
     2. ETHERNET_802.2
     3. ETHERNET_SNAP
Select new frame type: 1
   Previously loaded module was used re-entrantly
:
```

You can choose to add another frame type. When asked if you want to
add another frame type for a previously-loaded board, type **Yes** or **Y**
and press Enter to obtain the list of supported frames. For the purpose
of this example, select the Ethernet II frame and the previous driver is
used re-entrantly.

Of the supported frames, the Ethernet II is used by many large systems such as DEC and SUN Microsystems. The 802.3 is the standard setup by IEEE and is the Novell default. ETHERNET SNAP currently is used by Macintosh EtherTalk system.

The TCPIP support NLM is required to supply the protocol. This NLM is loaded simply by using the LOAD command, as shown in figure B.12.

Figure B.12:
Loading the TCPIP support NLM.

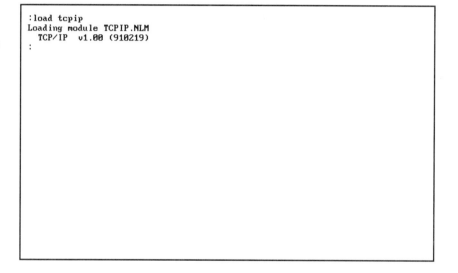

```
:load tcpip
Loading module TCPIP.NLM
  TCP/IP  v1.00 (910219)
:
```

Binding Protocols

Now you are ready to bind the new protocol to the driver as you did when binding IPX. The command is **BIND IP to NE2000**. A list of NE2000 boards and frame types that are available for use is displayed. Select the required card. In this case, select the Ethernet II frame or board 2. Type **2** and press Enter.

You then are prompted for the IP address, which is nothing like the native MAC addressing Novell uses. In the TCP or IP environment, each portion of the address has a particular meaning. Each portion must be assigned to prevent problems because TCP networks are generally quite large and each node must have a unique address while conforming to the numbering conventions of the network. In a large network, it can be difficult to trace if two nodes have the same IP address. Figure B.13 displays a screen print of this information.

Figure B.13:
Binding IP to
NE2000.

```
:bind ip to ne2000
Several boards are using the NE2000 LAN driver
     1. NetWare NE2000   v3.11 (910131) using I/O Port 300h to 31Fh, Interrupt 3h
 Frame type: ETHERNET_802.3
     2. NetWare NE2000   v3.11 (910131) using I/O Port 300h to 31Fh, Interrupt 3h
 Frame type: ETHERNET_II
Select board to bind: 2
IP address: 192.68.205.1
IP: Bound to board 3.  IP address 192.68.205.1, net mask FF.FF.FF.0
IP LAN protocol bound to NetWare NE2000   v3.11 (910131)
:
```

You can return to the Install utility by pressing Alt-Esc and selecting Create the AUTOEXEC.NCF File. After you select this option, the system should remember all the commands you entered and automatically insert them into the AUTOEXEC.NCF file (see fig. B.14).

Check the file for accuracy. Notice that the PC500386 driver that was loaded from drive C is not entered properly. This problem is simple to solve. Place **C:** before the driver, or place a copy of the driver in the SYS:SYSTEM directory so that your backup device protects this file too.

 Notice the parameter "name" in the AUTOEXEC.NCF file. This parameter is useful because it enables you to name the individual drivers and BIND to the name.

Although this example does not illustrate this technique, it is a simple matter to replace the LAN driver name with the assigned name, such as **BIND IPX to CDI net=3**.

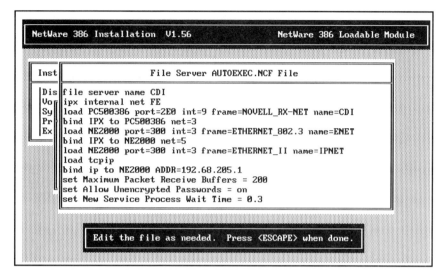

```
Inst          File Server AUTOEXEC.NCF File
Dis  file server name CDI
Vo   ipx internal net FE
Sy   load PC500386 port=2E0 int=9 frame=NOVELL_RX-NET name=CDI
Pr   bind IPX to PC500386 net=3
Ex   load NE2000 port=300 int=3 frame=ETHERNET_802.3 name=ENET
     bind IPX to NE2000 net=5
     load NE2000 port=300 int=3 frame=ETHERNET_II name=IPNET
     load tcpip
     bind ip to NE2000 ADDR=192.68.205.1
     set Maximum Packet Receive Buffers = 200
     set Allow Unencrypted Passwords = on
     set New Service Process Wait Time = 0.3

       Edit the file as needed.  Press <ESCAPE> when done.
```

Figure B.14:
The AUTOEXEC.NCF file settings.

Modifying the 3.11 Operating System

Changing Hardware

This section teaches you how to spot possible configuration problems with your server. These problems can require file-server expansion to solve. Common solutions to configuration problems include adding memory, splitting the network into multiple LAN cards, or adding one or more new disk channels.

Adding Memory

Many people overlook the importance of system memory. NetWare 3.11 is a high-level multitasking system that requires many times more memory than the average workstation. Most 3.11 file servers should not have fewer than 8M of memory, and should have much more memory if large disk volumes are being used.

As a rule of thumb, the total number of cache buffers listed on the main MONITOR screen should be between 800 and 1000. The amount of

Cache Buffers listed under Resource Utilization should not be fewer than 20 percent.

If either of these statistics vary outside of these ranges, Novell suggests that you add memory in increments of one megabyte until the problem is solved.

Additional LAN Cards

As a rule of thumb, all numbers listed under the monitor LAN driver statistics, with the exception of Total Packets sent and received, should be as low as possible, if not zero. Different LAN cards display various statistics, but a high level of error and retries generally represent a defective card or a high level of traffic. The simplest solution to a traffic problem is to install another LAN card to handle some of the traffic load.

 To identify a problem can require special equipment and a high level of traffic pattern knowledge for that particular topology. If you think you are experiencing problems because statistics found in the monitor program, ask your vendor for suggestions.

Disk Channels

Disk Channel performance is difficult to diagnose. A particular disk controller has a limit on the number ofreads and writes it can do in any given second, but most network file server loads are not consistent. Word processors, spreadsheets, and database applications present a different load to the disk controller. This inconsistency is compounded by the number of users and the work loads created in the office environment.

If the actual disk-access time appears to be slow, the system administrator can watch a few key Monitor statistics. Two in particular, Dirty Cache Buffers and Current Disk Requests, can inform you of the file server's capability to handle the current load.

The Current Disk Requests shows the number of disk requests in the queue waiting to be serviced. The Dirty Cache Buffers is the number of file blocks in memory waiting to be written to disk. If these numbers are high, the disk system may be overworked or the file server may be too slow to process the request in memory. An overworked disk channel requires that you install another disk channel to assist with the load. But before you invest in additional hardware, talk to a reputable vender for a solution.

Optimizing the Environment (Set Commands)

The SET commands available at the console are intended to be used in customizing the system environment. Listed here are just a few of the most common commands you can use to help performance and solve problems that you may encounter.

The first two commands must be set in the STARTUP.NCF file and are not required on all systems, but should be used on any system that uses a high performance ARCNET controller and runs TURBO-II packets.

STARTUP.NCF

```
set maximum physical receive packet size = 4202
set minimum packet receive buffers = 100
```

The following set commands can provide additional performance under the proper conditions and are helpful on most file servers:

AUTOEXEC.NCF

```
set Allow Unencrypted Passwords = on
set Maximum Packet Receive Buffers = 200
set New Service Process Wait Time = 0.3
set Maximum Outstanding NCP Searches = 100
set Maximum Directory Cache Buffers = 700
```

If you want to favor writes, use the following:

```
set maximum concurrent disk cache writes = 100
```

If you want to favor reads, use the following:

```
set maximum concurrent disk cache writes = 50
```

Upgrading to v3.11

When you upgrade to NetWare 3.11, keep in mind that there are a few things you cannot do. You cannot back up your 286 file server and restore to the new 386 system. If your backup device saves the security information (which it should), system corruptions will occur when you restore to the new NetWare 386 system. The system rights and file and directory attributes are different and will not restore correctly. You must pass all data through the Novell UPGRADE program to convert the file information properly.

If you are not reusing your old file server to upgrade, you will not encounter a problem, and the upgrade can be very smooth. Some tape drive manufactures offer drivers for the Novell UPGRADE program, and you may want to call your vendor for current information.

History of the NetWare DOS Shell

T his appendix relates the history of the major changes that have occurred in the NetWare DOS shell beginning with version 3.01. The lowercase x indicates a variable that was replaced with the number of the DOS version being used. For example, if you boot your PC using DOS 5.0, use NET5.COM, XMSNET5.EXE or EMSNET5.EXE.

NETx.COM, XMSNETx.EXE, EMSNETx.EXE
3.01 Rev. A
released on 5-8-90

This was the initial release of the 3.01 shell.

NETx.COM, XMSNETx.EXE, EMSNETx.EXE
3.01 Rev. B
released on 6-6-90

This shell corrected the problem of the workstation hanging when Brightwork's SiteLock program was loaded.

NETx.COM, XMSNETx.EXE, EMSNETx.EXE
3.01 Rev. C
Released only to developers on 9/7/90

This shell version corrected the following problems:

- Slow network response time when using the Preferred Server option in the SHELL.CFG or NET.CFG file.
- DOS directories incorrectly displayed under Windows when using DOS 4.0 and EMSNETx or XMSNETx.
- Fake roots were deleted when using the volume name in a path.
- `Device not ready` error appeared on the workstation when printing to a captured LPT device.
- Enhanced memory shells did not send the header information to the printer. The header information contained the escape codes necessary for the printer.
- When used with NetWare 2.x versions, the Dynamic Memory Pool 1 was not released properly with the enhanced memory shells, causing the server to hang.

NETx.COM, XMSNETx.EXE, EMSNETx.EXE
3.01 Rev. D
released on 9-7-90

The NetWare DOS shells v3.01 rev. D was released to all users and contains all the 3.01 rev. C changes.

NETx.COM, XMSNETx.EXE, EMSNETx.EXE
3.01 Rev. D
released on 9-18-90

Another release of version D corrected the following two problems:

- NVER returned Rev. C instead of Rev. D.
- When running the older Rev. D shell on NetWare v2.15 or earlier, the capability to perform an external program execution from the login script requires the user to have Open rights at the root.

NETx.COM, XMSNETx.EXE, EMSNETx.EXE
3.01 Rev. E
released on 11-27-90

This release corrected the following concerns:

- When using the DOS 4.0 TRUENAME internal command, (an undocumented DOS command that returns the full pathname, including file server name and volume), false information was returned which made Emerald System's backup fail.

- Microsoft Link displayed a scratched file error when linking a large number of files.

- The rename function caused the wrong error code to be returned to applications such as Platinum Accounting by Advanced Business Microsystems. This error also showed up in the NETGEN utility with the message: Cannot find DRVRDATA.DAT.

- Earlier shells were not correctly maintaining the default server after logout when an X.25 bridge was used.

- ELS NetWare servers gave you one less connection than the maximum when using remote boot.

- Enabled file caching in EMSNETx and XMSNETx shells. (File caching was not enabled in earlier releases of the enhanced memory shells.)

- Added the /? option to the command line which displays version and usage information.

- Added support for the VERSION.EXE command.

- Added a message that warned that a TSR program was loaded when trying to unload the shell.

NETx.COM, XMSNETx.EXE, EMSNETx.EXE
3.02
released on 2-06-91

Release 3.02 corrected the following problems:

- File caching was turned off in version 3.01 rev E. Among the applications experiencing problems due to file cache inadequacies were Paradox, Lotus 123 and Quattro, DESQview and NetRemote.

- Added the new NET.CFG configuration parameters—Environment Pad and DOS Name

- The new shell now relinquishes all connections. (Previous shells held one connection open when shells were unloaded.)

- Cache was turned off when setting `Cache Buffers=0` in the NET.CFG file.

- Capturing to a file no longer results in truncated print files.

NETx.COM, XMSNETx.EXE, EMSNETx.EXE
3.21
released on 7-18-91

Version 3.21 incorporated the following changes:

- The Generic Shell is introduced and works with DOS 3.x, 4.x, and 5.x.

- Using the Preferred Server function no longer causes some machines to hang randomly.

- The /c = option was added to provide flexible naming of the shell configuration file, and the /f option was added to unload the shell if it was loaded high.

- A "creation date" code was added to the shell when running NETX i.

- Added support for EMS memory handle names.

- Added support for international date and time formats.

- Fixed the DOS NAME parameter problem with the EMS and XMS shell. (The EMS and XMS shells would hang when loading if the DOS NAME was used.)

- Fixed the problem with "P_STATION" returning bad information in the Login script. This problem only occurred with the v3.2 shell.

- Fixed a problem with being denied simultaneous access to a shared file.

- Fixed cache problem which was causing a WordPerfect diskfull error.
- Corrected "call 5" functions for programs ported from CPM to DOS.
- Included a feature that displays what version of DOS is currently running when loading the shell.
- Resolved a problem where Btrieve files were being corrupted when the server was turned off without being downed.
- DOS 5.0 Load High did not work properly with NET5.COM.
- Fixed the problem with DOS 5.0 MEM. The program did not displaying program names correctly after the shell was loaded.
- DOS ATTRIB command was unable to find hidden directories on network drives.

NETx.COM, XMSNETx.EXE, EMSNETx.EXE
3.22
released on 7-31-91

Problem with remote boot and DOS 5.0 was corrected. Previously, the shell looked to the F: drive rather then the A: (virtual) drive.

NETx.COM, XMSNETx.EXE, EMSNETx.EXE
3.26
released on 2-11-92

Shell revised to work with Windows v3.1

Using the Programs on the Bonus Disk

N The *Inside Novell NetWare, Special Edition* bonus disk contains a variety of programs designed to assist you in managing and using your NetWare network. This appendix contains brief descriptions of the programs along with installation instructions. Most of the programs are delivered in compressed .ZIP files which first must be decompressed by using PKUNZIP. For your convenience, a copy of PKUNZIP is enclosed. Instructions for unzipping files are included at the end of this appendix.

ASAP! for Networks

File: ASAP!.ZIP

ASAP! is a groupware office automation package with features that may surprise you. Some of the tools in this package are as follows:

- An address book
- A calendar/scheduler
- A group chat facility
- A phone messaging system
- A to-do list with alarms

The main menu screen for ASAP!, shown in figure D.1, gives you an idea of its features. Pull-down menus control everything, so that users require little training.

Figure D.1:
The main menu
screen of ASAP!

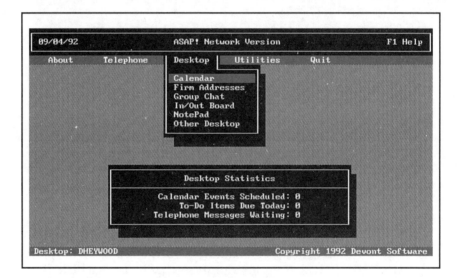

Figure D.2 shows the ASAP! calendar. On the left is a view of the day's appointments. Other options, such as week-at-a-glance, also are available.

To install ASAP!, unzip the distribution file into a temporary directory. Print the manual contained in ASAP.TXT and follow the installation instructions.

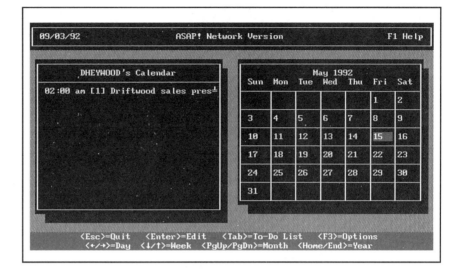

Figure D.2:
The ASAP!
calendar.

BIND

File: BINDSU.ZIP

BIND is a DOS bindery viewer structured with a NetWare menu utility interface. BIND enables you to easily browse through any properties in your server's bindery.

To install, simply unzip the distribution file, then copy BIND.EXE and BIND.LBR into SYS:PUBLIC. Documentation is included in README.DOC.

BINDSCAN

File: BINDSC.ZIP

If you prefer working with Microsoft Windows, here is a Windows bindery viewer.

To install, unzip BINDSCAN.ZIP, then use the Windows Setup utility to add BINDSCAN to your Windows programs. The user's guide is found in BINDSCAN.WRI.

CHAT

File: CHAT120.ZIP

CHAT is a two-person chat utility that can be loaded as a pop-up TSR or as a transient DOS program. It comes in two versions. CHAT1 uses a single window; CHAT2 places each conversation in a separate window. A CHAT1 dialog is shown in figure D.3.

Figure D.3:
A dialog with CHAT.

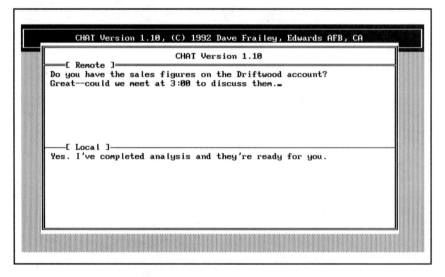

```
        CHAT Version 1.10, (C) 1992 Dave Frailey, Edwards AFB, CA
                            CHAT Version 1.10
        ━[ Remote ]━
        Do you have the sales figures on the Driftwood account?
        Great--could we meet at 3:00 to discuss them._




        ━[ Local ]━
        Yes. I've completed analysis and they're ready for you.
```

To install, unzip CHAT.ZIP and place the desired .COM file in SYS:PUBLIC. The documentation is contained in a file named CHAT.DOC. In the DOC file, you discover that the program author, Dave Frailey, maintains a BBS that distributes his and other authors' programs. If you like CHAT, you may want to check out Mr. Frailey's other offerings. USPACE, also included on this disk, is another of Mr. Frailey's utilities.

P.S. Menu

File: PSMN15.ZIP

Menus make PCs easier to use, especially when they are on a LAN. P.S. Menu is attractive, slick to use, and easy to configure.

P.S.Menu uses a push-button graphic interface that supports a mouse. Figure D.4 is a screen shot of the sample version's startup screen.

Figure D.4:
A sample P.S.Menu screen

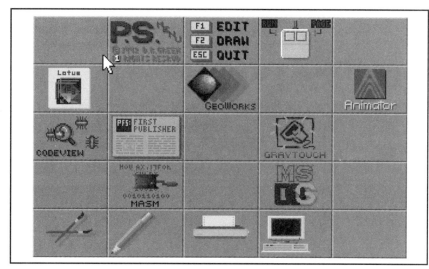

The screens for P.S. Menu consist of rows and columns of pushbuttons. Each button can be assigned a program startup task and an icon.

To install P.S. Menu, unzip PSMN15.ZIP into a temporary directory, then type PSINSTALL. The installation procedure walks you through the rest of the procedure.

As this book goes to press, a new version of P.S. Menu is nearing completion. If you like version 1.5, make sure that you contact the author and check out the new version.

ExpressIT!

File: EXPRESS.ZIP

A network without electronic mail is incomplete. Even doubting Thomases find that e-mail quickly incorporates itself into their working habits. E-mail is a great way to communicate.

ExpressIT! is an outstanding electronic mail program that works well with NetWare Lite. You have received a 30-day demonstration copy of the product on the bonus disk. ExpressIT! is a full-featured mail program, yet it is so easy to operate that users require little or no training.

Figure D.5 shows an ExpressIT! screen being used to compose a message.

Figure D.5:
E-mail message
being composed in
ExpressIT!.

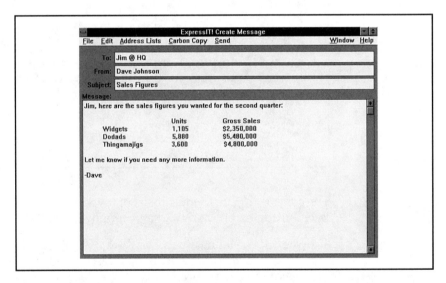

To install ExpressIT! on a NetWare server, unzip the distribution file into a temporary directory. Then follow the installation instructions in the file EXPRESSR.DOC.

The creators of ExpressIT! also offer a variety of useful tools to support electronic mail and LAN management. Check out their other offerings in the program documentation.

USPACE

File: USPACE.COM

USPACE—another contribution from the author of CHAT—is a simple utility with an important function. USPACE makes it easy to obtain reports about the disk space owned by your LAN users. Reports may be directed to the screen or to a file.

PKUNZIP

The PKZIP file compression utility is an industry standard. Most programs on bulletin boards and on CompuServe are distributed in the form of .ZIP files, created by PKZIP. Your book disk includes PKUNZIP—a program for decompressing .ZIP files. You probably will want to install PKUNZIP in a directory on your DOS PATH.

To unzip the files on your book disk perform the following steps:

1. Copy the .ZIP file into the desired directory.
2. Enter the command `PKUNZIP filename` where `filename` is the name of the .ZIP file.
3. Delete the original .ZIP file, which is no longer required.

PKUNZIP is included on your disk for simplicity. No LAN administrator should be without a copy of the complete PKZIP program, however. If you do not have a copy of PKZIP, you can download a demonstration copy from CompuServe or from most bulletin boards. Or you can contact PKWARE directly for a license.

Using Shareware

New Riders Publishing is enthusiastic about the programs included on your bonus disk. With the exception of ExpressIT!, the programs are *shareware*. Shareware programs are demonstration copies distributed free of charge. The copyright owner requests that you register the program if you are going to use it after an evaluation period.

ExpressIT! is a 30-day demonstration version of a commercial program.

If you examine the software market, you may notice that often the most innovative features are incorporated into shareware programs. Developers of these programs have a direct stake in the success of the program, and they must be creative and responsive to user needs.

Registration fees are almost always modest, and give the program developer an incentive to make a good program better. They also guarantee you a receptive ear when you call the software developer. Almost without fail, these developers will listen to your ideas, and you may find your idea in a program update.

New Riders Publishing cannot provide technical support for these programs. The documents accompanying each program describe your technical support options.

New Riders Publishing hopes that you enjoy the programs on your bonus disk, and encourages you to support the programs you like by registering your copies.

NetWare Command Reference

ADD NAME SPACE   :

Purpose

Stores non-DOS files, such as Macintosh files, on a NetWare volume. This command is available only at the file server console.

Syntax

```
ADD NAME SPACE name TO VOLUME volumename
```

Options

Macintosh	Use for Macintosh files
OS2	Use for OS/2 files

515

NFS	Use for Unix files
FTAM	Use for Unix files

Rules and Considerations

To set up a volume for the storage of non-DOS files, make sure that the appropriate NetWare Loadable Modules (NLMs) for the non-DOS files have been loaded. Next, configure the volume for the new name space.

Before you can use this command, you must load the appropriate name space module. Extra server memory is required for each name space you add to a volume. Use the ADD NAME SPACE command once for each non-DOS naming convention you intend to store on a NetWare volume.

To use Macintosh files on your NetWare 3.11 server, you must run MACINST and specify your server as a target file server after you have added name space.

Examples

To add Macintosh name space support to the NetWare volume SYS, type the following form of the command at the console:

ADD NAME SPACE MACINTOSH TO SYS

To see the name space support currently set up on your server, type the following command at the file server console:

ADD NAME SPACE

The screen displays the following message:

```
Missing name space name
Syntax: ADD NAME SPACE <name space name>
[TO [VOLUME]] <volumename>

Loaded name spaces are:
DOS
MACINTOSH
```

Important Messages

None

Notes

 After you set up a NetWare volume to store non-DOS files, you can reverse the name space only by loading and running the VREPAIR utility and destroying all non-DOS file data.

You must use the ADD NAME SPACE command for every volume that needs to store non-DOS files.

See also

LOAD NAME SPACE
STARTUP.NCF
MACINST
VREPAIR

ALLOW   F> 3.11

Purpose

Enables you to change, view, or set the inherited rights mask (IRM) of a file or directory. The ALLOW command resides in the SYS:PUBLIC directory.

Syntax

ALLOW *path\filename rightslist*

Use the following rights in place of the *rightslist* variable. Except for ALL, use the first letter only.

Options

ALL	Specifies all rights
No Rights	Specifies no rights, does not remove Supervisory
Read	Opens and reads files
Write	Opens and writes to files
Create	Creates and writes to files
Erase	Deletes a file or directory
Modify	Renames files or directories; modifies file or directory attributes
File Scan	Views files and directories
Access Control	Enables changes to security assignments

You may use only the boldfaced letters rather than the entire word. Add a space between rights.

Rules and Considerations

You must change all of the IRM rights of a directory or file at the same time. Each time you use the ALLOW command to change the mask, it overrides the previous mask; you cannot change the mask incrementally.

You cannot remove the S(Supervisory) right from the IRM of a directory or file.

Examples

To change the IRM of subdir1 to Read and File Scan, type the following:

```
ALLOW SUBDIR1 R F
```

To change the IRM of file1 in subdir1 to Read, Write, and File Scan, type the following:

```
ALLOW SUBDIR1\FILE1 R W F
```

Important Messages

NetWare may display the following message when you issue the AL-LOW command:

```
No Entries Found!
```

If this message appears, make sure that you specified a file or directory that exists and that you spelled it correctly. Also, make sure that you specified the correct path, and that you have File Scan rights in the directory.

The following message may appear if the Access Control right is not set correctly:

```
Directory Name (mask) Not Changed.
```

If this message displays with the name of your directory, make sure that the Access Control right is set in the directory.

Notes

 When you change the IRM of a directory or file, you are changing the effective rights of all users in that directory or file.

See also

RIGHTS

ATOTAL   F> Purpose

The ATOTAL utility is designed to be used with Novell's Accounting feature. ATOTAL lists the following accounting totals:

- Connect time in minutes
- Service requests
- Blocks read
- Blocks written
- Disk storage in blocks per day

Syntax

```
ATOTAL
```

Options

None

Rules and Considerations

Before you run ATOTAL, make sure that NetWare's accounting feature has been installed. See Syscon for information on installing the accounting feature. This command must be run from the SYS:SYSTEM directory.

Important Message

NetWare may display the following message when you attempt to issue the ATOTAL command:

```
ACCOUNTING SERVICES TOTAL UTILITY, Version 2.02
Unable to open sys:system\net$acct.dat
file not found. Perhaps accounting is not
enabled?
```

If this message appears, make sure that the accounting has been installed on your file server. Also, make sure that accounting has been running for at least one-half hour and that you have logged out of the server and then logged back in.

Example

To generate a summary list of the accounting services, from SYS:SYSTEM (or with a search drive mapped to SYS:SYSTEM), use the following command:

    ATOTAL

This displays the summary list on the workstation's screen.

Notes

 ATOTAL generates a great deal of data, and you may not derive much value from simply displaying the data on-screen. A much more practical idea is to redirect the output data to a file, using standard DOS redirection commands, and then print the file.

To redirect ATOTAL data to a file, type the following:

    ATOTAL > *filename.ext*

In this generic syntax, ***filename.ext*** is the name of the file in which you want to direct the ATOTAL data. To print the file, type **NPRINT *filename.ext***. This command sends the ASCII text file *filename.ext* to the default print queue on your file server.

The DOS redirection procedure creates a standard ASCII file, which you can import into a word processing or spreadsheet program for further processing.

See also

SYSCON

ATTACH

Purpose

Provides access to services provided by another file server after you have logged into a file server.

ATTACH.EXE is stored in SYS:LOGIN and SYS:PUBLIC

Syntax

ATTACH *fileserver_name/username* /P /G

Options

fileserver_name	The name of the file server to which you want to attach.
fileserver_name\username	The file server name and user name for the file server to which you are attaching.
private	For OS/2 sessions only. This option enables you to attach to a server in single session.
global	For OS/2 sessions only. This option enables you to attach to a server in all sessions.

Rules and Considerations

The ATTACH command assigns a connection number to a workstation and attaches the workstation to an additional file server. ATTACH does not execute the system login script. After you are attached, however, you have access to files, applications and other resources. If you do not include the file server name and user name in the command,

NetWare prompts for them. If the user name requires a password, NetWare prompts for the password, as well. You can attach to as many as seven file servers other than the one you currently are using.

You can use the ATTACH command without entering the file server name or user name. After you type **ATTACH**, NetWare displays the message `Enter server name` to prompt for the file server name. NetWare then displays the message `Enter user name` to prompt for the user name. Enter the name of the user for that file server. If that file server requires a password, NetWare prompts for the password by displaying the message `Enter your password`. When you enter the password, NetWare should display the following message:

`Your station is attached to server servername`

If you do not know the name of the file server to which you want to attach, use the SLIST command to obtain a list of file servers that are available.

You can attach to seven file servers at one time. Log in to the first file server and attach to seven others.

Important Message

If the ATTACH command fails, NetWare may display the following message:

```
No response from file server.
```

If this message appears, a bad connection may exist between the file server onto which you are connected and the file server to which you are trying to attach.

Example

To attach the user Jacob to the file server FS1, issue the following command:

```
ATTACH fs1\jacob
```

Notes

 If you try to attach to an eighth file server, NetWare displays the following message:

```
The limit of 8 server connections has been
reached
```

If you already are attached to seven file servers and you want to attach to another one, you must first log out from one of the servers to which you are attached. Log out by issuing the following command:

LOGOUT *fileserver_name*.

You then you can attach to another file server.

 Too many file server attachments can affect your system's performance. If performance is slow, log out from the file servers whose services you do not need, then re-attach when you need those services.

You also can use the MAP command to attach to another file server. Simply issue the MAP command and NetWare prompts you for the file server name, user name, and a password (if one is required for the user name you specify). NetWare runs the MAP command and attaches you to the file server at the same time.

One final way to attach to another server is to issue the CAPTURE or NPRINT commands with the /S=*servername* switch. You will be asked for a username and password if the user guest has a password or has been deleted.

See also

WHOAMI
MAP
LOGIN
SLIST

BIND   : 3.11

Purpose

Links the LAN drivers to a communication protocol and to a network
board in the file server. The communication protocol must be linked
to the board, or it will be unable to process packets. Each network
board and protocol is bound separately.

Syntax

    BIND *protocol* to *board_name* *protocol_parameter*

or

    BIND *protocol* to *LAN_driver* [*driver_parameters*]
    protocol_parameter

Options

protocol   Normally, you would use IPX,
                        Internetwork Packet Exchange, protocol
                        although you may use other protocols
                        such as IP.

LAN_driver   The Name of driver you loaded for the
                        network board.

board_name   The board name you assigned when you
                        loaded the driver.

DMA=*number*   The DMA channel the network board is
                        configured to use (if any).

FRAME=*name*   Frame type the driver is to use for this
                        network board.

INT=*number*   The hardware interrupt the network
                        board is configured to use.

`MEM=number`	The Shared memory address the network board is configured to use (if any).
`PORT=number`	The I/O port address (in hex) the network board is configured to use.
`SLOT=number`	The slot in which the network board is installed (valid only for EISA and IBM Micro Channel equipped machines).
`driver_parameter`	You should include a driver_parameter when you have more than one network board of the same type in the file server.
`NET=number`	The unique network address number for the cabling system that is attached to the board.
`protocol_parameter`	Use for the parameters unique to the selected communications protocol. IPX has only one: NET.
`ADDR=number`	The unique IP address for that machine.

Refer to the documentation that comes with other third-party protocols for their specific protocol parameters.

Rules and Considerations

The following information applies when you load multiple network boards of the same type. When binding a protocol to a board name, you do not need to include the driver_parameters because each board has a unique name that identifies its hardware settings. If you choose not to name the boards, you must let the operating system know which protocol goes to which board. This is accomplished by binding the protocol to the LAN driver, then specifying which board to bind to by listing that board's hardware settings. These settings, or driver_parameters, should be enclosed in square brackets.

If you loaded the driver with more than one frame type for a single network board, select a hexadecimal number that is different from all other network numbers (IPX internal network numbers and cabling systems).

Do not use the same number that was used for another frame type on the cabling system.

Before you use BIND, you must install the board and load the driver.

Unless a communication protocol has been linked (bound) to the network board, that board cannot process packets.

Bind a protocol to each LAN driver you load. If you load a LAN driver more than once, bind a protocol for each set of driver parameters.

Examples

To bind IPX to the NE2000 LAN card, with a network address of 105, type the following:

```
BIND IPX to NE2000 NET=105
```

Repeat the process for each LAN driver in the file server.

To bind the IPX protocol to the NE2000 LAN card, with a network address of 105, a port address of 340, an interrupt of 4, and a frame type of Ethernet_802.3, use the following command:

```
BIND IPX to NE2000 [PORT=340 INT=4
FRAME=ETHERNET_802.3] NET=105
```

You must issue this command each time the file server is booted; otherwise, you can place the command in the AUTOEXEC.NCF file. Include complete LAN-card configuration information in this file. Add the line after the LOAD LAN driver command.

Important Message

To determine which LAN drivers need a protocol bound to them, type **CONFIG** at the file server console. Bind a protocol if the LAN driver information ends with the following message:

```
No LAN protocols are bound to this LAN board
```

Notes

If the network board is attached to an existing cabling system, NET=*number* must use that system's network address. Failure to comply results in router-configuration errors on other file servers and routers on the network.

 NET=*number* is always required when binding the IPX protocol. If you fail to enter this parameter at the command line, the network operating system prompts for the network address.

See also

ULOAD

BINDFIX

Purpose

Helps solve problems with the NetWare bindery files. In v3.x, the bindery files are called NET$OBJ.SYS, NET$PROP.SYS, and NET$VAL.SYS. In v2.1x to v2.2, the bindery files are called NET$BIND.SYS and NET$BVAL.SYS. You may encounter one or several problems with the bindery, such as the following:

- You cannot change a user's password.
- You cannot change or modify a user name.
- You cannot modify a user's rights.
- You receive the unknown server error message during printing, even when you are printing on the default file server.
- At the file server console, you see error messages that refer to the bindery.
- Most symptoms occur in the SYSCON utility.

BINDFIX.EXE and the bindery files are stored in the SYS:SYSTEM directory. Invoke the BINDFIX command from the SYS:SYSTEM directory.

Syntax

```
BINDFIX
```

Options

None

Rules and Considerations

Log in to the file server as user SUPERVISOR. Make sure that all other users are logged out of the file server. Before running BINDFIX, disable LOGIN at the file server console or in the FCONSOLE utility.

Important Messages

BINDFIX closes down the bindery files and then rebuilds them. After it rebuilds the files, it displays a list of the tasks it is performing. After it rebuilds the files, BINDFIX re-opens them.

BINDFIX displays the following prompt:

```
Delete mail directories for users that no longer
exist? (y/n):
```

If you answer Yes, BINDFIX deletes all corresponding mail directories for nonexisting users from the SYS:MAIL directory. BINDFIX then prompts as follows:

```
Delete trustee rights for users that no longer
exist? (y/n):
```

If you answer Yes, BINDFIX scans all mounted volumes on the file server and deletes nonexisting users from all trustee lists.

BINDFIX renames the NET$OBJ.SYS, NET$PROP.SYS, and NET$VAL.SYS files to NET$OBJ.OLD, NET$PROP.OLD, and NET$VAL.OLD, and creates new NET$OBJ.SYS, NET$PROP.SYS, and NET$VAL.SYS files in v3.x. In v2.1x and v2.2, the NET$BIND.SYS and the NET$BVAL.SYS are renamed to NET$BIND.OLD and NET$BVAL.OLD. If BINDFIX run on v2.x finishes successfully, the following message appears:

```
Please delete the files NET$BIND.OLD and
NET$BVAL.OLD after you have verified the recon-
structed bindery.
```

Do not delete the .OLD files immediately. If you delete the .OLD files, you will not be able to restore the bindery if a problem occurs.

Notes

Make sure that all users are logged out of the file server before you run BINDFIX.

 After BINDFIX reconstructs the bindery files, do not delete the .OLD files from the SYS:SYSTEM directory. Keep these files, so that you can restore the bindery if a problem arises with the newly-constructed bindery files.

After all of your users' groups and trustee assignments have been made with a new installation, you might want to execute BINDFIX to get an original backup copy of your bindery files. Copy .OLD files onto a floppy disk for safe keeping. If BINDFIX is unable to reconstruct the bindery files, and if BINDREST is not restoring the bindery, copy the .OLD files back into the SYS:SYSTEM directory and try BINDREST again.

See also

BINDREST
BROADCAST
CLEAR STATION
DISABLE LOGIN

FCONSOLE
MONITOR

BINDREST   F>

Purpose

Reverses the effect of the BINDFIX command. The BINDREST command restores the backup bindery files created by BINDFIX. The backup bindery files are called NET$OBJ.OLD, NET$PROP.OLD, and NET$VAL.OLD in v3.x. In v2.1x and v2.2, the files are called NET$BIND.OLD and NET$BVAL.OLD. BINDREST returns these files to their original versions and names (NET$OBJ.SYS, NET$PROP.SYS, and NET$VAL.SYS in v3.x or NET$BIND.SYS and NET$BVAL.SYS). You only need to use BINDREST if BINDFIX fails. If you lose your bindery files and you have a backup copy of the bindery files on floppy disk, copy these files to the SYS:SYSTEM directory and execute BINDREST.

Syntax

```
BINDREST
```

Options

None

Rules and Considerations

Before using the BINDREST command, log in to the file server as user SUPERVISOR and make sure that all other users are logged out of the file server. Use the FCONSOLE or USERLIST command to ensure all users are logged out of the file server. Use FCONSOLE or CLEAR STATION to clear all logged in users. Use DISABLE LOGIN to prevent users from logging in to the file server while BINDREST is running.

Important Messages

If you invoke BINDFIX then delete the .OLD files after BINDFIX runs, you cannot use BINDREST to restore the bindery files.

If you delete the old v3.x bindery files, NetWare displays a message similar to the following:

```
ERROR: File NET$OBJ.OLD does not exist.
ERROR: File NET$PROP.OLD does not exist.
ERROR: File NET$VAL.OLD does not exist.

      Unable to restore old bindery files.
```

If you have a backup of the .OLD files on a floppy disk, copy them to the SYS:SYSTEM directory and rerun BINDREST.

Note

Make sure that all users are logged out of the file server before you invoke the BINDREST.

See also

BINDFIX
BROADCAST
USERLIST
CLEAR STATION
DISABLE LOGIN
FCONSOLE
MONITOR

BROADCAST

Purpose

Sends a message to all users logged in or attached to the file server or to a list of connection numbers. You must issue the BROADCAST command from the file server console.

Syntax

```
BROADCAST "message" TO username
```

Options

username	The user's login name.
connection number	The connection number listed by the USERLIST command.
Press Space	Enter a space on the same line as the command to specify another user name or connection number. Place the space between user names or connection numbers.

Rules and Considerations

To determine a connection number, refer to Connection Information in the MONITOR screen at the file server console, or use the USERLIST command from your workstation.

The message can be up to 55 characters long. If you do not specify the connection number or user name, NetWare sends the message to all attached users.

All logged in users receive the messages, except the following:

- Users who have used the CASTOFF ALL command.
- Users who logged in using an ACS or NACS.
- Users who are logged in on a remote workstation.

Some graphics applications that are being used will not show the message you received, but you will hear a beep. Press Ctrl-Enter to continue.

Users who receive the message will see it appear on the 25th line of the screen. The message should not interfere with the screen display. The workstation locks and nothing happens until the user clears the message by pressing Ctrl-Enter.

Important Messages

None.

Examples

Suppose that you want to send the message "Meeting in room 1A in 10 minutes" to all users. Issue the following command:

```
BROADCAST Meeting in room 1A in 10 minutes
```

You do not need to enclose the message in quotation marks when you are sending a message to all users.

If you want to send the same message to Tim, Jane, Jacob and connection number 6, issue the following command:

```
BROADCAST "Meeting in room 1A in 10 minutes" to
Tim, Jane, Jacob and 6
```

Notes

 A message received at a workstation prevents further work until the message is cleared from the screen.

 Use the CASTOFF ALL command at the workstation to prevent it from receiving messages.

See also

MONITOR
CASTOFF ALL

CAPTURE

Purpose

Redirects printed output from applications not designed to run on a network or from the screen to a NetWare print queue. CAPTURE also can save printed data to a file.

Syntax

    CAPTURE *options*

Options

The optional switches used by CAPTURE consist of one or more of the following:

AU (AUtoendcap)   Automatically closes out a print job when you exit an application. Autoendcap is enabled by default.

NA (NoAutoendcap)   Requires the use of the ENDCAP utility to terminate the effects of CAPTURE. Use NoAutoendcap to move in and out of your applications without prematurely closing the print queue file(s) you are creating.

B (Banner)   A banner name can be any word or phrase up to 12 characters in length that you want to appear on the lower part of the banner page. To represent a space between words, use an underline character; the underline character will print. The default is LST.

NB (NoBanner)   Tells NetWare not to print a banner page.

C (Copies=*n*)	*Replace n* with with the number of copies you want to print (1 to 999). The default is 1 copy.
CR (CReate=*filespec*)	Creates a print file in which to store instead of sending the print job to a file server's print queue. *Filespec* can be any legal DOS file name and can include path information; you can create the print file, however, only on a network drive.
FF (FormFeed)	Sends a form-feed code to the printer at the end of each print job so that the next print job can start at the top of the next sheet of paper. If your application sends a form-feed code at the end of the print job, an extra page will be fed through the printer wasting paper. Form feeding is enabled by default.
NFF (NoFormFeed)	Disables the sending of form-feed codes at the end of a print job.
F (Form=*formname* or *n*)	Replace *formname* with the name of the form on which you want your print job to print. Replace *n* with the form number onto which you want your print job to print. Use the PRINTDEF utility to define form names or numbers (or both) before using this option.
J (Job=*jobconfig*)	Replace *jobconfig* with the name of a predefined print job configuration you want to use. You must use the PRINTCON utility to define print jobs before using this option.

K (Keep)	Tells CAPTURE to keep all data it receives during a print capture in case your workstation locks up or loses power while capturing data. This option is useful if you capture data over a period of several hours. If your workstation loses its connection to the file server, the server sends the data to the print queue after the server realizes your station is no longer connected to it.
L (Local=*n*)	Indicates which local LPT ports you want to capture. Valid choices are 1, 2, or 3. The default is 1. The local LPT ports defined here are "logical" connections, not "physical" ports. You can print to and capture from all three LPT ports even though your workstation might only have one physical LPT port installed.
NAM (NAMe=*name*)	*name* can be any word or phrase, up to 12 characters in length, that you want printed on the upper part of the banner page. The default is the user's name used when you logged in to the file server. The NoBanner option defeats the purpose of using this switch, because no banner page is printed.
Q (Queue=*queuename*)	*queuename* is the file server queue name to which you want to send the print job. This option is useful if multiple queues are mapped to one printer. If you fail to specify a queuename, CAPTURE defaults to the queue to which Spooler 0 has been assigned.
S (Server=*name*)	*name* is the name of the file server to which you are sending the print job and the server on which the print queue is located. The default is the default server you first logged in to.

SH (Show)	Displays a list of the currently captured LPT ports. SH does not affect the capture status of an LPT port. It merely returns the currently active CAPTURE options (if any). You cannot use SH with other CAPTURE options.
T (Tabs=n)	Use this option only if your application program does not support print formatting; most do. n is the number of characters in each tab stop, from 0 to 18. The default is 8.
NT (NoTabs)	Ensures that all tabs arrive at the printer unchanged. By default, this option also specifies the file to be a binary or "byte stream" file. Use this option only if your application program has its own print formatter. Most applications produce embedded printer-specific codes. This option ensures that those codes arrive at the printer intact.
TI (Timeout=n)	Enables you to print from an application without forcing you to exit it. It sends the print data to the print queue in a specified number of seconds after the application finishes writing to the file or after waiting the specified number of seconds for additional print output. After the specified amount of time, CAPTURE begins again. For best results TI should not be set to less than 5 seconds or greater than 60. n = number of seconds, 1 to 1,000. Timeout is disabled by default.

You can list multiple options.

Rules and Considerations

The create=*filespec* switch must use a network drive.

The FormFeed switch might not be necessary on some laser printers that are installed as network printers. Many laser printers automatically issue a form feed at the end of a page or partial page of text.

You must use the PRINTDEF utility to define forms before you use the Forms switch.

You cannot use SH with any other CAPTURE options. It must be used alone.

If your TI setting is not long enough, you might experience printing problems, especially if you are printing graphics. Increase the TI setting if parts of files are being printed or if files do not print at all.

You can define commonly used CAPTURE options in PRINTCON as job configurations and use the Job option to indicate which configuration profile to use.

If you fail to specify options with the CAPTURE command, data is printed according to the default print job configuration defined in PRINTCON.

Output should be sent to print queues rather than printers. Printer numbers and print server names are not supported in CAPTURE.

The data you capture is not printed or sent to a file unless you end the CAPTURE command and send your data to a network printer or a file. This can be done by using either the AU or TI switch, or by using the ENDCAP utility.

To use the ENDCAP utility effectively to send captured print jobs to the printer, disable AUtoendcap and TImeout in the CAPTURE command.

Important Messages

None.

Example

To capture print jobs to the queue called Laser on the file server Training Solutions, type the following:

```
CAPTURE  S=TRAINING_SOLUTIONS  Q=LASER_Q  NB  TI=5
NFF
```

The job does not print a banner, the timeout is five seconds, and no form feed follows the print job.

For best results, and to prevent your workstation from possibly hanging, use the CAPTURE command in your login script.

If you use the CAPTURE command at the DOS prompt, it overrides the command issued in your login script, unless you merely issue a CAPTURE SHow.

Notes

 Use AU to save several different screen prints or printouts from the same application to a single print-queue file. AU does not automatically terminate the capture of an LPT port. To terminate an active LPT capture, you must issue the ENDCAP command.

If you experience problems (such as half-completed pages) when printing from your application, increase the value of TI until the problem stops or until you reach 60, whichever comes first. It is extremely rare when an application, even an intense database query, will pause longer than 45 seconds between print output bursts.

Your workstation might hang if you press Shift-Print Screen when none of your LPT ports are captured and no local printers are attached to your workstation. To prevent this, include the following line in the NET.CFG file on your boot disk:

```
LOCAL PRINTERS = 0
```

 You can save data in a print file to a server to which you are not attached. If you specify a server to which you are not attached, CAPTURE attaches you as the user GUEST unless GUEST requires a password, or GUEST has no effective rights to any of the server's print queues or disk space. You cannot create a file or send a file to a queue without rights.

It often is preferable to capture to a print file when you are plotting from CAD packages in the NetWare environment. This usually causes far fewer problems than trying to capture the plot output to a file server queue. After the plot file has been created, you can use the NPRINT utility to send the plot file to the queue.

See also

ENDCAP

NPRINT

NET.CFG

SPOOL

CASTOFF

Purpose

Prevents messages sent from the file server console or other workstations from reaching your station and interrupting unattended operations (such as printing or compiling).

Syntax

CASTOFF

or

CASTOFF ALL

Options

A or ALL   Blocks messages from both the file server console and other workstations on the network

Rule and Considerations

The CASTOFF command blocks messages sent by other workstations. CASTOFF ALL blocks all messages, including those sent from the file server console.

Before starting any process that can run unattended (such as compiling, printing, remote LAN hookup, and so on), you should use CAST-OFF ALL to prevent messages from interrupting the unattended process.

Important Messages

None

Example

```
CASTOFF ALL
```

Note

 To enable your station to receive incoming messages again, use the CASTON utility.

See also

CASTON
SEND

CASTON

Purpose

Enables your workstation to resume receiving messages if you used the CASTOFF utility to block incoming messages.

Syntax

```
CASTON
```

Options

None

Rules and Considerations

When a workstation receives a message, the station cannot continue processing until the user acknowledges the message by pressing Ctrl-Enter.

Important Message

The following message appears on-screen after CASTON is invoked:

```
Broadcast messages from the console and other
stations will now be accepted.
```

See also

CASTOFF
SEND

CHKDIR   F> 3.11

Purpose

Lists information about directories and volumes. When invoked, CHKDIR displays the following types of information:

- Directory space limitations for the file server, volume, and directory

- The volume's maximum storage capacity in kilobytes, and the directory's maximum storage capacity (if the directory has a space restriction in effect)
- Kilobytes currently in use on the volume and in the specified directory
- Kilobytes available on the volume and in the specified directory

Syntax

```
CHKDIR path
```

Options

path   The directory path leading to and including the path you want to check.

Rule and Considerations

The *path* option must be a legal DOS path name. You can substitute NetWare volume names for DOS drive letters.

Important Messages

None

Example

Suppose that you want to see information about a directory named SYS:DATA. Enter the following command:

```
CHKDIR SYS:DATA
```

NetWare displays information similar to the following:

```
Directory Space Limitation Information For:
TRAINING_SOLUTIONS/SYS:DATA
```

```
Maximum     In Use      Available
631,600K    452,693K    178,907K Volume Size
38,776K     178,907K    \DATA
```

See also

CHKVOL

CHKVOL

Purpose

Shows the amount of space currently in use and the amount of space available on the volume. The CHKVOL command displays volume space in bytes, the byte count taken by files, the number of bytes available on the volume, and the number of directory entries left. You can view this information on all volumes, and all file servers to which you are attached.

Syntax

CHKVOL *fileserver_name\volume_name*

Options

fileserver_name	The name of the file servers volume to view
volume	The name of the volume to view
*	Specifies all file servers you are attached to, or all volumes

Rules and Considerations

The use of CHKVOL is not limited by security, you may view CHKVOL to view volume information for any file server to which you are attached.

Important Messages

The CHKVOL command displays information similar to the following:

```
Statistics for fixed volume TRAINING_SOLUTIONS/SYS:

Total volume space:              640,048 K Bytes
Space used by 7,105 files:       152,672 K Bytes
Space remaining on volume:       487,376 K Bytes
Space available to username:     487,376 K Bytes
Directory entries available        2,121
```

`Directory entries available` does not refer to the number of directories you still can create on this volume. One directory entry is used by a DOS file, subdirectory, and trustee list. Macintosh files use two directory entries.

Examples

To check the volumes called SYS on all file servers to which you are attached, issue the following command:

CHKVOL */SYS

You can express wild cards in many different ways. If you want to see volume information for all the volumes on the file server named TRAINING, for example, issue the following command:

CHKVOL TRAINING/*

If you want to see the SYS volumes on file servers named TRAINING and SOLUTIONS, issue the following command:

```
CHKVOL */SYS
```

If you want to see information about all volumes on all the file servers to which you are attached, issue the following command:

```
CHKVOL */*
```

You also can specify drive letters that are mapped to volumes that you want to view.

Note

 If NetWare displays the message The specified volume not found, either you mistyped the volume name or the volume does not exist. Check the volume name and try again.

See also

FILER (Volume Information)
WHOAMI
ATTACH

CLEAR MESSAGE   : 2.2

Purpose

Clears the message at the bottom of the file server's display when you are using the MONITOR command.

Syntax

```
CLEAR MESSAGE
```

Options

None

Rules and Considerations

The CLEAR MESSAGE command clears a message from the bottom of the file server's display. The command does not clear the entire screen and does not affect the MONITOR screen.

The CLEAR MESSAGE command is coded into the operating system.

Important Messages

None

See also

BROADCAST
SEND

CLEAR STATION :

Purpose

Removes all file server resources from the specified workstation, and breaks the link between the file server and the workstation.

Syntax

```
CLEAR STATION station_number
```

Options

None

Rules and Considerations

The CLEAR STATION command is coded into the operating system. When you invoke CLEAR STATION, all the workstations' open files are closed and the communication link to the file server is broken. If the workstation had drive mappings to other file servers, the user can continue working on those file servers' drive mappings. If no drive mappings exist to other file servers, however, the user must reboot the workstation and reload IPX and NETx before accessing any file server.

Important Messages

None

Example

To clear station number two, issue the following command:

```
CLEAR STATION 2
```

To view a list of station numbers, you can issue the MONITOR command at the v3.11 file server console or use USERLIST at a workstation. The connection number is listed in the screen's left margin.

Note

Because the CLEAR STATION command closes open files, data may be lost when you use the command. CLEAR STATION normally is used when a workstation locks up and leaves open files on the file server.

See also

FCONSOLE
USERLIST

CLIB   :LOAD 3.11

Purpose

Provides NetWare Loadable Module (NLM) developers with a set of global functions and routines that an NLM can utilize. This global library of C routines and functions should be used if you are using an NLM, such as the BTRIEVE NLM or the PSERVER NLM which relies on CLIB to function properly.

CLIB is not fully functional unless the STREAMS NLM is loaded. If you fail to load STREAMS prior to loading CLIB, the NetWare v3.11 operating system attempts to load STREAMS for you.

Syntax

```
LOAD path CLIB
```

Options

path   The full DOS path name to the directory that contains the CLIB NLM. The path name can begin with either a valid DOS drive letter or a valid NetWare volume name. If you do not specify a path, NetWare v3.11 attempts to locate and load the NLM from the SYS:SYSTEM subdirectory.

Rules and Considerations

NetWare sets a time zone for CLIB when the utility loads. By default, NetWare uses the Eastern Standard time zone. Use the SET TIMEZONE command to set the time zone so that it is appropriate for your geographical area.

Be sure to save the command in the AUTOEXEC.NCF file so that CLIB is loaded and the appropriate time zone is set each time the file server is rebooted.

Important Messages

None

Examples

To load the CLIB utility, issue the following command:

```
LOAD CLIB
```

To make sure that the additional modules necessary for CLIB to operate are loaded at boot time, add the following commands to the
server's AUTOEXEC.NCF file:

```
LOAD STREAMS
LOAD CLIB
```

This example assumes the STREAMS and CLIB NLMs are located in
the SYS:SYSTEM subdirectory.

Notes

You must load the CLIB NLM before you load any NLM that requires
CLIB. If you want, you can place the STREAMS and CLIB NLMs can
be placed on the DOS partition of the file server's hard disk.

The CLIB NLM is just one example of a loadable function library module. Some NLMs depend on other NLMs to function properly. To
improve system performance and reliability, Novell recommends that
you load the following NLMs in addition to CLIB. If you are using
non-Novell supplied third-party NLMs that are incompatible with the
current version of NetWare v3.11, these additional NLMs prevent the
offending NLM from loading and/or corrupting the network operating system. It is strongly recommended that you load these NLMs in
the following order:

LOAD STREAMS

LOAD CLIB

LOAD MATHLIB

LOAD TLI

LOAD IPXS

LOAD SPXS

To automatically load these NLMs at boot time, edit your
AUTOEXEC.NCF file to include these commands.

See also

SET TIMEZONE

LOAD

CLS   : 3.11

Purpose

Clears the file server's console screen.

Syntax

    CLS

Options

None

Rules and Considerations

The cleared screen shows only the command prompt and the cursor.

Important Messages

None

See also

    OFF

COMCHECK

Purpose

Tests the communication between network stations, file servers, and
routers. The command does not require the file server or router to be
running. Use COMCHECK to help locate possible cable problems,

duplicate node addresses, and potential problems with cable linking devices. COMCHECK checks the entire communications path before the network is up and running.

Syntax

    COMCHECK

Options

None

Rules and Considerations

Before you execute COMCHECK, make all cable connections to workstations, file servers, routers, and cabling devices. IPX must be loaded first. COMCHECK uses IPX to communicate to each cabled node on the cable system. Each node requires a unique ID. As you execute COMCHECK on the node, the utility prompts for a unique ID. You can use any name, such as NODE1, FILESERVER1, ROUTER3, and so on.

Example

    IPX
    COMCHECK

COMCHECK prompts you to enter a unique node name to identify the station. You can find the COMCHECK program on the disk labeled WSGEN. If you experience problems loading IPX, make sure that IPX is configured for the LAN card you are using, and that the setting on the LAN card matches that of IPX. The following message should appear on the screen:

```
NetWare Communication Check v2.00 Friday October
30, 1991 2:00 pm
NetworkNode  Unique UserYr Mo Dy Hr Mn Sc *
00000000     000000F3    Node1 91/10/30  02:09:21
*
00000000     00001A34    File Server9 1 / 1 0 / 3 0
0      2     :     1     4     :     1      2
00000000     000000BF    Node2 91/10/30 02:18:01
```

- **Network.** Displays 0s if the shell is not loaded.
- **Node.** Displays the node ID of the LAN card installed.
- **Unique User.** Displays the unique name you gave to this node.
- **YrMoDy Hr Mn Sc.** Shows the time and date. The time is updated every 15 seconds to show that the node is communicating.
- ***.** Indicates that this is the current workstation.

If the station does not show any of this information after 15 seconds, check all cabling, connectors, cabling devices, and LAN cards. Make sure that each of the nodes has a unique node ID.

You can change the broadcast delay period by pressing Esc and selecting Broadcast Delay from the menu. This is specified in seconds, and tells the system the number of seconds or broadcasts from a particular station. The default setting is 15 seconds.

The Dead Timeout Period specifies the amount of time COMCHECK waits after a workstation does not send out packets and then declares the node dead. This time period must be at least 10 seconds greater than the broadcast delay period. A workstation that is declared dead will appear on the other workstations as a bold entry. The default Dead Timeout Period is 60 seconds.

See also

IPX

COMPSURF   :Down 2.1

Purpose

Performs a low-level format and surface analysis (or integrity test) on standard MFM, RLL, ARLL, ESDI, and SCSI hard disks and prepares them for use under Novell NetWare.

Syntax

```
COMPSURF
```

Options

None

Rules and Considerations

The COMPSURF utility may require several hours to test each hard disk properly. Be sure to allow sufficient time.

You must install hard disks before you execute the COMPSURF utility.

You should use COMPSURF to reformat disks only as a last, extreme measure to attempt to correct major disk drive problems (such as when it has become impossible to write and read data to and from the disk). COMPSURF destroys all data contained on a hard disk.

Do not execute COMPSURF on NetWare Ready drives because any NetWare ready information on the disk will be erased.

New hard disks no longer require testing with COMPSURF. The IN-STALL command prepares new hard disks by using the ZTEST (track zero test) utility rather than COMPSURF.

Most hard disks are shipped with a manufacturer's bad block table that identifies, by head and cylinder number, any media defects (such as bad blocks) found by the manufacturer prior to shipment. If the hard disk you will be formatting (or reformatting) with COMPSURF has a manufacturer's bad block table, you should enter the bad blocks from this list prior to running COMPSURF.

If you are using SCSI hard disks, you also must run DISKSET, or an equivalent third-party utility, to configure the Host Bus Adapters (HBA) connected to any installed SCSI disk subsystems.

Important Message

The following message appears when you issue the COMPSURF command:

```
The COMPSURF command destroys all data on the
hard disk!
```

Make sure that you have a backup of the disk's data before you execute the command.

Examples

You can run the COMPSURF utility by issuing the following command:

COMPSURF

Prepare to execute the COMPSURF utility by backing up the existing disk files and down the file server. This step is only required on existing NetWare installations.

Locate the disk manufacturer's test printout. This will contain a list of media defects (such as bad blocks) detected by the manufacturer at the time of assembly. You are prompted to enter these blocks after you enter the COMPSURF utility. The manufacturer's bad block list is usually printed on a sticker attached to the hard disk housing. Often the list will be duplicated on a paper printout shipped with the disk.

If you do not have a hard copy printout of the bad block table, you might have to remove the cover from the file server or disk subsystem to locate the bad block table sticker on the hard disk housing. These defects should be entered into COMPSURF to enable COMPSURF to map out known media defects and prevent their use under NetWare. This will ensure greater data integrity.

If you want a printout of the media defects detected by COMPSURF, prepare and install a parallel printer. The printer must be connected to the first parallel port (LPT1) on the file server. You will be given an opportunity to print the media defect list before exiting COMPSURF.

COMPSURF can run without a parallel printer attached. If you run COMPSURF without a printer, however, you must refrain from selecting any option that indicates printing test results. If you do select a print option when no printer is attached, COMPSURF might hang up the computer.

Before executing COMPSURF on a problem disk, you should try to copy as many data files as possible to a disk that is operational.

Be sure you have correctly identified all network hard disks in your server's hardware configuration, including disks both inside the file server and inside external disk subsystems. If necessary, execute DISKSET to identify SCSI hard disks in external disk subsystems or inside the file server. If necessary, run the SETUP (or similar) utility supplied by the computer manufacturer to identify internal disk drives.

Before executing COMPSURF, make sure that you can identify the disk drive on which you want to run COMPSURF by channel number, controller address, and drive number.

If needed, refer to the documentation accompanying your hardware for information on how to determine controller addresses and drive numbers.

If you are using a disk that is defined in the CMOS of your computer, most likely you will be using the ISADISK driver. If this is true, this unit functions on Channel 0.

You can low-level format and test only one hard disk at a time. Execute COMPSURF on each disk you want to be low-level formatted and tested.

Start COMPSURF by locating the program. Under NetWare v2.1x, it usually is located on the UTILEXE diskette. Under NetWare v2.2 and NetWare v3.11, it is located on the SYSTEM-2 diskette.

To load and execute COMPSURF, insert the appropriate disk into drive A, and type **COMPSURF** at the DOS prompt.

The Comprehensive Surface Analysis header appears on the screen, along with a list of the hard disk drives COMPSURF can find attached to the file server.

Select the hard disk you want to test. Do not be concerned if the head, cylinder, and sectors-per-track values displayed on the screen do not correspond to the actual values for the disk. Certain types of disk drives do not supply this information, and COMPSURF uses default values for these disks.

Select the appropriate program operational parameters for the drive you have selected. The parameters that appear depend on the type of disk you are testing and whether or not it has been previously formatted with COMPSURF. For most disks, the list will be similar to the following:

- Specify whether or not to format the disk.
- Specify whether or not to keep the current bad block list.
- Specify if you want to enter the media defect list.
- Select the number of passes for the sequential read/write test.
- Select the number of reads and writes to be performed in the random test.
- Confirm the operation parameters you have just selected.

A more detailed discussion of each prompt follows:

- **Format the disk:** This prompt appears only when you are retesting a disk that has been previously low-level formatted by COMPSURF. Any hard disk that has never been low-level formatted or tested with COMPSURF will be formatted automatically. If you answered Yes to the Format disk prompt and if the hard disk you have selected requires an interleave factor value, select the appropriate interleave factor. Interleave should be selected based on the following criteria:

1. For internal hard disks in all NetWare file servers and IBM PC/AT-type file servers that run off original IBM or Western Digital 1003 series controllers, use the default interleave value of 2.

2. For internal hard disks in all IBM PC/AT and 100 percent compatible NetWare file servers that run off Western Digital 1006 series controllers (or 100 percent compatibles), select an interleave value of 1.

3. For internal hard disks in all IBM PC/AT and 100 percent compatible NetWare file servers that run off Western Digital 1007 series ESDI controllers (or 100 percent compatibles), select an interleave value of 1.

4. For internal hard disks in an IBM PS/2 file server, select an interleave value of 1.

5. For other types of hard disks (such as embedded SCSI or third-party external disks), check with the disk supplier to determine the appropriate interleave value.

6. For internal hard disks in all IBM PC/AT and 100 percent compatible NetWare file servers that run off controllers not listed above, check with the controller manufacturer to determine the appropriate interleave value.

- **Current bad block list:** Each hard disk drive maintains a list of media defects. These media defects are areas of the disk that are physically unable to hold data reliably. This list is sometimes referred to as the bad block table. Answer Yes if you want COMPSURF to keep the current list of bad blocks or rebuild a new bad block table. If you answer No, the media defect list is cleared.

- **Media defect list:** The media defect list also is known as the bad block list. If the disk you are testing was not shipped with a manufacturer's media defect list, answer No to the prompt and go on to the next section. If the disk was shipped with a manufacturer's media defect list, enter the bad block list manually at the file server's keyboard when prompted.

  The bad blocks you enter from this list, as well as any additional bad blocks found by the COMPSURF utility, will be written to the disk's bad block table. It is important to enter the manufacturer's bad block list, if possible, to ensure that these blocks are included in the NetWare-compatible bad block table stored on the disk. This will prevent NetWare from using these potentially unreliable areas of the disk to store your valuable data.

- **Sequential Test:** This COMPSURF routine writes and reads various patterns to the disk sequentially to analyze the integrity of the disk's surface. Any bad blocks that are found during this process are added to the disk's bad block table so that the file server will not attempt to store data in them.

  Each pass of the sequential test takes roughly 30 to 45 minutes for the average 20M hard disk—and longer for hard disks with larger storage capacity.

  You can specify that the sequential test be performed from zero to five times. The COMPSURF criteria used to determine the reliability of the disk is based on three passes of the sequential test, however. It is strongly recommended that you not skip this section of COMPSURF.

- **Random Test:** This COMPSURF routine writes and reads data patterns to random locations on the disk to locate additional bad blocks. This procedure also will test the head positioning mechanics of the disk. As with the sequential test, any bad blocks that are found are included in the disk's bad block table so that the file server will not attempt to store data on them.

The default number of write/reads (I/Os) shown in the prompt is the recommended minimum number of random I/Os to ensure an adequate sampling of the disk's head-positioning mechanism. You can increase or decrease this number of I/Os.

It takes approximately three minutes for the random test to perform 1,000 I/Os. As an example, a random test performed on an average 20MB hard disk would require 16,000 random I/Os and would take 45 to 50 minutes.

- **Enter the bad block list:** If the COMPSURF OPERATIONAL PARAMETERS window shows that media defects will be entered by hand, you must enter the manufacturer's bad block list from the file server's keyboard. An empty bad block window appears on the screen.

  Bad blocks are identified by head and cylinder number. Each hard disk has a specific number of read/write heads and cylinders. The number of heads and cylinders for the currently selected disk should be displayed on the second line of the COMPSURF screen header.

Media defects can be added to the list by performing the following:

1. Press Insert. The following prompt should appear:

   ```
   Enter head number:
   ```

2. Type the head number of one of the bad blocks on the manufacturer's bad block list. Heads are usually numbered starting with zero, such as zero relative. If your disk has seven heads, for example, they are numbered from zero to six.

3. After you have typed the head number, press Enter. The following prompt should appear:

   ```
   Enter cylinder:
   ```

4. Type the cylinder number of the bad block as it appears in the manufacturer's list. Like heads, cylinders are also numbered starting with zero (such as zero relative).

5. After you have typed the cylinder number, press Enter. The head and cylinder numbers should be displayed in the list on the screen. If you make a mistake and type an incorrect head or cylinder number, you can correct it by simply highlighting the incorrect entry and pressing Delete.

6. Repeat these steps until you have entered all of the bad blocks on the manufacturer's bad block list.

7. Confirm the bad block list. After you have entered all of the bad blocks from the manufacturer's bad block list, press Esc. If you need to add or delete bad blocks to or from the table, answer No and return to the `Enter the bad block list` prompt. If the table is complete and correct, answer Yes to the prompt and continue.

- **Format and test the disk:** You do not need to make any more keyboard entries until the COMPSURF testing process is complete, but you should monitor the progress of the test as outlined in the process that follows. The information for each test assumes that you selected the recommended COMPSURF operational parameters, such as low-level formatting the disk and repeating the sequential surface analysis three times.

- **Formatting the disk:** While the disk is being low-level formatted, the following message should appear on the screen:

```
The Drive is Being Formatted
Please Wait
```

The formatting process can last anywhere from a few minutes to several hours, depending on the storage capacity and the type of hard disk being tested. The average 20MB hard disk, for example, takes roughly 15 to 25 minutes to low-level format.

```
The track zero test:
```

After the disk has been successfully low-level formatted, the track zero integrity test begins. This test ensures that track zero on the selected disk is 100 percent free from any media defects. Any defects on track zero would render the drive unbootable under NetWare, and might render the drive unusable altogether.

During this test, the screen displays information in a format similar to the following:

```
Track Zero Test
Block # Pattern Pass BadBlocks
0 a5a5   1/20    0
```

As the track zero test progresses, the numbers displayed in each column change to reflect what is occurring on the drive. This test will make 20 passes of track zero writing and reading various binary patterns to ensure it has no media defects.

```
Run the Sequential Test:
```

When the track zero test is successfully completed, the sequential test begins. This test searches the entire disk surface for media defects (such as bad blocks). Media defects are defined as blocks on the disk that cannot reliably store data.

The disk's bad block table consists of both bad blocks that you entered by hand and those discovered during the sequential test sequence. While the sequential test is running, you should see a screen similar to the following:

```
Sequential Test
Block # Pattern Pass BadBlocks
0 a5a5   1/20    0
```

The `Block #` column indicates the block currently being tested. This number counts down to zero for each of the five binary data patterns.

The `Pattern` column indicates the binary data pattern currently being written to the disk.

The `Pass` column indicates the number of passes of the sequential test that have been completed out of the total number of passes specified in the program operational parameters.

The `Bad Blocks` column indicates the number of bad blocks on the disk. This number is a total of those entered by hand and those located during the sequential test. This number might increment during the sequential test.

You can interrupt the sequential test at any time to view or to print a list of the bad blocks that have been located so far. You also can turn off the screen update to slightly speed up the execution of the program.

- **Display the bad block table:** This information appears on the screen in a format similar to the following. Do not worry about duplicate entries in the list; this is common and results from the fact that one track can have one or more bad blocks:

```
Head Cylinder

1     234
2     476
```

Program execution continues while you view the list.

- **Print the bad block table:** If you have attached a parallel printer to the first parallel printer port (LPT1) on the file server, you can print a list of the bad blocks found so far. After the testing process is complete, you will have another opportunity to print the complete bad block list.

  Do not select the `Print the bad block table:` option if you have not attached a parallel printer to the file server. The computer will disconnect if you do, resulting in the loss of all located bad blocks and requiring you to restart COMPSURF from scratch.

- **Turn off the screen update:** Turning off the screen update enables the sequential test to proceed without constantly refreshing the screen display. This can marginally reduce the time required to complete the sequential test. You can exercise this option at any time during the sequential test. Updates to the screen information cease until you re-enable screen updating.

- **Turn on the screen update:** Resumes updates to the various columns on the screen.

- **Run the Random Test:** After the sequential test successfully completes, the random test automatically begins. If you specified zero passes of the sequential test, a random test initialization procedure will be executed before the actual random test begins. This initialization procedure prepares the disk's data storage area to prepare for the random I/O test.

  As with the sequential test, you can interrupt the random test at any time to view or to print a list of the bad blocks that have been located so far. You also can turn off the screen update to marginally speed up the operation of the program.

- **Record the final bad block table:** When all of the COMPSURF formatting and testing procedures have successfully concluded, a message similar to the following appears:

  ```
  Surface Analysis Completed  disk passed.

  Display Bad Block Table
  Print Bad Block Table
  ```

  If the disk did not successfully pass the COMPSURF testing series, this also is indicated on the screen. Failure to successfully pass a COMPSURF test requires replacing the hard disk.

  After completing the COMPSURF testing, press Esc to exit the program. You can display the bad block table on the screen and record the information by hand if you want, or, if you have a parallel printer attached to the file server, you can print a hard copy of the final bad block table.

  You should maintain a permanent record of the disk's bad block table. If you do not, you will be unable to re-enter the bad block table should it ever be deleted.

Notes

 Some manufacturers ship hard disk drives with the designation "NetWare Ready." You do not need to use the COMPSURF utility on the drives. In addition, advances in NetWare v2.2 and NetWare v3.11 Hot Fix techniques, as well as the ZTEST utility in NetWare v2.2, have made the COMPSURF utility somewhat unnecessary.

Beginning with NetWare v2.2, COMPSURF supports formatting the hard disk with a 1:1 interleave.

See also

DISKSET
INSTALL
ZTEST
HOT FIX

CONFIG   :

Purpose

Lists the following information about the file server:

- File server name; internal network number (NetWare v3.x).
- Loaded/Linked LAN drivers.
- Hardware settings on network boards.
- Node (station) addresses (ID) of network boards.
- Communication protocol bound to the network board (NetWare v3.x).
- Network number of the cabling scheme for a network board.

- Frame type assigned to the board (NetWare v3.x). Ethernet and Token-Ring boards can have more than one.
- Board name assigned (NetWare v3.x).
- Number of File Server Processes (NetWare v2.x).
- Linked active disk driver and settings (NetWare v2.2).

Syntax

```
CONFIG
```

Options

None

Rules and Considerations

Use the CONFIG command to view a list of hardware settings on network boards before installing additional memory cards, network adapters, or disk coprocessor boards in the server. This will help you avoid conflicts before installation.

Under NetWare v2.x, use CONFIG to list the number of file server processes.

Use CONFIG to list all assigned network numbers and node addresses.

Under NetWare v3.x, use MODULES and MONITOR to display information about NetWare loadable modules (NLM) linked to the core operating system.

Under NetWare v3.x, use INSTALL to display configuration information about disk drivers (Look in either the STARTUP.NCF or AUTOEXEC.NCF file).

Under NetWare v3.x, use DISPLAY NETWORKS to list all network numbers being used by other file servers on your network. This will help avoid router errors and internal IPX network number conflicts.

Important Messages

None

Example

To use CONFIG, issue the following command at the console:

```
CONFIG
```

Under NetWare v2.2, CONFIG displays information similar to the following:

```
Hardware Configuration Information for Server
TRAINING_SOLUTIONS

Number of File Server Processes: 7

LAN A Configuration Information:
Network Address: [19910ACE] [ 32]
Hardware Type: NetWare RX-Net
Hardware Settings: IRQ = 9, I/O = 2E0, RAM Buffer
at D000:0

LAN B Configuration Information:
Network Address: [19910ACE] [01A034845D1B]
Hardware Type: Novell NE1000
Hardware Settings: IRQ = 3, I/O = 300, No DMA or
RAM
```

Under NetWare v3.11, CONFIG displays information similar to the following:

```
File server name: TRAINING_SOLUTIONS386
IPX internal network number: BADCAFE

NE-2000 LAN Driver V3.10 (900308)
 Hardware setting: I/O Port 300h to 31Fh, Inter-
rupt 3h
 Node address:00001B0280A3
 Frame type: ETHERNET_802.3
 Board name: BACKBONE
 LAN protocol: IPX network 00000001
```

See also

DISPLAY NETWORKS (NetWare v3.x)
INSTALL (NetWare v3.x)
MONITOR

CONSOLE   F> 2.2

Purpose

Switches a non-dedicated file server or router to the Console screen.
Once in the Console screen, you can issue console commands.

Syntax

```
CONSOLE
```

Options

None

Rules and Considerations

After using the CONSOLE command to switch the file server or router
to console mode, use the DOS command to switch back to the work
station mode.

Important Messages

None

See also

DOS

DCONFIG   : 2.2

Purpose

Changes the configuration options of the IPX.COM file and NET$OS.EXE operating system file. Enables you to modify the IPX.COM to match the configuration setting of the network board in the workstation should it require change after generation. Also enables modification of various parameters in the NET$OS.EXE operating system file after generation.

Syntax

    DCONFIG *filename options*

You can specify more than one option on a command line.

Options

-i volume/drive: filename	Uses input from specified file. This option is valid for IPX.COM only.
SHELL: *node address, configuration #;*	Valid for IPX.COM only.

Rules and Considerations

You cannot use the DCONFIG command to insert or delete network card drivers from NET$OS.EXE, or to change the network card for which IPX.COM was originally generated.

When you issue DCONFIG with just the filename (such as IPX.COM or NET$OS.EXE), NetWare displays a list of the adjustable parameters' current settings.

If you type DCONFIG alone (with no options) on the DOS command line, NetWare displays a brief list of the available options.

Although the SHELL option shown previously lists a node address option, this is seldom used. Most network cards used today determine the node address automatically.

If you do not want to change part of an option (such as net address), leave that field blank.

Important Messages

None

Examples

To change the configuration of the LAN adapter used by IPX.COM to option 2, type the following:

```
DCONFIG IPX.COM SHELL:, 2;
```

To change the configuration of the LAN adapter used by NET$OS.EXE to option 3., type the following:

```
DCONFIG NET$OS.EXE A: ,,3;
```

To change the IPX.COM file at the workstation, change to the directory containing the boot files. To view the current configuration for the IPX.COM file, type:

```
IPX I
```

NetWare should display an informational screen similar to the following:

```
Lan Option: NetWare Ethernet NE2000 V1.00EC
(801004)
Hardware Configuration:IRQ=3, I/O Base=300h,
no DMA or RAM
```

You also can type **DCONFIG IPX.COM** to receive an informational screen similar to the following:

```
Shell Driver: NetWare Ethernet NE2000 V1.00EC
(801004)Node address is determined automatically.
* 0: IRQ = 3, I/O Base = 300h, no DMA or RAM
  1: IRQ = 3, I/O Base = 280h, no DMA or RAM
  2: IRQ = 3, I/O Base = 2A0h, no DMA or RAM
  3: IRQ = 3, I/O Base = 2C0h, no DMA or RAM
  4: IRQ = 4, I/O Base = 300h, no DMA or RAM
  5: IRQ = 4, I/O Base = 2A0h, no DMA or RAM
  6: IRQ = 4, I/O Base = 2C0h, no DMA or RAM
  7: IRQ = 5, I/O Base = 300h, no DMA or RAM
  8: IRQ = 5, I/O Base = 280h, no DMA or RAM
  9: IRQ = 5, I/O Base = 320h, no DMA or RAM
 10: IRQ = 7, I/O Base = 280h, no DMA or RAM
```

The asterisk (*) indicates that the active configuration option in IPX.COM is active, and displays the other options and the option numbers associated with each setting. To change IPX.COM to a different option number, such as option 4, type:

DCONFIG IPX.COM SHELL:,4

Following are examples of common changes made to NET$OS.EXE using the DCONFIG utility:

DCONFIG NET$OS.EXE BUFFERS:*xxx*

The *xxx* variable represents the desired number—150 is the maximum you can select in NETGEN. You can add more here. INSTALL in v2.2 enables you to use up to 1000 communications buffers.

To change a LAN adapter to another available configuration, use the command:

DCONFIG NET$OS.EXE A:,,*xx*

The *xx* variable represents the desired configuration # for LAN A Adapter configuration and network address can be changed simultaneously if you want.

Notes

 Type **DCONFIG** *filename.ext* to display the current configuration of the selected file (IPX.COM or NET$OS.EXE). Before making any changes to the file, use this option and redirect it to a printer to create a handy reference. For the OS, this command would be **DCONFIG NET$OS.EXE > LPT1**.

If you want to make temporary changes to the IPX.COM configuration, you also can use the O# option in NET.CFG, SHELL.CFG, or load IPX.COM using the desired option number on the command line (such as IPX O#4). After the correct option is selected, you can use the ADCONFIG utility to make it permanent.

See also

NET.CFG
NETGEN
SHELL.CFG
WSGEN
INSTALL

DISABLE LOGIN

Purpose

Prevents users from logging in to the file server.

Syntax

```
DISABLE LOGIN
```

Options

None

Rules and Considerations

The DISABLE LOGIN command does not affect users who already are logged in to the file server. It only prevents a user from logging in after you issue the command at the file server console.

Important Message

After you issue **DISABLE LOGIN** command, NetWare should display a message similar to the following:

```
Login is now disabled.
```

This confirms that the command has worked.

See also

ENABLE LOGIN
FCONSOLE (Status)
LOGIN

DISABLE TRANSACTIONS : 2.2

Purpose

Manually disables the NetWare Transaction Tracking System (TTS). This command is used primarily by application developers who need to test transactional applications while TTS is disabled.

Syntax

```
DISABLE TRANSACTIONS
```

Options

None

Rules and Considerations

The NetWare TTS uses only 40 bytes of memory; it can, however, use as much as 400KB of memory if it is handling extremely large records. TTS is an integral part of the file server operating system that will protect the bindery and other files that have been flagged as transactional from becoming corrupted. TTS will remain disabled until you issue the ENABLE TRANSACTIONS command or reboot the file server.

Disabling transactions is not an effective way to increase memory at the file server. The protection TTS provides you is worth the additional memory used at the file server.

Important Messages

None

See also

ENABLE TRANSACTIONS
FCONSOLE (Status)
SETTTS
FLAG

DISABLE TTS   : 3.11

Purpose

Manually disables the NetWare Transaction Tracking System (TTS). This command is primarily used by application developers who need to test transactional applications while TTS is disabled.

Syntax

```
DISABLE TTS
```

Options

None

Rules and Considerations

The NetWare Transaction Tracking System uses only 40 bytes of memory; it can, however, use as much as 400KB of memory if it is handling extremely large records. TTS is an integral part of the file server operating system that protects the bindery and other files that have been flagged as transactional from becoming corrupted. TTS will remain disabled until you issue the ENABLE TTS command or reboot the file server.

Disabling transactions is not an effective way to increase memory at the file server. The protection TTS provides you is worth the additional memory used at the file server.

Important Messages

None

See also

> ENABLE TTS
> FCONSOLE (Status)
> SETTTS
> FLAG

DISK : 2.2

Purpose

Monitors and displays the status of network disk drives. Shows which disks and disk channels are functioning normally and which ones are not.

Syntax

> **DISK** *volumename*

or

> **DISK** *

Options

When you issue the DISK command alone (without switches), NetWare displays a screen that provides information on all known disks and disk channels installed in the server.

volumename   Causes DISK to display information specific to the volume you specify

*   Displays an overview of disk volumes

When you issue the DISK command alone (without switches), NetWare displays information about all known disks and disk channels installed in the server.

Rules and Considerations

You must issue the DISK command from the file server console.

Important Messages

None

Examples

The following three examples demonstrate the use of the DISK command by itself, with the * switch, and with a specific volume name.

If you want to check the status of all the disks on your system, issue DISK by itself, as follows:

```
DISK
```

NetWare displays information about all the system's disks, as follows (your system information may be different from the example shown here):

```
PHYSICAL DISK STATUS AND STATISTICS
        cha   con   drv   stat   IO Err   Free  Used

  00     1     0     0    OK       0      699    8
  01     1     0     1    OK       0        0    8
  02     2     0     0    NO HOT   0        0    0
  03     2     0     1    OFF      0        0    0
```

This table includes the following types of information:

First column	The physical drive number
cha	The channel number on which the interface board is installed
con	The address of the controller for that disk
drv	The disk address (as seen by the controller)

stat	The disk's operational status; the following values are possible:

OK	Drive set for Hot Fix and not mirrored
NO HOT	Hot Fix turned off for this drive (Reinstall Hot Fix as soon as possible; the drive will shut down automatically.)
DOWN	Drive is out of service or not operating (Repair if possible, or remove from system if necessary.)
M *xx*	Drive is part of a mirrored pair; xx is the number of the other drive in the pair
D *xx*	Drive was originally set up for mirroring, but is now dead (Repair or replace drive and remirror.)

IO Err	The number of input/output errors that have occurred on this drive
Free	The number of unused blocks in the Hot Fix redirection area
Used	The number of used blocks in the Hot Fix redirection area (Hot Fix uses 6 blocks by default.)

If you want to see a list of all the file server's installed volumes, use the * switch, as follows:

DISK *

NetWare displays the following information (your list may be different from the one shown in this example):

```
               FILE SERVER VOLUMES

Volume Name  Phy Drv    Mir Drv
SYS            00          01
VOL1           02
ACCT           03
```

This table includes the following types of information:

Volume Name   The name assigned to each file server volume

Phy Drv   The physical drive number assigned to each drive

Mir Drv   The physical drive number of the secondary drive in a mirrored-pair set

If you want to see information about a specific volume, include the volume's name with the DISK command. In the following example, the volume is named SYS:

DISK SYS

NetWare displays the following information:

```
Information For Volume SYS
Physical drive number        : 00
Physical drive type          : ISA Disk type 09
IO errors on this drive      : 0
Redirection blocks available : 223
Redirection blocks used      : 9
Mirror physical drive number : 01

Other volumes sharing these
physical drive(s):
VOL1
```

NetWare first displays information about the unmirrored or primary disk on the controller that contains the requested volume. If the disk is part of a mirrored pair, NetWare also reports information about the secondary disk.

Note

In the preceding examples, the physical drive numbers are the drive numbers assigned to each disk by the operating system.

DISKSET   A> :LOAD

Purpose

Loads identification information about external hard disks attached to a Novell Disk Coprocessor Board (DCB) into the DCB's EEPROM chip.

You can load DISKSET at any time on a downed file server to perform the following functions:

- Place configuration information about the hard disks attached to the DCB into the DCB's EEPROM chip. This configuration information enables the file server to communicate with the attached hard disks through the DCB.
- Back up the NetWare Ready configuration information from a NetWare Ready drive to a floppy disk.
- Restore NetWare Ready configuration information from a backup floppy disk to the NetWare Ready drive.

Syntax

Use the following syntax for v2.2:

    DISKSET

Use the following syntax for v3.11:

    LOAD DISKSET

Options

None

Rules and Considerations

If you are running v2.2, the file server must be downed before running the disk setup program.

If you are running v3.11, the file server must be up and running to load the disk setup program.

Important Messages

None

Example

```
A:DISKSET
```

In this example, the DISKSET utility loads from a DOS disk in drive A. When the utility is loaded, NetWare prompts you to specify the address of the controller you want to use. The system then presents a screen similar to the following:

```
Choose Controller Address
    1
    2
    3
    4
    5
    6
    7
```

After you select the DCB, you are ready to select a disk and controller type from the menu list. The screen should look similar to the following:

```
Select a DISK/CONTROLLER
CDC WRENIII HALF-HEIGHT
CDC WRENIII/EMBEDDED SCSI
FJ-M2243/A4000
FJ-M2243/A4000 , FJ-M2243/A4000
Fujitsu M2246AS/EMBEDDED SCSI
Generic SCSI
Generic SCSI , Generic SCSI
MAXTOR-1140/A4000
MAXTOR-1140/A4000 , MAXTOR-1140/A4000
MAXTOR-1140/A4070
```

```
MAXTOR-1140/A4070 , MAXTOR-1140/A4070
MAXTOR-3280/EMBEDDED SCSI
MINISCRIBE 4020
MINISCRIBE 4020 , MINISCRIBE 4020
Pyxis 27/A4000
NETWARE READY/EMBEDDED SCSI
Pyxis 27/A4000 , Pyxis 27/A4000

Toshiba MK56/A4000
Toshiba MK56/A4000 , Toshiba MK56/A4000
Toshiba MK56/A4070
Toshiba MK56/A4070 , Toshiba MK56/A4070
Vertex V150/A4000
Vertex V150/A4000 , Vertex V150/A4000
Vertex V150/A4070
Vertex V150/A4070 , Vertex V150/A4070
Vertex V170/A4000
Vertex V170/A4000 , Vertex V170/A4000
Vertex V170/A4070
Vertex V170/A4070 , Vertex V170/A4070
Vertex V185/A4000
Vertex V185/A4000 , Vertex V185/A4000
Vertex V185/A4070
Vertex V185/A4070 , Vertex V185/A4070
```

If you have a NetWare Ready or other generic embedded SCSI hard disk, select `NetWare Ready/Embedded SCSI` or `Generic SCSI` from the list of options.

Repeat the preceding steps to configure the remaining hard disks and DCBs installed in your system.

Notes

The DISKSET program that ships with NetWare v2.x should be located on the SYSTEM-1 disk.

The controller address (for Novell's DCB) is controlled by a PAL chip on the board. If you require a different setting, you must contact your Novell reseller or Novell's After Market Products division.

The Novell DCB is controlled by an 80188 CPU chip, which is located on the board. This chip loads instructions from ROM that also is contained on the DCB. Newer versions of NetWare (especially NetWare v3.x) require specific versions of this ROM to operate properly. For more information, contact your Novell reseller or Novell's After Market Products division.

DISMOUNT

Purpose

Dismounts a NetWare drive partition or disk, rendering that volume unavailable to users. When a partition or disk is dismounted, you have the opportunity to maintain or repair the volume, or (in the case of NetWare v3.x) upgrade the disk drivers while the server is running.

Syntax

```
DISMOUNT volumename
```

Option

volumename   The name of the volume you want to take out of service

Rules and Considerations

Use the BROADCAST console command to inform users that you are dismounting the volume before you actually take the volume out of service. This warning will enable users who are using that volume to close any files they have in use.

If you have a NetWare volume that is not used very often, dismount it until you need it. Mounted volumes take up memory and reduce overall system performance.

Important Messages

None

Example

Suppose that you want to dismount a NetWare volume named VOL1. To take the volume out of service, use DISMOUNT as follows:

```
DISMOUNT VOL1
```

This command enables you to service the drive or change disk drivers.

See Also

MOUNT

DISPLAY NETWORKS

Purpose

When entered at the server console, the DISPLAY NETWORKS command displays the following information on the server console's screen:

- Network numbers, both cable and internal IPX (NetWare v3.x only)
- The number of hops (networks crossed) required to reach the network (0 hops is the server at which you issue the command)
- The estimated time in ticks (each tick equals 1/18 second) required for a packet to reach the other network
- The total number of networks recognized by the internal router

Syntax

```
DISPLAY NETWORKS
```

Options

None

Rules and Considerations

You must issue DISPLAY NETWORKS from the file server console.

Important Messages

None

Example

To make sure that your file server can read all the network numbers, type the following command at the file server console:

```
DISPLAY NETWORKS
```

This command displays the total number of networks recognized by the internal router.

Notes

On a Novell NetWare network, each file server maintains an internal router table. This table lists the network and node addresses of each file server and router that this server recognizes. If you have trouble using the LOGIN and ATTACH commands, try using the DISPLAY NETWORKS command to determine whether the server or network in question is "visible" to the other servers and routers on the network.

See Also

DISPLAY SERVERS
RESET ROUTER

DISPLAY SERVERS

Purpose

When entered at the server console, the DISPLAY SERVERS command displays the following information on the server console's screen:

- The file servers recognized by the internal router
- The number of hops (networks that must be crossed) required to reach the server

Syntax

```
DISPLAY SERVERS
```

Options

None

Rules and Considerations

You can issue the DISPLAY SERVERS command only at the file server's console.

Important Messages

None

Example

If you are having trouble attaching to a file server, you can issue the DISPLAY SERVERS command as follows, to determine whether all the system's file servers recognize one another:

```
DISPLAY SERVERS
```

Note

On a Novell NetWare network, each file server maintains an internal router table. This table lists the network and node addresses of each file server and router that this server recognizes. If you have trouble using the LOGIN and ATTACH commands, try using the DISPLAY SERVERS command to determine whether the internal router table recognizes the server in question.

See Also

DISPLAY NETWORKS
RESET ROUTER

DOS : 2.2

Purpose

This command switches a nondedicated file server or router from console mode to DOS mode.

Syntax

DOS

Options

None

Rules and Considerations

This command is valid only at a file server that is running NetWare v2.x in nondedicated mode. NetWare v3.x file servers cannot run in nondedicated mode.

If the workstation session (or task) hangs, the file server or router task also may hang, breaking any and all connections maintained by the file server or router. The loss of connection causes users to lose files and access to their applications, printers, disk storage, and other services.

If a nondedicated file server or router hangs when in DOS or console mode, ask all users to try to save their work (to a local disk, if necessary) and log out. Then bring the nondedicated machine up again to see if the problem is corrected.

Even if the nondecicated file server or router is still operating and functional, you must reboot the computer to return the workstation task to normal operation. As a result, however, the nondedicated file server or router will go down.

Important Messages

None

Example

After you have issued console commands, you may want to switch back to the DOS session and continue using your applications. To move back to the DOS session, issue the DOS command at the nondedicated file server or router console, as follows:

    DOS

Notes

On a nondedicated file server running NetWare v2.x, the DOS session has the highest service priority. In other words, virtually all other service requests generated by other users are serviced after the nondedicated DOS session. Further, because the DOS session is polled (not interrupt-driven, as are the network adapter cards), this overhead exists even if no programs are executed in the DOS session. If at all possible, you should change your server to run in dedicated mode.

If you are running your NetWare v2.x file server in nondedicated mode, you are sacrificing approximately 30 percent of your server's performance or more. You can determine the system's minimum performance sacrifice by switching the file server to console mode (with all users logged out) and observing the server's utilization. The utilization data is displayed in Monitor mode. The percentage displayed represents the amount of overhead required just to maintain the DOS session on your nondedicated file server.

 If the file server locks up and its keyboard does not respond, go to another workstation on the network and log in as supervisor. When you are in the system, issue FCONSOLE and select Down The Server. This command shuts down the server in an orderly fashion and should help avoid the corruption of files that might have been left open. This procedure may take several minutes.

See Also

CONSOLE
FCONSOLE
MONITOR

DOSGEN   F>

Purpose

DOSGEN creates a boot image file called NET$DOS.SYS in the SYS:LOGIN directory. NET$DOS.SYS is a copy of the files on the system's book disk. This file enables diskless workstations to boot from remote boot image files, which reside on the server's hard disk.

Syntax

```
DOSGEN source filename
```

Options

source	The drive in which DOSGEN can find the boot disk. If you omit this drive indicator, NetWare assumes that you want to use drive A.
filename	The output file name. If you do not specify an output file name, NetWare use the name NET$DOS.SYS.

Rules and Considerations

For proper operation, DOSGEN requires you to map two drives, as follows:

```
MAP F:=SYS:SYSTEM

MAP G:=SYS:LOGIN
```

If your network has several servers, copy the Remote Boot image files onto each server that may come up as the Remote Boot station's default server. Then, if the default server is busy when a Remote Boot station boots, the next available server becomes the default server.

Important Messages

If NetWare displays the `Error opening boot disk image file` error message, you probably are attaching to another file server that does not contain the Remote Boot image file. Either log in to the other possible default file servers as supervisor and run DOSGEN on each, or copy the SYS and BAT files in SYS:LOGIN from the default file server to the other file servers on the network.

If you receive the `Batch file missing` error message, make sure that the AUTOEXEC.BAT file is in SYS:LOGIN for every file server to which you can attach.

Example

The following form of the DOSGEN command should be run from drive G. This example retrieves the boot files from drive A and uses the files to create a remote boot image file called NET$DOS.SYS in the LOGIN subdirectory:

```
F:DOSGEN A:
```

To use this command to create a remote boot image file, complete the following steps:

1. Boot a suitable workstation from a floppy or hard disk, and log in as supervisor.
2. Insert the configured boot disk for the Remote Boot workstation into drive A.
3. Map drive F to SYS:SYSTEM.
4. Map drive G to SYS:LOGIN.
5. Change to SYS:LOGIN by making drive G current.
6. To run DOSGEN, type **F:DOSGEN A:**, as shown earlier. During the program's execution, your screen should contain the following information:

```
Floppy Type f9 = Quad Density, 15 Sectors per
track
Total Floppy Space 2400 Sectors
Setting Up System Block.
Setting Up FAT Tables.
Setting Up Directory Structures.
Traversing Directory Structures.
Processing IBMBIO   COM
Processing IBMDOS   COM
Processing CONFIG   SYS
Processing COMMAND COM
Processing IPX      COM
Processing NET3     COM
Processing AUTOEXECBAT
Processing NET      CFG
Transferring Data to "NET$DOS.SYS"
```

7. Copy the AUTOEXEC.BAT file from the boot disk in drive A into the SYS:LOGIN subdirectory. NetWare may display the `Batch file missing` error message when you log in, if the AUTOEXEC.BAT file is not copied to SYS:LOGIN and the default user directory.

8. Copy the AUTOEXEC.BAT file from the boot disk to the default directory specified in the user's login script (usually the user's home directory).

9. Flag the NET$DOS.SYS file in SYS:LOGIN Shareable Read/Write.

The next example, which also should be run from drive G, assumes that you will be creating several remote boot image files. Like the first example, this form of the DOSGEN command retrieves the needed files from a disk in drive A, and uses the data to create a remote boot image file in the LOGIN subdirectory. This form of the DOSGEN command, however, names the new file ARCNET.SYS:

```
F:DOSGEN A: ARCNET.SYS
```

To use this command to create a remote boot image file, complete the following steps:

1. Boot a suitable workstation from a floppy or hard disk, and log in as supervisor.

2. Insert the configured boot disk for the Remote Boot workstation into drive A.

3. Map drive F to SYS:SYSTEM.

4. Map drive G to SYS:LOGIN.

5. Change to SYS:LOGIN by making drive G current.

6. To run DOSGEN, type **F:DOSGEN A: ARCNET.SYS**, as shown earlier. During the program's execution, your screen should contain the following information:

```
Floppy Type f9 = Quad Density, 15 Sectors per
track
Total Floppy Space 2400 Sectors
Setting Up System Block.
Setting Up FAT Tables.
```

```
Setting Up Directory Structures.
Traversing Directory Structures.
Processing IBMBIO  COM
Processing IBMDOS  COM
Processing CONFIG  SYS
Processing COMMAND COM
Processing IPX     COM
Processing NET3    COM
Processing AUTOEXECBAT
Processing NET     CFG
Transferring Data to "ARCNET.SYS"
```

7. Copy the AUTOEXEC.BAT file from the boot disk in drive A to the SYS:LOGIN subdirectory. NetWare may display a `Batch file missing` error when you log in if the AUTOEXEC.BAT file has not been copied to SYS:LOGIN and the default user directory. In the example, the AUTOEXEC.BAT file should contain only the name of a second batch file. This second batch file should contain the true desired contents of a boot AUTOEXEC.BAT. Because you are configuring for several remote boot image files, give a unique name and BAT extension (such as ARCNET.BAT) to each AUTOEXEC.BAT file from each boot disk, and copy them all into the SYS:LOGIN subdirectory. When each Remote Boot workstation boots, the operating system reads the AUTOEXEC.BAT file and goes to the renamed batch file to execute the desired boot commands.

8. Copy the renamed AUTOEXEC.BAT file from SYS:LOGIN to the default directory specified in the user's login script (usually the user's home directory).

9. Flag the ARCNET.SYS file in SYS:LOGIN Shareable Read/Write.

10. Record the network number and node address of the station that will use the Remote Boot image file you just created. You will need this information when you create the BOOTCONF.SYS file.

When you create multiple Remote Boot image files, you also need a BOOTCONF.SYS file in the SYS:LOGIN directory. The

BOOTCONF.SYS file lists the names of all the custom Remote Boot image files (except the default NET$DOS.SYS file), and the network and node address of each station that uses the customized remote boot image file. It is nothing more than an ASCII text file in the SYS:LOGIN subdirectory that routes the correct remote boot image file to the correct workstation. Take the following steps to create the BOOTCONF.SYS file:

1. Move to the SYS:LOGIN directory.

2. Use a DOS text editor (such as EDLIN) to create the BOOTCONF.SYS file in the SYS:LOGIN directory. The file should contain a line for each Remote Boot image file you created. Use the following format for entering the required information:

   0x (the number zero plus x)

   The network address

   A comma (,)

   The node or station address

   An equal sign (=)

   The remote boot image file name

Following this format, your file should look something like this:

```
0xBADCAFE,02F=ARCNET.SYS
```

This example is for an ARCNet workstation. An Ethernet workstation would have a much longer node address.

3. To complete the setup, flag the SYS and BAT files in SYS:LOGIN as Shareable Read/Write. For example:

```
FLAG *.SYS SRW

FLAG *.BAT SRW
```

Notes

If one user can successfully log in but other users are unsuccessful when trying at the same time, verify that the *.SYS files were flagged Shareable Read/Write. You may also need to grant users the Modify right to the SYS:LOGIN subdirectory.

Use the TRACK ON command at the server console and watch for GET NEAREST SERVER REQUESTS from the workstation. This will give you an idea as to whether the boot ROM on the workstation is successfully sending packets to the file server.

Load MONITOR at the file server console and see if the diskless workstations are opening the BOOTCONF.SYS file, the NET$DOS.SYS file, or other boot disk image files.

If a workstation using a boot ROM does not boot, and you have another workstation with a disk drive configured the same as the first workstation (that is, if both have the same type of network board using the same configuration options), see if the second station will boot with the boot disk you used during DOSGEN. By booting with the boot disk in the second workstation, the booting proecedure should execute in the same manner as booting from the server with the Remote Boot image file on the first workstation.

DOWN   ⋮

Purpose

The DOWN command shuts down the NetWare operating system so that you can safely turn off the file server. When you issue the DOWN command, the following events occur:

- All cache buffers are written to disk.
- All open files are closed.
- All directory and file allocation tables are updated (if appropriate).

Syntax

    DOWN

Options

None

Rules and Considerations

Make sure that all users are logged out before you issue the DOWN command. Use the MONITOR command to make sure that all users have logged out and all files are closed.

Do not issue the DOWN command or turn off the server if database or word processing files are still open. Close these files from within the appropriate application, and then use DOWN.

Important Messages

None

Example

Before you can perform any kind of hardware maintenance to the file server, you must turn it off. Before turning off the server, issue the DOWN command, as follows:

DOWN

When you issue the command, NetWare should display a message similar to the following:

```
Server Training-Solutions has been shut down.
Please reboot to restart.
```

Notes

If you fail to use the DOWN command before turning off the file server, you will corrupt any files that may be open. Further, you may cause irrepairable damage to the File Allocation Table (FAT) and Directory Entry Table (DET) on the hard disks. If the FAT and DET become corrupted, you probably will not be able to reboot the server and access your data.

Any changes to data files remain in cache buffers and are not written to disk until a minimum time (the default is three seconds) has elapsed or the files are closed. These changes are lost if you do not use DOWN before turning off the file server.

If the MONITOR screen shows a list of the files that are still open, it also should display the station connection numbers that opened them. If files remain open after all users have logged out, you can close these files from the server by using the CLEAR CONNECTION command. You should use this procedure, however, only as a last resort! If the files are not closed by the application that opened them, they may become corrupted.

See Also

BROADCAST
CLEAR CONNECTION
MONITOR

ECONFIG   F>

Purpose

The ECONFIG command lists Ethernet configurations, configures workstation shells to use the Ethernet II protocol standard, and embeds NetWare's unique protocol number (8137) in the workstation shell file IPX.COM.

Syntax

```
drive1: ECONFIG drive2: IPX.COM SHELL:packet
protocolnumber
```

Options

drive1: Indicates the location of the ECONFIG.EXE file.

drive2: Indicates the location of the IPX.COM file.

packet Specifies the data that is to be transmitted, and its form of transmission. A packet can be one of the following:

> **Netware.** Use **N** if the driver is to use the IEEE 802.3 standard frame format.

> **Ethernet II.** Use **E** if the driver is to use the Ethernet standard frame format.

protocolnumber Specifies the Ethernet protocol number. By default, this is Novell's IPX protocol number (8137). You can specify any number currently registered with your server.

Important Messages

None

Example

This example assumes that the WSGEN disk (which contains ECONFIG.EXE) is in drive A, and that the IPX.COM file is in drive B. The following form of the command lists the current Ethernet configuration for IPX.COM:

```
A:ECONFIG B:IPX.COM
```

If the shell file is Ethernet-configurable, but has not yet been configured, you should see the following information on your screen:

```
SHELL: Novell Ethernet (IEEE 802.3 compatible)
```

If the shell file already has been configured with ECONFIG, you should see the following information:

```
SHELL: Ethernet Typefield: 8137 (Assigned Novell
type constant)
```

To embed NetWare's protocol number 8137 into the IPX.COM file, type the following form of the ECONFIG command:

A:ECONFIG B:IPX.COM SHELL:E

NetWare displays the following information:

```
SHELL: Ethernet Typefield: 8137 (Assigned Novell
type constant)
```

EDIT   :LOAD 3.11

Purpose

The EDIT command creates or modifies an ASCII text file from the NetWare v3.11 file server console.

Syntax

LOAD *path* EDIT

Option

path   Determines the full path to the directory containing the EDIT module. You may begin with either a DOS drive letter or a NetWare volume name. If you do not specify a path, the operating system looks for EDIT in SYS:SYSTEM. You can use the SEARCH command to set up additional paths for automatic searching.

Rules and Considerations

You may find EDIT particularly useful when you want to create NCF batch files that automatically execute file server commands. Although you can edit such files in the INSTALL NLM, EDIT provides an alternative means to create or edit them.

You can use EDIT with ASCII text files on either DOS or NetWare partitions. The EDIT NLM can edit ASCII files up to 8K.

Important Messages

None

Example

To load the editor at the file server, issue the EDIT command as follows:

```
LOAD EDIT
```

At the `File to Edit` prompt, enter the complete directory path for the ASCII file that you want to create or edit. After you create or edit the file, press Esc to exit from EDIT. When the confirmation box appears, select Yes to save the file with the changes you have made during this editing session. Otherwise, you can select No to abort and exit without saving the changes.

See Also

SEARCH

EMSNETX.COM or EMSNETX.EXE

Purpose

The EMSNETx command loads the NetWare shell driver and moves most of the commands in NETx.COM from DOS memory to LIM expanded memory. This arrangement frees approximately 34K of the DOS 640K base memory. About 6K must remain in base memory to handle various interrupts and some data.

Syntax

EMSNET*X*

Options

-I   Enables you to see which version of the shell driver you are using, without actually loading it into memory

-U   Unloads the shell driver from memory, but must be the last TSR
program loaded for this to function properly

Rules and Considerations

IPX.COM must be loaded before you attempt to load EMSNETX.EXE.

Older versions used the *X* to represent the version of DOS you are running at the workstation; for example, MS-DOS v5 requires you to issue the command as **EMSNET5**.

All NETX.COM parameters in the shell configuration files
SHELL.CFG and NET.CFG work with the expanded memory shell.

Important Messages

None

Example

Issue the following form of the command to load the shell driver into
expanded memory:

EMSNETX

Notes

 For ease of use, copy the EMSNETX.EXE (or COM) file to the workstation's boot disk and include the file name (EMSNETX) in the AUTOEXEC.BAT file. This automatically loads the shell driver when you boot your workstation.

The expanded memory shell works with all NetWare versions and operates under the same conditions as the regular NetWare DOS shell v3.01 and above.

The expanded memory shell replaces the current NETX.COM shell option and is intended for use by users who have LIM expanded memory.

You can use the following parameter in the SHELL.CFG or NET.CFG file to determine the number of times you can re-enter the expanded memory shell:

```
ENTRY STACK SIZE
```

See Also

NET.CFG
SHELL.CFG
XMSNETX

ENABLE LOGIN   :

Purpose

After you have used the DISABLE LOGIN command, you must use ENABLE LOGIN to enable the system's users to log in to the file server.

Syntax

```
ENABLE LOGIN
```

Options

None

Rules and Considerations

The ENABLE LOGIN function is built into the file server's operating system.

When you disable login and then down the file server, you do not need to issue ENABLE LOGIN. The command is issued automatically when you reboot the file server.

Important Messages

None

Example

To reverse the DISABLE LOGIN command, issue the following:

```
ENABLE LOGIN
```

See Also

DISABLE LOGIN
LOGIN
FCONSOLE (Status)

ENABLE TRANSACTIONS : 2.2

Purpose

If the NetWare Transaction Tracking System (TTS) has been disabled—either automatically or manually—you must manually re-enable TTS by using the ENABLE TRANSACTIONS command.

Syntax

```
ENABLE TRANSACTIONS
```

Options

None

Rules and Considerations

ENABLE TRANSACTIONS is a part of the operating system. During normal operation, TTS is enabled. The file server automatically disables TTS if the TTS backout volume (usually SYS) becomes full, or if the file server does not have enough memory to run TTS. You also can manually disable TTS by using the DISABLE TRANSACTIONS command. Transactions that were initiated while TTS was disabled cannot be backed out after TTS is re-enabled.

If the file server is rebooted while TTS is disabled, TTS is automatically re-enabled when the file server is rebooted.

Important Messages

None

Example

If you have disabled TTS and want to re-enable it, issue the following command:

```
ENABLE TRANSACTIONS
```

See Also

DISABLE TRANSACTIONS
SETTTS
FCONSOLE (Status)

ENABLE TTS   : 3.11

Purpose

If the NetWare Transaction Tracking System (TTS) has been disabled—either automatically or manually—you must manually re-enable TTS by using the ENABLE TTS command.

Syntax

```
ENABLE TTS
```

Options

None

Rules and Considerations

ENABLE TTS is a part of the operating system. During normal operation, TTS is enabled. The file server automatically disables TTS if the TTS backout volume (usually SYS) becomes full, or if the file server does not have enough memory to run TTS. You also can manually disable TTS by using the DISABLE TTS command. Transactions that were initiated while TTS was disabled cannot be backed out after TTS is re-enabled.

If the file server is rebooted while TTS is disabled, TTS is automatically re-enabled when the file server is rebooted.

Important Messages

None

Example

If you have disabled TTS and want to re-enable it, issue the following command:

```
ENABLE TTS
```

See Also

DISABLE TTS

FCONSOLE (Status)

ENDCAP

Purpose

Use the ENDCAP command to terminate the capturing of one or more of your workstations' LPT ports. Always use the CAPTURE command before using the ENDCAP command.

Syntax

```
ENDCAP option
```

Options

ENDCAP ends capturing to LPT1, unless you enter one of the following options:

Local *n*	Indicates the LPT port from which you want to end capturing. Replace *n* with the number of the desired parallel port, such as 1, 2, or 3.
ALL	Ends the capturing of all LPT ports.
Cancel	Ends the capturing of LPT1 and deletes the data without printing it.
Cancel Local *n*	Ends the capturing of the specified LPT port and deletes data without printing it. Replace *n* with the number of the desired parallel port, such as 1, 2, or 3.
Cancel ALL	Ends the capturing of all LPT ports and deletes the data without printing it.

Rules and Considerations

Use the ENDCAP command only after having issued the CAPTURE
command.

Important Messages

LPTx set to local mode.	Indicates that port LPT*x* (LPT1, 2, or 3) has been set to local operation and the CAPTURE function has been canceled

Example

To end capturing to LPT1, issue the following command:

ENDCAP

To end capturing to LPT2, issue the following command:

    ENDCAP L=2

To end capturing to LPT1 and delete the print job without printing it, issue the following command:

    ENDCAP CL=1

See Also

CAPTURE

EXIT :3.11

Purpose

Returns the file server console to DOS after you have used the DOWN command. EXIT enables you to access files on the DOS partition, or to reload SERVER.EXE with new parameters.

Syntax

    EXIT

Options

None

Rules and Considerations

If you use the console command REMOVE DOS to remove DOS from memory, you cannot use the EXIT command to return to DOS.

Important Messages

None

Example

After you have shut down the file server, you can return to the DOS prompt by issuing the following command:

```
EXIT
```

Note

You can use EXIT to warm boot the file server if you have issued the REMOVE DOS command.

See Also

DOWN
REMOVE DOS

FLAG   F>

Purpose

Displays or changes files attributes.

Syntax

```
FLAG path flaglist
```

Options

path
:   Designates directory path that leads to the name of the file you want to view or change.

flaglist
:   Specifies one or more of the following attributes (use the bold character to express the attribute):

Shareable	Allows a file to be opened by more than one person at a time. Shareable is often used in conjunction with Read Only and is also used to mark application programs (that is, EXE or COM files).
Read **O**nly	Prevents you from writing to, deleting, or renaming a specified file. The Read Only flag often is used in conjunction with Shareable on application program files.
Read/**W**rite	Specifies the file as a data file, which means that data can be written to it. This is a default setting for files.
Normal	Specifies the NonShareable and Read/Write flags together. All files loaded on the network are set this way by default.
Transaction Tracking System	Specifies the file is transactional. This flag is designed to be used with NetWare's Transaction Tracking feature, which prevents database corruption in case of system failure. The Transaction Tracking System ensures that when a file is modified, either all changes are made or no changes are made, thus preventing data corruption.

Indexed	Forces NetWare to keep a special File Allocation Table to speed data access. Used with data files using more than 64 cache blocks. Automatic in v3.11.
Hidden	Prevents a file from displaying when a DOS DIR command is executed. The file will appear, however, if you have the File Scan right in that directory, and you use the NDIR command. You cannot copy or erase Hidden files.
SYstem	Flags a file as a system file and is used for the system function. A system file does not appear when you use the DOS DIR command, but it will appear when you use the NetWare NDIR command if you have the File Scan right. You cannot copy or delete system files.
Archive	Attaches automatically to all files that have been modified since the last backup was performed.
Execute Only	Allows the program file to execute, but prevents it from being copied. This special flag is attached to COM And EXE files. Files with this flag set are not backed up, nor can this flag be removed. The file must be deleted and reinstalled to remove this attribute. This attribute can only be set by the supervisor in the FILER utility.
SUBdirectory	Displays or changes file attributes in the specified directory and its subdirectories.

Rules and Considerations

You must be attached to the file server before you can view or change file attributes of files on that server.

You cannot change file attributes in a directory unless your effective rights in that directory include the Read, File Scan, and Modify privileges.

Use the - or + constants to add or delete all file attributes except Normal and SUBdirectory. When attributes are added or deleted in the same command, keep the + attributes separate from the - attributes.

Important Messages

None

Example

If you want to flag as Shareable Read Only every file on the CDI server in the MS-DOS v5.00 directory under Public, enter the command:

```
FLAG CDI\SYS:PUBLIC\IBM_PC\MSDOS\V5.00\*.* SRO
```

Notes

MS/PC-DOS files should be flagged as Shareable Read Only.

If you enter the command FLAG /?, a help screen displays.

The *filename* parameter in the syntax also supports standard DOS wildcard characters.

 Use the Execute Only flag with extreme care. Some application programs will not execute correctly if they are flagged with this option. If you are going to use this flag, make sure you have a copy of the EXE or COM file before you set this flag. The only way to remove this flag is to delete the file.

See Also

FILER

NDIR

FLAGDIR   F> 3.11

Purpose

Lists or changes the attributes of directories and subdirectories.

Syntax

FLAGDIR path flaglist

Options

path   Specifies the path to the directory you want to view or change.

flaglist   Specifies one or more of the following attributes (use the bold character to specify the attribute):

Normal   Cancels all other directory attributes. Normal is automatically overridden if you include any other option.

Hidden   Prevents a directory from listing when the DOS DIR command is used. The directory will appear if you have the File Scan right and you use the NetWare NDIR command. With these privileges, you can access a Hidden directory, but you cannot copy or delete Hidden directories.

SYstem	Flags a directory as a System directory, which stores the network's operational files. A directory flagged as System will not appear when you use the DOS DIR command. A System directory will appear if you use the NetWare NDIR command and if you have the File Scan right.
Private	Protects data from casual directory-browsers. You can use the Private option to hide the directory names of all directories below the flagged directory. Although you cannot see any files on the system because you have no rights, you can see directories and use the DOS CD command to move through the directory structure. Can be used only in v2.2.
Delete Inhibit	Prevents users from erasing a directory even if they have Erase rights for that directory. Can be used only in v3.11.
Rename Inhibit	Prevents users from renaming directories even if they have Modify rights for that directory. Can be used only in v3.11.
Purge	Marks files that you want to purge immediately after deletion. These files cannot be recoved by using SALVAGE. Can be used only in v3.11.
Help	Displays the FLAGDIR help text.

Rules and Considerations

You cannot set attributes on local drives.

You cannot copy or delete system directories.

Important Messages

None

Example

To flag the TGEN subdirectory as private and to prevent other users from seeing the subdirectories under it when they use the DOS DIR command, type the following:

```
FLAGDIR TRAINING_SOLUTIONS\SYS:USERS\TGEN P
```

See Also

FILER

GRANT

Purpose

Grants trustee rights to a user or a group.

Syntax

```
GRANT rightslist FOR path TO USER username
```

or

```
GRANT rightslist FOR path TO GROUP groupname
```

Note that the specifiers USER and GROUP are required if the user or group to be modified has the same name as another user or group.

Options

path	Specifies the path for granting trustee rights
username	Specifies the name of a valid user on the file server to whom you want to grant trustee rights
groupname	Specifies the name of a valid group on the file server that is to be granted trustee rights
rightslist	Represents one or more of the following options (use the bold character to express the desired option):

All	Grants all rights except supervisory rights in v3.11
Create	Enables users to create files but not to write to them
Erase	Enables users to delete or erase files
Modify	Enables users to modify file names or attributes
Access Control	Enables a user or a group to control access to the directory
Read	Enables users to read from a file in the directory
File Scan	Enables users to "see" file names during a DOS DIR command
Write	Enables users to write to files
Supervisor	Gives all available rights to user. 3.11 only.
ALL BUT or ONLY	Switches that you can use before the *rightslist* option

Rules and Considerations

You must be attached to a server before you can grant trustee rights on the server.

Before you can grant rights to a user (or group), the user must exist on the network.

If you elect to grant rights to a user, you can grant rights to only one user with each GRANT command.

If you revoke trustee rights, the user remains a trustee of the directory unless he or she is removed from the trustee list.

Important Messages

None

Example

The following example grants the Read, Write, File Scan, and Modify rights to the user TGENDREAU for the PUBLIC subdirectory on the file server TRAINING_SOLUTIONS:

```
GRANT R W F M FOR TRAINING_SOLUTIONS\SYS:PUBLIC
TO TGENDREAU
```

See Also

ATTACH
MAP
REMOVE
REVOKE
SESSION
SYSCON

HELP

Purpose

Enables you to view on-line information about NetWare. HELP provides information on NetWare concepts, system messages, and utilities. You can use HELP to search for information in databases or infobases.

Syntax

    HELP *command*

Option

command   Specifies the command that you would like more information about.

Rules and Considerations

The HELP utility is placed in the SYS:PUBLIC directory during NetWare installation. Use the cursor keys to move around in HELP, or use the following keys:

+ or -   Rotates windows without closing them

Tab   Moves the cursor to the next link

Shift-Tab   Moves the cursor to the previous link

Esc   Closes windows, exits a search or exits the help utility

If your workstation has graphics support, you can use the left-right arrow keys to access graphics screens. If you have a mouse, point and click on the menu name. If you use a keyboard, access the menus with the following keystrokes:

Alt-S plus arrow keys	Enables you to scan menus
Alt-F	Accesses the file menu
Alt-D	Activates menus at the top of the screen

Following Links

Links are used to connect related information from different parts of the infobase. Use the TAB and SHIFT-TAB keys to position the cursor on the link, and then press ENTER. A new window will display the information.

Searching for Words or Phrases

When the cursor is in a window and not under a link, press the space bar. The search window appears and the query window will be active. Type the word or phrase you want to find (enclose phrases in quotation marks), and then press ENTER. A new window appears displaying the segments of the infobase where the searched words occur. You can use the TAB or SHIFT-TAB keys to move through the information. If you want to see where the information appears in the complete infobase, press ENTER at the marker.

The following operands illustrate the different types of searches you can specify. These operands can be typed in upper- or lower-case letters.

- **AND**. Use the AND operator to search for combinations of words. You can use a space between each word to represent the AND operator. For example, to search for all occurrences of print and queues together in a segment, type `print queues`.
- **OR**. Use the OR operator to search for occurrences of words either together in the segment or separately. Use the forward slash character (/) to represent the OR operator. For example, to search for all occurrences of the words print or queues or both in the same segment, type `print/queues`.
- **NOT**. Use the NOT operator to search for all occurrences of a word except when it is used with another specific

word. Use the circumflex symbol(^) to represent the NOT operator. For example, to search for all occurrences of the word print, except when it is used with the word queues, type `print^queues`.

- * and ?. Use the asterisk (*) and question mark (?) to search for variations or words. For example, to search for all words that begin with prin followed by more than one unspecified character, type `prin*`.

You also can perform a proximity search in a specific order to search for words that occur within a certain number of words from each other. Place the words that you want to search for inside quotation marks, followed by the number of words that you want to search within. For example, to search for the words print and queues within four words, type `"print queues"4`.

You can use the ampersand (@) symbol to perform a proximity search in any order. For example, to search for the words print and queues within five words in any order, type `"print queues"@5`.

You can print the information you find in HELP in several ways. Follow these steps to print information:

1. Press Ctrl-B to begin blocking text.
2. Use the cursor keys or a mouse to group the text together.
3. Press Ctrl-Printscrn after you block the text.
4. Select PRINT and highlight the desired settings, then press Enter.

The block of text will print.

Blocks of information can also be sent to a file and printed later by choosing the menu option Redirect document to ____.

Example

```
HELP NPRINT
```

By typing HELP followed by a command you need help with, the HELP utility will display information on the command that you typed.

Important Messages

None

Notes

 If you need help using the HELP utility, press the F1 key inside the HELP window.

See Also

NFOLIO

HOLDOFF   F> 2.2

Purpose

Enables you to close a file that you have been using so that other users can access it. HOLDOFF reverses the effects of the HOLDON command.

Syntax

```
HOLDOFF filename.ext
```

Options

None

Rules and Considerations

You do not need to use the HOLDOFF command unless you previously used the HOLDON command.

Example

```
HOLDOFF LOTUS.COM
```

The preceding example reverses the effects of the HOLDON command that was issued on the file LOTUS.COM.

Important Messages

None

See Also

HOLDON

HOLDON   F> 2.2

Purpose

Holds a file open while you use it and prevents other users from writing to the current file.

Syntax

```
HOLDON filename.ext
```

Options

None

Important Messages

None

See Also

HOLDOFF

INSTALL   :LOAD 3.11

Purpose

Enables you to install the v3.11 operating system on a file server's hard disk drive(s). INSTALL also is used to load the SYSTEM and PUBLIC files onto the file server; format and mirror hard disks; and create NetWare partitions, volumes, and file server boot files. Use the F1 key for help while the install utility is active. Press F1 twice for an overview of the installation process.

Syntax

```
LOAD path INSTALL
```

Option

path   Specifies the path or drive letter that the computer uses to load the install utility.

Rules and Considerations

Before you can use the INSTALL command, you must execute the SERVER program to bring up the v3.11 file server. The SERVER program can be found on the SYSTEM-1 disk. To execute the server command, insert the SYSTEM-1 disk in drive A and type **SERVER**. After you press Enter, information similar to the following will appear on the screen:

```
Novell NetWare 386 v3.11
Processor speed: 265
(Type SPEED at the command prompt for an explanation of
the speed rating)
Total server memory: 8 Megabytes
Copyright 1988, 1990 Novell, Inc. All Rights Reserved.
```

```
File server name:
```

Give the file server a unique name from 2 to 47 characters. The name cannot contain a period or spaces. After you name the file server, you will be asked to enter an internal network number. The internal network number must differ from other network numbers. The internal network number is a hexadecimal number (base 16) that uses 0-9 and A-F. The number can be 1 to 8 digits long.

Next, load the appropriate disk driver modules. Type **LOAD** *path disk driver.* Your disk driver should be either an ISADISK for AT type controllers, DCB for Novell Disk Coprocessor Boards, PS2ESDI, PS2MFM or PS2SCSI for PS/2 type controllers. The manufacturer of the disk controller you are using will provide you with these drivers. Consult your controller and disk drive documentation for more detailed information.

Now you are ready to load the INSTALL utility. To do so, insert the SYSTEM-2 disk in drive A in the file server and type **LOAD INSTALL** at the prompt.

Example

LOAD A:INSTALL

The preceding example loads INSTALL.NLM from drive A.

Important Messages

None

See Also

DISKSET

LOAD

IPX.COM

Purpose

The Novell IPX (Internetwork Packet eXchange) is a communication protocol that creates, maintains, and terminates connections between network devices such as workstations, file servers, and routers.

Syntax

IPX *options*

Options

I   Enables you to see how the IPX file is configured. The I option does not load IPX into memory.

Additional switches for the v3.02 shells include the following:

D	Display hardware options
O*num*	Loads IPX using the hardware option (*num*)
C=*path filename*	Use an alternate configuration file
?	Display this help screen

Rules and Considerations

At each workstation, two components in combination often are called the *shell*.

The first component is the *Internetwork Packet Exchange/Sequenced Packet Exchange (IPX/SPX)* interface. This interface provides the hardware communications routines that enable the workstation to communicate with its installed network card. The network card communicates with other network devices such as file servers.

The other component, called *NETX* monitors DOS calls from the application that is running on the workstation. NETX determines whether the DOS calls are for a file server or the local PC.

NETX intercepts and prepares requests. Before NETX hands requests to IPX, IPX.COM uses a LAN driver routine to control the station's network board and address. The LAN driver routine also is used to route outgoing data packets for delivery on the network. IPX reads the assigned addresses of returning data and directs the data to the proper area within a workstation's shell or the file server's operating system.

Important Messages

None

Notes

 The following message appears if you type IPX after you loaded the IPX.COM file at the workstation:

```
IPX/SPX already loaded.
```

Try to execute the NETx.COM file or log in to the file server or do both to use the IPX command.

See Also

NETX
PROTOCOLS

IPXS   :LOAD 3.11

Purpose

Used by other loadable modules that require STREAMS-based IPX protocol services.

Syntax

```
LOAD path IPXS
```

Option

path   Defines the full directory path to the directory that contains the loadable module. You can use DOS drive pointers such as A: or B:, or use a NetWare volume name. If no path is specified, the operating system assumes that the loadable module is in the SYS:SYSTEM subdirectory.

Rules and Considerations

Before you unload a protocol-stack NLM such as IPXS, unload all other loadable modules that may potentially use IPXS.

If your loadable module requires STREAMS-based IPX protocol services, load the following additional modules in the order listed before you load IPXS:

1. Load the STREAMS module
2. Load the CLIB module
3. Load the TLI module

Important Messages

None

Example

```
LOAD IPXS
```

The preceding example loads STREAMS-based IPX protocol services.

LISTDIR

Purpose

Lists subdirectories and subdirectory information.

Syntax

```
LISTDIR path options
```

Options

path
Specifies the directory path for which you want more information. The path can include the volume, directory, and subdirectory.

option
Specifies one or more of the following options:

/Rights
Lists the Inherited Rights Masks of all subdirectories in a specific directory.

/Effective rights
Lists the effective rights for all subdirectories of the specified directory.

/Date or /Time
Lists the date or time or both that a subdirectory was created.

/Subdirectories
Lists a directory's subdirectories.

/All   Lists all subdirectories,
                              their Inherited Rights
                              Masks, effective rights, and
                              their creation dates and
                              times.

Important Messages

None

Example

To list all subdirectories, inherited rights masks, effective rights, and
creation dates for everything in the WP51 directory, enter the command:

```
LISTDIR TRAINING_SOLUTIONS\SYS:APPS\WP51 /A
```

LOAD   : 3.11

Purpose

This command loads NetWare Loadable Modules (NLMs) at the file
server console.

Syntax

```
LOAD path NLM parameter
```

Options

path   Represents the full path to the directory that contains
                      the loadable module. The path variable can begin with
                      either a valid DOS drive letter or a valid NetWare
                      volume name. If you do not specify a path and the
                      SYS: volume has not been mounted, the operating sys-
                      tem (OS) assumes that the NLM is in the default DOS

partition or directory. After the volume SYS: has been mounted, the OS assumes the loadable module is in the SYS:SYSTEM directory.

NLM Specifies the name of one of the following types of NLMs:

Disk drivers

LAN drivers

Name space

NLM utilities

Consult either NETWARE, your reseller, or a third-party dealer for other available NLMs.

`parameter` Settings are specific to each NLM. Refer to the NLM's documentation for more information.

Rules and Considerations

To load modules automatically each time the server boots, store the appropriate LOAD commands in the AUTOEXEC.NCF or STARTUP.NCF file. See AUTOEXEC.NCF and STARTUP.NCF for more information.

 All NLMs should be certified by Novell, Inc. If you run any third-party NLMs, check with NETWARE or your Novell Authorized Reseller for a list of Novell approved NLMs. If you load a module that is not approved, your server may ABEND (an ABnormal END) and data may become corrupted.

NLMs will not load under any of the following conditions:

- The server cannot find the loadable module.
- The server does not have enough free memory.
- The module is dependent on another module that is not loaded.
- You used an invalid parameter.
- LOAD is not entered before the module name.
- You used an invalid command in the NCF files.

Important Messages

None

Example

To load the industry standard disk drive that supports many different hard disk drive controllers, enter the command:

```
LOAD ISADISK
```

Notes

An NLM links itself into the OS and allocates a portion of server memory for its own use.

Some NLMs will check the system memory for the existence of required NLMs at load time and automatically preload the required NLMs if necessary.

LOGIN

Purpose

Accesses the named or default server and invokes your login script on that particular file server.

Syntax

LOGIN *option fileserver/login_name scriptparameters*

Options

option   May be one or more of the following:

                                  /Script

| | /NoAttach |
| | /Clearscreen |

fileserver	Identifies the file server you want to log into
login_name	Specifies your user name or login name (account name, for example)
scriptparameters	Specifies the parameters set in your login script

Rules and Considerations

You may include a LOGIN command in your AUTOEXEC.BAT file. Then when you boot your workstation, it will attach itself to the logically closest file server. This becomes your default server.

If you automatically log in to several servers simultaneously, you can synchronize your password on all the servers where you use the same login or user name. If you change the password, LOGIN prompts if you want to synchronize passwords on all servers.

A LOGIN implies a LOGOUT, and thus logs you out of other servers. To access another server and remain logged in to your default server, use the ATTACH command instead.

Important Messages

None

Notes

LOGIN shows the last time the user logged into the file server.

If the password notification is set to yes in SYSCON, users are notified when their passwords will expire each time they log on.

See also

ATTACH
LOGOUT

LOGOUT

Purpose

Logs you out of file servers you are attached to.

Syntax

```
LOGOUT fileserver
```

Option

Replace *fileserver* with the name of the server you want to log out of. If you do not specify a file server, you will be logged out of all file servers you are attached to.

Rules and Considerations

When you log out of a server, drive mappings to that server disappear. You must have a search drive mapped to the PUBLIC directory of at least one of the servers you are still attached to, or you cannot execute any NetWare utilities.

Important Messages

None

See also

ATTACH
LOGIN

MAKEUSER

Purpose

This utility creates and deletes user accounts on a regular basis. Makeuser is commonly used to set up user accounts for new students each semester, create accounts for temporary employees, or to batch add many users at once. Workgroup managers often use MAKEUSER to create their users.

Syntax

```
MAKEUSER
```

Options

None

Rules and Considerations

To create and delete users with the MAKEUSER command, you first must create a USR script file. This file contains the keywords necessary to create the user(s), assign rights, assign trustee restrictions, assign a home directory to new users, or delete existing users from the system.

To modify or process a USR file, you must be in the directory where that file is located. You can use any ASCII text editor to create USR files, but the file must be saved in ASCII format and have a USR extension.

You must process the USR file with MAKEUSER before the accounts are created or deleted.

The keywords used in a USR file to create and delete users in MAKEUSER are as follows:

#ACCOUNT EXPIRATION month day year

#ACCOUNTING balance, lowlimit

#CLEAR or #RESET

#CONNECTIONS number

#CREATE user name [option ...]

#DELETE user name

#GROUPS group

#HOME_DIRECTORY path

#LOGIN_SCRIPT path

#MAX_DISK_SPACE vol, number

#PASSWORD_LENGTH length

#PASSWORD_PERIOD days

#PASSWORD_REQUIRED

#PURGE_USER_DIRECTORY

#REM or REM

#RESTRICTED_TIME day, start, end

#STATIONS network, station

#UNIQUE_PASSWORD

Important Messages

If USR file contains errors, you might see a message similar to the following:

```
Error   :  Line 001, Undefined keyword
Warning:  Line 002, Group expected
Please fix the error in the file and try it again.
```

Notes

 Create a directory for all USR files. When you create a USR file, the MAKEUSER command places the file in the current directory.

See also

USERDEF

Purpose

Lists, creates, or changes logical drive mappings in the NetWare environment.

Syntax

```
MAP parameters drive:=path
```

Options

parameters can be one of the following:

INSert	Alters search drive mappings
DELete	Deletes a drive mapping
REMove	Deletes a drive mapping
Next	Maps next available drive letter to the specified path
ROOT	Maps the drive as fake root (useful for Windows applications)
drive	The drive letter mapped to the directory you want to work with
path	Directory path you intend to work with

Rules and Considerations

When attempting to map a drive to a specified path, the path named in the MAP command must exist.

You must be attached to a file server before you can map drives to it.

Important Messages

None

Examples

To list all currently active mappings, type the following:

```
MAP
```

Your screen display should resemble the following:

```
Drive A:   maps to a local drive
Drive B:   maps to a local drive
Drive C:   maps to a local drive
Drive D:   maps to a local drive
Drive E:   maps to a local drive

Drive F:= TRAINING_SOLUTIONS/SYS:
Drive G:= TRAINING_SOLUTIONS/SYS:USERS/GUEST /
SEARCH1:=Z:. [TRAINING_SOLUTIONS/SYS: /PUBLIC/]
SEARCH2:=Y:. [TRAINING_SOLUTIONS/SYS: /PUBLIC/
IBM_PC/MSDOS/V5.00]
```

To map a fake root for applications (such as Windows applications) that write files to or create directories off the root directory, type the following:

```
MAP NEXT ROOT SYS:WINAPPS
```

If you then type **MAP** to view the active drive mappings, you should see the following screen display:

```
Drive A:   maps to a local drive
Drive B:   maps to a local drive
Drive C:   maps to a local drive
Drive D:   maps to a local drive
Drive E:   maps to a local drive

Drive F:= TRAINING_SOLUTIONS/SYS:
Drive G:= TRAINING_SOLUTIONS/SYS:USERS/GUEST /
Drive H:= TRAINING_SOLUTIONS/SYS:WINAPPS /

SEARCH1:=Z:. [TRAINING_SOLUTIONS/SYS: /PUBLIC/]
SEARCH2:=Y:. [TRAINING_SOLUTIONS/SYS:/PUBLIC/
IBM_PC/MSDOS/V5.00/]
```

The space between the end of the path and the last slash indicates that this is a fake rooted drive.

To map an additional search drive, type the following:

MAP S16:=SYS:APPS\FOXPRO

By typing **S16:** for the search drive, you automatically assign it to the last available search drive position open.

Notes

Drive mappings are valid only for the active session unless you save them in your login script.

From a fake root, you cannot use the DOS CD (change directory) command to return to the original root directory. To change to the original root, you must remap the drive. Or you can type the CD command and reference the volume level as follows:

CD SYS:TRIVIA

The MAP command accepts either forward slashes (/) or backslashes (\) as part of the path. To maintain consistency with DOS, however, it is suggested you use only backslashes (\) in the path designation.

See also

SESSION

MATHLIB   :LOAD 3.11

Purpose

Loads a library of support routines, if your server has a math coprocessor (such as a 386 machine with a math coprocessor or a 486DX machine).

Syntax

```
LOAD path MATHLIB
```

Option

path   Specifies the path to the directory containing the NLM. Can begin with either a DOS drive letter or a NetWare volume name.

Rules and Considerations

If you do not specify a path, the operating system assumes the NLM is in SYS:SYSTEM.

If you need MATHLIB, the following modules need to be loaded in the exact order listed as follows:

   STREAMS
   CLIB
   MATHLIB

Important Messages

None

Notes

To make sure that the modules necessary for MATHLIB load automatically when the file server boots, add the following commands to the AUTOEXEC.NCF file.

LOAD STREAMS
LOAD CLIB
LOAD MATHLIB

See also

INSTALL

MATHLIBC :LOAD 3.11

Purpose

Loads a library of support routines if your server does not have a math coprocessor (such as a 386 machine without a math coprocessor).

Syntax

```
LOAD path MATHLIBC
```

Option

path   Represents the full path to the directory containing the NLM. Can begin with a valid DOS drive letter or NetWare volume name.

Rules and Considerations

You must load CLIB before you load MATHLIBC.

The following modules must be loaded in the exact order listed as follows:

STREAMS
CLIB
MATHLIBC

If you do not specify a path, the operating system assumes that the NLM resides in SYS:SYSTEM. (Use SEARCH to set up additional paths for searching.)

Important Messages

None

Notes

To make certain that the NLMs necessary to support MATHLIB load when the file server boots, add the following commands to the AUTOEXEC.NCF file:

```
LOAD STREAMS
LOAD CLIB
LOAD MATHLIBC
```

See also

INSTALL

MEMORY : 3.11

Purpose

Views the total amount of the memory the operating system can address in the file server.

Syntax

MEMORY

Options

None

Rules and Considerations

NetWare v3.x addresses all memory installed in an EISA computer. If you have either a microchannel or ISA computer, the operating system only addresses up to 16M of memory. Use the REGISTER MEMORY command to enable the operating system to address the memory above 16M.

Important Messages

None

Example

To display all of the memory the operating system can address, type the following:

MEMORY

See also

REGISTER MEMORY

MENU   F>

Purpose

Invokes a custom menu that you have created. See Chapter 9 for information on creating custom menus.

Syntax

MENU *filename*

Options

None

Rules and Considerations

When using the MENU command, you must specify the extension of the option file name unless you use the extension MNU.

Example

MENU main

Important Messages

None

MODULES   : 3.11

Purpose

Displays information about the modules currently loaded at the file server. You see the short name of the module, the long name of the module, and version information about your LAN and DISK driver modules.

Syntax

MODULES

Options

None

Important Messages

None

See also

LOAD

MONITOR

Purpose

Locks the console, enables the screen saver, and enables you to monitor how efficiently the network is operating. When used with NetWare 3.11, the MONITOR command displays the following:

```
Utilization and overall activity
Cache memory status
Connections and their status
Disk drives
Mounted volumes
LAN xdrivers
Loaded modules
File lock status
Memory usage
```

Syntax

```
LOAD path MONITOR parameter
```

Options

path
: Full path beginning with a DOS drive letter or NetWare volume name. If you do not specify a path, and volume SYS has been mounted, the operating system assumes the module is in SYS:SYSTEM unless other search paths have been added.

parameter can be one of the following:

ns
: (No screen saver). Disables the screen saver option. If you do not use ns, a utilization snake appears on the screen after a few minutes of console keyboard inactivity. To redisplay the MONITOR screen, press any key.

nh
: (No help). Prevents MONITOR HELP from loading.

p
: Displays information about the file server microprocessor

Rules and Considerations

None

Important Messages

```
This module is ALREADY loaded and cannot be loaded
more than once.
```

If MONITOR is already loaded, the preceding message appears. If it does, do one of the following:

Press Alt-Esc to move through the activated screens until the MONITOR screen appears.

Press Ctrl-Esc and select Monitor Screen from the list of available screens.

Notes

The MONITOR command can perform the following tasks:

- List active connections
- List physical record locks
- Clear a connection
- List open files
- List system disk drives
- List volume segments per drive
- Change the "Read After Write Verify" status
- Flash the hard disk light
- Activate/deactivate a hard disk
- Mount/dismount a removable media device
- Lock/unlock a removable media device
- List LAN drivers and statistics
- List system modules
- List resources used by system modules
- Lock the console
- Unlock the console
- Check file status
- View mounted volumes
- View memory statistics
- View tracked resources
- Exit

MONITOR   : 2.2

Purpose

Tracks and displays the activities of all workstations that are logged in to or attached to the file server. Also displays the activities of VAPs and enables you to see what files each station is using and possibly locking. MONITOR also displays the file server's utilization.

Syntax

```
MONITOR number
```

Option

Replace *number* with the station you want to monitor. If you omit *number*, stations 1 through 7 are displayed by default.

Rules and Considerations

Include a station number if you want to monitor the activities of one specific workstation. This information can be obtained using the FCONSOLE command.

The MONITOR command screen displays information on six stations at once.

MONITOR also displays the operating system version and the percentage of file server utilization.

When a workstation requests a transaction, MONITOR displays up to five files and a file status message. A file server running NetWare in dedicated mode also can display two status letters. File status also can have an identifier, and the request area often will display a message.

Important Messages

None

Example

```
MONITOR
```

Notes

Execute MONITOR if you suspect an application has crashed at a particular workstation. The display might show W for 20 minutes on a small file, indicating a Write operation has locked the workstation.

Every file shown has an accompanying DOS task number to the left of the status field.

The request area to the right of each station number indicates the most recent file server request the workstation made. The following is a list of valid requests that NetWare might display:

```
Alloc Resource Record
Begin Trans File
Clear File
Clear File Set
Clear Record Set
Close File
Clr Phy Rec
Clr Phy Rec Set
Copy File
Create File
Dir Search
End of Job
End Trans
Erase File
Floppy Config
Get File Size
Lock File
Lock Phy Rec Set
Lock Record
Log Out
Log Pers File
Log Phy Rec
Log Record
Open File
Pass File
Read File
Rel Phy Rec
Rel Phy Rec Set
```

```
Rel Record Set
Rel Resource
Release File
Release File Set
Release Record
Rename File
Search Next
Semaphore
Set File Atts
Start Search
Sys Log
Unlock Record
Win Format
Win Read
Win Write
Write File
```

See also

OFF

MOUNT   :

Purpose

Places the volume in service. By mounting the volume, users have access to the information about that volume. The MOUNT command can be used while the file server is running.

Syntax

MOUNT *volume_name* or **ALL**

Options

volume_name   Specifies the volume name you want to put into service or mount

ALL   Enables you to mount all volumes without specifying the names of each volume

Rules and Considerations

If you have volumes that are not used often, it is wise to leave them
dismounted until you need them. When you mount a volume, it uses
file server memory; this lessens the amount of memory you have available for file caching.

Important Messages

```
Volume  volume_name could NOT be mounted.
Some or all volume segments cannot be located.
```

This message is displayed if the volume you specified does not exist
or has a problem.

See also

DISMOUNT

NAME

Purpose

Displays the name of the file server.

Syntax

NAME

Options

None

Rules and Considerations

When you invoke the NAME command, you see the name of the file server in a format similar to the following:

```
This is server TRAINING_SOLUTIONS
```

Important Messages

None

NCOPY   F>

Purpose

Copies one or more files from one location to another.

The NCOPY command works much like the DOS COPY command. The big difference between the two is that NCOPY performs the copy at the file server itself. The DOS COPY command reads data from the file server and then writes the data back to the file server over the network. The NCOPY command is much faster and does not slow down the network as much as the DOS COPY command would.

The NCOPY command is placed in the PUBLIC directory during installation.

Syntax

```
NCOPY path FILENAME to path FILENAME option
```

Leave a space between the source file name and the destination directory path. The NCOPY command supports wildcard characters and up to 25 directory levels. When the copied file lands in the destination directory, it retains the original's date and time.

Options

/**A**	Copies only files that have the archive bit set. Will not reset the archive bit.
/**C**OPY	Copies files without preserving the attributes or name space information.
/**E**MPTY	Copies empty subdirectories when you copy an entire directory with the /S option.
/**F**ORCE	Forces the operating system to write sparse files.
/**I**NFORM	Notifies you when attributes or name space information cannot be copied.
/**M**	Copies only files that have the archive bit set, and will reset the archive bit after copying.
/**P**RESERVE	Copies SYSTEM and HIDDEN files and preserves attributes.
/**S**UBDIRECTORIES	Copies all the files and subdirectories.
/**V**ERIFY	Verifies that the original file and the copy are identical.
/**H**elp /?	Displays usage guide.

Rules and Considerations

You may use wildcards to copy more than one file at a time. The NCOPY command automatically preserves a file's attributes.

Important Messages

None

Examples

To copy all the dbf files from drive G: to drive H:, type the following:

```
NCOPY G:*.dbf H:
```

To copy all of the dat files from the REPORTS directory to the ARCHIVE\JULY directory, type the following:

```
NCOPY SYS:DATA\REPORTS\*.DAT SYS:ARCHIVE\JULY
```

You then see the source and destination of the file as well as the names of the files being copied; it should resemble the following:

```
From     TRAINING_SOLUTIONS/SYS:DATA/REPORTS
To       TRAINING_SOLUTIONS/SYS:ARCHIVE/JULY
   MASTER.DAT to   MASTER.DAT
   MAILING.DATto   MAILING.DAT
 2 files copied.
```

See also

FILER

NDIR   F>

Purpose

Lists detailed file and subdirectory information, including NetWare specific information. The NDIR command can perform the following functions:

List files and subdirectories

Search a volume for a file

List specific files

Use wildcards to list related files

Use an option to list files

Use several options to list files

List Macintosh files

Syntax

NDIR *path option* . . .

Options

path   Identifies the directory path leading to and including the directory and file you want to list. You can include a file chain of up to 16 filenames.

option   Can be one of the following:

             Attribute options

             Format options

             Restriction options

             Sort options

A list of the more commonly used options follows. Use a space between multiple options.

RO   Lists files that have the read only attribute set.

S   Lists files that have the shareable attribute set.

A   Lists files that have their archive attribute set. Files are displayed in the backup format, which lists the last modified and last archived dates. The archive flag is set whenever a file is modified.

EX   Lists files that are flagged as execute only.

H   Lists files or directories that have the hidden attribute set.

SY   Lists files or directories that have the system attribute set.

T   Lists files that have been flagged as transactional.

I   Lists files that have been flagged as index files.

P	Lists files or directories that have the purge attribute set. (NetWare 3.x only.)
RA	Lists files flagged as read audit. (NetWare 3.x only.) (Not currently implemented.)
WA	Lists files flagged as write audit. (NetWare 3.x only.) (Not currently implemented.)
CI	Lists files flagged as copy inhibited. Restricts copyrights of users logged in from Macintosh workstation. Only valid for files.
DI	Lists files or directories flagged as delete inhibited. Prevents users from erasing directories or files even if they have the erase right.
RI	Lists file and directories flagged as rename inhibited. Prevents users from renaming directories and files even if they have the Modify right.
D	Lists time and date stamp information about files. Shows the date last modified, last archived, last accessed, and the date created.
R	Lists your access rights on selected files (NetWare 3.11 only); lists inherited and effective rights on files and subdirectories, and shows file flags. On NetWare 2.x systems, no rights are associated with files, therefore the rights field will be empty.
MAC	Lists Macintosh subdirectories or files in a search area. When you list only Macintosh files or subdirectories, they appear with their full Macintosh names.
LONG	Lists all Macintosh, OS/2, and NFS long file names for the file under all loaded name spaces in a given search area.
HELP	Lists the NDIR command format and available command options.
OW	Lists files created by a specific user.
SI	Lists files by their sizes.
UP	Lists files by their last update date.

CR   Lists file by their creation date.

AC   Lists file by their last accessed date.

AR   Lists files by their archive date.

FO   Lists only files in a directory.

DO   Lists only subdirectories in a directory.

SUB   Applies the NDIR command to all subdirectories and subsequent subdirectories in a directory.

Rules and Considerations

Use a forward slash (/) before the first element of the option list and backslashes (\) in path names.

Each NDIR command can include up to 16 filenames.

Important Messages

None

Example

To list all files in all subdirectories on the NetWare volume SYS, type the following:

```
NDIR SYS:*.* /SUB FO
```

The FO option excludes the listing of any subdirectory names found during the directory search.

Note

You may combine several restriction options in a single NDIR command line. For a full listing of all options and logical operators supported, use NDIR /HELP or refer to the documentation included with NetWare.

See also

FILER

FLAG

NETBIOS   F> 3.11

Purpose

Enables workstations to run applications that support IBM's NETBIOS networking calls. You also can view NetWare NETBIOS version information, determine whether NETBIOS has been loaded, determine which interrupt it is using, or unload NETBIOS.

Syntax

NETBIOS *options*

Options

Inquire   Views version information, whether NETBIOS has been loaded, and which interrupt it is using. Using this switch will not reload NETBIOS.

Unload   Unloads NETBIOS from memory.

Important Messages

None

Example

NETBIOS

NETX.COM   F> 3.11

Purpose

Provides an interface between the application and DOS. NETX inter-cepts all interrupt 21h DOS requests and inspects each one. After in-spection, the shell either passes the request to the DOS interrupt routine or keeps it and converts the request into the appropriate NCP request, and sends it to IPX/SPX for transmission to the file server.

Older versions of the shell included NETx.COM. The X in NETx.COM is replaced with the version of DOS you are using at the workstation—NET3.COM for DOS 3.x, NET4.COM for DOS 4.x, and NET5.COM for DOS 5.x. There is a generic version of NETx.COM called NETX.COM.

Syntax

    NETX *option*

Options

/I	Displays information about the shell type and the revision level of the NETx file.
/U	Unloads the NETx shell from the workstation's memory. NETx must be the last terminate and stay resident (TSR) program loaded.
PS=servername	Specifies your preferred server. The shell at-tempts to attach you to the server you specify rather than the first available.

Rules and Considerations

NETX.COM must be loaded after IPX.COM has been loaded.

Important Messages

```
Not running on top of DOS 3.x.
```

This message means you tried to load the wrong version of NETX. Use the VER command to find the version of DOS you are using and execute the proper NETX.COM command.

See also

IPX/SPX

NMAGENT.NLM :LOAD 3.11

Purpose

Manages LAN drivers by collecting and storing information about them as they are loaded.

Syntax

```
LOAD path NMAGENT
```

The path should be specified only if the NMAGENT.NLM file is not in the SYS:SYSTEM directory.

Options

None

Rules and Considerations

The NMAGENT (Network Management Agent) command must be loaded prior to any LAN drivers being loaded to enable it to register the LAN drivers. If NMAGENT has not been loaded, NetWare will attempt to load NMAGENT before it honors a request to load a LAN driver.

Examples

To load NMAGENT from the SYS:LOGIN directory, type the following:

```
LOAD SYS:LOGIN/NMAGENT
```

To load NMAGENT from the SYS:SYSTEM directory of file server FS1, type the following:

```
LOAD NMAGENT
```

Note

 See the Netware System Administration manual for a list of the resources that are tracked by NMAGENT.

NPRINT

Purpose

Sends a file from the disk to a NetWare print queue. The NPRINT command is the NetWare substitute for the DOS PRINT command.

Syntax

```
NPRINT filespec options
```

Options

NPRINT supports the following options:

Banner=*banner name*   Determines whether a banner (a word or phrase up to 12 characters) is printed. Spaces are entered by using the underscore character (above the minus on most keyboards). The default is the name of the file you are printing.

Copies=*n*	Specifies the number of copies to print from 1 to 999.
Delete	Deletes a file immediately after it is printed.
Form=*frm*	Specifies the name or number of a previously defined form. The default is the form specified in your default print job configuration if it has been defined.
Form**F**eed	Sends a form feed to the printer after the job has printed. The default is enabled.
Job=*jobname*	Specifies which print job configuration to use. Print job configurations can be created using PRINTCON. A single print job configuration can define the settings for all of the options for NPRINT with a single option.
NAMe=*username*	Specifies the name that appears on the top part of the banner page. The default is the user's login name.
No**B**anner	Prints without the banner page. The default is for the banner page to print.
No**F**orm**F**eed	Does not send a form feed to the printer after the job has printed. The default is to send a form feed to the printer after a job has printed.
No**NOTI**fy	Prevents the operating system from notifying you when a print job has finished printing. (This option is only necessary if NOTIfy is enabled in your print job configuration and you want to ignore it.)
No**T**abs	Stops NetWare from altering your tabs before they are sent to the printer.
NOTIfy	Notifies you when the print job has been sent to the printer.

Queue=*queuename*	Identifies which queue the job is sent to. Queues may be defined with PCONSOLE.
Server=*servername*	Specifies which server the print job should be sent to for printing. The default is the current server.
Tabs=*n*	Indicates the number of spaces between tabs, ranging from 0 to 18. The default is 8 spaces.

Rules and Considerations

To use the NPRINT command, you first must create print queues. You can manage print queues with the PCONSOLE menu utility program.

If you execute NPRINT with the filespec to print and no options, the file will be sent to the print queue specified in the default print job configuration. If no default print job configuration has been set, the print job will be sent to, for example, PRINTQ_0, or the name of your default queue.

Print job configurations should be created with the PRINTCON menu utility program before use.

Forms should be defined with the PRINTDEF menu utility program prior to using them in print job configurations.

Important Messages

```
Access to the server FS1 denied.
```

This error occurs if you attempt to use NPRINT to print to server FS1 using the Server=FS1 option, and you were denied access to the server. The GUEST account is usually used to attach to another server for printing purposes. If the GUEST account has a password assigned, you will get this error message.

To correct the error, attach to the server you are trying to print from and supply your correct user name and password for that server, or get the supervisor to remove the password requirements for the GUEST user.

```
Illegal banner specification. (length 1 - 12)
```

This error occurs if you attempt to use the `banner=` option without entering a banner name, or if you enter a banner longer than 12 characters.

To print a print job without a banner use the NB option instead of trying `banner=(nothing)`.

Examples

To send 10 copies of the OLDMEMO.TXT file in the root directory of drive A: to the printer serviced by the print queue HPLASER, type the following:

NPRINT A:\OLDMEMO.TXT Q=HPLASER C=10 NB NOTIFY

The print job prints without a banner, and the user is notified when the print job has been completely sent to the printer.

To send one copy of the MYMEMO.TXT file in the current directory to the printer serviced by PRINTQ_1, type the following:

NPRINT MYMEMO.TXT Q=PRINTQ_1

The print job prints with a banner showing the user's name on the upper half and MYMEMO.TXT on the lower half. The user will not be notified when the print job is completed.

To send the number of copies of the file 123DATA.PRN in the current directory to the printer serviced by the print queue defined in the print job configuration called TOSHIBA, type the following:

NPRINT 123DATA.PRN J=TOSHIBA

This print job configuration contains settings for tabs, notification, form feeds, banners, copies, and so on. Print job configurations are created with the PRINTCON utility.

Notes

Be careful when using the Delete option when printing a file you cannot reproduce. In the case of a paper jam, or even in some instances when a printer is turned off, when you send something to its print queues, you could be left without your printout and without the file necessary to re-create the printout.

 Use the NB (NoBanner) option when sending EPS (encapsulated postscript) files to a postscript printer to be certain that the banner information does not interfere with the printing of the postscript information.

Use the NFF option when the file you are printing contains a form feed as the last character. If so, an extra blank page is printed after your print file. If this is the case, print the file with the NFF option.

Use PCONSOLE to cancel erroneous print jobs you have started printing using NPRINT.

Refer to Chapter 8 for information on setting up print jobs using the following NetWare Menu Utilities: PCONSOLE, PRINTCON, and PRINTDEF.

See also

CAPTURE

NVER

Purpose

Reports the versions of NetBIOS, IPX/SPX, LAN driver, workstation shell, workstation DOS, and file server operating system for your file server and workstation.

Syntax

NVER

Options

None

Example

NVER

The NVER displays the following sample output:

```
NETWARE VERSION UTILITY, VERSION 3.12
IPX Version: 3.02
SPX Version: 3.02

LAN Driver: NetWare Ethernet NE2000 V1.03EC (891227) V1.00
            IRQ = 2, I/O Base = 340h, no DMA or RAM

Shell:      V3.10 Rev. A
DOS:        MSDOS V5.00 on IBM_PC

FileServer: FS1
Novell Dedicated NetWare V2.2(100) Rev. A (02/11/91)
```

Notes

 Use DOS redirection (>) to redirect NVER output to a file or printer. You will find the version information handy when trying to diagnose software problems or find differences between two workstations.

Refer to the NetWare manuals for information on the SYSCON and FCONSOLE menu utilities, which report file server software version information and performance statistics.

See also

IPX

NETx

OFF :

Purpose

Clears the file server console screen, similar to CLS in DOS.

Syntax

OFF

Options

None

Example

OFF

Important Messages

None

Notes

 Using OFF to clear an active MONITOR screen adds to the life of your video display and increases performance slightly.

PAUDIT F>

Purpose

Displays the system's accounting records including login time, logout time, service charges and intruder detection information.

Syntax

PAUDIT

Options

None

Rules and Considerations

To use PAUDIT, the accounting services first must be installed on your file server using SYSCON.

Example

To display systems information, type the following:

PAUDIT

The screen returns information such as the following:

```
12/15/92 21:34:37  File server FS1
   NOTE: about User DKLADIS during File Server services.
   Login from address 99000001:00001B0ACD9C.
12/15/92 22:40:07  File Server FS1
   NOTE: about User DKLADIS during File Server services.
   Logout from address 99000001:00001B0ACD9C.
12/16/92 7:49:12  File Server FS1
   NOTE: about User SUPERVISOR during File Server services.
   Login from address 99000001:0080C820A5FB.
12/16/92 9:23:56  File Server FS1
   NOTE: about User SUPERVISOR during File Server services.
   Logout from address 99000001:0080C820A5FB.
12/16/92 9:24:36  File Server FS1
   NOTE: about User LBUCK during File Server services.
   Login from address 99000001:00001B0ACD9C.
```

Important Messages

None

Notes

PAUDIT.EXE is located in SYS:SYSTEM. Make sure you change to SYS:SYSTEM before you try to run PAUDIT.

 Press Pause on newer 101-key keyboards to stop the scrolling, or press Ctrl-S on older keyboards.

You can redirect output from PAUDIT to a file with the DOS redirection operator (>), such as: **PAUDIT > TODAY.AUD**.

You can reset the accounting detail by erasing the NET$ACCT.DAT file in the SYS:SYSTEM directory.

See also

ATOTAL

PRINTER

Purpose

The PRINTER console command enables many options for controlling NetWare printers. This command is available in NetWare 286 only. Most of these functions may be performed using PRINTCON under both NetWare 286 and 386.

Syntax

PRINTER *options*

or

P *options*

Options

The PRINTER command has many functions, as shown in the following list. Be sure to substitute a valid printer number for the variable n. Valid printer numbers range from 0 to 4.

PRINTER	Lists information about printers attached to the file server, including on-line status, mounted forms, form number mounted, and the number of queues that are being serviced.
PRINTER HELP	Lists printer commands available from the file server console.
PRINTER n ADD QUEUE queuename [AT PRIORITY]	Adds an existing queue to printer n.
PRINTER n CONFIG	Shows the configuration for printer n.
PRINTER n CREATE port	Creates a NetWare printer process for a particular port. Valid port options are COM1, COM2, LPT1, LPT2, and so on.
PRINTER n CREATE COMx options	Changes configuration of a serial printer n attached to the file server's serial printer port x.

The options that are not specified remain unchanged. These options include the following:

Baud is the baud rate in bits per second

Wordsize is the number of data bits

Parity is the type of parity

XonXoff is handshaking

Stopbits is the number of stop bits

Poll is the polling period

`PRINTER n DELETE QUEUE queuename`	Stops a printer from servicing a particular queue temporarily. The queue may be added again with `PRINTER n ADD QUEUE queuename`.
`PRINTER n FORM FEED`	Sends a form feed to printer n.
`PRINTER n FORM MARK`	Prints a line of asterisks (*) marking the current top of form for printer n.
`PRINTER n MOUNT FORM frm`	Changes the type of form mounted in printer n to form number *frm*. Use PRINTDEF to define forms.
`PRINTER n POLL period`	Sets the polling period (Amount of time the printer process waits to check printer queues for print jobs). The polling period default is 15 seconds and may be set from 1 to 60 seconds.
`PRINTER n QUEUE`	Displays a list of printer queues and priority levels.
`PRINTER n REWIND p PAGES`	Restarts the current print job on printer n, first rewinding the print job p number of pages. If the print job does not contain form feeds, or you attempt to rewind more than 9 pages, the print job will restart at the beginning.
`PRINTER n START`	Restarts a printer that has been stopped with `PRINTER n STOP`.
`PRINTER n STOP`	Stops printer n. The printer can be restarted with `PRINTER n START`.

Rules and Considerations

Valid printer numbers range from 0 to 4.

Important Messages

None

Example

To use the PRINTER console command to set up NetWare core print-ing for a laser printer attached to LPT1: as printer 0 on the file server and assign it to an existing print queue named HPLASER, type the following:

```
PRINTER 0 CREATE LPT1

PRINTER 0 ADD HPLASER
```

To print a line of asterisks at the top of the page to check form align-ment on a matrix printer attached to the file server as printer 2, type the following:

```
PRINTER 2 FORM MARK
```

To re-start a printout a couple of pages back after a printer jam on a printer attached to the file server as printer 1, type the following:

```
PRINTER 1 REWIND 2 PAGES
```

Note

 The PRINTER command controls and creates print jobs that also are controlled through several NetWare menu utilities. Information on these menu utilities can be found in Chapter 8. See PCONSOLE, PRINTDEF, PRINTCON, and SYSCON for more information on creating and controlling printer pro-cesses and print jobs.

See also

PSC
PSERVER (DOS executable)
PSERVER (loadable module)
PSTAT

PSC   F> 3.11

Purpose

The PSC command offers many of the same features as the NetWare PCONSOLE menu utility regarding printer status checking and print server control. If you use PSC, these status checking and print server control features are available from the DOS command line.

Syntax

PSC PS=*printservername* P=*printernumber* options

Replace `printservername` with the name of the print server you want to check or manage.

Replace `printernumber` with the number of the printer you want to check or manage.

See the Switches section for a list of valid options.

Options

Option	Meaning	Description
AB	ABort	Cancels the current print job and continues with the next print job in the queue.

Option	Meaning	Description
CD	CancelDown	Use this option to reverse the effects of the "Going down after current jobs" selection in PCONSOLE
STAT	STATus	Displays the status of the printer.
PAU	PAUse	Pauses printing temporarily.
STO	STOp	Stops the printer. Use **STOP Keep** to resubmit the current job. Without Keep, the current job is deleted.
STAR	STARt	Starts the printer after it has been paused or stopped.
M	Mark	Prints a line of asterisks on the current line.
FF	Form Feed	Advances the printer to the top of the next page. The printer first must be paused or stopped.
MO F=n	MOunt Form	Replaces n with the number of a form that has been defined in PRINTDEF.
PRI	PRIvate	Changes a remote printer to a local printer so that network users cannot access it.
SH	SHared	Changes a private printer back to shared status.

Rules and Considerations

Print server operators can use any of the PSC features; regular NetWare users can use only the status checking features.

You can include PS= or P= or both with the PSC command.

Printer numbers are defined first using the PCONSOLE menu utility when the print server is set up. They may then be used with PSC from the DOS command line.

Important Messages

```
You must specify the print server name.
```

In the preceding message, PSC requires that you specify a print server name. If you want to set a default print server, use the SET PSC command. The following message appears if a syntax error appears in the PSC command:

```
The specified action is not supported.
```

To correct this problem, retype the PSC command line carefully and check spelling and syntax.

Example

To stop an unwanted printing of the current job on print server ACCTNG, enter the following:

```
PSC PS=ACCTNG P=1 STOP
```

To notify NetWare that you have changed the type of paper loaded in printer 2 on printserver ADMIN to a paper type of 35, enter the following:

```
PSC PS=ADMIN P=2 MO F=35
```

Notes

 Many of these functions can be performed with PCONSOLE if a menu-driven utility is preferred. PSC is particularly helpful in batch files.

See also

PRINTER

PSERVER.EXE   A>DOS EXECUTABLE
(DOS executable)   3.11, 2.2, 2.1x

Purpose

Use PSERVER to configure a personal computer as a dedicated print
server.

Syntax

PSERVER *fileservername* **printservername**

The *fileservername* parameter is optional. Specify a valid print server
name for the *printservername* parameter.

Rules and Considerations

Before you can run PSERVER, you must first use the NetWare
PCONSOLE command to configure the print server.

Print servers created with the PSERVER command can support up to
16 printers and can service queues up to 8 file servers.

To run PSERVER, you must have access to IBM$RUN.OVL,
SYS$ERR.DAT, SYS$HELP.DAT, and SYS$MSG.DAT.

See the Chapter 8 for more information on the PSERVER.EXE program.

Important Messages

If you have a print server named LASERS and the following message
appears, you already started a print server named LASERS:

There is already a print server named LASERS running.

If you want to load a second print server with the same configuration
as LASERS, create another print server and give it a different name.

If the following message appears when you try to print from your workstation on the network, your workstation does not have enough SPX connections:

```
There are not enough SPX connections to run the print
server.
```

To create more SPX connections, add the following line to the SHELL.CFG file in the workstation's boot directory:

```
SPX CONNECTIONS=60
```

Example

To load a print server named ACCTNG on the ADMIN file server, enter:

```
PSERVER ADMIN ACCTNG
```

Note

 Use the PCONSOLE command from any workstation to shut down a print server that was started with the PSERVER command.

See also

PSERVER.NLM (loadable module)
PSC

PSERVER.NLM :LOAD 3.11

Purpose

Loads a print server on a NetWare 3.11 file server. PSERVER is a loadable module.

Syntax

`LOAD` *path* `PSERVER` ***printservername***

The path should be specified only if the PSERVER.NLM file is not in the SYS:SYSTEM directory.

Rules and Considerations

Before you can load PSERVER, you must use the PCONSOLE NetWare menu utility to set up print queues, print servers and, printers.

The PSERVER.NLM command can support a total of 16 printers, including as many as 5 local printers depending on the number of parallel and serial ports on the server. The PSERVER.NLM command can support up to 16 remote printers run using the RPRINTER command.

Important Messages

None

Example

To start a print server called MAIN that has already been configured with the PCONSOLE menu utility, switch to the file server console and enter the following command:

`LOAD PSERVER MAIN`

Note

 It is usually desirable to load PSERVER automatically each time you boot the file server. To do so, use the INSTALL command to include a `LOAD PSERVER` *printservername* command in the server's AUTOEXEC.NCF file. Replace *printservername* with the name of the print server you want to load.

See also

PSERVER.EXE (DOS executable)

PSTAT   F> 2.2

Purpose

Displays printer status information.

Syntax

PSTAT S=servername P=printer

Options

S=*servername*   Designates the name of a valid file server.

P=*printer*   Designates *printer* is either a valid printer name or printer number.

Rules and Considerations

Before you can use the PSTAT command to check printers on a server, you must first attach or log in to the server.

You do not need to supply the name of the server (S= option) if it is the default server.

Important Messages

None

Notes

An off-line printer will be listed as on-line until you attempt to print to it.

Use the PCONSOLE NetWare menu utility to obtain individual print job status.

See also

PRINTER

PSC

PURGE

Purpose

Prevents previously erased files from being salvaged.

Syntax

```
PURGE filepath /ALL
```

Options

filepath   An optional parameter that accepts wild-card characters.

/ALL   Deletes all recoverable files in the current directory and in all subdirectories.

Rules and Considerations

If you type Purge with no options, all of the recoverable files in the current directory will be removed. The Purge command used with no

options has the same effect as entering a file path with the *.*
wildcards.

Important Messages

None

Example

To permanently remove all recoverable erased files on a file server
volume, log in as SUPERVISOR and enter the following command at
the volume root directory:

```
PURGE /ALL
```

To purge only your DOC files in the SHAREDOC directory on file
server FS2 on volume DATA, enter the command:

```
PURGE FS2/DATA:SHAREDOC\*.DOC
```

Note

 See related information in Chapters 9 and 10 on the SALVAGE
and FCONSOLE menu utility programs.

QUEUE : 2.2

Purpose

Creates and maintains NetWare print queues. Displays a list of print
queues including information about the number of jobs in each print
queue, print queue name, and the number of printers servicing each
queue.

Syntax

```
QUEUE options
```

or

    Q *options*

Options

HELP	Displays a list of valid options.
queuename CHANGE JOB *jobnumber* TO PRIORITY *prioritylevel*	The *quename* variable is the name of a valid print queue. The *jobnumber* variable is replaced by a particular print job whose priority you want to change. The *prioritylevel* variable is the new priority level for the print job that you want to change. A priority level of 1 will move the print job to the top of the queue; a priority level of 1 plus the number of jobs in the queue will move the job to the end of the queue.
QUEUE *queuename* CREATE	Use the *queuename* variable for the name for the new print queue. Used in lieu of PCONSOLE to create print queues from the console instead of a workstation.
QUEUE *queuename* DELETE JOB *jobnumber*	In the *queuename* location, specify the print queue that contains the print job(s) you would like to cancel. The *jobnumber* is the actual number of the particular print job. If you type an asterisk for the job number, all print jobs in the queue will be deleted.
QUEUE *queuename* DESTROY	Completely destroys the print queue *queuename* and all of its print jobs.
QUEUE *queuename* JOBS	Displays a list of print jobs for the *queuename* print queue.

Rules and Considerations

Do not use the QUEUE command on a network running the NetWare Name Service.

Important Messages

If the message `Queue already exists.` displays after you enter the QUEUE command, you are attempting to create a queue with the same name as an existing queue. Change the name and reenter the command.

The message `The specified Queue does not exist.` displays if you enter the name of a queue that does not exist on this server. Correct the name and reenter the command.

The message `Unknown Queue Command.` displays if you enter the QUEUE command incorrectly. Retype the command and then check the syntax.

Examples

To create a print queue for dot-matrix printers, enter the following at the console:

QUEUE MATRIX CREATE

To create a print queue specifically for the sales staff, enter the following at the console:

QUEUE SALES CREATE

To list all the print jobs in a print queue named HPLASER, enter the following command at the console:

QUEUE HPLASER JOBS

To display a list of queues and their current status at the console, enter the command:

QUEUE

Notes

Use the PCONSOLE utility instead of the QUEUE command on NetWare Name Service (NNS) Networks.

 See related information in Chapter 8 on the PCONSOLE menu utility.

See also

PRINTER

PSC

REGISTER MEMORY : 3.11

Purpose

Enables NetWare to recognize more than 16M of system memory.

Syntax

```
REGISTER MEMORY memstart memlen
```

Options

None

Rules and Considerations

The memory length *memlen* must end on an even paragraph boundary divisible by 0x10.

Important Messages

None

Example

To make the file server recognize 4M of additional memory starting at the 16M boundary, enter the following command at the console:

```
REGISTER MEMORY 0x1000000 0x100000
```

REMIRROR   :2.2

Purpose

Restores a duplexed or mirrored drive pair when one drive has been replaced.

Syntax

```
REMIRROR drivenumber
```

Options

None

Rules and Considerations

In the *drivenumber* place, specify the drive that needs to be updated. The REMIRROR command updates the hard disk drive to contain the same information as the mirrored drive.

Important Messages

```
Mirror drive will be auto remirrored.
```

If the preceding message appears after the system boots, the file server noticed during the boot that the mirror drive had been replaced or had previously failed. The file server automatically attempts to REMIRROR the drive if the drive previously failed or was replaced; you do not have to enter REMIRROR manually in this situation.

The following sample error message indicates that mirroring has failed on the file server CSOS drive 01, which affects the SYS volume:

```
Mirroring turned off on CSOS. Drive 01 failed.
Mirroring turned off on SYS.
```

To correct this problem, you enter **REMIRROR 01**

Example

To update drive 01 so that it matches drive 00 in a mirrored pair, enter the command:

REMIRROR 01

Notes

 Remirroring hard disk drives is often a slow process. During the remirror operation, file server response is slow because one drive's information is being copied in the background.

 If you do not shut down the file server after a mirrored drive pair has failed, REMIRROR will need to copy only the information that has changed since the mirror process failed. If you shut down the server, REMIRROR must copy the entire contents of one drive to the other drive, which is a lengthy process.

See also

UNMIRROR

REMOTE   :LOAD 3.11

Purpose

Enables you to use the RCONSOLE utility to run the file server console from a workstation.

Syntax

LOAD *path* **REMOTE** *remotepassword*

Option

remotepassword   Replace this variable with the password that you want all remote administrators to use.

Rules and Considerations

The path need only be specified if REMOTE.NLM is not found in the SYS:SYSTEM directory.

The *remotepassword* variable defaults to the SUPERVISOR password if no password is specified.

You can load RSPX only after REMOTE is loaded so that you can access the RCONSOLE utility.

Important Messages

None

Examples

To load remote file server console support using the password "SE-CRET," enter the following command at the console:

```
LOAD REMOTE SECRET
LOAD RSPX
```

To load remote file server console support using the SUPERVISOR password, enter the following at the console:

```
LOAD REMOTE
LOAD RSPX
```

To load remote file server console support from the SYS:NLM subdirectory using the password ABCDEFG, enter the following at the console:

```
LOAD SYS:NLM/REMOTE ABCDEFG
LOAD RSPX
```

Note

 You can access the remote console even when the file server console is in use, and both can display different information.

See also

RS232

RSPX

REMOTE F>

Purpose

Deletes users and groups from file and directory trustee lists.

Syntax

REMOVE USER *username* FROM *path option*

or

REMOVE GROUP *groupname* FROM *path option*

The *username* and *groupname* variables indicate either a user or a group that is to be removed from a directory or file trustee list. Indicate the path to the directory or file in the *path* variable.

Options

/S   Removes the user or group from all subdirectories in the specified path.

/F   Removes the user or group from files in the specified path.

Rules and Considerations

The USER and GROUP specifiers are only necessary when users and groups have the same name; otherwise the REMOVE command automatically distinguishes between users and groups.

If you enter REMOVE with only a user or group name, the user or group is removed from the trustee list of the current directory.

Important Messages

```
User or group "HORST" not found.
```

In the preceding example, the message indicates that no user or group named HORST exists on this server. Reenter the command with the correct name.

```
CSOS/APPS:ALLDOCS
User "FRED" no longer a trustee to the specified
directory.

Trustee "FRED" removed from 1 directories.
```

The preceding example message confirms that the user FRED was successfully removed as a trustee from the directory ALLDOCS on disk volume APPS of file server CSOS.

```
CSOS/APPS:DATENTRY
Group "TEMPS" no longer a trustee to the specified
directory.

Trustee "TEMPS" removed from 1 directories.
```

The preceding example message confirms that the group TEMPS was successfully removed as a trustee from the directory DATENTRY on disk volume APPS of file server CSOS.

```
CSOS/SYS:JUNK
No trustee for the specified Directory.
```

The previous sample error message displays when a user or group exists, but they are not a trustee of the specified directory or file.

Examples

To remove the group TEMPS as a trustee from the DATENTRY subdirectory on volume APPS of server CSOS, enter the command;

```
REMOVE GROUP TEMPS FROM CSOS\APPS:DATENTRY
```

To remove the user FRED from the trustee list of the ALLDOCS subdirectory on volume APPS of file server CSOS, enter the command:

```
REMOVE FRED FROM CSOS/APPS:ALLDOCS
```

To remove tthe user FRED from the trustee list of all the subdirectories of the ALLDOCS directory on volume APPS of file server CSOS, enter the command:

```
REMOVE FRED FROM CSOS/APPS:ALLDOCS /S
```

Notes

 Refer to the Netware documentation on SYSCON and FILER NetWare menu utilities for related information.

The /S option only removes the user or group from the trustee lists of every subdirectory of the specified directory path; the /S option does not affect the trustee rights to the specified directory.

See also

GRANT

MAKEUSER

REVOKE

TLIST

REMOVE DOS : 3.11

Purpose

Removes DOS completely from a NetWare 3.11 file server memory, eliminating access to DOS.

Syntax

```
REMOVE DOS
```

Options

None

Rules and Considerations

After you remove DOS from the file server, the system will perform a warm boot when you issue the EXIT command at the file server console; the system does not return to DOS.

If you remove DOS from the file server, Network Loadable Modules (NLMs) cannot be loaded from floppy disk drive partitions or the server's DOS hard drive partitions.

Important Messages

```
DOS access has been removed from file server.
```

The previous message displays after DOS is successfully removed from memory. To reload DOS access, you must shut down the file server and reboot.

Example

To remove DOS access from the file server, enter the command:

`REMOVE DOS`

Using this command ensures that unauthorized NLMs cannot be loaded at the file server console.

Note

If you use the REMOVE DOS command to disable DOS access on the file server, you still can copy NLMs into the SYS:SYSTEM subdirectory from a workstation.

RENDIR

Purpose

Renames a file server subdirectory without affecting the trustee rights to that directory.

Syntax

`RENDIR` *dirpath newname*

Rules and Considerations

If you have no trustee rights to a directory, you cannot change its name.

The RENDIR command renames a directory, but it does not affect the directory's trustee or user rights.

Important Messages

```
Directory renamed to DEPTDOCS.
```

The preceding message confirms that you successfully renamed a sample directory to DEPTDOCS.

```
The path specification (directory name) was incorrect.
```

The preceding message displays if you try to rename a subdirectory that does not exist or one that does not exist on the specified directory path. Correct the original directory path and name and retry the command.

Example

To rename the MYDOCS subdirectory to DEPTDOCS on the DOCS partition of file server FS3, type the command:

```
RENDIR FS3/DOCS:MYDOCS DEPTDOCS
```

If you want to give the current directory a new name, you can use a period (.) to specify the current directory path. To duplicate the previous example, use the Change Directory command (CD) to make the FS3/DOCS:MYDOCS subdirectory current, and then enter:

```
RENDIR . DEPTDOCS
```

Notes

 Changing directory names with RENDIR does not update MAP commands in DOS batch files or NetWare login scripts. If you do use RENDIR to rename a directory that you previously accessed using MAP commands, rewrite any affected MAP commands in the login scripts and batch files.

 You can find additional file management capabilities in the NetWare FILER menu utility. This utility is described in Chapter 6.

RESET ROUTER

Purpose

Updates inaccurate or corrupted router tables that result from file server or network bridge failure.

Syntax

```
RESET ROUTER
```

Rules and Considerations

The RESET ROUTER command is used only when inaccurate or corrupted router tables must be rebuilt.

Important Messages

```
Router has been reset.
```

According to the preceding message, the router table for this server has been rebuilt.

Example

To rebuild the router on a NetWare file server, go to the file server console and enter the command:

```
RESET ROUTER
```

Note

 The router tables are automatically updated every two minutes. Use the RESET ROUTER command on every network file server to update the router table sooner than the automatic two minute time period.

See also

TRACK ON
TRACK OFF

REVOKE   F⟩

Purpose

Enables you to revoke individual trustee rights for files or directories from users and groups.

Syntax

REVOKE *rightslist* *path* **FROM** USER *username* /SUB or /FILE

REVOKE rightslist *path* **FROM** GROUP *groupname* /SUB or /FILE

Options

rightslist   The rightslist can consist of one or several of the following rights attributes. Each attribute must be separated by a space:

Right	Description	NetWare 2.2 or 3.11
ALL	All	BOTH
A	Access Control	BOTH
C	Create	BOTH
E	Erase	BOTH
F	File Scan	BOTH
M	Modify	BOTH
R	Read	BOTH
S	Supervisor	3.11
W	Write	BOTH

path   Optional variable that defaults to the current directory if no path is specified.

username   Specifies a single existing user who will have his or her rights revoked.

groupname   Specifies a single existing group that is to have its rights revoked.

/SUB   Affect subdirectories of the selected directory.

/FILE   Affect files of the selected directory.

Rules and Considerations

The *rightslist* variable can consist of one or several rights separated by spaces.

If the path is omitted, REVOKE will default the current directory.

The /FILE and /SUB flags may not be use in the same command.

The /SUB (subdirectory) flag used with REVOKE affects only subdirectories of the selected directory; the directory is not affected.

You must include the USER or GROUP identifiers only if the user or group you want to modify has the same name as another user or group.

Important Messages

    No trustee for the specified directory.

The preceding message displays if the specified directory does not exist. Check the spelling and retry the command.

    User or group "ACCNTG" not found.

In the preceding example, no user or group was found with the name ACCNTG. Check the user or group name and retry the command.

    CSOS/DOCS:SPECDOCS
    Trustee's access rights set to [RWC MFA]

    Rights for 1 directories were changed for DEDE.

The preceding example confirms the E (Erase) trustee right was successfully revoked from user DEDE in the SYS:SPECDOCS directory.

Examples

To block the user DEDE from erasing files in the SPECDOCS subdirectory on volume DOCS of the default file server, enter the command:

```
REVOKE E DOCS:SPECDOCS FROM USER DEDE
```

To remove completely the user STEPHEN from the subdirectory SHAREDOC on the VOL1 volume on file server SP1, enter the command:

```
REVOKE ALL SP1/VOL1:SHAREDOC FROM USER STEPHEN
```

Continuing with the last example, to revoke the erase right for all the files in the SHAREDOC subdirectory for group ADMIN, enter the command:

```
REVOKE E SP1/VOL1:SHARDOC FROM GROUP ADMIN /FILE
```

Notes

 When you revoke rights, make sure you do not alter the rights for the EVERYONE group in the LOGIN, MAIL, and PUBLIC system directories. If these rights are changed, the system will not work as expected.

 For more information on the SYSCON menu utility, see the Chapter 7. This chapter lists additional features for maintaining trustee rights for users and groups.

See also

GRANT

REMOVE

RIGHTS

Purpose

Displays your effective rights to a file or subdirectory.

Syntax

RIGHTS

or

RIGHTS *path*

Options

path   Specifies a valid NetWare volume, a directory,
                subdirectory, or file path. The path can be listed, for
                example, as **FS1/SYS:SYSTEM**.

Important Messages

```
Specified path not locatable.
Usage:  RIGHTS [path]
Rights = All | Read | Write | Create | Erase | Modify
              | Filescan | Access Control
```

If the previous message appears, you specified a directory path that
does not exist. Correct the directory path and try again.

Examples

The following sample output lists a user with all rights to the
MISCDOCS directory of volume PROGS on file server CSOS:

```
CSOS\PROGS:MISCDOCS
Your Effective Rights for this directory are [RWCEMFA]
```

```
May Read from File.   (R)
May Write to File.    (W)
May Create Subdirectories and Files.   (C)
May Erase Subdirectories and Files.    (E)
May Modify File Status Flags.     (M)
May Scan for Files.   (F)
May Change Access Control.  (A)

You have ALL RIGHTS to this directory area.
```

The following example output lists a user with limited rights to the PUBLIC directory of volume SYS on file server CSOS:

```
CSOS\SYS:PUBLIC
Your Effective Rights for this directory are [R    F ]

May Read from File.   (R)
May Scan for Files.   (F)
```

Notes

 See the NetWare menu utilities SYSCON and FILER for menu driven access to directory and file rights.

See also

GRANT

REMOVE

REVOKE

RPRINTER

Purpose

Connects a workstation printer to the network as a remote printer. RPRINTER also is used to disconnect workstation printers from the network.

Syntax

```
RPRINTER printservername printer flag
```

Options

`printservername`	Specify the print server that includes the printer you want to connect to the network.
`printer`	Specify the printer number for the remote printer. This number represents the printer configuration that was defined using the PCONSOLE command.
`-R`	Disconnects the remote printer
`-S`	Displays the status of the remote printer
	No flag connects the remote printer

Rules and Considerations

RPRINTER runs as a TSR (Terminate and Stay Resident) program on the user's workstation. For this reason, the RPRINTER utility requires workstation memory.

If a user's local printer is connected to the network as a remote printer, the user must print to a captured network printer port rather than print directly to the local printer port.

If more than one remote printer is attached to a workstation, the RPRINTER TSR must be loaded for each printer.

The NetWare shells must be loaded on the workstation before the RPRINTER TSR is loaded.

To run RPRINTER, the workstation must have access to the following files:

IBM$RUN.OVL
RPRINT$$.EXE
RPRINTER.HLP

SYS$ERR.DAT
SYS$HELP.DAT
SYS$MSG.DAT

Important Messages

```
No print servers are operating.
```

If the preceding message appears, no printer servers are running. Start a printer server and try to connect the remote printer.

```
RPRINT$$.EXE not found.
```

If the preceding message appears, the RPRINTER utility was not installed with the capability to access all the necessary files. Reinstall RPRINTER so that all the files listed in the Rules and Considerations section are available when you run RPRINTER.

Examples

To load RPRINTER on a workstation that has been set up properly for remote printer 2 on print server ADMIN, enter the command:

RPRINTER ADMIN 2

To remove the remote printer defined in the previous example, enter the command:

RPRINTER ADMIN 2 -R

To check the status of remote printer number 2 on print server ADMIN, enter the command:

RPRINTER ADMIN 2 -S

Notes

 To support a remote printer, the workstation must not be rebooted. If a workstation supporting remote printers is rebooted, the RPRINTER TSR must be reloaded for each remote printer connected to the workstation.

The commands for connecting remote printers can be loaded by the AUTOEXEC.BAT file of the workstation if the NetWare shells are loaded before the RPRINTER utility is run.

For example, include the following commands in AUTOEXEC.BAT:

```
CD\NET
IPX
NETX
RPRINTER ADMIN 2
CD \
```

The preceding example assumes that IPX, NETX, RPRINTER, and all required files are located in C:\NET.

RS232   :LOAD 3.11

Purpose

Enables you to access the file server console over asynchronous communications ports or a modem. The RS232 command is used with the REMOTE.NLM.

Syntax

```
LOAD RS232 comport speed
```

Options

comport   Valid options for this variable are 1 for COM1 or 2 for COM2.

speed   Valid options for this variable are 2400, 4800, or 9600 for the data transfer rate of the modem.

If you do not enter the *comport* or *speed* variables when RS232 is loaded, you will be prompted to do so.

Example

To load remote support for a 9600 bps modem attached to COM2 on the file server, enter the command:

```
LOAD RS232 2 9600
```

Notes

 REMOTE.NLM must be loaded before RS232 so that you can use the RS232 NLM as a remote console.

See the Remote Management section of the *NetWare System Administration* manual for more information on the RS232 NLM.

See also

REMOTE

RSPX

RSPX

Purpose

Used with the REMOTE.NLM, RSPX enables you to access the file server console from a workstation using the RCONSOLE utility program.

Syntax

```
LOAD RSPX
```

Options

None

Rules and Considerations

To run a remote console, you must first load REMOTE and then RSPX.

Example

To load RSPX.NLM after REMOTE.NLM is loaded, enter the command:

```
LOAD RSPX
```

Notes

 Use the RCONSOLE menu utility to access the remote console using REMOTE.NLM and RSPX.NLM from any NetWare workstation on the LAN.

See also

REMOTE

RS232

SEARCH : 3.11

Purpose

Sets a path at the file server to search for NLMs and network configuration (NCF) files.

Syntax

```
SEARCH option
```

Options

If the SEARCH command is entered by itself with no option, the current search paths display.

ADD *number* **searchpath**   Adds a new search path. The *number* variable is optional and refers to the desired position for inserting the new search path. The **searchpath** variable refers to the new search path.

DEL **number**   Deletes an existing search path. The *number* variable refers to an existing search path and must be included.

Rules and Considerations

Unless SEARCH is used, NetWare examines only the SYS:SYSTEM directory when looking for NLM and NCF files.

If you use the SEARCH ADD command without specifying a number, the new search path is appended to the end of the search paths.

Important Messages

None

Examples

To search the SYS:NLM and SYS:SYSTEM directories for NLM and NCF files, enter the following command:

    SEARCH ADD SYS:NLM

To list the current search paths, enter the following command:

    SEARCH

To delete the search path in the second position, enter the following command:

```
SEARCH DEL 2
```

Note

 Use SEARCH if you keep NLMs in directories other than the SYS:SYSTEM directory. If you use SEARCH, you do not need to specify the path for the LOAD command every time you load these NLMs.

See also

LOAD
SECURE CONSOLE

SECURE CONSOLE   : 3.11

Purpose

Removes DOS from the file server and prevents the use of the OS debugger. SECURE CONSOLE also limits the loading of NLMs from only the SYS:SYSTEM directory, and SECURE CONSOLE permits only console operators to change the system date and time.

Syntax

```
SECURE CONSOLE
```

Options

None

Example

To secure the file server console on a NetWare 386 file server, enter the following command:

```
SECURE CONSOLE
```

Note

 The server must be rebooted to reverse the effects of SECURE CONSOLE.

See also

REMOVE DOS
SEARCH

SECURITY

Purpose

Displays a list of possible security problems. This list can include users, passwords, login scripts, and access privileges.

Syntax

```
SECURITY /C
```

Options

/C   Optional switch that continuously lists potential security violations without pausing at the end of every screen page.

Rules and Considerations

To use the SECURITY program, you must log in as the SUPERVISOR or as a supervisor equivalent. The SECURITY program is run from the SYS:SYSTEM directory.

Important Messages

```
Usage: security [/Continuous]
```

If the preceding message appears after you enter the SECURITY command, then you ran the SECURITY program with incorrect syntax. Reenter the command again with the correct syntax.

The following sample output of the SECURITY program shows the types of violations you may encounter:

```
SECURITY EVALUATION UTILITY, Version 2.23

User BRANDON
  Has password expiration interval greater than 60 days
  Has no password assigned
  No Full Name specified

Group ADMIN
  No Full Name specified

User DANNY (Full Name: Danny R. Kusnierz)
  Is security equivalent to user SUPERVISOR
  Has password expiration interval greater than 60 days
  Has no password assigned

User DEDE (Full Name: Dede Kusnierz )
  Is security equivalent to user SUPERVISOR
  Has password expiration interval greater than 60 days

User GUEST
  Has no login script
  Has no LOGIN_CONTROL property
  No Full Name specified

Group EVERYONE
  No Full Name specified
```

```
User SUPERVISOR (Full Name: System Supervisor)
  Does not require a password
```

Example

To print a list of potential security violations on a printer at the LPT1 port, enter the following command:

SECURITY > LPT1:

Notes

 Run SECURITY every time you modify the rights of a user or a group to ensure that you did not mistakenly introduce any security breaches into the system.

See also

GRANT

REVOKE

SETPASS

SEND (command line utility)

Purpose

Enables you to send short messages from your workstation to any of the following: logged in users or groups, the file server console, a particular workstation, or a set of workstations.

Syntax

SEND *"messagetext"* TO *destination*

Options

messagetext Specifies the message, which can be a maximum of 44 characters minus the length of the sending user's name.

destination Specifies the user or group that will receive the message. Using any of the following formats, this variable can designate users, groups, the file server console, specific workstations, or all workstations:

USER *userlist* Enables you to send messages to one or several users. The USER specifier is optional. The *userlist* variable is an optional file server name followed by the name of a user. Multiple users are separated by commas.

GROUP *grouplist* Enables you to send messages to one or several groups. The GROUP specifier is optional. The *grouplist* variable consists of an optional file server name followed by the name of a group. Separate multiple groups with commas.

servername /CONSOLE Enables you to send messages to the file server console. The optional *servername* variable specifies a file server; CONSOLE specifies the file server console.

servername/ EVERYBODY Enables you to send messages to all workstations. The optional *servername* variable specifies a file server; EVERYBODY specifies all workstations.

STATION *servername* /*stationlist* Enables you to send messages to specific workstations. The STATION specifier is optional. The following variables are optional: *servername* defaults to the current server; *stationlist* consists of a station number. Additional station numbers are separated by commas.

Rules and Considerations

A SEND message can be up to 44 characters in length minus the length of your user name. The Supervisor, for example, can send a message only a maximum of 34 characters in length because the word Supervisor is ten characters long.

If no file server name is specified, the default file server is used.

Users must be logged in to receive messages.

The workstation and login name of the sending user are displayed with the message text.

To send messages to users or groups on another server, you must be attached to that server.

Important Messages

```
User/Group FS1/ALL does not exist.
```

If the preceding message displays, the user or group you specified does not exist. Reenter the message with a valid user or group name.

```
Message sent to CSOS/SUPERVISOR (station 1).
```

In the preceding example, the message was sent successfully to user SUPERVISOR logged in on station 1.

```
Message not sent to CSOS/HEATHER (station 2)
```

According to the preceding example, your message was not sent to the user HEATHER. Either HEATHER used the CASTOFF utility so that her workstation cannot receive messages or her workstation's incoming message buffer is full. To undo the effects of CASTOFF, HEATHER must use the CASTON utility to re-enable message receipt. If the cause is a full message buffer, HEATHER must read enough messages to make room in the buffer.

Examples

To send a note to all members of the group STAFF about the 4:00 staff meeting, enter the command:

> SEND "Remember - Staff mtg at 4:00" TO GROUP STAFF

or the command:

> SEND "Remember - Staff mtg at 4:00" TO STAFF

To send a note to the file server console to request that the console operator mount form 2 into printer 3 on the file server, enter the command:

> SEND "Pls mount form 2 in printer 3" TO CONSOLE

To send a personal note to user JESSICA, enter the command:

> SEND "How about dinner tonight @ 8:00" TO JESSICA

Notes

If you send a message to a user who is not currently logged in, the message will not be saved. To send messages that are longer than the maximum size allowed for your ID, you must purchase an electronic mail, or email, package. Email packages enable you to send messages to users who are not currently logged in.

Receiving a message stops all processing under DOS. For this reason, do not send messages to unattended workstations, unless you are ready to explain why you stopped the user's computer from completing its task while the user was away from his or her desk.

See also

BROADCAST
CASTOFF
CASTON
SEND (console command)

SEND (console command)   : 3.11

Purpose

Enables you to send short messages from the file server console to specific users, all users, or to workstations.

Syntax

```
SEND "messagetext"
```

or

```
SEND "messagetext" TO userlist
```

or

```
SEND "messagetext" TO stationlist
```

Options

messagetext	Specifies a message that can be up to 55 characters in length.
userlist	Specifies the user(s) who is to receive the message. Multiple users are separated by commas.
stationlist	Consists of a station number. Additional station numbers are followed by commas.

Rules and Considerations

A user must be logged in to receive a message from the console with the SEND command.

If a user list or station list is not specified, the message is sent to all workstations.

Example

To remind all logged in users that the system will be shut down for maintenance this afternoon at 5:00, enter the command:

```
SEND "Don't forget! Server shutdown today at
5:00"
```

To send a message from the console to the user MICHAEL, enter the command:

```
SEND "Stop sending junk messages to the console!"
TO  MICHAEL
```

To send a message from the console to workstations 14 and 17, enter the command:

```
SEND "Please LOGOUT now!!!!" TO 14,17
```

Notes

 NetWare 2.2 uses the BROADCAST command instead of the SEND command.

 Workstations receiving messages halt all processing under DOS. Do not send messages to unattended workstations unless you are willing to explain why you interrupted the user's computer as it processed tasks while the user was away from his or her desk.

See also

BROADCAST

CASTOFF

CASTON

SEND (command line utility)

SERVER   C> 3.11

Purpose

Installs or boots a NetWare 386 file server.

Syntax

```
SERVER
```

Options

None

Rules and Considerations

After NetWare executes SERVER.EXE, it attempts to run the commands in STARTUP.NCF and AUTOEXEC.NCF if these files have been created.

Important Messages

```
*** This machine does not have an 80386 microprocessor ***
NetWare 3.11 CANNOT BE RUN ON THIS MACHINE!!!
```

The preceding message informs you that NetWare 386 must be run on a system with an 80386 or higher processor. Install NetWare 386 on a file server with an 80386 or higher processor.

```
Insufficient memory to run NetWare 3.11
   (requires at least 1 megabyte of extended memory)
```

The preceding message informs you that NetWare 386 requires 1M of extended RAM (usually reported as 1640K) or 2M of RAM on most systems to load. Add memory to the file server and reload SERVER.EXE.

Example

To begin the installation process on a new file server that has an 80386 or higher CPU, the required amount of extended RAM, and the network card or cards already installed, enter the command:

SERVER

To start the file server process on a NetWare 386 file server that has NetWare installed, enter the following command at the DOS prompt:

SERVER

Notes

 A few options are available with the SERVER command. Refer to the NetWare 386 installation manuals for more information on the available SERVER.EXE options.

See also

DOWN

LOAD

REMOVE DOS

SECURE CONSOLE

SET   : 3.11

Purpose

Enables you to display or change the values that tune the performance of the NetWare 386 operating system.

Syntax

SET *variable* = *value*

Options

The SET command entered without a variable displays the current parameter settings.

variable   Specifies a variable to change its setting.

value   Specifies a value to be assigned to the variable. Consult the *System Administration* manual for a list of variables and their allowed values.

Rules and Considerations

See Chapter 10 for more information on the SET commands.

Important Messages

None

Example

To display at the console the current parameter settings on a NetWare 386 file server, enter the command:

    SET

To change the system parameter for NetWare 386 file servers that accept encrypted passwords and the parameter that forces older NetWare 286 file servers to accept passwords, enter the command:

    SET ALLOW UNENCRYPTED PASSWORDS=YES

Notes

 For a list of valid SET parameters, refer to the NetWare System Administration manual.

See also

    SET TIME

SET TIME

Purpose

Enables you to set the time or date or both from the console on a NetWare file server.

Syntax

```
SET TIME mo/dy/yr hh:mm:ss
```

Options

None

SET TIME entered without any parameters displays the current system time.

Rules and Considerations

You can set the date and time independently or together.

To set the time, substitute the hour in 24 hour format for hh, the minutes for mm, and the seconds for ss.

Times entered greater than 24 hours will be changed to 24 hours. For example, 25:15:00 becomes 01:15:00.

Important Messages

None

Examples

To set the date and time to 1 minute before midnight on New Year's Eve, 1999, enter:

    SET TIME 12/12/99 23:59:00

To set the time to 3:15 in the afternoon, enter:

    SET TIME 15:15:00

To change the date to February 10th, 1993, enter:

    SET TIME 2/10/93

Notes

 Workstation dates and times will not correspond to the corrected file server date and time until the workstation shells are reloaded.

 Time may also be entered in 12 hour format if it is followed by AM or PM.

Years entered prior to 1980 will be listed after the year 2000. You can change the date to some date up to but not including the year 2080.

See also

SET

TIME

SETPASS

Purpose

Enables users to change their passwords if they have the rights to do so.

Syntax

```
SETPASS servername
```

Options

servername   Optional variable that is set to the name of the file
              server that stores the password you want to change.

Important Messages

```
You are not connected to file server ABRACADABRA.
```

In the preceding example, you entered **SETPASS ABRACADABRA**
and thought that your current password would be changed to ABRA-
CADABRA. To change your password correctly, enter **SETPASS** without any parameters and follow the prompts.

```
Access denied to NRP1/BRANDON, password not
changed.
```

The preceding example message shows the current password for user
BRANDON was entered incorrectly at the SETPASS prompt. Retry the
command by entering your current password.

Example

In the following example, BRANDON changes his password using the
SETPASS prompts. Note that the passwords he types are not displayed
on screen when they are entered. BRANDON presses Enter after responding to the prompts.

```
F:\USERS\BRANDON>SETPASS

Enter old password for NRP/BRANDON:NCC1701

Enter new password for NRP/BRANDON:NCC1701A

Retype new password for NRP/BRANDON:NCC1701A

The password for NRP/BRANDON has been changed.
```

Notes

 NetWare security relies largely on users who must keep their passwords secret. Use SETPASS often to change your password, which helps to maintain a high level of security. You also can increase the security of your passwords by not using words associated with family, hobbies, friends, and so on. The best passwords are arbitrary combinations of letters and numbers.

See also

SECURE CONSOLE
SECURITY

SLIST

Purpose

Lists file servers that are available for your workstation.

Syntax

SLIST *servername* /C

Options

servername   Specifies a file server. If you enter SLIST with a file server name, the file server displays if it is available.

/C   Specifies that SLIST continuously scroll the screens instead of pause at the end of every screen page.

Rules and Considerations

If you enter SLIST without a file server name, a list displays of every available file server.

Important Messages

```
Server CSOS2 not found.
```

The preceding message shows the requested file server, CSOS2, is not available. In this case, the preceding command was **SLIST CSOS2**.

Example

The following is example output from the SLIST command:

```
Known NetWare File Servers    Network     Node Address   Status
--------------------------    -------     ------------   -------
CSOS                          [19910001][ 2608C0B39CA]  Default
Total of 1 file servers found
```

See also

LOGIN

MAP

SMODE

Purpose

Enables you to set or view the method a program uses to search for data files and overlays.

Syntax

SMODE *filepath* *searchmode* **/SUB**

Options

filepath

Consists of an optional path and a file specification (wild cards are allowed).

searchmode

Specifies the type of search method you want to use. Valid search modes include the following:

0   The shell default. Program follows instructions in SHELL.CFG.

1   If the program specifies a directory path, it will search only that path. If no path is specified, the search extends through all search drives.

2   If the program specifies a directory path, it searches only that path. If no path is specified, only the default directory is searched.

3   Similar to the preceding search mode. If, however, the search is Read Only, the search is extended to directories in the search drives.

4   (reserved, do not use)

5   If the program specifies a directory path, it searches that path followed by the search drives. If no path is specified, the default directory is searched, followed by the search drives.

6   (reserved, do not use)

7   If the program specifies a directory path, that path is searched first. Then, if the open request is Read Only, the program searches the search drives. If no directory path is given, the program searches the default directory. Then, if the open request is Read Only, the program searches the search drives.

If *searchmode* is not specified, the current search modes of the selected files display.

/SUB Extends the effect of the commands to all subdirectories of the requested directory. A filepath must be used if /SUB is included.

Rules and Considerations

SMODE operates on executable files and ignores non-executable files.

Important Messages

```
No EXECUTABLE files could be found with pattern "*.*"
```

The preceding sample message displays when SMODE is executed in a directory that has no executable files. Change to a directory that contains executable files or specify the path to the desired files.

```
Mode 4 is reserved.
```

The preceding sample message displays when you attempt to set a reserved search mode. To correct this problem, assign a valid search mode.

Example

To set the program 123.EXE so that it does not search for data files on search drives, enter the command:

SMODE 123.EXE 2

Notes

The default for most executable files is search mode 0 (shell default). You can set the default shell variable SEARCH MODE = searchmode in the NET.CFG file which should be located in the directory from which you load your DOS workstation shells.

See also

MAP

SPEED   : 3.11

Purpose

Displays a number that represents the relative speed of a NetWare 386 file server.

Syntax

    SPEED

Options

None

Important Messages

None

Example

To display the relative speed of a NetWare file server, enter the command:

    SPEED

Notes

 The reported speed of a NetWare file server is relative. A speed of 300 compared to a speed of 150, for example, shows that the first file server is twice as fast as the second. For an accurate comparison of two file servers, both servers must run the same version of NetWare 386.

SPOOL : 2.2

Purpose

Creates, maintains, and lists spooler mappings to print queues.

Syntax

```
SPOOL
```

or

```
SPOOL printernumber TO QUEUE queuename
```

Rules and Considerations

If you enter SPOOL without a printer number or a queue name, the current spooler mappings display.

Valid options for the *printernumber* variable range from 0 to 4.

Valid *queuename* options include any existing print queue name.

Important Messages

```
Spooler 0 is directed into printer HPLASER
Spooler 1 is directed into printer MATRIX1
```

A SPOOL status message similar to this displays when the SPOOL command is entered with no options.

Examples

To spool printer 1 to a print queue named HPLASER3, enter the command:

```
SPOOL 1 TO QUEUE HPLASER3
```

To display a list of current spool mappings, enter:

SPOOL

Notes

 You can include SPOOL commands in the AUTOEXEC.SYS file to have these commands automatically load when a NetWare 2.2 file server is started.

See also

CAPTURE
NPRINT
PRINTER
QUEUE

SPXCONFG   :LOAD 3.11

Purpose

Configures NetWare 386 SPX parameters.

Syntax

LOAD SPXCONFG *option...option*

Options

A=   Sets SPX watchdog abort timeout in ticks (A *tick* is 1/18 of a second)

V=   Sets SPX watchdog verify timeout (in ticks)

W=   Sets SPX Ack wait timeout (in ticks)

R=   Sets SPX default retry count

S=   Maximum concurrent SPX sessions

Q=1   Quiet mode: suppresses display of the settings

H   Displays a help screen

Rules and Considerations

You must specify a path if SPXCONFIG.NLM is not installed in the SYS:SYSTEM directory.

Important Messages

None

Example

To load SPXCONFG, enter the command

```
LOAD SPXCONFG
```

and an SPXCONFG menu is displayed.

```
LOAD SPXCONFG A=500
```

SPXS   :LOAD 3.11

Purpose

Used with NLMs that support the STREAMS-based IPX protocol services.

Syntax

```
LOAD SPXS
```

Options

None

Rules and Considerations

To properly load STREAMS-based IPX/SPX protocol services for an NLM that requires these services, load these NLMs in the following order:

1. Load STREAMS.NLM first
2. Load CLIB.NLM second
3. Load TLI.NLM third
4. Load IPXS.NLM fourth
5. Load SPXS.NLM last

Important Messages

None

Example

To load SPXS, enter the command:

```
LOAD SPXS
```

See also

CLIB
IPXS
STREAMS
TLI

STREAMS   :LOAD 3.11

Purpose

Provides an interface among NetWare and other transport protocols. STREAMS is loaded before CLIB or STREAMS-based protocol services.

Syntax

```
LOAD STREAMS
```

Options

None

Rules and Considerations

STREAMS must be loaded before CLIB is loaded.

To properly load STREAMS-based IPX/SPX protocol services for an NLM that requires it, load these NLMs in the following order:

1. Load STREAMS.NLM first
2. Load CLIB.NLM second
3. Load TLI.NLM third
4. Load IPXS.NLM fourth
5. Load SPXS.NLM last

Important Messages

None

Example

To load STREAMS, enter the command:

LOAD STREAMS

Notes

 For more complete information on the use of STREAMS and STREAMS-based protocol services, see Chapter 5.

See also

CLIB
IPXS
SPXS
TLI

SYSTIME

Purpose

Enables you to view and change the date and time on your workstation to that of a file server.

Syntax

SYSTIME

or

SYSTIME *fileserver*

Options

fileserver   Specifies a file server that is to be used to set the date and time of a user's workstation.

Rules and Considerations

If a file server is not specified, SYSTIME configures your workstation's date and time to that of the default file server.

Important Messages

```
Current System Time:   Monday   November   11,  1992   3:06 pm
```

The preceding example displays when the SYSTIME command is used without any parameters.

```
    You are not attached to server HELP.
```

The preceding example displays when a non-attached file server is specified. Attach to the requested file server or reenter the command with a valid file server name.

Example

To set the workstation date and time to that of the default file server, enter the command:

SYSTIME

Notes

 If you change the time on the file server with the SET TIME console command, you can synchronize the workstation clock with the file server clock by using SYSTIME.

See also

SET TIME
TIME

TIME

Purpose

Displays the date and time at the file server console.

Syntax

```
TIME
```

Options

None

Rules and Considerations

TIME displays only the system date and time. You must use SET TIME to change the date or time.

Important Messages

None

Example

To display the current system date and time at the file server console, enter:

```
TIME
```

Notes

See the NetWare manuals under menu utilities SYSCON and FCONSOLE for more information on checking and changing the file server system clock.

See also

SET TIME
SYSTIME

TLI   :LOAD 3.11

Purpose

Supports STREAMS and CLIB and enables them to use transport protocols such as SPXS and IPXS. *TLI* is a NetWare 386 NLM that stands for Transport Layer Protocol.

Syntax

```
LOAD TLI
```

Options

None

Rules and Considerations

Both STREAMS and CLIB must be loaded before loading TLI because TLI supports STREAMS and CLIB.

One of the STREAMS protocol modules, such as SPXS or IPXS or both, must be loaded after TLI is loaded.

Important Messages

None

Example

To completely load STREAMS support with IPXS and SPXS at the file server console, enter these modules in the following order:

1. Load STREAMS.NLM first
2. Load CLIB.NLM second
3. Load TLI.NLM third
4. Load IPXS.NLM fourth
5. Load SPXS.NLM last

See also

CLIB
IPXS
SPXS
STREAMS

TLIST

Purpose

Displays a list of trustees for the specified file or directory.

Syntax

TLIST *dirpath option*

or

TLIST *filepath option*

Options

dirpath   Specifies a NetWare directory on the currently logged
               file server.

filepath   Specifies a NetWare file path on the currently logged
               file server.

option   Lists group or user trustees or both, depending on the
               specified option. Leave *option* blank to list both group
               and user trustees. Specify GROUPS to list group trust-
               ees, or specify USERS to list to user trustees.

Rules and Considerations

Wildcards are supported for directory and file specifications.

If you do not specify USERS or GROUPS in the *option* parameter, both
will be displayed.

Important Messages

```
NRP\PROGS:UTILITY
No trustees found.
```

The preceding example shows that the specified directory has no
group or user trustees. Use GRANT or SYSCON to assign trustees.

```
Path does not exist.
```

The preceding message displays when a directory or file specification
is entered that does not exist. Enter the correct directory or file specification.

Examples

To display the trustees of the SHAREDOC directory on volume DATA
of file server NRP if you are currently logged into this file server, enter
the command:

TLIST NRP/DATA:SHAREDOC

The previous command displays the following output:

```
NRP\DATA:SHAREDOC
User trustees:
   DEDE  [RWCEMFA]  Dede Kusnierz
   FRED  [RWCEMFA]  Fred Flinstone
   ──
Group trustees:
   SECS  [      ]
```

To list the user trustees of the PUBLIC directory on the default file server, enter the command:

TLIST SYS:PUBLIC USERS

To list the group trustees of the PUBLIC directory on the default file server, enter the command:

TLIST SYS:PUBLIC GROUPS

Notes

 To specify quickly the current directory or the parent directory, use the period (.) and double period (..) DOS specifications instead of typing the entire directory name.

See also

GRANT

REMOVE

REVOKE

RIGHTS

TOKENRPL   :LOAD 3.11

Purpose

Loads file server support enabling stations without floppy disk drives but with Token-Ring network adapters to boot from the file server.

Syntax

```
LOAD TOKENRPL
```

Options

None

Rules and Considerations

TOKENRPL supports remote program loading only on Token-Ring network adapters.

The NetWork adapters in the workstations that do not have floppy disk drives must also support RPL (Remote Program Load).

Important Messages

None

Example

To enable Token-Ring workstations that do not have floppy disk drives to attach to a NetWare 386 file server when they first boot, enter the following command at the file server console:

```
LOAD TOKENRPL
```

Notes

Working with workstations that do not have floppy disk drives requires much planning. See the NetWare Administration manual for a complete explanation of TOKENRPL.

See also

DOSGEN

TRACK OFF

Purpose

Turns off the display of router traffic from the file server console.

Syntax

```
TRACK OFF
```

Options

None

Rules and Considerations

The TRACK OFF command is needed to turn off the display of router activity only after it has been turned on with TRACK ON.

Important Messages

None

Example

To disable the display of router activity from the file server console, type the following:

```
TRACK OFF
```

See also

ROUTER.EXE
TRACK ON

TRACK ON

Purpose

Displays router activity, including connection, network, and server requests, for troubleshooting or information.

Syntax

```
TRACK ON
```

Options

None

Rules and Considerations

The TRACK ON command can be entered at the file server console or at the console prompt of a router running ROUTER.EXE.

TRACK ON displays connection, network and server requests.

IN requests are those the file server or router is receiving. OUT requests are those the file server or router is sending.

Important Messages

None

Example

To enable display of the routing activity of the file server at the file server console, type the following:

```
TRACK ON
```

See also

ROUTER
TRACK OFF

UNBIND   :3.11

Purpose

Removes a communications protocol from a LAN driver for a network adapter card that was added to the LAN driver with BIND.

Syntax

```
UNBIND protocol FROM landriver
```

Options

protocol	The previously bound communications protocol, usually IPX
landriver	The name of the LAN driver from which to remove the communications protocol

Rules and Considerations

A protocol must have been added to a LAN driver with the BIND command in order for you to unbind it.

Currently supplied NetWare LAN drivers include NE1000, NE2, NE2000, NE232, RXNET, and TOKEN, although any vendor supplied LAN driver may be specified.

Important Messages

None

Example

To remove the IPX protocol from the NE232 LAN driver at the file server console, type the following:

```
UNBIND IPX FROM NE232
```

Notes

 When you unbind a protocol from an LAN driver, the LAN that was supported by that driver and all the workstations supported by that protocol can no longer communicate through the file server.

See also

BIND

UNLOAD   : 3.11

Purpose

Removes a NetWare Loadable Module (NLM) from file server memory.

Syntax

```
UNLOAD nlmspec
```

Options

nlmspec   The name of the NLM to unload from memory

Important Messages

None

Example

```
UNLOAD NE232
```

Notes

 Use UNLOAD to remove unnecessary maintenance modules such as INSTALL that have been loaded for temporary use. After the NLM is unloaded, the memory it previously occupied returns to caching, which usually increases system performance.

WARNING Do not use UNLOAD to remove any NLM's necessary to the operation of your file server. This appears obvious, but the always "up" nature of a 386 file server might make you forget when you unload the particular NLM that some maintenance tasks require that you inform the users that the LAN will be unavailable, or a particular feature they expect to use will be unavailable.

See also

LOAD

UNMIRROR : 2.2

Purpose

Manually shuts down mirroring on a dedicated file server.

Syntax

```
UNMIRROR drivenumber
```

Options

drivenumber   Substitute the drive number of one drive of a mirror pair

Rules and Considerations

After mirroring has been shut down on a particular drive, that drive no longer is updated with disk drive activity.

Hot fix remains in effect for the other drive in the mirror pair.

Important Messages

```
Invalid physical drive specified.
```

The preceding message indicates that you did not specify a drive number when entering the UNMIRROR command. Retry the command with the correct drive number specified.

```
Physical drive and its mirror do not exist or are
totally shut down.
```

This message indicates that you have specified a drive number that does not exist, or is not available. Retry UNMIRROR with the correct drive number specified.

Example

To turn off mirroring on drive 01, which you intend to replace with a new drive after you shut down the server, type the following:

```
UNMIRROR 01
```

Notes

 The UNMIRROR command generally is useful only if: the mirroring feature is not working correctly; one of the drives in a drive pair keeps failing enough to slow performance but

not enough for the operating system to disable mirroring; or if you intend to remove the specified drive after shutting down the file server.

 Disabling mirroring leaves you with only hot-fix protection on the remaining drive.

If you accidentally unmirror a drive, be careful to specify the correct drive number when you invoke REMIRROR, or the newer information will be overwritten with the older information of the unmirrored drive.

See also

DISK
REMIRROR

UPS   :LOAD 3.11

Purpose

Loads hardware support for an uninterruptable power supply on a NetWare 386 file server.

Syntax

    LOAD UPS *upstype ioport discharge recharge*

or

    LOAD UPS

Options

upstype   The type of UPS (DCB, STANDALONE, MOUSE, EDCB, KEYCARD, OTHER)

ioport	The mouse port, communications port or network card supporting the UPS, expressed in hexadecimal (consult the UPS documentation)
discharge	The estimated time required to discharge the UPS in minutes
recharge	The time to recharge the UPS in minutes

Rules and Considerations

If the **UPS** command is entered without parameters, you will be prompted to supply parameters.

The UPS must be one supported by the UPS.NLM, or you will have to use the NLM supplied with the UPS.

UPS.NLM must be loaded before UPS support is enabled.

Important Messages

```
WARNING: UPS hardware configuration error was
detected. Check for errors in you UPS hardware
configuration settings.
```

If you receive the preceding message, the UPS NLM was not loaded because of a configuration error. LOAD the UPS NLM again, correcting the settings for the on-line and low battery configuration.

```
UPS is shutting down server GROUP1. Commercial
power has failed and the battery is too low.
```

This message indicates that file server GROUP1 has been automatically shut down by the UPS software because it recognized a power failure and the battery was too low or ran down because commercial power was out too long. To correct, wait until commercial power is restored and then restart the file server process.

Example

To install UPS hardware support and be prompted for the parameters, type the following:

    LOAD UPS

Notes

 Use INSTALL.NLM to put the LOAD UPS parameters line into your AUTOEXEC.NCF to make sure that UPS support is loaded when the file server is booted.

See also

UPS STATUS
UPS TIME

UPS   : 2.2

Purpose

Displays the status of an uninterruptable power supply.

Syntax

    UPS

Options

None

Important Messages

    UPS Monitoring Disabled

You receive this message if no UPS is attatched to your system, or if there is no SERVER.CFG file enabling the UPS.

```
UPS enabled on NPR3
```

This message displays at file server boot time to indicate that the SERVER.CFG contained proper information and UPS monitoring has been enabled.

Example

To check the current status of a UPS attatched to the file server at the file server console, type the following:

UPS

To enable the UPS on a NetWare 286 file server to include the appropriate command lines, enter the command:

UPS TYPE=n

Replace *n* with one of the following numbers:

1   for standalone monitor boards

2   for Host bus adapter (e.g. DCB)

3   for SS keycard

4   for PS/2 mouse ports

To specify 10 minutes as the amount of time that users have to log out after a loss of commercial power, enter the command:

UPS DOWN=10

To specify 30 seconds as the amount of time in seconds that passes before users are notified that commercial power has been restored, enter the command:

UPS WAIT=30

Notes

 Refer to the manuals supplied with the UPS to find out the valid setting for the UPS DOWN= setting in the SERVER.CFG file. If the time you set for the server to shut down is longer than the battery will last, users will not be given ample notice to complete their work and the file server will be shut off by the UPS before the operating system has had a chance to down the file server.

See also

DOWN

UPS STATUS : 3.11

Purpose

Checks the status of the UPS attatched to the file server.

Syntax

```
UPS STATUS
```

Options

None

Rules and Considerations

UPS must be loaded before UPS STATUS is a valid command.

Important Messages

```
??? Unknown Command
```

The preceding messages informs you that you have not loaded the UPS.NLM file for UPS support. You must LOAD UPS before UPS STATUS is available.

Example

To check the current status of the uninterruptable power supply attatched to the file server, type the following:

```
UPS STATUS
```

Notes

 When you invoke the UPS STATUS command, the times displayed are usually based on those entered with the UPS TIME command and are therefore not guaranteed. If UPS recognizes less power than was expected from one of the more intelligent UPS devices, or if battery power fails, the file server will be terminated regardless of the displayed status.

See also

UPS

UPS TIME

UPS TIME : 3.11

Purpose

Sets or changes the estimates for UPS battery discharge and recharge times.

Syntax

```
UPS TIME dischargetime rechargetime
```

Options

dischargetime   The length of time the battery will keep the file server running after commercial power loss.

rechargetime   The length of time the UPS needs to recover after it has been used to run the file server after commercial power loss.

Rules and Considerations

The UPS loadable module must be loaded before UPS TIME is a valid command.

Example

To set the UPS battery backup time to 15 minutes and the recharge time to 30 minutes, type the following:

```
UPS TIME 15 30
```

Notes

 Do not enter times that do not conform to the ratings for your UPS. Under certain conditions, your equipment can be severely damaged if a battery backup was run down to a complete loss of power before the file server and UPS were shut down.

Enter valid times for the discharge, as this will guarantee that the file server is not prematurely switched off by the UPS before the software shuts down the file server process.

See also

UPS

UPS STATUS

USERLIST

Purpose

Displays a list of logged in users and some status information for those users.

Syntax

USERLIST *userspec* /C /Option

Options

userspec	An optional file server specification followed by a user name for which you are requesting status
/A	Display network address information with the user list display
/O	Display object type information with the user list display
/C	Display a continuous list without pausing at the end of each screen page for long lists

Important Messages

```
User Information for Server CSOS
Connection   User Name        Login Time
----------   ----------       ----------
No users named FS2.
```

This message shows that the requested user named with the USERLIST command was not found. In this case it appears as if the slash was not typed after the file server name. Type the slash after the file server name and try again.

```
You are not attached to server FS2.
```

This messages shows that you tried to check the user list on file server FS2, but that you are not attached to it. Log in to it or attach to it, and then retry the USERLIST command.

Example

If you type **USERLIST /A**, you receive output as follows:

```
User Information for Server NORTH386
Connection User Name     Network Node Address Login Time
---------- ---------     ------- ------------ ----------------
1          * SUPERVISOR [CDC]    [ 1B1EFDDB]  9-14-1992 9:10 am
2          *SU1         [   5]   [ 1B191D38]  9-14-1992 9:30 am
```

If you type **USERLIST /O**, you receive output as follows:

```
User Information for Server NORTH 386
Connection User Name       Login Time         Object Type
---------- ---------       ------------------ -----------
1          * SUPERVISOR    9-14-1992  9:10 am User
2          *SU1            9-14-1992 10:28 AM User
```

Notes

 The asterisk in the user listing shows which entry shows the information for your workstation. Thus, if you are logged in on more than one workstation, you can determine which connection you are without having to use the WHOAMI command.

See also

SLIST

TLIST

WHOAMI

VAP   : 2.2

Purpose

Displays a list of loaded value-added processes on a NetWare 286 file server.

Syntax

    VAP

Rules and Considerations

The VAP command displays not only a list of all loaded VAPs, but also the console commands the VAP will accept.

VAPs are loaded by copying them to the SYS:SYSTEM directory of the file server. The VAPs are loaded after the file server is booted.

Because VAPs also can be loaded on routers, the VAP command also works at the (:) prompt on routers.

Important Messages

    No Value Added Processes loaded.

This message is displayed if you have not loaded any VAPS. To load VAPs, they must be copied into the SYS:SYSTEM directory. They are enabled after the server is booted.

Example

To view a list of all loaded VAPS and the command available to them, type the following:

    VAP

See also

OFF

VER   : 2.2

Purpose

Checks the file server's NetWare operating system version, release, and user count information from the file server console.

Syntax

VER

Options

None

Important Messages

```
Dedicated Netware V2.2(100) Rev. A 2/11/91
```

This sample message displays operating system version, user count, revision, and release date.

Example

To check the version information, type the following:

VER

See also

NVER
VERSION

VERSION

Purpose

Displays version information for NetWare EXE files containing version information.

Syntax

```
VERSION filespec
```

Options

filespec   Specifies the location of the file to check on the file server including the file server and directory name as well as the file name.

Rules and Considerations

Wild cards are supported.

If you invoke VERSION against a file without version information, the file's checksum is calculated.

Important Messages

```
NET$OS.EXE:
  Version Dedicated NetWare V2.2
  (C) Copyright 1983-1991 Novell Inc.
  Checksum is 61FD.
```

The preceding message displays example output from the VERSION command.

Example

To display the previous output, type the following:

```
VERSION SYS:SYSTEM/NET$OS.EXE
```

See also

NVER

VER

VERSION   : 3.11

Purpose

Displays the NetWare 386 operating system version and copyright information at the file server console.

Syntax

```
VERSION
```

Options

None

Important Messages

None

Example

To display the NetWare 386 operating system version number and copyright information at the file server, type the following:

```
VERSION
```

See also

NVER

VOLUMES   : 3.11

Purpose

Displays a list of available drive volumes from the file server console.

Syntax

    VOLUMES

Options

None

Rules and Considerations

The VOLUMES command lists only volumes that are currently mounted.

Example

For a list of mounted volumes, type the following at the file server console:

    VOLUMES

See also

DISMOUNT
MOUNT

VREPAIR :LOAD 3.11

Purpose

Repairs problems with a NetWare hard drive recovering access to the data on the drive.

Syntax

```
LOAD VREPAIR
```

Rules and Considerations

Other volumes can be accessed while a defective volume is being repaired by VREPAIR.

The VREPAIR command should be invoked whenever file allocation table (FAT) errors, disk read errors, mirroring errors at boot time, or power failures have corrupted a volume.

Important Messages

```
    Error reading in volume directory.
```
or
```
    Invalid available entry.
```
or
```
    Invalid deleted file block.
```
or
```
    Invalid directory number code.
```
or
```
    Invalid user restriction node...too many trust-
    ees.
```
or
```
    Invalid Maximum Space defined in Subdirectory.
```

or

```
Invalid volume header / root directory entry.
```

The preceding messages indicate that NetWare 386 had trouble mounting a volume. Invoke VREPAIR to repair.

Example

To invoke the VREPAIR command on a damaged NetWare volume, type the following:

LOAD VREPAIR

Notes

 The VREPAIR command sometimes causes loss or damage to files. You should have a good backup and be prepared to replace some data after executing VREPAIR, although the command usually does not cause data loss.

WATCHDOG   : 2.2

Purpose

Monitors file server connections.

Syntax

**WATCHDOG START=*startsecs* INTERVAL=*intervalsecs*
COUNT=*intervalcount***

Options

startsecs   Specify in seconds how long you want the file server to check a new connection. The time can be between 15 and 1,200 seconds with 300 seconds as the default.

intervalsecs	Specify how long the interval between checks should be, in seconds. The *intervalsecs* variable ranges from 1 to 600, with a default of 60 seconds.
intervalcount	The number of intervals that must go by before clearing an active connection, ranging from 5 to 100 with a default of 10.

Important Messages

None

Example

To enable WATCHDOG with the defaults, type the following:

```
WATCHDOG
```

To enable WATCHDOG with your own settings, type the following:

```
WATCHDOG START=10 INTERVAL=5 COUNT=20
```

Notes

 Place the WATCHDOG command in the AUTOEXEC.SYS to load it automatically when the file server is booted.

See also

MONITOR

WHOAMI

Purpose

Displays connection, identification, and security information for the current user.

Syntax

```
WHOAMI [servername] option
```

Options

If you type **WHOAMI** and do not include parameters, you receive the user name, server name, workstation connection, NetWare version, and login time.

servername	Unless a file server is specified, information is provided for all attached servers.
/ALL	Displays group membership and security equivalence along with the basic WHOAMI information.
/G	Displays group information along with the basic WHOAMI information.
/O	Displays object supervisor information along with the basic WHOAMI information.
/R	Displays effective rights for each attached volume along with the basic WHOAMI information.
/S	Displays security equivalences along with the basic WHOAMI information.
/SY	Displays general system information along with the basic WHOAMI information.
/W	Displays workgroup manager information along with the basic WHOAMI information.

Rules and Considerations

You must be logged in to a file server to run WHOAMI.

If you type **WHOAMI** without any parameters, the user name, server name, workstation connection, NetWare version, and login time display.

Only one option at a time can be entered with WHOAMI.

Important Messages

```
You are not attached to server DANNY.
```

This messages indicates what happens if you enter **WHOAMI** followed by some text — in this case, **WHOAMI DANNY**. To correct, type **WHOAMI** without any options, or try one listed in the examples that follow:

Examples

If you type **WHOAMI**, you receive information similar to the following:

```
You are user DENISE attached to server NRP2, connection 7.
Server NRP2 is running Dedicated NetWare V2.2(100) Rev. A.
Login time: Tuesday  November  12, 1991  4:14 pm
```

If you type **WHOAMI /ALL**, you receive information similar to the following:

```
You are user BOB attached to server FINI, connection 1.
Server FINI is running Dedicated NetWare V2.2(50) Rev. B.
You are a workgroup manager.
Login time: Thursday  November  14, 1991  7:14 am
You are security equivalent to the following:
    EVERYONE (Group)
You are a member of the following groups:
    ACCOUNTING
    EVERYONE
    SHIPPING
[RWCEMFA]  SYS:
[RWCEMFA]  VOL1:
Server CSOS is not in a Domain.
```

See also

USERLIST

WSGEN F>

Purpose

An installation utility that creates an IPX.COM file specific to a particular workstation's configuration.

Syntax

    WSGEN

Options

None

Rules and Considerations

The WSGEN command requires at a minimum a LAN driver disk for the network adapter card to complete execution.

WSGEN requires DOS 3.0 or higher to run.

Important Messages

None

    WSGEN

Notes

 Use IPX I after generating an IPX.COM file with WSGEN to check its version, suported LAN adapter, and configuration option.

See also

DCONFIG
IPX
NETx

WSUPDATE

Purpose

Updates NetWare shells on workstations with newer versions.

Syntax

```
WSUPDATE source dest
```

or

```
WSUPDATE /F=scriptfile
```

Options

source	Location and name of source file
dest	Location and name of file to be replaced with newer version
scriptfile	*scriptfile* is a file created to contain a list of source destination pairs for automatic execution

Rules and Considerations

WSUPDATE replaces files with newer versions only.

Important Messages

None

Example

To update the workstation shells easily, copy the updated shells into one of the search drives on the network and type the following on a MS-DOS V5 workstation using the regular memory workstation shell:

```
WSUPDATE F:\PUBLIC\NET5.COM A:\NET5.COM
```

To update the workstation shells at login time, create a WSUPDATE configuration file for each user's workstation and execute the WSUPDATE program from the users login script. If the user's WSUPDATE script file was named WSUPDRK.CFG, you would type the following into the login script:

```
IF DAY_OF_WEEK = 2, RUN #WSUPDATE /F=WSUPDRK.CFG
```

Notes

A sample WSUPDATE script might resemble the following:

```
F:XMSNET5.COM A:XMSNET5.COM
F:IPX.COM  A:IPX.COM
```

 Do not accidentally replace the IPX.COM file on a workstation with an IPX.COM generation intended for another workstation. Although the NETx flavors are generic, the IPX.COM file must be generated for a particular workstation adapter card.

See also

EMSNETx

IPX

NETx

XMSNETx

XMSNETX

Purpose

Loads the DOS NetWare shell program into extended memory on 286 and higher CPUs, with more than 1M of RAM conserving lower RAM for application software.

Syntax

```
XMSNETX option
```

Options

/C=*filespec*	Specify the directory location and the file name for the shell configuration file, usually NET.CFG for the default
/I	Displays version and configuration information without loading the workstation shell
/PS=*fileserver*	*fileserver* specifies the preferred default file server; the shell creates a connection with this file server even though another file server responds faster
/U	Unloads the XMSNETX workstation shell from the workstation memory
/?	Displays usage options for the XMSNETX command

Rules and Considerations

If you type XMSNETX with no option, the DOS workstation shell loads.

XMSNETX files can be found on the WSGEN disk and should be copied to the workstation boot disk.

The file server should be running before you attempt to connect to it or access it with the workstation shells.

IPX.COM must be loaded before XMSNETX to allow connection to a file server.

XMSNETX requires an XMA memory driver such as DOS 5's HIMEM.SYS before it can access extended memory for the NetWare DOS shells.

Important Messages

```
NetWare V3.10 - XMS - Workstation Shell for PC DOS
V5.x  (910307)
(C) Copyright 1990 Novell, Inc.  All Rights Reserved.
```

The preceding is an example output message from the /I option, showing the version and release date of the workstation shell along with the copyright information.

Example

To load the workstation shell into workstation extended memory with HIMEM.SYS installed in the CONFIG.SYS file on a system running DOS 5, type the following:

XMSNET5

To unload the XMSNET4 workstation shell from a workstation's memory, type the following:

XMSNET4 /U

To check the configuration and version of an XMSNETx file on a DOS 5 version of XMSNETX.EXE, type the following:

XMSNETX /I

Notes

 Use the NET.CFG file to set several options for the IPX and XMSNETx flavors of the workstation shells. You can use the /C switch to make sure the configuration file is found when loading XMSNETX.

See also

EMSNETX

IPX

NETX

Index

E

J-K

L

M

N

Q

R

T

X-Y-Z

Add to Your New Riders Library Today with the Best Books for the Best Software

Yes, please send me the productivity-boosting material I have checked below. Make check payable to New Riders Publishing.

❏ **Check enclosed.**

Charge to my credit card:

❏ **VISA**   ❏ **MasterCard**

Card # _____

Expiration date: _____

Signature: _____

Name: _____

Company: _____

Address: _____

City: _____

State: _____ ZIP: _____

Phone: _____

The easiest way to order is to pick up the phone and call 1-800-541-6789 between 9:00 a.m. and 5:00 p.m., EST. Please have your credit card available, and your order can be placed in a snap!

Quantity	Description of Item	Unit Cost	Total Cost
	Inside CorelDRAW!, 2nd Edition	$29.95	
	AutoCAD 3D Design & Presentation*	$29.95	
	Maximizing Windows 3 (Book-and-Disk set)	$39.95	
	Inside AutoCAD, Special Edition (for Releases 10 and 11)*	$34.95	
	Maximizing AutoCAD: Volume I (Book-and-Disk set) Customizing AutoCAD with Macros and Menus	$34.95	
	AutoCAD for Beginners	$19.95	
	Inside Autodesk Animator*	$29.95	
	Maximizing AutoCAD: Volume II (Book-and-Disk set) Inside AutoLISP	$34.95	
	Inside AutoSketch, 2nd Edition*	$24.95	
	AutoCAD Reference Guide, 2nd Edition	$14.95	
	AutoCAD Reference Guide on Disk, 2nd Edition	$14.95	
	Inside CompuServe (Book-and-Disk set)	$29.95	
	Managing and Networking AutoCAD*	$29.95	
	Inside AutoCAD, Release 11, Metric Ed. (Book-and-Disk set)	$34.95	
	Maximizing MS-DOS 5 (Book-and-Disk set)	$34.95	
	Inside Generic CADD*	$29.95	
	Inside Windows	$29.95	
	AutoCAD Bible	$39.95	
	*Companion Disk available for these books	$14.95 ea.	

❏ **3½" disk**

❏ **5¼" disk**

Shipping and Handling: See information below.	
TOTAL	

Shipping and Handling: $4.00 for the first book and $1.75 for each additional book. Floppy disk: add $1.75 for shipping and handling. If you need to have it NOW, we can ship product to you in 24 to 48 hours for an additional charge, and you will receive your item overnight or in two days. Add $20.00 per book and $8.00 for up to three disks overseas. Prices subject to change. Call for availability and pricing information on latest editions.

New Riders Publishing • 11711 N. College Avenue • P.O. Box 90 • Carmel, Indiana 46032

1-800-541-6789   **1-800-448-3804**

Orders/Customer Service   **FAX**

To order: Fill in the reverse side, fold, and mail